Along the Diagonal

Along the Diagonal

Art/Essays/América

Roberto Tejada

Foreword by Mary K. Coffey

FORDHAM UNIVERSITY PRESS
NEW YORK 2026

Fordham University Press also publishes its books in a variety of electronic formats. Some content that appears in print may not be available in electronic books.

Visit us online at www.fordhampress.com.

For EU safety/GPSR concerns: Mare Nostrum Group B.V., Doelen 72, 4831 GR Breda, The Netherlands, gpsr@mare-nostrum.co.uk

Library of Congress Cataloging-in-Publication Data available online at https://catalog.loc.gov.

Printed in the United States of America

28 27 26   5 4 3 2 1

First edition

CONTENTS

FOREWORD BY MARY K. COFFEY

Along the Diagonal: Art/Essays/América is a lyrical and incisive collection of essays drawn from poet, essayist, *cronista*, art historian, and critic Roberto Tejada's published and unpublished work since 2010. Some of these essays have appeared in journals and exhibition catalogs, others have reached a public only through conference and event presentations. These are essays born of the author's experiences, not only his travels and periods spent living in different parts of the Americas, but also his family's immigration from Colombia to Los Angeles, where the author grew up and found community in the burgeoning punk music scene of the 1980s. Some are, thereby, highly personal, following the format of the ekphrastic memoir to provide on-the-ground accounts of essential moments or periods in the development of art worlds in Los Angeles, São Paulo, and Mexico City. Others are more historiographic, providing foundational accounts of important but understudied genres of visual culture. They treat ephemeral histories that threaten to disappear entirely from the record without chroniclers like Tejada who were there. Chapters on Los Angeles's changing urban landscape are suffused with an aching melancholy as they track the challenges of belonging within the virulent efforts of Anglo settlers to eradicate *América* and replace it with (US) America. Together, these essays are invaluable not only for the historical record, but also for Tejada's skill at situating them within important national, political, and economic contexts that illuminate the contingent circumstances in which fragile art worlds are born and, at times, die.

Along the Diagonal is a deeply archival work that tacks between avant-garde literary and visual art with dexterity, bringing the poet's eye for formal and linguistic play to the visual in ways that are allusive, generative, and creative. Tejada's critical methodology inhabits and violates borders between nations, genres, and disciplines to produce a hybrid form that is autobiographical, critical, erudite, and aesthetically experimental. He attributes his method to the formative influence of Mexico City's art world and cites novelist, critic, historian, and curator Olivier Debroise to draw a distinction between a kind of art writing that is "fanciful" and "impressionistic" and his own, which is grounded in "literary art writing associated with avant-garde language practices." This declaration comes late in the text, but it captures the tone of the volume as a whole. Tejada's writing requires a dedicated reader—one who is committed to the critical purchase of the historical avant-gardes and invested in the speculative force of ekphrasis.

As a leading Latinx scholar, Tejada approaches questions of identity—gender, sexual, class, national, racial, or ethnic—in undoctrinaire ways. He does not respect the discipline's tendency to delimit fields by national geographical borders. He consistently hails a hemispheric América and refuses to confine identity to the discursive patterns or compulsory scripts that prevail in any one region, state, or political period. In short, his *latinidad* is capacious, generous, and open-ended. These essays restore the hemispheric scope of the Americas, an agenda Tejada shares with both artists (see his essays on José Clemente Orozco, David Alfaro Siqueiros, Jennifer Allora & Guillermo Calzadilla) and writers (see references to Gloria Anzaldúa or Raquel Gutiérrez). At the same time, his essays push against narrow conceptions of Latinx identity as well as isolated histories of civil rights movements, showing how journalists, poets, artists, and critics crossed racial, ethnic, national, and urban lines to forge solidarities and "assemblies," a term that has particular resonance in Tejada's writing.

Along the Diagonal asks the reader to wander at oblique angles through the gridded and occupied landscapes of Latin/America, encountering beauty and loss, and forging fugitive assemblies along the way. It is a timely meditation on what art does for us and why attending to its moments of emergence and disappearance is a commitment to the better angels of our fraught histories.

Along the Diagonal

Introduction: Diagonally Speaking

Tell all the truth but tell it slant

—EMILY DICKINSON

Staggered at an angle and resting in zigzags across the polished concrete floor, three elongated supports feature wooden blocks that double as colossal dice, two in soft pink, the other in baby blue. Nestled in the shallow trays of unstained wood, eight blocks to a row, each die reveals a word incised onto each of its six sides, exposing the raw lumber under the painted surface so that each group forms several bilingual lines of discernible but disconnected phrases in lowercase and all caps. One spells out: "MY denial rage BE silence forever NEW fear." Another: "PUTA religion que very SUAVE MUCHO chisme AY TÚ." Equal parts minimalist floor sculpture, three-dimensional concrete poem, and the material result of a socially engaged process, the oblique floor-level arrangement is the work of Mexican American artist Celia Álvarez Muñoz. (A detail of the installation, *A Brand New Ball Game* [1994/2020], is featured on the cover of this book.) The triad, as it was on display in its 2020 iteration at Art League Houston, serves here to reflect styles of attention and making that inform my own writings on art.

In creating the installation, originally commissioned in 1994 for Capp Street Projects in San Francisco, Álvarez Muñoz worked with Black and Latinx LGBTQ+ youth who submitted their complex personal histories and affective family relationships to a collective workshop process whose critical method involved experiments with chance, subversive affirmation, and the materiality of language. At the height of the HIV/AIDS epidemic, Álvarez Muñoz held a space for these youth to craft candid, at times bilingual anecdotes, spirited wordplay, and free associations that reflected the fear and ambivalence of the moment: ". . . CLINIC FLUIDS LATEX . . ." ". . . protect sex practice terrifying responsibility . . ." ". . . attitude chisme tradition family home. . . ."[1] The process gave way to narrative sketches and a general lexicon that the artist printed as photomechanical proofs and stencils, typographically varied, while isolating some of the language to be later transferred onto the pink and blue dice—and, for the original 1994 exhibition, onto the gallery walls. The work can be viewed as having materialized the encounter that artworks enable insofar as the aesthetic process occasions the continuities and discontinuities between subject and object, the instability of viewer and viewed overbrimming with variable identifications and disavowals that expose a selfhood in the material fact of language and the flux of becoming, even as the interactions of art can prepare a participant-witness for unprecedented eventualities. As one youth workshop participant observed: "Things change. ANYTHING CAN HAPPEN. YOU NEVER KNOW (what will happen next)."[2]

A Brand New Ball Game reflects the lifetime corpus of Álvarez Muñoz insofar as it dwells—as do my essays that follow—on histories and geographies along interpersonal, political, and conceptual borders. It provides an opportunity to rehearse elective affinities that join Álvarez Muñoz's material concern and critical perspective—transversal in relation to media and subject matter—with the poetics of form I favor in the essays assembled here in *Along the Diagonal: Art/Essays/América.* I situate work like that of Álvarez Muñoz within canons of US conceptual art and a genealogy of Latin American–descendant expressive culture that the artist herself theorizes by animating a cross-cultural Latinx archive of living heritage and artifacts in the form of prints, photographs, wall drawings, artist's books, performances, and multimedia installations. All the while she code-switches between artistic grammars, between genres and formats, between Spanish and English vernaculars, between locations along the Texas-Mexico borderlands, and between regional cultures, the mass media, and idioms of the avant-garde (chapter 13, "Celia Álvarez Muñoz: 'Ideas Are the Drivers'").

The essays assembled in *Along the Diagonal* are similarly the result of my personal circumstance and critical inclinations; they are grounded in the contingencies of time and place and the idiosyncrasies of the essay as a thought-form. My focus likewise navigates between expanses across Latin America, the Caribbean, and Latinx locations in the United States, with the purpose of testing the confines of category and with an aim to defy those versions of modern and postmodern cultural descriptions that only emphasize or overstate the exceptional status of national or cultural identities. To this end, the essay form allows me to suggest indirect or furtive connections between artworks and actors in the hemispheric key of América, even as I describe and examine the material differences between Latin American and Latinx cultural forms (chapter 5, "Diaspora Assemblage: 'Held Together by Stardust,'" and chapter 6, "Frameworks of Intelligibility: Latin American/Latinx Art").

Latinx art and its criticism differ appreciably from Latin American art histories, even as both often intersect in the dislocations specific to some makers and their work, to occasions of display within institutional and commercial settings, and to fields of knowledge that encompass comparative cultural studies, transnational hemispheric perspectives, and the experimental humanities. Latinx art can expand knowledge about the colonial past and diasporic present by looking to the endeavors and practices advanced within the US, but whose heritage, originating in Mexico, Central and South America, or the Caribbean, visually marks a corpus distinct from strictly US American or Latin American frameworks, canons, and markets. Animating complex cultural narratives with innovative forms and conceptual verve, together these artists cut a diagonal line, so to speak, across understandings of national art in the US and the Americas. The essays that comprise *Along the Diagonal: Art/Essays/América* inhabit assorted art scenes across Latin America and within US Latinx contexts. Assembling an array of visual and art-historical materials, I relate aesthetic encounters, in some cases from my own lived experience, unique to objects and actions in the visual imagination that extends along the diagonal of an inclusive, expansive understanding of a hemispheric América.

My title builds on Alexander Galloway's reference to the diagonal's "ubiquitous technology"[3] capable of cutting across disciplines, and to the earlier example offered by sociologist of the sacred and onetime surrealist Roger Caillois, whose connections to América were various,[4] and whose writings also inform my perspective on multimedia installations by the Puerto Rico–based artist duo Allora & Calzadilla (chapter 14, subtitled "Wonderstruck on the Edge of Decline"). In *Mask of the Medusa* (1964; *Méduse et Cie*, 1960), a collection that featured the author's canonical essays "The Praying Mantis" and "The Three Functions of Mimicry," Caillois remarked that the "advancement of knowledge" is, unavoidably, a contingent endeavor. While often facing the "tacit disapproval" of attempts "to relate phenomena belonging to different 'kingdoms,'" a speculative method demarcating what he called the "diagonal sciences" may well invite one to look beyond connections grounded in resemblance and to strive toward uncovering inconspicuous relationships that hold promise without guarantee. He wrote, "Mostly it is chance, allied to a certain boldness of imagination, which puts us on the road to . . . discovery."[5]

The essay form turns to the staggered, the oblique, the crosswise—to imaginations that aim here to make legible a long-view history of Latinx artists in the US, together with their counterparts in Latin American regions of origin, and cultural critics like Ramón Gutiérrez, Tomás Ybarra-Frausto, Mari Carmen Ramírez, Chon Noriega, Ed Morales, and Claire F. Fox, among others who trace a legacy of art practices from a hemispheric perspective.[6] These writers historicize a dynamic that begins with the Spanish colonization of the Indigenous Americas and the enslavement of Africans, resulting in Hispanic and Latino panethnicities that further developed, according to Gutiérrez, with "the United States military's takeover of what became the American Southwest at the end of the Mexican War in 1848," and more recently with "the mass decolonization civil rights movement undertaken by radicalized minorities in the United States during the mid-1960s and early 1970s"[7]—conditions that energized the Chicano art movement. I explore these circumstances in essays that blend memory, history, theory, and criticism, while staging intersecting themes around immigration, language, difference, and identity. I do so by drawing together scenes that convey personal and family stories as well as a Latinx cultural history of Los Angeles (chapter 1, "Diagonal and Self-Possessed: Group Portrait with Liminal Figures").

In 2011, art historian and curator Kellie Jones organized the landmark exhibition *Now Dig This! Art and Black Los Angeles, 1960–1980* at the Hammer Museum in Los Angeles.

As part of the Getty Foundation's Pacific Standard Time initiative, her exhibition offered me a space to recount Southern California episodes by way of montage form. In an "extended play" version of my contribution to that exhibition catalog, I transpose a series of sketches about a wide range of artists, musicians, poets, and journalists. These stories serve as a meditation on the place of memory, media, and power during the interethnic civil rights and art movements in Los Angeles from the 1960s to the 1980s (chapter 2, "'Everything I See Needs Rearranging': Los Angeles Snapshots"). The city appears again as a protagonist in the spatial imagination of LGBTQ artists included in the 2017 exhibition *Axis Mundo: Queer Networks in Chicano L.A.*, curated by C. Ondine Chavoya and David Evans Frantz, which I relate to the work of the Colombian American poet and performance artist Jennif(f)er Tamayo (chapter 17, "Latinx Art in the Future Imperfect: *Axis Mundo*, Jennif(f)er Tamayo").

Thereafter, *Along the Diagonal: Art/Essays/América* traverses a sequence of landscapes and themes with a focus now on the connected histories of Latinx and Latin American art, sometimes based in urban centers that include Los Angeles, Mexico City, São Paulo, and Miami, as well as the Caribbean archipelago and the US-Mexico borderlands. A disenchantment with the developmental account has often inspired me to write narratives about art that pursue alternate techniques and arcs capable of connecting episodes around subjects and locations, in order to encompass the contemporary visual cultures of a hemispheric América, all the while exploring the intricate networks of modern and late-modern mentalities contained in artifacts, art objects, and situations of exchange. This open history of Latin American–Latinx art turns to a mixed lineage of writers whose cultural accounts seek to reflect, at the level of form and language, objects and circumstances animated by the written word, similarly situated in distinct cultural contexts and historical processes born of colonial and modern experiences. With a preference for high contrast, in some essays I join disparate storylines to provoke a broader and deeper understanding of the American hemisphere's image environment. I turn to the novel *The Savage Detectives* by Roberto Bolaño, for example, as a backdrop to tell art stories about the political and economic life of Mexico City, where I lived and worked in the late 1980s and throughout the 1990s, a period that witnessed the rise of neoliberalism, and the increasing integration of Mexico's art world into a globalized market (chapter 3, "Mexico City: Art Stories with Roberto Bolaño").

My essays look to participate in a conversation around contemporary art and criticism and the fields of Latin American and Latinx art as separate and interfacing locations of expression and knowledge, along with a personal investment in writing that can reimagine the archives jointly revealed by visual artists and cultural observers but in a language that can ironize or perform the historical processes such repositories reveal. The range encompasses the origin of photography in nineteenth-century Brazil by way of the more recent archive emerging from a Latin American photography forum in São Paulo (chapter 8, "Tropics of Broadband: Camera Culture and Experience in São Paulo"); the enduring impact of the surrealist journal *Tropique*, founded by Aimé Césaire, Suzanne Césaire, and René Ménil, on Allora & Calzadilla and their exhibition *Specters of Noon* at The Menil Collection in Houston (chapter 14); or news files of the *Los Angeles Times* that, in tandem with the theoretical writings underpinning the Chicano art movement of the 1970s–1980s, flash forward so as to shed light on my own personal journals and interaction in the Mexico City art world of the 1990s (chapter 1, "Diagonal and Self-Possessed: Group Portrait with Liminal Figures," and chapter 4, "Family Resemblance in 1990s Mexico: Francis Alÿs, *The Fabiola Project*").

Throughout, I rehearse my faith in the speculative possibilities of close visual description and its capacity to illuminate the historical imagination. And because I entrust the exposition of artworks to a literary viewpoint, and to the incongruity between visual evidence and written account, the writing style of the essays can range in voice and mood. Suggested in the stakes of moving along a bias (rather than merging with or rejecting the oblique) is an approach therefore that bedevils disciplines. Moreover, a diagonal passage between Latin American and Latinx experience perseveres in the unsparing domains of historical narratives able to relate the development of art practices connecting diasporic histories and local experience, a contemporary Latinx archive linked to urban processes and art world dynamics. The historical, disciplinary, and sociopolitical differences between artists and their work in regional Latin American settings or US Latinx diasporic relationships matter insofar as they mark the discrepancies—on the move, in flux—of cultural translation, so rhyming with my approach to questions of ethnic, racial, sexual, and national identities.

More than a few essays explore the site of contemporary avant-garde practice in its vexed relation to the unfinished project of modernism; to uncanny, elliptical, or poetic temporalities, and to institutional sites of cultural production (chapter 5, "Diaspora Assemblage: 'Held Together by Stardust,'" among others). In my attempt to develop a diasporic Latinx understanding of the modern in its expanded field, I give voice to the personal account, as well as to that of historians, critics, and curators, as I interrogate the categories of Latin American and Latinx art, drawing on the violent histories of América in artworks that habitually serve as the theoretical basis for this expanded locality (chapter 6, "Frameworks of Intelligibility: Latin American/Latinx Art").

In two shorter essays I take up the modernism of Mexican muralists José Clemente Orozco and David Alfaro Siqueiros—in an inter-American and transhistorical context. I interpret the internationalist perspective of Orozco's 1931 mural cycle *Call to Revolution and Table of Universal Brotherhood* at the New School for Social Research in New York City (chapter 10, "Center of Gravity: José Clemente Orozco"); and, in the work of Siqueiros, a form of homoerotic figuration employed by the muralist in oblique connection to photographic studies made by Colombian cameraman Leo Matiz and an iconic contemporary painting by Mexican artist Javier de la Garza (chapter 12, "The Capture of Cuauhtémoc: David Alfaro Siqueiros, Leo Matiz, Javier de la Garza"). The use of preconquest figures like Cuauhtémoc in the painting by de la Garza extends across the political imaginary to overlap with the mythic Indigenous pantheon evoked by artists like Celia Álvarez Muñoz in her *Petrocoatl, Aztec God del Fin del Mundo* (1992). That work, reconfigured for her 2020 exhibition at Art League Houston, spoke of world catastrophe in diagonal lines that connect 1492 to 1992 and to the global crisis of 2020: the COVID-19 pandemic (chapter 13, "Celia Álvarez Muñoz: 'Ideas Are the Drivers'").

Foregrounding media specificity and the particular connotations of format, both the 2016–17 exhibition and accompanying book *CLAP! 10×10 Contemporary Latin American Photobooks, 2000–2016* prompted an incursion into the legacies of a still largely underappreciated genre, the photobook.[8] I turn to historical, social, and political contexts that have given way to the legitimacy of the book-object—a repertoire from the past that informs present-day canons of Latin American photography, particularly from Mexico and Brazil, since the 1970s, and the inter-American debates about the role of photography, camera culture, and its regional institutions in a dialogue across borders (chapter 7, "The Latin American Photobook in Context"). At the invitation of Esther Gabara for her exhibition *Pop América, 1965–1975*, I turn to *El corno emplumado*, edited by Margaret Randall and Sergio Mondragón in Mexico City, a 1960s journal that served as an internationalist vehicle for poetry from the Americas and far beyond, with visual work by emerging artists, including those associated with the pop art movement. As both a literary magazine and a network of social exchanges, *El corno emplumado* featured work by Mexican artists like Mathias Goeritz and Felipe Ehrenberg, which I counterpose with printworks made by Brazilian artist Antônio Henrique Amaral and the writings of art critic Mário Pedrosa, alongside Chicano pioneers like Rupert García, Mel Casas, and Judith Baca. Print culture and printed matter can serve as a diagonal line by which to orient the work of Latin American and Latinx artists who formally transfigured the grammar of pop art and a social critique specific to the 1960s and 1970s (chapter 9, "Printed Matters and Pop Art in América").

The inter-American context expands to include episodes like that of Argentine artist Miguel Angel Ríos, who left Argentina and its military dictatorship of the 1970s, moving first to New York and subsequently to Mexico where he has lived and worked for over four decades. His video films address the question of modernity and its ghosts that haunt the crisis of mass global migration and asylum seeking (chapter 11, "White Stone, Bramble, Gravity, Chance: Miguel Angel Ríos"). An inter-American configuration attains meaningful inflection to the degree that contemporary US-based Latinx artists are joined in their various assessments of US geopolitical and mass media dominance in the hemisphere and of homogenous understandings of cultural identity. In this sense, Luis Gispert (Cuba-USA) exposes the art world and its objects made for consumption in the language of advertising and hip-hop subculture to critique the overdeterminations of ethnic, social, and sexual identities (chapter 15, "Luis Gispert: Radical Feedback"). Art writer Raquel Gutiérrez (Mexico–El Salvador–USA) honors the photographic work of the late artist Laura Aguilar (Mexico-USA) by crafting sentences that make palpable both the personal loss and geopolitical "wounding" of history for descendants of Latin American and Mexican migrants in the US—productive sites of what Gutiérrez refers to as Brown ambivalence and pleasure (chapter16, "Geographies of Language and Light: Laura Aguilar, Raquel Gutiérrez").

In an experimental text and performance-based work, Jenni(f)er Tamayo (Colombia-USA) transmutes the Nickelodeon cartoon *Dora the Explorer* in order to ventriloquize the obscene fantasy formations around corporate forms of Latinidad, the US nation-state, and its role in the hemisphere, as well as the cultural apparatus that denigrates or fetishizes

Latinx identity (chapter 17, "Latinx Art in the Future Imperfect: *Axis Mundo*, Jennif(f)er Tamayo"). By contrast, Jesús Macarena-Ávila (Mexico-Colombia-USA) turns to the crisis of public health in paintings and mixed-media works that address the 2020 COVID-19 pandemic, resulting from his ongoing research into activist history, the surveillance state, and persistent residues of colonial violence for Latinx subjects within the hierarchies of power and social rank and beyond the insulated echo chamber of the art world (chapter 18, "Jesús Macarena-Ávila: The Essential Work").

The book ends with an essay on the critically inclined work of Chicana photographer Christina Fernandez (Mexico-USA), whose political and conceptual underpinnings I connect to the New Topographics method of Lewis Baltz and Robert Adams, to the writings of critic Robert A. Sobieszek and artist Robert Smithson, to the 2008 real estate crisis in Southern California, and to the Los Angeles of Roman Polanski and Robert Towne's 1973 neo-noir *Chinatown* (chapter 19, "Christina Fernandez: Something Lost, Missing, or Unattainable"). Photographs by Fernandez allow my writing about them to inhabit the urban field of Los Angeles as a model for writing art history; that is, a city may be apt to monumentalize even as it is unable to tell the whole story. Spatial, economic, and social disparities lead me, photographically speaking, to find language for the discontinuous geography of Los Angeles in detours that draw critical contrast between sites of production, embodied urban fact, optical experience, and the contingencies of depiction—the political differences between the overlooked and visually underplayed.

This method reflects the demands of an image economy foreseen by media and communication theorist Vilém Flusser, the Czech exile from Nazi Germany who, from 1941 to 1972, worked as a researcher at various institutions in São Paulo, Brazil, where his impact and legacy have been lasting (chapter 8, "Tropics of Broadband: Camera Culture and Experience in São Paulo"). I join the perspective of Flusser, whose ideal model was often that of the metropolis, when I turn to the urban field concerned as much with visual objects of inquiry as with the sentence as an architectural unit capable of composing an environment of thought in the ethical encounter between subjects and objects, even as I seek to have the essay form thrive as an alternately systemic, gestural, and metaphoric field. Flusser's writing leads me to a cultural poetics of the present, so to speak, wherein to stage a sequence of actualities that enliven the space between perception and imminent action, between expectation and modified perspective. My desire is for writing to be restless in relation to the gestural effects of culture and time, to enact the eye's relation to visual detail and at the level of the letter—verbal performances adequate to account for historical change. In this, I connect currents of modern thought dissatisfied with inevitabilities or that seek to traffic not in obligatory relations but in coincidental ones, including those in concrete zones that so command the occasion and cadence of exchange as to disrupt the homogeneity of expository time.

The US American poet Robert Duncan memorably aligned the qualities of attention to a form of rehearsal, a return to a "made place . . . as if it were a given property of the mind / that certain bounds hold against chaos, // that is a place of first permission."[9] I situate *Along the Diagonal: Art/Essays/América* within a poetics of attention and its rehearsals, seeking to enliven that which cannot be confined entirely to recorded accounts, even of the recent past. In the episodes I relate—telescoping abruptly between location and time—Latin American and Latinx artists attend to their surroundings, often urban sites for enacting the boundaries of curiosity, fantasy formation, and foreboding, as well as for fashioning selfhoods communicable to the degree that anyone can dwell on the political horizon of contingency. This concern for a poetics of attention has been greatly influenced also by the work of improvisation-based musician, composer, and sound artist Pauline Oliveros (1932–2016), a Mexican-descendant, openly lesbian innovator, originally from Houston, Texas. Her practice of "deep listening" encourages the experience of one's environs beyond the auditory faculties. It suggests levels of awareness amplified during moments that call attention to the act of listening itself so as to prepare participants for the sociability of the democratic experiment. Oliveros and music artist David Dove cofounded Nameless Sound (2006), an innovative music education initiative in Houston committed to groundbreaking contemporary music and to "a vision of personal and community growth through creative music."[10]

My evolving thoughts on the cadences of attention owe much also to the many elective affinities I've shared with fellow writers whom I name and thank in the acknowledgments. Poet and cultural critic Dale Martin Smith describes attention as the flux of a welcoming that inaugurates identity "based not on an occupation, but as passage." In his poetics of attending as a form of self-reflective initiation, Smith takes up Michelangelo Antonioni's *The Passenger* and the filmmaker's "attention to the passing of subjectivities through bodies and places. His art invites passage through the perceptive textures of another's encounter with alien circumstances, a diminishment of self-command." And then in line breaks that voice the lyric self, Smith affirms "*When you see what you see/It's inside your seeing, how the image/settles its quickening/to your nature.*"[11] And I'm indebted as well to the meetings and communal practices convoked by Friends of Attention, "a loose, informal network of creative collaborators, colleagues, and actual friends who share an interest in 'ATTENTION'—the puzzles and promises of the focused mind and the directed senses." Having emerged in the wake of the 2018 São Paulo Biennial, Friends of Attention—D. Graham Burnett, Alyssa Loh, Peter Schmidt, and an attending assembly—practice an ongoing commitment to "ATTENTION ACTIVISM" that broadens the horizon of "attention's relation to human flourishing."[12]

In what follows, I also animate my own giving of attention as a rehearsal with a view to shared intimacy, and as an immersive strategy of openness to indwelling and variability; the process of embodiment to which a sentence can aspire when prompted by the sensation of looking and discerning. I regard writing about objects and actions as being analogous to the media and experience wagered by artists in their effort to make meaning: a force constitutive of society, especially when encounters, at once likely and unlikely, so come into focus as to suggest a model of history adequate to América, both its imaginaries of place and properties of first permission.

ONE

Diagonal and Self-Possessed: Group Portrait with Liminal Figures

What I seek is permission for a storyline, clauses of invention, the chance to find cover in the episodes, a cascading commitment to making shape and being shaped. Here, I understand the power of "feeling at home" in a form, or in form as such, and it doubles always into foreboding, into impending eviction. Given to conflict in the process of composition—equal parts reverie and self-loathing—I trust the method of "objective chance" that André Breton claimed makes "a mockery of what would have seemed most probable."[1] I give in to the doubling, to a place punctuated with visual interludes, and what I know as my own story appears largely to subsist over time by means of a lens, small mementos from the past, perishable scraps of history, little evidences of experience, both proper and foreign to myself, composed of drawings, prints, films, and photographs. To find a foothold, I recall the ventriloquizing passage voiced by the fictitious narrator of Chris Marker's 1983 essay film *Sans soleil*: "The first image he told me about was of three children on a road in Iceland, in 1965. He said that for him it was the image of happiness and also that he had tried several times to link it to other images, but it never worked. He wrote me: one day I'll have to put it all alone at the beginning of a film with a long piece of black leader; if they don't see happiness in the picture, at least they'll see the black."[2] A decade earlier, in 1971 Amiri Baraka wrote of desires for, and attitudes about, the engagement in action of a "personality as part of the total world community," of personhood in the geopolitical racialized imaginary from a largely Euroethnic base of operations. Baraka wrote that "a counterform in the closed field of white definition" marks that place where "Ethics and

Aesthetics, as Wittgenstein sd, are one," by which Baraka meant the projection of experience "hopefully beneficial in some way to the world."[3]

So I begin with a photograph, an Ektachrome slide of an immigrant couple posing for the camera at Griffith Park Observatory in Los Angeles just before or after Baraka published his "Counterstatement" (plate 1). The hazy blush of a polluted sky hangs heavy over the decline of the sluggish hills, rendering the Hollywood sign a blur at the summit of Mount Lee in the background. The couple comes here with a photographer, likely a relative, too early in the day to watch the sunset, maybe mid-morning, at any rate posing between the 1930s streetlamp and, beyond the frame, the sundial and Astronomers Monument from whose vantage point the portrait is rendered. With the lawn singed beige and brown by weeks of winter drought, the quad that leads to the Planetarium appears devoid of others. Or is it only the illusion of the photograph's framing? For this couple, a husband and wife in their mid-thirties, there's a visual disagreement in this opportunity for self-presentation. She wears a puffy hairstyle and red long-sleeve minidress; the purse suspended from her left arm obliges a delicate but studied gesture that configures a feminine performance. With cigarette in hand, he wears his hair slicked back, and over the pink shirt and floral necktie, a poncho, or *ruana* (the name of that item in the Andes region of Colombia). A testimony to immigrant achievement in the prosperity promised by Los Angeles in the Cold War years, between 1960 and 1970, when a Latin American diaspora, primarily from Mexico, but also from Central and South America, made its way to this urban refuge.

The husband's affirmation of his ethnic difference further marks the couple in public space—a defiance. She refuses to comply as well, but by other means. Her eyes avoid the camera's lens and our gaze as latter-day onlookers, as though she was already skilled in so many narrative displacements about the social divisions in California, and the cultural expectation and racialized meanings applied to her body in the "closed field of white definition." Once, where she was from, she had committed to habit and memory, accepted as fact, the entitlements of lighter skin.

Once, where she was from, hierarchies of color allowed for the over-reporting of class status. Here, any visual haziness in the potent systems of subordination sharpens into the field of perception, made absolute and unambiguous, owing to something here inaudible: a heavily accented English. Every encouragement "to pass" conceals the heavily enforced borderlines of speech acts, even as time and again she will have endured, with the unruffled dignity or aspirational pride of the petit-bourgeois outsider allergic to victimhood, the ineluctable nature of US American attitudes of exception and white supremacy.

Where are you from? When asked, she ironizes with imaginative lines of flight. Sometimes the reply is simply "South America," a term whose perplexing political cloudiness plays evasive even as it assumes—rightly—her opponent's liable ignorance of geography. It preempts embarrassment of the other and a need for explanations—a little act of ingenuity and generosity. Increasingly, and because this is California, the rejoinder is "Mexico"—with the particulars, however, that make a fiction plausible, that enhance a narrative of passing. And so, to avoid any association with her native Colombia—that is in the media grotesque, with narcotics and criminality—she adds "from Mérida, Yucatán." Her preference for passing—not quite not white, not quite not a Mexican national—is a vernacular knowledge of her body as a sign of "difference that exceeds the body." But she also knows, as Samira Kawash in another context observed, "the visible becomes an insufficient guarantee of knowledge. As a result, the possibility of a gap opens up between what the body says and what the body means."[4]

Similarly, an accent is a surplus so culturally determined in social space, it can never be understood properly on its own terms but rather only as a measure of other competencies. Poet Rosa Alcalá writes: "An article in *Time* magazine on voice activation technology discusses the failure of this innovation to recognize female or 'foreign' voices with thick accents. . . . I sometimes worry that the ways in which we define poetry and separate it into exclusionary camps is like creating a technology that recognizes only a few representative voices—or no voice at all—and can only accomplish a limited set of commands."[5]

My father died in early 2016, and in the time elapsed since his passing the meanings of his loss have become forever entangled in the mess that is the time of the now, what Naomi Klein refers to as the large-scale shocks to society, the opportunistic occasions to advance an agenda auspicious for corporations and the brutal accumulation of wealth; to the conditions that gave way to a return of the repressed, to the preservation of whiteness and toxic masculinity; to the assault on immigrants and Indigenous rights, to anti-Black violence and other forms of racial aggression and religious intolerance; to unpredictable levels of cyber-surveillance and the single-minded repeal of all our social safety nets. There is a particular form of immigrant sorrow that is loath to overstate the family narrative even as it finds no place for all the fixed or misremembered scenes of prohibition and shame, all the violence and survival, all the contingencies and chances, the kindnesses and care, as anything but empty if not in a method of kinship with actors in the past and present for whom the odds of time and place have not been favorable.

Although my father was capable of gentleness, and there were moments in my adult life when we came close to being close, he was largely absent, and ever the silent witness of my mother's aptitude for severity, beholden to aspirational decorum and to those Catholic pieties that serve as a cover story to disavow the precarious flux of sexual and social life. Even as my father and I were sort of strangers to each other, I found a renewed indebtedness to his lifelong commitment to dreaming, despite what was for him—a physician who never practiced in the US and therefore a subsistence-wage professional, an immigrant who abided in the perplexing order of that uncertainty—the uneven playing field and the undeniable consequences of disadvantage. Insomuch as the concept of clear and open communication was alien to my upbringing, the charge to find the words that are true, to acknowledge the task as embodied, however embedded in the undeniable privileges in my possession, became a place of antagonism, of early and belated instructions about how I was to self-present and find mobility in a world, by means of provisional personas liable to render a self—myself—as something legible. It became—as Philip Roth once remarked, a coup for me of recognition—a task of having likewise, over and over again, "to fight for my fluency, every paragraph, every sentence."[6]

In the hospital, on his deathbed, my father experienced abrupt recollections from his youth, as when he had committed to memory the Spanish Golden Age poet Pedro Calderón de la Barca and the well-known soliloquy recited by the imprisoned Segismundo in the baroque drama *La vida es sueño*:

¿Qué es la vida? Un frenesí.
¿Qué es la vida? Una ilusión,
una sombra, una ficción,
y el mayor bien es pequeño:
que toda la vida es sueño,
y los sueños, sueños son.

What is life? It's madness.
What is life? An illusion
a shadow a fiction
and all kindness is nothing:
interlude of a life dreamt
by a dream inside another dream.[7]

I gained the dubious ability at times to so create a network of alliances as to dodge the sight lines of oppression and the physical or psychic battery of its vengefulness. The ferocity of family prepared me, perversely, for the equally unpredictable violence of system; for the times it has sought to render a body hyper-visible—in the way especially that sex and ethnicity refuse the false solace of categories—or when it (system) prefers the technologies of indifference or disregard. (Here, lines by Dodie Bellamy come to my rescue: "I'm alone, thrust upon my own alterity—but who is ever not alone? To me, being queer means doing without the false solace of categories."[8]) Habit and nuance give way to the presentation of a person—biological inheritance and learned enactments wherein, as in the poem by Robert Duncan, often I am permitted to return, rehearse, regard, and resemble, even as the union of inner weather and outer shell did not always provide the skills to navigate the unrelenting grip of cultural authority and its dismissals.[9] So I came then to see childhood, my own, in images like those by Graciela Iturbide, as inquiries into the division of private and public life in terms of age, into the developing mind and body suspended between the spontaneous life of the imagination and the margins of social constraint. I saw it in the image of three boys depicted at a window (fig. 1), pressing their faces behind a curtain—one of them raising a toy pistol to the side of his head—as if to illustrate Walter Benjamin's observation of how, for children, the home often becomes "an arsenal of masks," and how "the child hidden behind a curtain himself becomes a blank thing moved by the wind, a ghost . . . enclosed by the material world, [a world] that is tremendously accurate, and approaching him in a way that is ineffable."[10] The photographer had encapsulated the early fear and fantasy of the inanimate—those diminutive terrors by which child and adult coexist on incommensurable fields of understanding. In another, *Gitana*, she monumentalized the antagonisms of child and guardian—that is, the line that divides formative identity from those of paternal intent, suspended in the contradiction

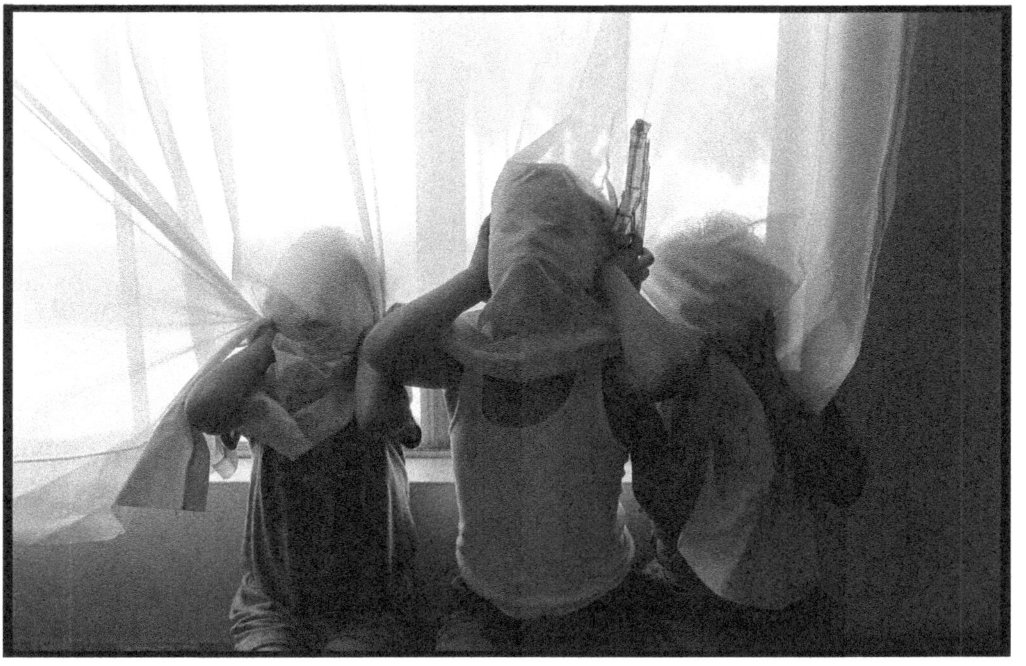

FIGURE 1. Graciela Iturbide, *Cholitos, White Fence, East L.A.*, 1986, gelatin silver print. Courtesy of the artist.

of vulnerability and victory, of retrospection and the radius needed to calculate the plenitude of experience as ever subject to scale.

I began to seek a society of alternate belonging, the varieties of masculine expression, bodies in public shape, the structures of social appearance—internal and external differences that make a subject distinguishable—and moreover to confirm my liminal status as an outsider-insider. And there were counterforms. Take this promo poster of the searing punk-pop trio The Plugz (fig. 2): Bandleader Tito Larriva is flanked by Barry McBride and Chalo Quintana.

Commenting on the scene's appeal for the many Latinos involved, Larriva exclaimed, "I think the 'fuck you' attitude of punk was great for Latinos. You could assimilate into a new culture that was evolving without compromising who you were, or having to be segregated." Sean Carrillo reminds us that "when the LA punk scene was born, Latinos were integrally involved, and throughout its lifespan the contributions of Ron Reyes and Dez Cadena of Black Flag . . . Gerardo Velazquez of Nervous Gender; Joe Ramirez of the Eyes, as well as the Brat [and] the Odd Squad . . . among others, were an undeniable part of its history and growth."[11] A list of those others includes Alice Bag (or Alicia Armendariz) of The Bags, Eddie Muñoz and Louie Ramírez of the Plimsouls, Charles Ramirez (aka Chuck Roast) of Suburban Lawns, and Juan Gómez of Human Hands.

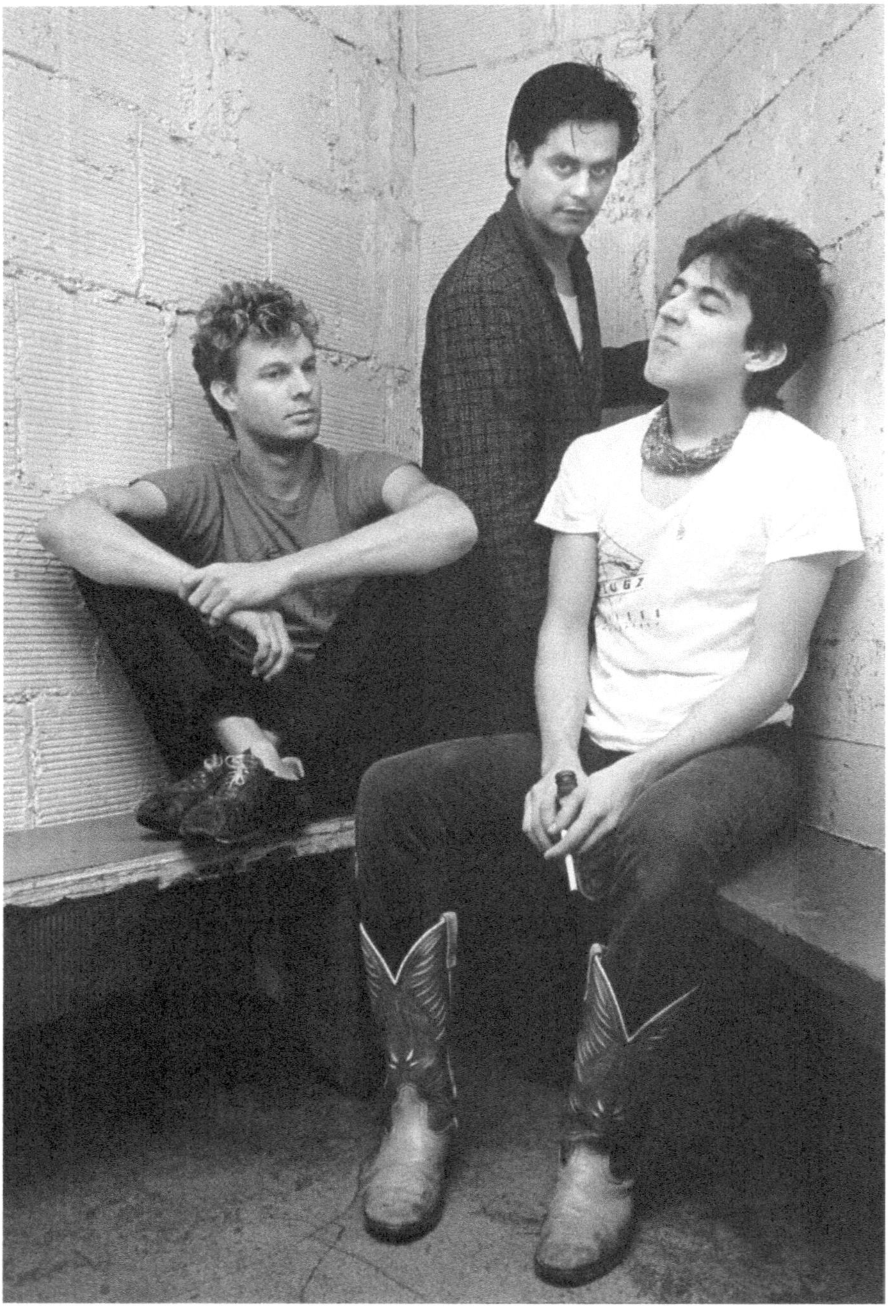

Figure 2. Michael Hyatt, *The Plugz, Olympic Auditorium, Los Angeles*, 1980. *Left to right:* Barry McBride, Tito Larriva, Chalo Quintana. Photo by michael-hyatt.com.

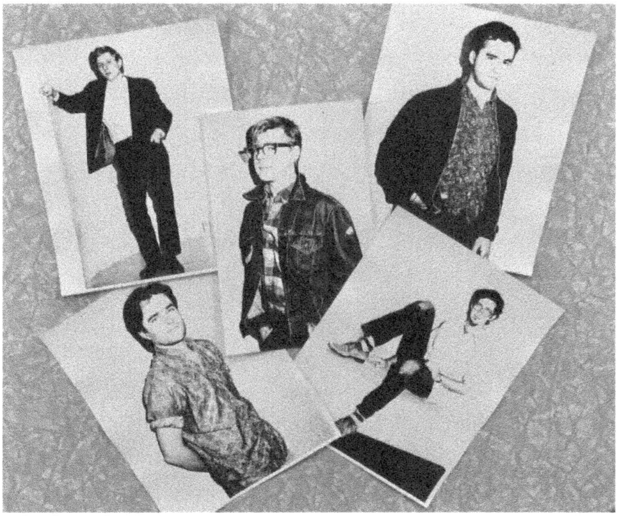

FIGURE 3. Artist unrecorded, Human Hands promotional photographs, ca. 1980. *Clockwise from top left:* Dennis Duck, Juan Gómez, Rick Potts, Bill Noland, and David Wiley (*center*).

The idiosyncratic short-lived quintet from Los Angeles, Human Hands (fig. 3) were Juan Gómez (guitar, bass, vocals), David Wiley (vocals, guitar, saxophone, percussion), Bill Noland (keyboards, cornet, vocals), Dennis Duck (drums & percussion, keyboards, vocals), and Rick Potts (bass guitar, saxophone, saw, vocals). They might have passed for office clerks, record store employees, or aerospace engineers who sought the "aural nightmare" of sonic shapes in comic-book colors, unyielding of the climate's hard edge and in spite of their relish for cartoon logic and the false problem, as in the track titled "Planes vs. Trains": "Trains can't fly into the air / Planes can't swim under the sea / Trains can't jump over buildings / Planes can't crawl into tunnels."[12]

On April 6, 1980, in the *Los Angeles Times*, writer Terry Atkinson offered the following assessment: "Human Hands is a quintet from Pasadena that has become one of the punk circuit's leading attractions. . . . This despite the fact that the group is hardly a typical hard-core outfit. Instead of spiky hair and black leather jackets, this punk band features an almost aggressively 'normal' look: lots of horn-rimmed glasses, haircuts that might have been done by the neighborhood barber, and clothes apparently bought at Sears. Though the group's music contains its share of slashing punk rhythms, its scope also includes influences like [Brian] Eno, Talking Heads, Wire and even Stockhausen." As if to overcompensate for their ordinary surface of "I tried so hard / To look like myself," lead singer David Wiley snarls, "But then I look so different / I look like everyone else." From "New Look": "I've got the new look / Does it look good to you? / I've got the new look / It's really nothing new."

A band's band, further showered with critical favor, in the years they played the circuit, Human Hands produced a catalog of tracks that never found their home in album format. Time passes and I learn that, after moving back to his native Phoenix, David Wiley had died of HIV/AIDS in 1986. And Juan Gómez went on to other bands (The Romans, among others) while serving also in his parallel life as an esteemed librarian at the Huntington in Pasadena. But from 1978 to 1981, the band engaged in the willful inversion of a punk noir aesthetics of indictment that informed much of punk's more politically inclined lyrics of the time. They countered outrage with joy by holding tight to desire and to the bodily absurd. "Go Existential": "I used a needle and thread/To sew a stitch in my head/My dreams came apart at the seams/Until I took a tailor to bed."[13]

"An ambitious outfit with lots of good ideas and uncommon influences," wrote Ira Robbins of Trouser Press, the Human Hands were "capable of disturbing art/jazz angles and fringey experiments . . . [and remain] a neat paragraph to West Coast rock history."[14] Juan Gómez and Dennis Duck had been responsible for most of the songwriting whose tone and themes were in keeping with contemporary Angeleno cartoon art like the Brothers Hernández's *Love and Rockets*, Matt Groening's *Life in Hell*, or David Lynch's anti-art comic strip *The Angriest Dog*. It was keyboardist Bill Noland, however, who penned one track whose lyrics endure and are as fine as any short poem of the moment, certainly one I wish I'd written. It's a poem about how the world has the potential—as it was in childhood—to terrify and to touch and to edify, a knowledge as enclosed in books, or otherwise curbed, but never entirely containable no matter how long we wait in the shadows in order to trust in the day. It's called "Lurk."[15]

Lurk
Something made me crouch
Like little night noises
That crease electric wires
Hallways and metal rooms

Convivial nighthawks
Reach me with their voices
While inside they've got shelves with
Bookends of human heads

The heads still live and talk
About the books next door
They compete for your attention
Regardless of what you're there for

School bus pulls up outside
And we look for a seat
Door seals us in metal room
We get ready for the day

All that I can see
And all that I can hear
Are surrounded by these walls

Diagonal and Self-Possessed: Born at the crossroads with the punk/performance art and music scene of Los Angeles in the late 1970s and early 1980s were budding intellectual passions for experimental theater. It included, for example, The Actors Gang, and its version of Alfred Jarry's *Ubu the King* (directed by a recent UCLA graduate, the actor Tim Robbins), as well as the electrifying social experience that was Luis Valdez's *Zoot Suit*, performed at the Aquarius Theater in 1979 (plate 2). Notably performed in the distinctive vocal and physical stylizations of actor Edward James Olmos, the mythical stage creation that was *Zoot Suit*'s El Pachuco endures in video documentation and in Valdez's own 1981 film adaptation of his 1978 play.

Clad in solid black drapes and matching fedora, gold crucifix worn over a high-collar crimson shirt, El Pachuco submits a smooth display of diagonal attitude and self-possession—immortalized as such in Ignacio Gomez's iconic 1978 poster and the Aquarius Theatre outdoor mural. Poet Joshua Escobar recently reminds me that "El Pachuco—a figure demonized at the height of 1940s racial tensions, and in the widely covered legal trials afterward—becomes terrifically inverted through Valdez's stagecraft, a wildly liminal figure able to slide between foreground and background to instigate and protect, whose voice nearly exceeds the framework of the play." His most memorable lines were those delivered in Brechtian self-referential (and rhyming) direct address: "I speak as an actor on the stage; the Pachuco was existential for he was an actor on the street, both profane and reverential," words that echo a method Valdez had already employed as early as 1967 in Delano, California, with El Teatro Campesino. Galvanizing around the leadership and collective resources of the United Farm Workers, in tandem with the stage guidance of budding director Valdez, Mexican American farmworkers further enhanced the ability to organize and advocate for change in labor practices by means of popular stagecraft.

***Rasquache* and Existential**: Tomás Ybarra-Frausto linked the "rough and tumble performance style" of El Teatro Campesino to the "delight and refinement" found in what is more generally deemed banal, lowly, or uncouth.[16] Although "witty and ironic," the ethos of *rasquache* was rarely "mean-spirited," even when Valdez and his company lampooned the contradictions proper to evolving Mexican American and Chicano cultural values, as in *Los Vendidos* (The Sellouts), first performed in 1967 for a Brown Berets meeting at Elysian Park in East Los Angeles—later a 1972 Emmy Award–winning public broadcasting teleplay. As El Teatro Campesino transitioned from its makeshift rural stages to an urban environment, its creators posed questions about the place of voluntarism in the circuitry of social production, and about commitments to ethnic self, family, society, and history—insofar as the promises of these values are the absurd stuff of tragicomedy. El Teatro Campesino had made charm and swift comic timing crucial to its own pedagogy of the oppressed, deflating the power of so-called social fact by empowering laborers to indulge in the productive play of role reversal. (Valdez: "Put the rancher on the stage but we'll do the acting!") In the style of the skeptical Pachuco—archetype of what is required to be an actor on the street—El Teatro Campesino's through line can be read allegorically as one that asked the existential questions driving the secret fear and fantasy of action and agency, especially when the cultural manifestations and living styles practiced by a people are subsumed in a recovery process that later renders them symbolic of a preordained authenticity. For a subject in social production, there are no guidelines for the collective enterprise that eschews a view of the past as fixed and unchanging—a museum—but rather optimistically as the open-ended possibility of the ephemeral archive.

Hazy sun seeps through a window, enhancing the indoor fluorescent light as it imbues the scene with a lulled manila glow (plate 3). The large windowpane at the upper right is framed in relation to the lighting fixture overhead, angled at the uppermost left. These spatial elements occupy the greater area of the picture—the room itself staggered into planes and angles, as in a stage set—even as you begin to configure the couple seated side by side on a couch, each immersed in reading, possibly out loud to one another from the printed matter held in their hands. The lean youth wears a white T-shirt and brown corduroy jeans that match his Adidas suede sneakers. He leans closer, just barely, to the friend with whom he shares a flocked upholstery couch of neo-California colonial design. That's his jacket and spiral notebook strewn on the floor next to him. She sports a black leather coat, shin-high, white-strapped sandals, and a deep-red patterned minidress accentuating her smooth crossed legs. With her hair styled in an updo, her face betrays a self-conscious or undecided smile. Does she ponder her companion's remark, or is it something about the pages in front of her that occupies her thoughts? Or, rather, is it the sudden presence of the photographer clicking the shutter? Are the ocher hues in this interior due to an overcast layer through the foliage or to the forty-year fade of a slide transparency? The moment hangs on such questions of physical relation and style across time, as it does on the different shades of their skin and the indeterminate time of day.

Oscar Castillo recalls that this image "was taken in the early 1970s on a visit that I made to the campus of California Polytechnic University, San Luis Obispo, to help deliver an art exhibit which was loaned to the Chicano university students by Mechicano Art Center. The two were studying in the student dorms and this was a candid shot. The exhibit arrangements were made by a graduate architecture student, whose name I unfortunately cannot remember."[17] Víctor Franco was the founder of Mechicano Art Center, and he had championed community arts and their "direct role in . . . the spiritual uplifting of the people, the masses of people that are downtrodden right now. The minority communities are spiritually dead and I think our main goal is to awaken them spiritually to the point where they can become politically conscious of their environment and what's happening to them and their lifestyle and hopefully to stimulate them to do something about their condition. . . . It's a tool for social change."[18]

In the early 1970s Castillo was in his mid-to-late twenties, not much older than the two students in the photograph. Chicano identity too was still in the making, working through its own internal conflicts and its association with the struggles of other oppressed peoples. A few years before the picture was taken, *Los Angeles Times* journalist Rubén Salazar reported that "relations between Mexican-Americans and Black activists in California colleges and universities—which are cool at best—have deteriorated as a result of a Chicano walkout during an educational opportunity workshop at UC Santa Barbara."[19] An alumnus of San Fernando Valley State College, later Cal State Northridge, Castillo was seasoned in the Mexican American student movement that advanced civil rights even as it ignited youthful conviction across university campuses. Students had already called for a curricular restructuring so that the education universities provided could speak to the knowledge and histories of underrepresented communities. United Mexican American Students of California, together with several nascent Chicano studies departments in the state, sponsored art exhibits, music events, and theatrical performances, while artist-run venues like Mechicano Art Center and Self Help Graphics & Art were generating exhibitions that sought to bring community art production into the critical spaces of higher learning. Castillo was among the handful of photographers who had documented the Chicano Moratorium, the anti–Vietnam War demonstration in East Los Angeles that led to police hostility and a subsequent outbreak resulting in considerable property damage, 400 arrests, and three fatalities. Most shocking was the death of Rubén Salazar, who had sought respite in the Silver Dollar Café from the violence being waged against the protesters outside. In the already disproportionate police offensive, Deputy Sheriff Thomas Wilson fired a tear-gas projectile at Salazar's head; the journalist was killed instantly.

Appropriate to the subject of reading are the permanent-marker graffiti on the wall behind the studious couple ("Victor de El Centro," "Manuel Carrillo de Aztlán"). For me, the photograph similarly holds a place for what Ramón Gutiérrez calls the "spatial concept of community," just prior to the protests or the collective demonstrations, and despite the interethnic arguments of the kind represented by the walkout at an educational opportunity workshop. Instead, the picture insinuates the promise of less visible moments of intimacy and alliance; that is, of politics by other means.[20] To the extent that the picture hinges on the desire to take action—are the youths studying or drawing up plans for an imminent demonstration?—the then and there of the picture can only be as undecided as that inscrutable smile, or as inadvertent as the connections still activated within the frame: proper names on the wall behind them, everyday life at California Polytechnic University, the gladness of working together in the complicity of joint effort, and the social possibility—our present—awaiting those eventual graduates beyond the amber glow.

Self-Portrait with Reflected Glimmer: In that glow or glimmer is marked the poetic justice required to tell narratives of sight and sound in transformation. To be in surplus of a scene is to be simultaneously attached to the setting and estranged from it. Looking back at episodes past, both lived and unlived, I can view such excess as a value, as that which makes something accessible to experience out of a general diminishing, a glimmer reflecting that unremarked violence at the picture's margin that gives surface reality a neutral semblance. My conflict is this: the impossibility of a viewpoint poised at the places that determine for me an inclusion in, or exclusion from, categories greater than the individual, but that so dislocate me from my surroundings as to resist too easy allocations of meaning . . . An ethics. There is no mystery other than the values that a self attributes to the situational world where, under a dimming glow, symbolic actions have a stake in escaping the instrumental life. The quality of light and subjectivity that is a provisional glimmer reminds us that the world can be readily stripped of its halo. When "all that is solid melts into air," and we are made to see the "real conditions" of our lives,[21] the syllabic self seeks reflection in settings of experience and experiment that cover a ground if only as a temporary residence. That transience may quicken us to substitute the vanishing with so many constituent parts, reanimated. The artwork or poem—even when deprived of a halo, even when released from its fixity and essence—is not without the radiance of a convenient forgetting, as when, in any quest account, the amulet found "is really a re-finding."[22] In its unhurried measure, inasmuch as speed for speed's sake endangers the sensual opportunity of the world, and every day—because so beckoning—its recurring custody, the words exact a style of integrity.

You can hear its command: Do we want humanity at the service of justice, or justice at the service of humanity?[23]

My desire is to assemble scenes and daydreams in search of a surrogate autobiography, memoir by other means, group portraits with liminal figures that make possible an understanding of our involvement with others, both familiar and unfamiliar—an ephemeral archive. I want this immigrant couple, from the perspective of the present, and the vantage point of Griffith Park in 1970, to gaze back at me with the historical consciousness of a present that views the past "only as an image which flashes up at the instant when it can be recognized and is never seen again." The experience of departure, disappearance, and the fleeting social relation that is the premonition of demise adjoin to Walter Benjamin's well-worn but always stunning formulation whereby "To articulate the past historically [is] to seize hold of a memory as it flashes up at a moment of danger."[24] I want the alternate futures that might have been possible for them once looming below in the city expanse to stagger now the conclusions of our historical circumstance, the present, as being anything but composed of so many loose ends, false starts, scrap remainders of experience or public opinion, the stuff of self-conscious gestures, cruel ironies, unsubstantiated exchange or contrasts, a frame through which to view the horizon of relations. I dodge from the infinite verbs that overpromise—to de-privilege, decentralize, de-modernize, decolonize—in favor of the more modest and immediate but nonetheless deviant tasks. In *Wartime Kiss*, Alexander Nemerov describes the act of making history, of being in the presence of the past, as a search for fragments—for images, for archival documents, for connections that "feel . . . like a disturbance on the surface of things."[25] Mexican artist Magali Lara provides an attendant animation of that disturbance in terms of self-estrangement, the custody of that which is prone to perish and guaranteed to die, a cellular striving ever to be more when patterns of the organism structure the imagination—life or lifelike varieties in mutual and ever regenerative transfigurations (fig. 4).

Wittgenstein famously described certain phenomena as such a "wonder at the existence of the world" that one is "inclined to use such phrases as 'how extraordinary that anything should exist' or 'how extraordinary that the world should exist.'" The philosopher of family resemblance came to see that "these nonsensical expressions were not nonsensical [but that he] had not yet found the correct expressions." What he sought in those terms was to "go beyond the world and that is to say beyond significant language." Ethics and aesthetics were for Wittgenstein this "absolutely hopeless" inclination "to run against the boundaries of language" or to brush up "against the walls of our cage."[26] That is to ask whether it is possible to be both autonomous and foreign to myself, diagonal and self-possessed. It never really works. The liminal figures I evoke in my doubling evanesce as suddenly as

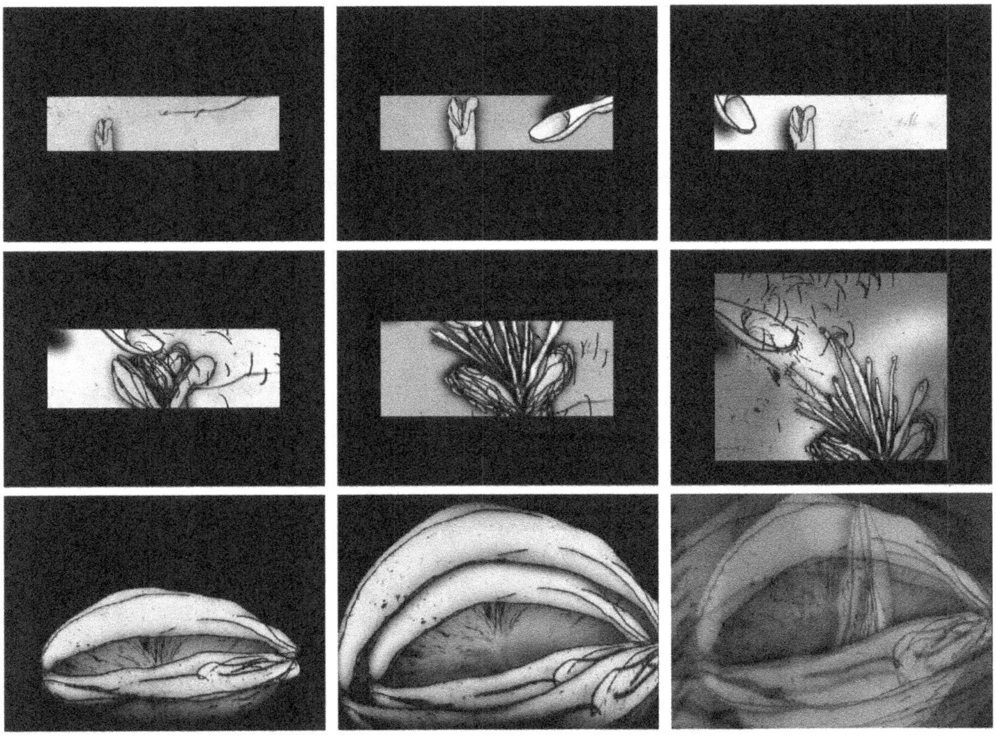

FIGURE 4. Magali Lara, *Lo otro*, 2004, 4′28″, video (stills); direction and animation by Luis Ordóñez, music by Ana Lara, based on print series *Alien*. Courtesy of the artist.

they appear, convenient placeholders of an action, or the projections of experience, both foreboding and hopeful. One day I'll have to line the words and images of my surrogate selves into a lecture that—like Magali Lara's animation—so produces irrepressible life as to ask whether those apparitions make legible an emotion, or so ground it as to be sufficient to its life form. That is, to speculate, with Judith Butler, about my refusal to grieve the masculine as a possibility of love;[27] to wonder, with my liminal figures, about the everyday evictions from an already impermanent home that makes of my racial identity an uncanny kinship with others. If I fail to see myself in the picture, at least I can find a provisional solace again in the amber glow, in a fight for fluency, in the finding and refinding, in the quest for the correct expression, my disturbance on the surface of things, an ephemeral archive . . .

All that I can see
And all that I can hear
Are surrounded by these walls.

How extraordinary that anything should exist.

TWO

"Everything I See Needs Rearranging": Los Angeles Snapshots

1.

Fireworks flare from a night sky otherwise low and unbroken over Wilshire Boulevard, but for a fleeting crisscross of searchlights enfolded now into the picture's past (fig. 5). The flash cascade of streams ignites aspects anyway of the privileged pageantry below as water jets propel cellophane flowers from a reflecting pool, the multitude along the length of a causeway pauses from its bustle up the plaza's double stairwell, and all the containable display above them reduces the polished crowds into illegible scrawl. One group assembles to observe on a level at the east end of three commanding pavilions that flank the raised plaza; another from a balcony jutting out from the west building, a sliver of which doubles in this photograph as a surrogate lefthand frame. In low-angle perspective against the carbon upper field, the phantom glow of the architecture appears to cast the composition into a theater of claims to perpetuity drawn back by so much luminous concrete receding into the uncertain depth of the emulsion. *Los Angeles Times* photographer Joe Kennedy framed the composition with a bare flagpole that cuts in from the right. On the lower edge, a solitary stone bench marks a diagonal. It provides a minimalist base from which to recognize, at least in light of the festivities beyond, another inflection to this moment—somebody's outsider status.

Under the heading "County Museum of Art Dedication Rites Held," the newspaper editors had cropped the photograph to a vertical fragment of the previous night's ceremonies—flagpole and bench now missing, the balcony crowd no longer present. The fêted new culture palace, however, still loomed out of reach and in spatial command of the

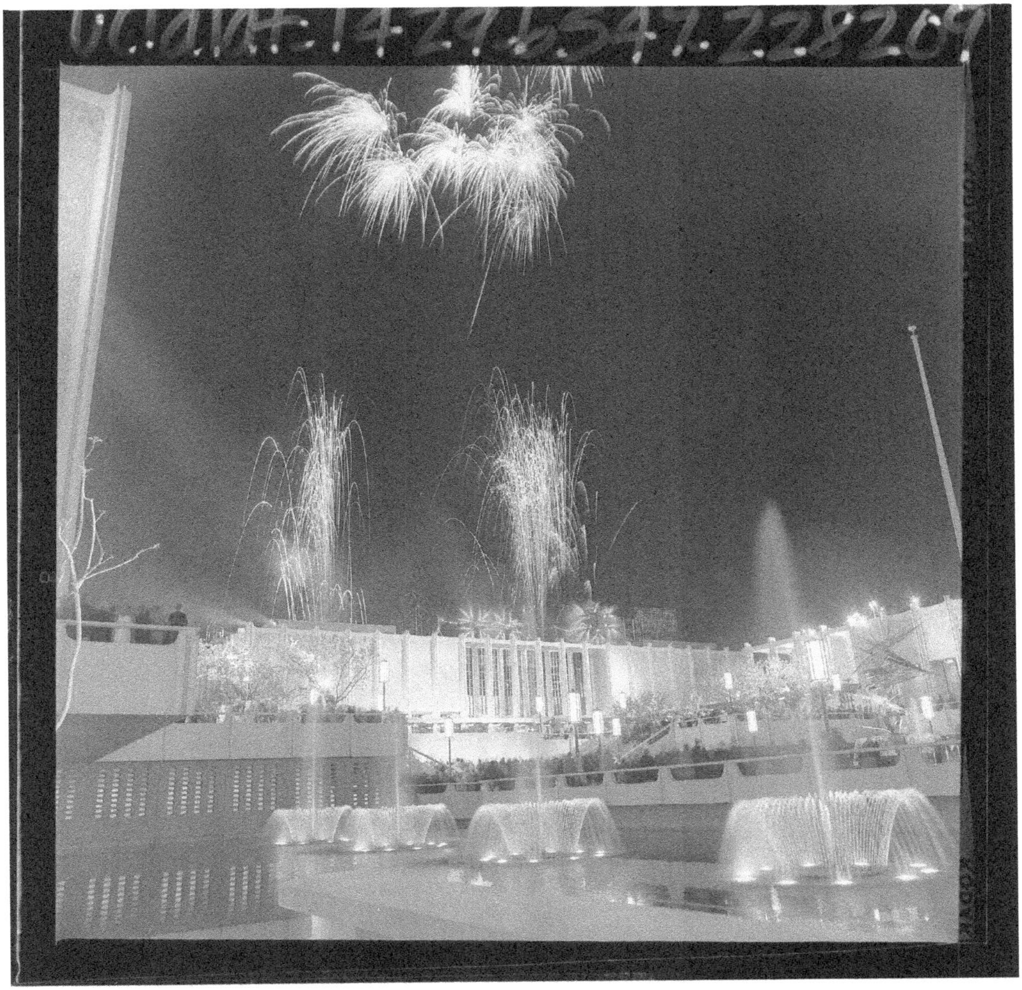

FIGURE 5. Joe Kennedy, "Fireworks above Los Angeles County Museum of Art during dedication ceremony," photograph, *Los Angeles Times*, March 31, 1965. Los Angeles Times Photographic Archive, UCLA Library Special Collection.

goings-on below. *Times* readers on Wednesday, March 31, 1965, might have paused at the subhead in smaller font—"Music, Oratory, Colorful Fireworks Mark Festivities Preceding Public Opening Today"—and, given all the fanfare, wondered what, exactly, they meant by public? Stakes were high for the Los Angeles County Museum of Art, a municipal endeavor "50 years in the making," and with its new home and architectural site in Hancock Park, the meaning of its geographic location was unambiguous.[1] A year before the dedication, *Harper's* had reported on the "cultural circus" of Los Angeles, its County Museum of Art dividing "amoeba-like," with "one part of it . . . about to have a more fashionable building and location." Of the original Exposition Park location, author Russell Lyme was prepared to accept that "[it] was once tolerably respectable and wealthy but . . . no longer a residential area in which anyone much wants to live who can afford to be elsewhere."[2]

In the months prior to the opening, the *Times* had featured accounts of the three-building campus and its construction, the largest art museum built in the country since 1940. With a total investment in amounts equal to the estimated value of the artwork it initially housed—about $20 million—and on land donated by the Los Angeles County Board of Supervisors (worth over $8 million), the architectural firm of William L. Pereira & Associates designed what was meant to be an institutional peer to the Music Center at the Civic Center. Private moneys totaling $11.5 million had been raised to fund construction of the Ahmanson Building, the Bing Theatre, and the Lytton Gallery. The largest of these was the four-level Ahmanson, housing the museum's permanent collection in halls that extended from an eighty-five-foot-high atrium. Making explicit news was a painting by Rembrandt, a "portrait of his son Titus," that the Norton Simon Foundation had purchased—and this gave way to speculation about its potential status as a long-term loan for the permanent collection, to be displayed in tandem with the inaugural exhibition of works by Pierre Bonnard.[3]

Mike Davis has related the territorial contest that was then ensuing between Downtown and Westside elites over cultural aspirations and geographic primacy for the city. The Los Angeles County Museum of Art had opened a few months after *Times* magnate Dorothy Chandler orchestrated the creation of Downtown's Music Center, with one of its buildings bearing her name. Meanwhile, the Hancock Park museum had been "heavily endowed by the Ahmansons and other Westside patrons," as though "to counterbalance the Music Center's pretensions to anchor Culture securely in Downtown."[4] In his 1964 *Harper's* article, Lyme had derided Los Angeles as "plugging culture in the best Chamber of Commerce tradition and backing up its aspirations for aesthetic conversion with steel and concrete temples of imposing dimensions."[5] While enduring speeches by the County Museum president (Edward W. Carter), city supervisors (Kenneth Hahn, Warren Dorn, and Ernest Debs), and board chairman (John Rex), to the strains of the National Anthem and Handel's *Music for the Royal Fireworks*, those assembled that evening—"a mixture of collectors, artists, dealers, curators, academics, amateurs, and of those who think it important for their social aplomb to be seen at such gatherings"—were cheerful converts to that aesthetic faith now materialized in steel and concrete.[6] The photograph encapsulates a group-specific, idealist fantasy formation about a style of municipal belonging.[7] Pereira's architectural design may have enticed with the promise of concrete civic space, even as its physical location and the symbolic central plaza contradicted any purported mission for this county institution in terms of demographics—and on a practical level, broad concourse perhaps rarely came to pass except at events like the one depicted. As a construction, it framed a cultural location for the right kind of public, the mutual production of a material site and imagined audience. Capturing a peculiar brand of Los Angeles triumphalism—dazzling, detached—Joe Kennedy's original negative of the eventually published print advances the ironies contained in this conspicuous display performed jointly by municipal elites and a new class of cultural consumers. The picture meant to inaugurate a strong unchallenged image of a Los Angeles whose culture classes could encourage a theater of common cause, a proscenium of historic scale, as though lacking antecedent and without contrary account, to serve as proxy for occasions of public assembly, generally deficient, except as on that Tuesday night, when occupied by largely concurrent interests. You can't help but be struck by the relative compliance and forthcoming tone of the *Times*, or by the undisputed truth of the new museum's institutional presence appearing in that conventional medium of public record. Such was its power of invention as to induce a form of convenient forgetting that made possible in Hancock Park this photographic pavilion of distraction. The picture survives what it meant to deflect, the invisible wreckage, so to speak, that enables any elation. Walter Benjamin had suggested that distraction serves as a kind of catharsis, a "physiological phenomenon" whose opposite in material fact and collective experience—applause for the benefactors, cheers for the civic authority—are so many dust clouds of demolition.[8] View the photo long enough with the tiniest shift of perception and the nighttime museum appears, under the weight of that multitude and the ignited display, on the verge of imploding.

2. *[Cover Story: "South of Chu Lai"]*

To ponder the evening sky only months after the County Museum dedication was to watch fumes now rise from the urban blaze. "A huge section of Los Angeles was virtually a city on fire," the *Times* reported, "as flames from stores, industrial complexes and homes lit the night skies."[9] On August 11, 1965, when "rocks, bricks, and bottles" first irrupted at the corner of 116th and Avalon Boulevard, and desperation unleashed into scenes of uprising in Watts and elsewhere—with firebombs setting storefronts and overturned cars ablaze, an escalating storm of law enforcement barricades followed by tear-gas missiles, mass arrests, and slayings, what the *Times* at first called a "melee" and later "virtual guerrilla warfare," that day found staff reporter Rubén Salazar en route to his assignment in Vietnam to dispatch from the paper's Saigon's bureau. One of two Mexican Americans at the *Times*, Salazar found opportunity in Vietnam to remark covertly on the crisis in Los Angeles. (Embarrassingly, the newspaper had no African American journalists on its staff to cover the Watts rebellion.) In an August 23 report, Salazar interviewed twenty-nine-year-old Marine Sgt. Harrison Madison, "a Negro formerly of Long Beach," stationed in Chu Lai, South Vietnam, on the "racial trouble in Los Angeles." Salazar's interview prompts the Marine at first to denounce the revolt as unfounded: "Violence is never justified when peaceful settlement is possible."[10] The cruel irony is not lost on Salazar, who in the same first paragraph describes the sergeant ordering his mortar section "to fire on nearby Viet Cong guerrillas." The rhetorical nuance builds with each paragraph Salazar unpacks in this brief report from the combat zone. Sergeant Madison tells of the remote position he and his men have secured in the village of Guong, about twenty-five miles south of Chu Lai. "The only way in or out is by helicopter," he specifies, and so the isolation has granted time to think about conditions in Watts. Reading newspaper accounts about the National Guard and its deployment in Los Angeles, Madison recalls the days he had been stationed at Camp Pendleton where—recently married at the time and with a first child—housing discrimination had prevented him from renting a house in Oceanside. In the background of the interview scene, as mortar fire rages, Madison bares his conflicted feelings.

As for the men in his troop, Madison confirms he is capable of keeping his command free of interracial strife: "'Some of those guys are white and some Black,' Madison said with a wry smile. 'They're doing a tough job and I'm not going to let them down—no matter what's going on in Los Angeles.'" But he admits feeling trepidation at the prospect of going home: "I thought things were getting better there between the races. Then I think about being able to rent a house in Oceanside and I think about our being here to stop communism from spreading to the United States and I get confused." Having served in the forces for eleven years, Madison relates that by the time he left Camp Pendleton in 1963 California's Rumford Act had enabled him to secure a house in Oceanside and that "Gov. Brown had done a lot to improve race relations." Salazar reminds the sergeant that the Rumford Act—the so-called Fair Housing Law—had since been repealed. "I have no way of knowing," Madison reacts, "but perhaps that helped foul things up in Los Angeles. . . . Being cooped up like we are here, surrounded by hostile forces, makes you uncomfortable, naggy and frustrated." At this juncture, a visual pause in the newsprint appears with a subheading "DIRECTS WHITE CREW," absorbing some of the impact of what follows, even as it drives the newsman's perspective home to Los Angeles. With Madison alternately voicing commands for his crew to supply additional mortar support—and with the phrase "uncomfortable, naggy and frustrated" still hanging in the air—the sergeant turns to Salazar in an aside to admit, "Maybe that's what happened in Watts."

3.

Rubén Salazar was not alone in his readiness to voice the social contradictions of US war efforts in Southeast Asia. While so many African American and Chicano soldiers risked their lives on behalf of anti-Communism—by some accounts, as "cannon fodder" for the defense of national interests—their families and communities at home faced flagrant white advantage, nonetheless organizing to defy discrimination and the flimsy odds at opportunity. Back in Los Angeles, the 1965 Watts revolt incited celebrity musician Johnny Otis to compose a written tribute that combined eyewitness accounts with political analysis and autobiography in alternate bursts of outrage, melancholy, and astonishment. *Listen to the Lambs* (1968) is a book as urgent as it is difficult to contain; it synchronizes personal stakes and historical consequences in a series of reflections on the past that inform his commentary in the present. Otis, with the second sight of the outsider-insider—a Greek American who did not object to, perhaps even encouraged, being mistaken for Black—repeatedly debunks the commonplace rationale of the convenient cover story that impugned outside agitators as the invisible cause of the Watts uprising. United with Salazar in this respect, Otis could not separate the urban dispossession ravaged on Watts from the war waged in Vietnam as anything other than the effects of white supremacy. In his superb intellectual biography of Otis, George Lipsitz underscores the efforts of the musician turned author to connect the workings of racism at home to US foreign policy. Otis saw through "the hypocrisy of a government . . . eager to police the world overseas, [but] unwilling to defend the lives, labors, and property of its own Black citizens"; *Listen to the Lambs* encouraged "a global rather than a purely national solution to racial oppression."[11] Early in the book, Otis supplements his own account with a chorus of persons who bore witness to the events unfolding inside the barricaded "curfew zone." Maxcy D. Filer, age thirty-five, a law student and president of the NAACP's Compton division, spoke of residents "who had cracked under the social pressure piled on through the years. . . . They knew they were going to die, but with some Negroes it has come to that: just die and get it over with; nothing to live for really, anyhow. Vietnam? We had it in Watts that Friday the thirteenth."[12] Citing contemporary opinion polls on the uprising and its basis in alleged "outside agitation," Otis indicts the facile willingness of whites to blame Communists underpinning over the material facts of "unemployment, living conditions, or police mistreatment" as being at the root of the rebellion.[13] Otis names the "stark racist overtones of the United States involvement in Vietnam," and the appalling "mass carnage visited upon the Vietnamese people—women, children, farmers—with the use of napalm, defoliation, the Lazy Dog bomb (thousands of slivers of razor-sharp metal), gas, and all the rest. This kind of indescribable horror and murder of innocent civilians would never be applied against a white nation."[14]

To account for the Watts emergency, the social sciences were prone to expound on the unprecedented violence of disempowered peoples in terms that spoke chiefly of geographic confinement, racial dissatisfaction, intolerable living conditions, and "weak normative bond[s] to the majority group."[15] By contrast, and to the degree that it "drew the line of demarcation between those who would cling to liberal rhetoric, ties to the Democratic Party and middle-class concerns, and those who would attempt to go beyond liberalism," the rebellion, Cornel West has claimed, was "a watershed event in the Black freedom movement." It made obvious the limits of reform by means only of partisan politics and created further gaps between upward Afro-American middle classes and the growing desperation in some sectors of Black urban life.[16] The poet Jayne Cortez persuasively evokes the "uprising of Black discontent" as a reprisal for the "sacrifices made as a consequence of white domination." What the establishment saw as foreign menace was making broadcast news, Cortez recalls, with the "Cuban revolution, and Algerian war for independence, the Vietnamese struggle between oppressed and oppressors," and "students shouting 'we want our freedom now' as the struggle to desegregate the US south heated up."[17] The xenophobic inclination of US American political attitudes, however, found in "outside agitation" a scapegoat that could redirect the power of televised images transporting world events into domestic spaces across the US social spectrum.[18] But mainstream media coverage was as disinclined as it was unapologetic when it came to conveying a local viewpoint of the rebellious in Watts. Whereas many Black leaders were vocal about the conditions that led to violent protest—racial discrimination, police brutality, housing segregation, and unemployment—many white officials denounced what they saw as provocation by enemies closer to home. All this informed opinion and the language from which each day suspended can be surmised in the response of one eyewitness: twenty-three-year-old Yale law student Stanley Sanders, describing the daytime skies over Santa Monica.[19] Of the few African American reporters to cover the Watts disturbance from within, Sanders informs Otis that media reports had alerted him about the possibility of "Cuban-guerrilla influence" and that he should keep one eye open for "Panama hats, the red arm bands, things that would smack of guerrilla effort." Additional radio and television accounts warned of witnesses spotting "Cuban hats and red arm bands, loading trucks with rifles and guns and what not. Whether that's true or not I don't know," Sanders recalls, "but what I *did* see while I was traveling along the freeway on Saturday, August fourteenth, was an airplane doing some skywriting. It spelled H-I-D-D-E-N, then there was a space, and this was followed by M-A-O-I and then a curlicue, which was obviously an unfinished S, and the rest of it, I suppose, would have come out spelling out 'HIDDEN MAOIST.'"[20] Sanders relates his attempts as a newswriter to identify the source of this public display meant to further enhance the already elevated state of panic and distrust in a Los Angeles stunned by recent events. "The skywriting stretched approximately from Santa Monica Beach to Redondo, over the ocean, so it could be read by someone in an easterly position."[21] Sanders is able finally to trace the airplane to its proprietor, but his phone call to the commercial holder leads only to uncooperative refusals to disclose information. What was the nature of the call, and how did he get this number anyway?

4.

Skywriting in its various forms—advertisement, paranoid warning, or authoritarian display—prompted a cryptic search that drove many others in Los Angeles to foreboding. "Write the rules / In the sky / But ask your leaders / Why, why," bellowed Arthur Lee, visionary bandleader of the LA psychedelic rock ensemble Love, whose landmark 1967 album, *Forever Changes*, comprises eleven tracks that build from gauzy exuberance to a kind of apocalyptic chill. Indelible among its lyrics are the opening lines of "The Red Telephone," which veer from "Sitting on a hillside" to "watching all the people die / I'll feel much better on the other side."[22] A prominent member of the Sunset Strip nightclub elite, Lee found himself during the Watts revolts having to care for his mother who lived in the West Adams neighborhood, and so zigzagging his way by car, possibly from Sunset and La Cienega to the northern edge of the barricades. Andrew Hultkrans provides a stunning cultural account of Los Angeles through the lens of Lee and *Forever Changes*, whose title submitted the twin tenses of an always already allusive future and the unswerving persistence of transformation. As a cultural journey though the trippy stupor of Southern California in the years after the Watts rebellion, Hultkrans tells of Lee's direct contact with the "cataclysm that many Angelenos viewed as the beginning of The End for their fair city—the Watts race riots of 1965."[23] When violence erupted, Lee neared many of the police barricades to safeguard his mother Agnes who, according to Hulktrans, "was light skinned enough to be mistaken for white." More than mere personal anecdote, the experience for Lee, "along with his awareness of being Black in a white world, [gave him an] innate sense that America's 'streets of gold' had been paved with bodies and blood of his ancestors, that the country had furthermore been 'settled' by white colonists through the near genocide of its native residents, and that the descendants of those colonists were currently massacring people of color in Southeast Asia. . . . [It] contributed to the fervent, fire-and-brimstone rhetoric coursing throughout *Forever Changes*."[24] The album's second track, "A House Is Not a Motel," intones the dubious project of a sovereign selfhood so long as you stay put in the gap that opens up between your allotted location and the world writ large. For Lee, entangled lines connected the social scene of the Sunset Strip to the Los Feliz hills, where he lived, together with his bandmates and a rotating company of crashers, in a neglected mansion on Cedarhurst Circle, and South Los Angeles, where he had spent an important part of his youth; and now all these places pointed across the Pacific to the war in Vietnam. Poised at the brink of what had promised to be momentous changes—"This is the time and this is the time and/It is time"—came instead the disorder and violence of the political present—"More confusions, blood transfusions." As the "news today" was giving way to the "movies of tomorrow," insomuch as the political present rendered in the communication media appeared as footage from a grotesque fiction, and the counterculture figured progressively in decline, anonymity was just another name now for the declining means to any end: "You are just a thought that someone/Somewhere somehow feels you should be here"—a vacant place far away from the throngs and the fireworks. By its third verse, the galloping jangle of Wild-West inflection transmogrifies into its own strain of orchestral fireworks music. In the evocative description of Hulktrans, "The band then abruptly cedes the floor to a primal, tom-heavy drum break, a kind of martial warning, a preemptory strike, for the twin electric guitars that swoop in like howling dive-bombers, tearing up the skies in a furious dogfight that spirals upward into the stratosphere. Meanwhile, Arthur babbles beneath the firestorm like a Pentecostal speaking in tongues, or an Indian shaman, or both. Are you sure you want to live here?"[25]

5.

Sgt. Madison to journalist Rubén Salazar; Maxcy Filer and Stanley Sanders to Johnny Otis; Cornel West, Jayne Cortez, and Arthur Lee . . . These voices make it possible now to look at another photograph (fig. 6) published in the *Los Angeles Times*, on March 28, 1966, practically a year to the date of the County Museum dedication fireworks. A hulking mass, off center, comes into full-foreground view, a freestanding structure that replicates the edges of the image itself, and it towers over the miscellaneous arrangements beyond the frame within the frame. Behind it, from a foliate balustrade propped on a plank are five cables or rebar stems that blossom into craggy flowers; flattened into a withered clump, the bouquet remains upright, and the differing patinas on the charred frame or flower vase enhance the bare facts of this recognizably displaced matter. The upstage corner of a plywood performance dais steadies the charred frame at a diagonal, one end of it butting up to the edge of the dais where two knotted ropes hang from the side. A row of iron and pressed-wood auditorium seats nestles against the back wall, a step up from the dais. There's a contest of shadow and light in the accidental arrangement of the surrounding items, but the charred mass at center fails to wholly eclipse the other artworks.

Some are pulled together in a makeshift rack to the left or installed salon-style along the back wall. Geometric and figurative compositions, the art on display includes a grid

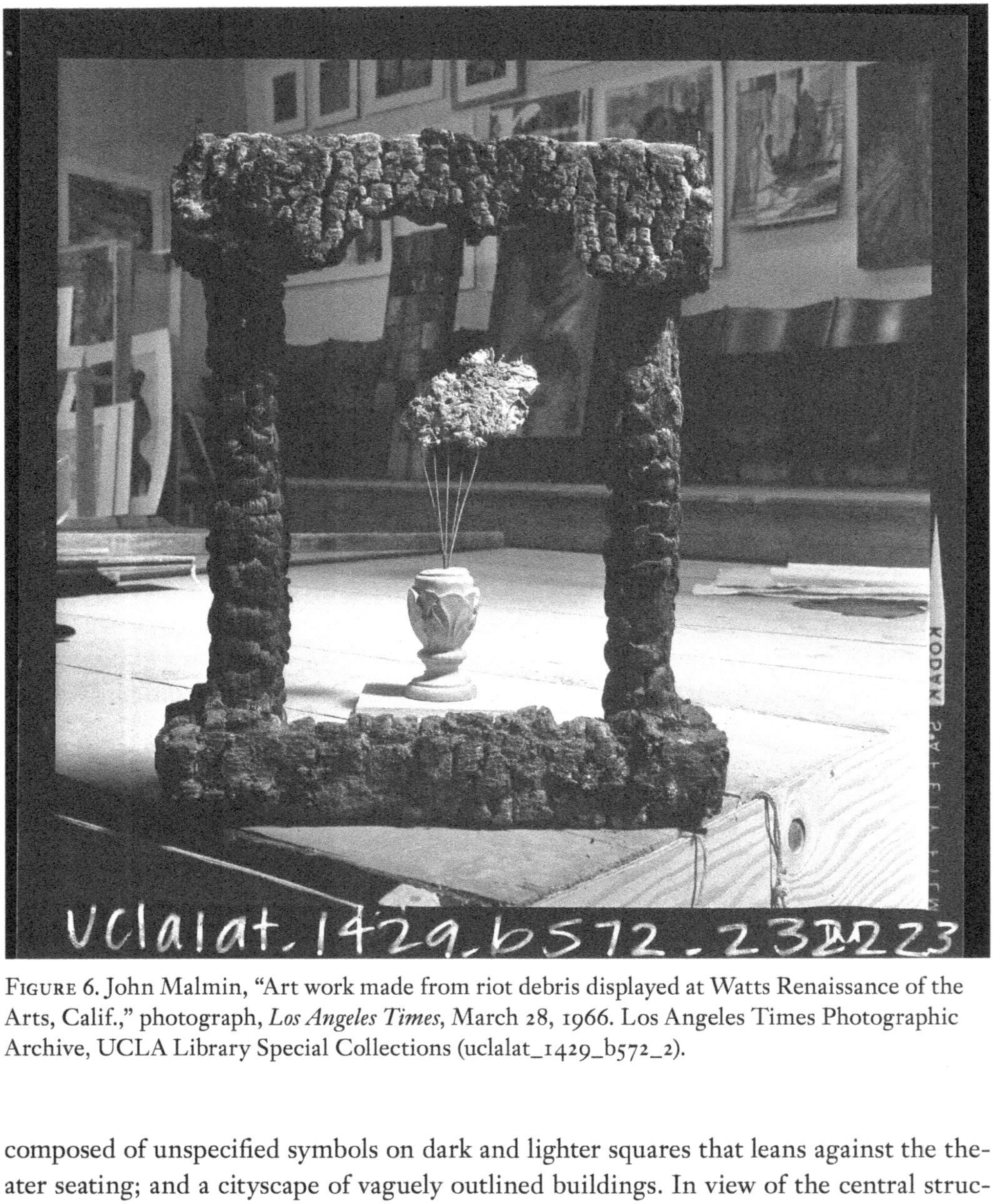

Figure 6. John Malmin, "Art work made from riot debris displayed at Watts Renaissance of the Arts, Calif.," photograph, *Los Angeles Times*, March 28, 1966. Los Angeles Times Photographic Archive, UCLA Library Special Collections (uclalat_1429_b572_2).

composed of unspecified symbols on dark and lighter squares that leans against the theater seating; and a cityscape of vaguely outlined buildings. In view of the central structure, most of the surrounding artworks appear more emphatically without frames. The charred mass, betrayed by its clumped surface, like wet sand or mud, or stone in the process of deterioration, appears anyway suspended in a semisolid state.

The photograph's maker remains unidentified, as was the image to remain unpublished—at any rate, it appears nowhere in that day's edition of the *Times*. The intended caption, at one time fixed to the verso of the print, reads: "DEBRIS—Sculptured effect is produced by a piece of burned roof and sheet metal prepared for display at the Watts Renaissance of the Arts."[26] In one of a handful of stories the *Times* ran on the cultural events in Watts that week, staff writer Art Berman's feature underscored how artists

Noah Purifoy and Judson Powell had combed through the uprising's devastation: "They were excited by what they found—hunks of melted neon signs, medicine bottles embedded in the molten remains of colorful plastic raincoats, twisted bits of metal, charred wood, pieces of smashed automobiles. . . . A charred window becomes a picture frame. A lump of lead and neon becomes a bouquet of flowers."[27] Powell and Purifoy had been teaching at the cultural center that was now an annex of Simon Rodia's Watts Towers, and with their students they had been transforming the result of their urban gleaning into works of assemblage art. These assemblages were displayed, as in the photograph, with more traditional artworks by hundreds of Watts-area artists at the Simon Rodia Commemorative Watts Renaissance of the Arts that took place April 3–9 at Markham Junior High School at 1650 E. 104th Street in Watts. A festival of visual and performing arts, it featured as well theater works, dance, music, photography, painting, and sculpture. To the *Times* reporter, whose copy makes allusions to the looting of the year before, Purifoy described the scraps they uncovered rather as "little jewels" of unprecedented shapes and forms. Berman made little effort to disguise his bias: "Unlike many Negroes who picked over the debris of the Watts riot seeking something of monetary value, Powell and Purifoy looked only for worthless junk."[28] Assemblages like the charred window and flower vase were displayed with contributions by other artists, including Mel Edwards, who, the *Times* added, had "recently exhibited at the County Museum of Art"—as well as with works by schoolchildren and adult students. A highlight of the festival was the exhibition of which the window and flower vase form part, entitled *66 Signs of Neon*, or as the *Times* described it, "works created out of the debris of last summer's Watts rioting."[29] In a long-overdue act of redress, the California Arts Commission, together with other South Los Angeles agencies, were showing resolve to narrow the discontinuities in the social geography of Los Angeles. The results were put on display in the featured *Times* photographs published that week: One depicted artist Noah Purifoy standing next to a different assemblage, a vertical construction of appliance parts crowned with a detached car window. Illustrating another story were two photographs of exhibition visitors, white women, in each case "smartly dressed," and we are to assume from places like Hancock Park, Beverly Hills, or Pasadena. A caption describes one Mary Jane Jones viewing "the remains of a neon sign at exhibition of Watts riot art," and a "Nancy Godwin, 22, [who] examines the rubble."[30]

The photograph of Purifoy and Powell's "window" survives on various levels. It serves as a stand-in for the Watts built environment, evidence of whose wreckage was now brought into interior space, and whose bald material realism now doubled as representational form—a shell to reframe ideas about the natural status of things. In the spaces separating the Watts Art Festival from the County Museum of Art dedication the year before, fireworks were to the display of municipal advocacy what "normative bonds to the majority group" were in relation now to the "charred window" and flower vase assemblage. With a flattened mood and desolate air that recall Atget's photographic framing of storefront displays, in this still life the sale-item artwork (meant to have generated revenue for workshops and art classes) appears destitute, perhaps makeshift but reliant on nothing in its immediate environment, and shockingly tender. Were he to have viewed this unassuming arrangement, Rubén Salazar might have also recalled the aftermath of mortar fire at Chu Lai and Sgt. Madison's belated outrage. And so the photograph turns Purifoy and Powell's material evidence into a scene that endures to contest the mostly demoded place of the social realm in some strands of modernist art ideologies—"Maybe that's what happened in Watts." It inhabits an uncanny setting of hospitality that submits these little jewels as objects for outlasting hostile forces, at once "uncomfortable, naggy, and frustrated." It tells a history "concealed and kept out of sight," at once a sign for home and an eviction.[31] "Do you really want to live here?"

6.

Like the Situationists in Paris, Purifoy, Powell, and other assemblage makers represented in the Watts Arts Festival employed the technique of so confronting urban space as to redirect the previous year's media spectacle around the rioting with the altered wreckage of that recent history. A photographic document of objects now lost to the historical record, Purifoy and Powell's window and vase serve to make claims about assemblage by African American artists as a fellow practice of spatial deviation—actions that reconfigure space to be experienced as "something one does not know one's way about in."[32] It spoke of the need to rearrange the geographies that, by means of institutionalized separation, keep some urban locations at a distance from the city's cultural capital. It sought, for Angelenos at large in the wake of the rebellion, to narrow the space between the vicinities of South Central and Watts, and greater metropolitan resources; between the causes of that social gap and the meaning ascribed to them in the hindsight of History. In an article for *Ebony* magazine, Stanley Sanders wrote that what he had "often mistaken for pointless spoutings was in reality a manifestation of this desperate search for truth about the riots."[33] Brought to light from the archives of the *Los Angeles Times*, the photograph makes it possible to think of Watts Festival assemblage art as a form of object-based journalism, facts gathered from scenes of disturbance juxtaposed into art-historical commonplace. Together, window frame and flower vase point to material conditions of a social breaking point. The photograph, by contrast, substantiates the truth-seeking to which Sanders alluded, as well as the reconfigured spaces transcending metaphor that assemblage art hoped to inaugurate. The "little jewels" endure in this image to speak of a resilience: Insomuch as resemblance is a shadow life, the charred window and vase look like their referent only to the degree that the picture obliquely points back to the cultural distractions of another city space documented photographically in the official fireworks during the County Museum dedication ceremony. Walter Benjamin suggested that "the survival of artworks should be represented from the standpoint of their struggle for existence. Their true humanity consists in their unlimited adaptability."[34] The anonymous photo of Purifoy and Powell's debris-inflected still life outlives the original occasion of display to remind us that no culture palace can conceal the fact that, once the fireworks are exhausted and the "splendid illumination is over, you can see that it came from a tawdry jumble of pipes."[35]

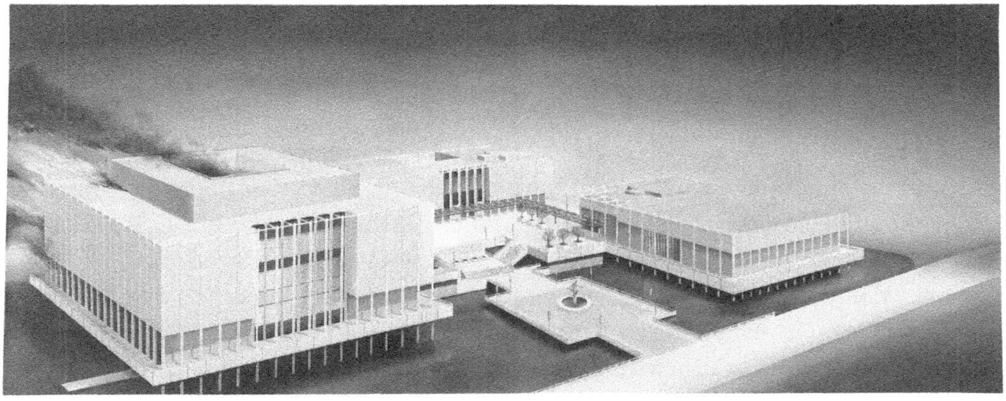

FIGURE 7. Ed Ruscha, *The Los Angeles County Museum on Fire*, 1965–68, oil on canvas, 53½ × 133½ in. (135.9 × 339.1 cm). Copyright Ed Ruscha, courtesy of the artist and Gagosian.

7.

There is an urgency with which Purifoy and Powell sought to redress the recent past by rebuilding with the chance unearthing from the wreckage. Even as it describes the number of works on display, the year and a surge of the present—1966—echo as well in the title *66 Signs of Neon*. The *Times* photograph of their picture frame and flower vase can be viewed in oblique relation to the contemporary devastation fantasy that was Ed Ruscha's *Los Angeles County Museum on Fire* (1965–68), a large-format painting that depicts William L. Pereira's three buildings ablaze (fig. 7). Set in unspecified pictorial space in hues of yellow and green, this familiar work very likely owes its most immediate visual referent to an uncredited bird's-eye photograph of the museum premises that appeared in a *Times* article on January 24, 1965, "County Museum of Art to Be Opened March 31."[36] Not long after the LACMA dedication and the Watts rebellion, Ruscha had begun work on his ambitious painting. Yve-Alain Bois has underscored the adversarial nature of the artist's self-styled concern for "visual noise," to such an extent that he never ceased "to depoliticize and de-dramatize one of his very few obvious assaults, *Los Angeles County Museum on Fire*." Alexandra Schwartz observes too that, even as its "monumental" scale (around 4½ by 11 feet) is rendered in "what Ruscha has often called an 'aerial oblique' perspective—with orange flames shooting discreetly off to the building's rear," the artist has disavowed readings of that canvas in reference to the Watts rebellion.[37] For Ruscha, even despite his own intentions, the natural order of the everyday, its face value coerced by a longer view, was not devoid of anxiety.

His detached but fastidious treatment of that apocalyptic daydream relates him to other artists caught up in the cultural contradictions of the 1960s. Ruscha executes banality with an increase in perversity, and things out of kilter were already for him the common condition—witness the bantamweight terrors of *Various Small Fires* or *Noise, Pencil, Broken Pencil, Cheap Western*, both of 1963. A different form of fear, for example, led Love's

Arthur Lee to hallucinating fire-and-brimstone prophesies overlooking the boulevards from a Hollywood hillside, watching "all the people die." But it is not *Los Angeles County Museum on Fire* that concerns me here so much as another work. In *Every Building on the Sunset Strip* Ruscha mounted a motorized Nikon to the back of a pickup truck (fig. 8). Driving eastbound and back, he clicked the extended cable-shutter at regular intervals, first on the south and then on the north side of the boulevard. Sequenced on upper and lower gutters of the page spread, with photos aligned into visible seams and breaks, the concept book aimed to encompass a world—like its twin, the self-styled "concept album"—for Ruscha, one of amazement disguised as mere automation. The successive pages of *Every Building* undermine mapmaking's delusional drive for exactitude when it aims to mirror the accidental features of urban disorder within the containable space of a book. In *Every Building* the Los Angeles Sunset Strip is shown to fluctuate wildly between chalet adorability and tawdry desolation, beginning with Schwab's Pharmacy—once a movie star haunt near Laurel Canyon Boulevard—and then an endless parade of faux Tudor façades next to courtyard apartments in vernacular California *moderne*. To the degree that telephone poles, bus stop benches, eucalyptus trees and palms coexisted with facades that could pass for any Main Street USA, so does the Whisky a Go Go and other music clubs, unremarkable in the light of day, extend horizontally on equal footing with a Texaco station or dry cleaners. With buildings so stripped of any glamour, indelible only are the billboards for Honda motorcycles, Kahlúa coffee liqueur, Johnnie Walker and J&B Scotch whiskies, the Sahara Hotel in Las Vegas featuring the Smothers Brothers and Vikki Carr, or the movie ad for *Arabesque*, starring Gregory Peck and Sophia Loren. This is the built environment that informs Love's *Forever Changes*. For example, in "The Daily Planet," the narrative depicts a citizen navigating the "go-stop boulevard"—a stand-in for the Strip—and it's certainly plausible to draw a correspondence between the urban billboard apparitions and the figure of "plastic Nancy / She's real fancy . . . Waiting on the war." That personification is similar to the one in the track "Andmoreagain," a selfhood that longs for a lifestyle of accumulated status and wealth. In short, the Sunset Strips of *Every Building* and "You Set the Scene" in *Forever Changes* contain all the geographies of leisure time that Purifoy and Powell's deteriorated window frame cannot give onto. "I see your picture / It's in the same old frame," sang Arthur Lee. In view of all the foregoing, the two lines are anteceded by an aphorism that best describes the poetics that *66 Signs of Neon* compelled: namely, "Everything I see needs rearranging."

Viewed in the context of *Every Building on the Sunset Strip*, the *Times* photograph of Purifoy and Powell's site-specific assemblage borders on the sacrosanct. Geographer Edward Soja asks that we pay careful attention to the creative dynamics of urban space. Because it is collectively produced and thus open to transformation, the urban environment and its civic interactions shape the social as much as the societal shapes the spatial. In the time zone of relation made visible in photography we can also trace the geographic effects that provide amendments for reframing the past. "As a starting point," writes Soja, this form of spatial justice "involves the fair and equitable distribution in space of socially valued resources and the opportunities to use them."[38] The photograph of Purifoy and Powell's window and *Every Building on the Sunset Strip* tell of those discontinuities. Two

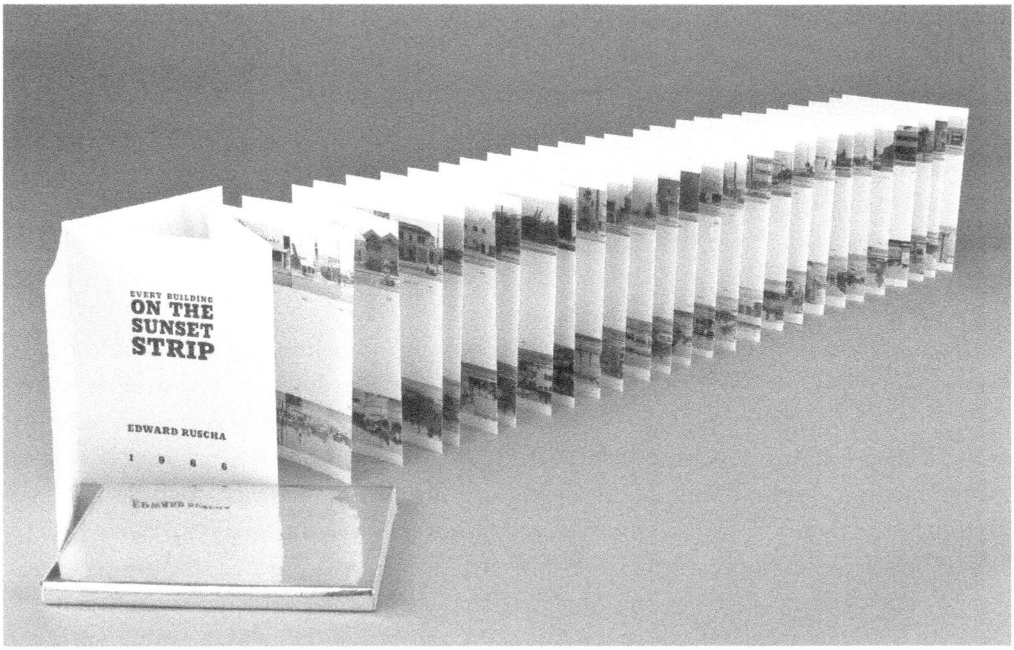

FIGURE 8. Ed Ruscha, *Every Building on the Sunset Strip*, signed artist's book, 1966, offset lithograph on paper in silver Mylar-covered box, 17.9 × 14 × 1.4 cm. Copyright Ed Ruscha, courtesy of the artist and Gagosian.

distinct practices in the technology of the image—an unpublished print meant for news copy, a self-published art book that undermines the window effect of a photograph—survive at this rhetorical juncture to submit an allegory of desire for spatial justice—the "same old frames" that oblige, if forever is to change, a visual rearranging.

8.

Lack of faith is what Arthur Lee intoned, and it was true to a declining historical confidence in the buoyant national self as once promoted in the popular press. The early 1960s were a time in which a purported Organization Man had given way to the Idea Man, and generational conquest spoke now in the language of efficiency and ambition, with a new corporate style and its greater stakes emerging for certain national protagonists. A 1962 special issue of *Life* magazine, for example, had devoted pages to "The Take-Over Generation," with a list of the "red-hot hundred" scientists, engineers, and cultural protagonists. This new brand of American demanded "responsibility," in *Life*'s prognostic, "not because he craves authority but because he can get the job done. He is, at this moment in history, starting to take over our destiny."[39] One of those generational victors, the Los Angeles architect and designer Richard Dorman was already by 1962 the president of two companies, the recipient of numerous awards and commissions, and a war veteran whose objective was to "get this country moving" by inciting a "hell" deemed "socially acceptable."[40]

A commissioned residence that Dorman designed was the subject of a feature in a 1966 edition of the *Los Angeles Times* "Home" section. Hired to photograph the house was Julius Shulman, the architectural cameraman whose images, for national and international audiences alike, stood for the staged seduction of an unruffled Los Angeles lifestyle in its commensurate built environment. Shulman's photographs encapsulate a brand of optimism, consistent with the modern project, whereby the designs of private and public space were meant to enhance the quality of life.

Economic expansion, advances in health sciences, space technology, and Cold War consumerism gave way to new forms of mass culture now receding into the American suburbs. To this, mid-century modern was a soft metropolitan rejoinder—household equivalent of the civic belonging performed at the Museum of Art dedication ceremony. Not given to effervescence, even Ed Ruscha has maintained that "Shulman's pictures have this force of romance to them; his work represents a certain ideal that happened years ago and yet it helped create the essence and ethos of this city."[41] Shulman's photography, in the *Times* spread entitled "Four Outstanding Architect Houses," included a high-angle shot of the Dorman house from the hillside street above, the San Fernando Valley a grid flickering in the expanse below, featuring the photographer's distinctive lighting of a residence from within, as though encased in encroaching nightfall. Another photograph recalls the sleek lines, high contrast, and vertiginous effects in the image he made of Pierre Koenig's Case Study House No. 22. The Dorman and Associates project comprises a series of steel, glass, and wood boxes articulated with exterior passageways that connect the decks and a pool overlooking the slope on which it is built. An interlocking network of discrete units composing a modernist hillside warren, Dorman called the four joined platforms "pods"—two of them feature skylight cupolas with the others "staggered back from the center." "At first glance," suggested the *Times*, "it looks like a cluster of those huts, which stand on stilts offshore in New Guinea."[42] With the "peaked roof" providing "volume and drama," the upper two-thirds of Shulman's photograph capture the ascendant diagonal beams and wood ceiling inside one of the modernist "huts." The geometric vault, activated by a triangular opening—the part visible from the skylight above, cathedral-like—draws focus away from the dwelling space below. Shulman's photograph of the Dorman interior uses one object to suspend the image at a visual centering: a metal sculpture on the face of the fireplace (fig. 9). The wall relief, by artist Mel Edwards, from the *Lynch Fragment* series, counts among a handful of works from the series that employ a circular convex base.[43] From the surface of a rose disk pertaining to cultivators used in mechanized farming, there appears to burst open a welded tangle of scrap metal, tool parts, hooks, chains, and other items formerly intended to shackle, puncture, carve, sever, and excavate. In one commonly held view, modernism had receded from its ambitious designs for society and wagered instead on private utopian havens for the advanced guard with economic means. The Edwards *Lynch Fragment* sculpture in this mid-century refuge from the urban core, surviving in Shulman's photograph, formerly in the *Los Angeles Times*, telescopes to the present tense as a historical placeholder for thinking about the artwork—a discreet hell that appears

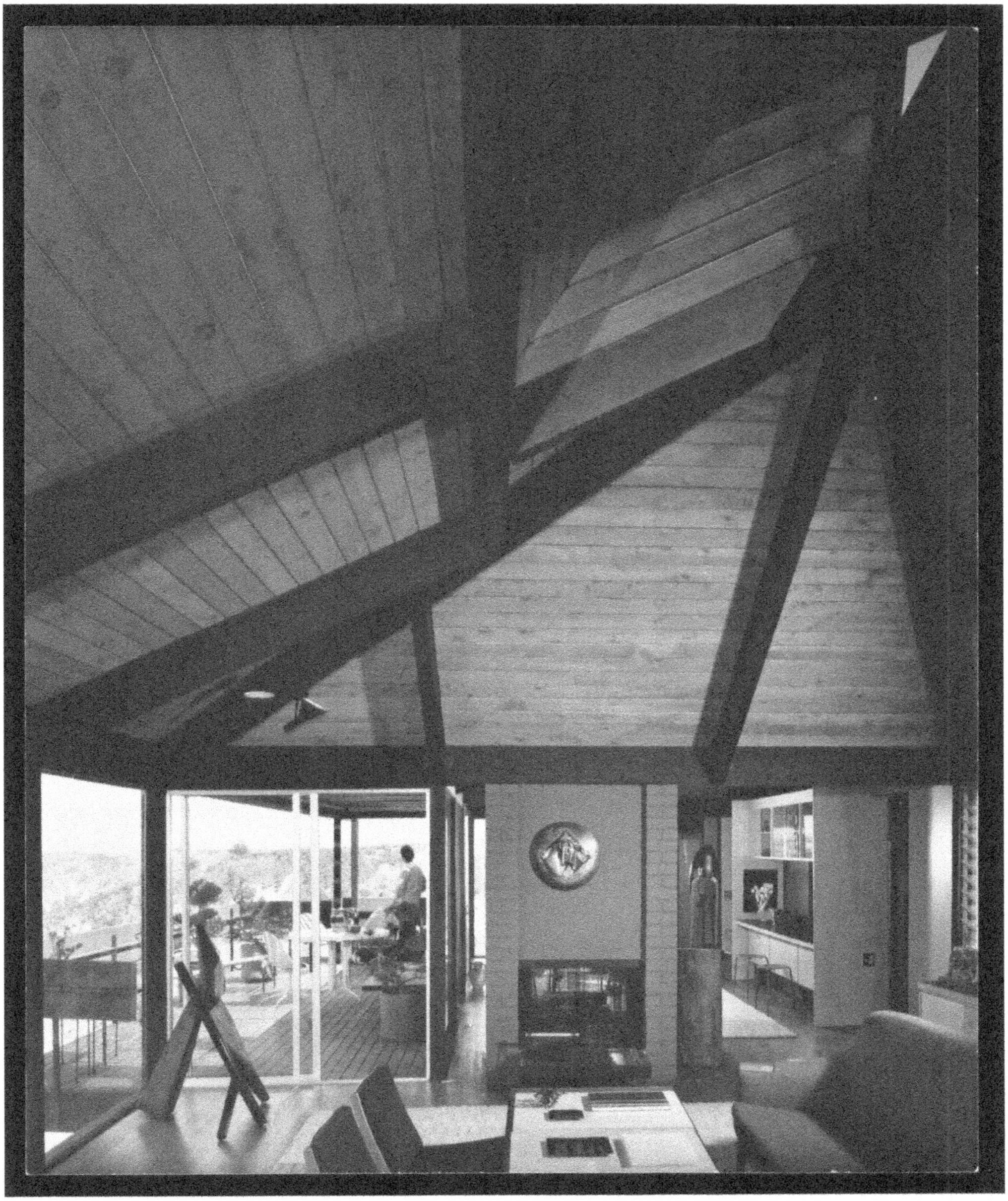

FIGURE 9. Julius Shulman, *Richard Dorman house, 196*, in Dan MacMasters, "Departure from the Stereotype," *Los Angeles Times*, May 22, 1966, p. 28. © J. Paul Getty Trust. Getty Research Institute, Los Angeles (2004.R.10).

socially acceptable—in its domestic environment and in photographs that over time betray inadvertent forms of visibility. A look into yet another space articulated by the *Lynch Fragment* series provides added layers of meaning.

Mel Edwards had moved to Los Angeles in the mid-1950s and studied at "Los Angeles City College for two years, at USC for a semester then Otis and back to USC for a year and a half." The artist hadn't really cared for sculpture as a medium until he "saw some welded things" and began to make sculpture in 1960. In a 1965 interview with LACMA curator Maurice Tuchman for the exhibition catalog to *Five Younger Artists*, Edwards likened his work to "icons or fertility figures [in] contemporary materials like steel and junk metal" and said that he drew from his "social background to give [himself] the impetus." The found objects included a meat hook in *The Lifted X* (1965) and "a blackball that came from a fireplace, in the same sculpture." Edwards appreciated the "reference to gonads there. I use chains—as in the *Chaino* and *Hang-Up*—both as a dynamic and symbolic thing." To Tuchman's suggestion that Edwards's work recalls "fragmented anatomies or flesh," Edwards responded: "I use the fragmented form idea from many sources—it might be flesh, a battleship gun, almost anything. But at all times I'm concerned with moving things in space."

Likewise concerned with the motion of bodies in space—of actors during a staged rehearsal—Jayne Cortez featured in a 1966 *Times* article about her role as director of acting classes for South Los Angeles youth at Studio Watts, part of the wider post-rebellion cultural resurgence. The account portrays her in a journalistic snapshot as she interrupts two young actors immersed in an improvised scene of dragging absurdist realism. She interjects with an assertion: "The only thing is . . . you forgot the real motivation of why you were there. Now let's try it again and keep your motivation in mind."[44] That reasoning has long been the core of her writerly poetics. Cortez takes apart the structures of cause and effect so as to repurpose the liability of any action. In her poetry the gaps between form and meaning and the aims of speech disclose a shape proper to energies brought without cease into view. Several years after the *Times* pages appeared on the Richard Dorman house and the Studio Watts Workshop, Mel Edwards and Jayne Cortez had the opportunity, now living in New York, to work together on a poet–visual artist collaboration that points back to the origins of this narrative in Los Angeles.

9. [Double Exposure: "Today on This Day"]

That structural violence exerts its conditions for an ordered society looms large even when defied on celebratory occasions. Jayne Cortez has spoken of locating her poetry in the unconscious and its concrete objects, employing visceral citations and a language of the lower body to render syllables immediate to their action. "I guess the poetry is like a festival," the author has remarked. "Everything can be transformed."[45] In 1971, Cortez printed *Festivals and Funerals*, a self-produced limited edition composed on an IBM Selectric II. At forty-four pages, the saddle-stitched book, now a rare object, was an extension of Cortez's Phrase Text imprint and a forerunner to her long-standing Bola Press.[46] The volume establishes a space of relation between the twenty-five poems and seven drawings produced for the edition by Edwards, each class of line remarking on its adjacent medium. So, too, does the collaboration hinge its two media in concrete spatial and temporal terms: Expectations and real time cut back and forth between typographic lines and ink markings. Cortez's poetry, unflinching insofar as it seeks to explore the brutal underside of expressive acceptability, makes such zones of interdiction possible in language that explodes with joyousness, even as it is capable of collapsing spaces at once social, psychological, geographic, and economic. These areas estrange speech because they strive to contain a world by rearranging its relations.

One of the opening poems in the collection submits, with no small amount of cruel irony, what the book as a whole exults. The "health department" appears to be shorthand for the institutional effect of municipal agencies, antipoverty programs, and other bureaucratic spaces not always able in their objective to ensure public well-being. Parallel leitmotifs include those of injury and amputation; flesh in its various states of combustion or breakdown; diseases congenital or infectious; and pathologies acute or chronic. Pan-African rituals blur into the violence of transatlantic slavery and again into the brutalities of the modern-day clinic. In this, her poems already shared elective affinities with Edwards's recombinant structures made of metal tools that stand for body parts that amalgamate to resemble ceremonial masks rising from the junk heap of modern consumption. Both artists explore drive—specifically that which is constitutive of Black sexuality—even as they wager political and aesthetic stakes on similar questions: What are the rhetorical and visual means by which to depict a social body so subsisting in everyday life as to contest the histories approved by the dominant order, but so proficient also as to celebrate even the defeats of that counterengagement?

In their collaborative working method, Cortez first sent the complete manuscript to Edwards, living at the time in upstate New York, who returned a large number of drawings grounded in the book's argument, structure, lexicon, and subject matter. Cortez then proceeded to select and visually order the drawings into the sequence of the book. The cover drawing to *Festivals and Funerals* relates formally to that on the interior title page (fig. 10). Positioned to the left is an upturned mask-like set of triangular teeth that form a grimace-flashing mouth. An eye-nipple nestles on a pair of breast-lips, overlapping vision and voluptuousness in a totemic ascent of glands, eyes, and nose. Although indistinguishable and in partial view, the configuration is rendered in solid bold lines and confident strokes, the marker's flat tip allowing Edwards to create thicker curved segments with a downward mark, and narrower lines on the horizontal and diagonal. These chain formations prompted from the unspecified space of the blank page materialize into long- and short-phrased gestures. Equally stressed between the flatness of the marking and the volume of the recommended form is what Cortez submits as a "second headed face" in an adjacent poem ("Initiation"). Together there emerges a chilling traction between the visual body parts and the ritual geography of cause that nominates "an arm for a rapist? / a leg for the servant?"

This prologue poem is followed by another riveting vision in "Today on This Day." An inauguration takes place, invoked by a subject in corporeal tatters, a baptismal offering in the fluid of tears. Proximity of terms, however—as "rags" is to "pop bottle"—suggest the liquid is combustible and that the launching is of a firebomb not unlike the kind unleashed on the streets of Los Angeles in 1965. The speaker releases sardonic well-wishing from a place of destitution, and the blistering temperatures turn progeny into corporeal decay. A single line, an eerie cheer for the "health department," invokes spectators to watch "a friday crowd" of injured bodies spread out on stretchers, as they are made to tumble into some storage place underground; these cadavers serve as surrogates for the decomposing foundation on which future admission is contingent.

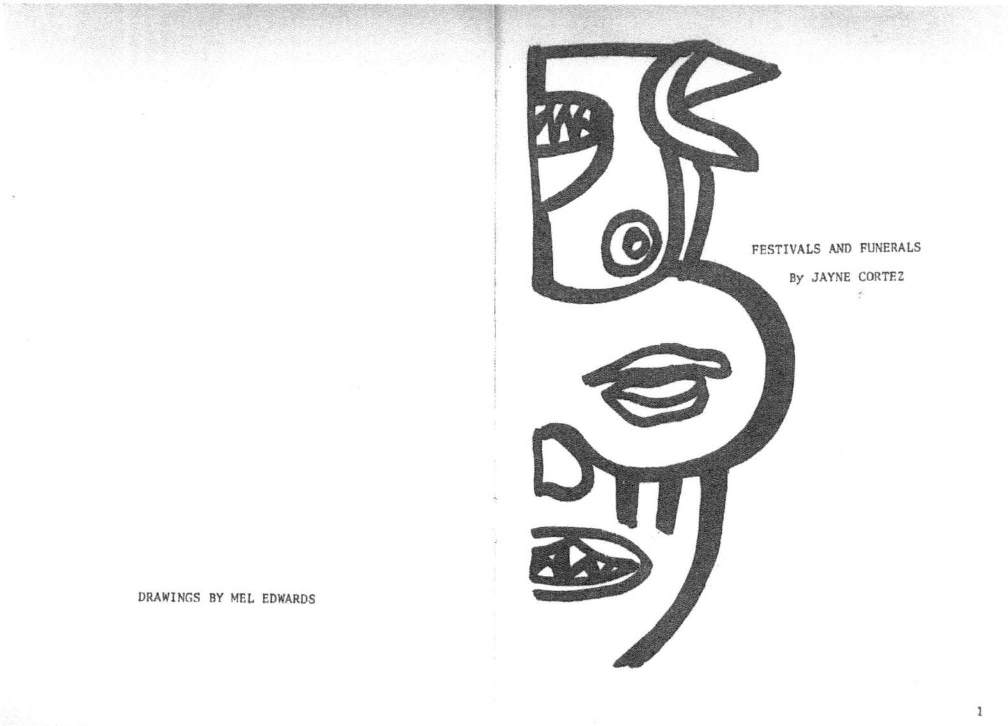

FIGURE 10. Jayne Cortez, *Festivals and Funerals* (New York: Phrase Text, 1971), poetry by Cortez with drawings by Melvin Edwards, interior cover. Private collection.

TODAY ON THIS DAY

Today on this day
I would like to push forward from
my shadow of rags
and offer this pop bottle of tears
I baptised in

good luck to you
from my torn suede shoes on
this same day of my daughters eyes
putrified
in donkey heat

Hooray for the health department

I feel damp before such an audience of
mascara and white coats waving
their bye bye's
to the friday crowd of occupied stretchers
bye bye
from the basement smell of their budget

bye bye
today on this day of jaws
in the fifth month of resemblance at
the end of a pretzel on the heart of
my son's remembrance
thump thump thump

Hands off my vomit number three recruiting
number four turning the exit to
enter my torn shoes in numbers
Warning
I take back my tears
my luck
my daughters eyes
today on this day of
No admittance No return Keep out
Cash only day of Shit

The sexual excitement and farewells at mid-poem are a defiance to spite the beau monde or scientific elites ("audience of/mascara and white coats waving"), and some of the visual citations are continuous in mood with the drawings by Edwards. The words "jaws" and "pretzel" betray oblique relation to the markings evocative of flaps and loops under an obtruding brush tip or traditional spear-like tool. This interlacing submits that likeness is to remembrance as the commemoration of a son or daughter is to History. The institutional or hallowed spaces proscribed to the speaker ("No admittance No return") recall, together with the drawing's archaic lines, that in the economics only of manufacture and consumption, money and human waste are of a piece. Several pages after this, precisely in the poem "Lynch Fragment," the conspiring visual and verbal poetics escalate. References to "whips" and "bones" and "mutilated flesh" communicate across the page—but never in one-to-one identity—with analogous noose, harness, or branch figures, aligned in the foreground of a midday sun or full-moon formation.

Lynch Fragment
My tongue whips blood through the
ribs of a cobra
I am a serpent
a parched cavity for lynched reptiles
iron rust of my musty scales sucking up the
secret strength of bad smells from two curved horns
clipped horns of a ram under the
bent pipe of my passionate sloping bone which
is the beauty mask that god wears like
the four part sun rising redly to the tip of
frozen nerves heard
beyond the muted cries of
mutilated flesh in a hole

a fox hole
a fixed hole where spirits erect themselves &
urinate inside my nostrils

Staged here are various affinities and incremental transmutations—of serpent into ram; of a divine mask into gashed tissue either defiled or consecrated with bodily fluids. If terror is the historical cause, and panic the internal root, of abjection—translated into animal odors and urinated cavities—it produces a body brutalized and thereby foreign to its own cultural and sexual figuration in the field of vision. For Georges Bataille and a strand of surrealism that saw picture and word as indivisible, the abject is a pageantry not of things that degrade but of all that we treasure. It appears as a bodily orifice—legitimate opening onto the world—and as the site of explosive impulses, as when the mouth is an organ of "muted cries," demented hilarity, or torture screams.[47] As with his small-format relief sculptures, Edwards creates pictorial enigmas in drawings that activate surplus energies in the depiction of Black histories, even as they ask where one linear idea begins and another ends in visual metaphors composed of patterns, profiles, and appendages. *Festivals and Funerals* is the effect of a meeting place between argument and image wherein no isomorphism is possible; however, the alliance—together in crisscrossed depiction, as voice to embodiment—is better able to articulate the taboo descriptions of a history shaped by American racial violence.

The abjections in *Festivals and Funerals* were meant at once to underline and to redirect "visceral feelings about Black bodies fueled by sexual myths of Black women and men," writes Cornel West. "The dominant myths draw Black women and men either as threatening creatures who have potential for sexual powers over whites, or as harmless, desexed underlings of a white culture. . . . The myths offer distorted, dehumanized creatures whose bodies—color of skin, shape of nose and lips, type of hair, size of hips—are already distinguished from the white norm of beauty and whose feared sexual activities are deemed disgusting, dirty, or funky and considered less acceptable."[48] Even as *Festivals and Funerals* counteracts by repossessing these revulsions, its abject image-texts fold backward in time to illuminate the assemblage by Purifoy and Powell. On that Markham Junior High School dais, but in this enhanced lighting, the charred picture frame and vase of *66 Signs of Neon* reappear in the photograph as a placeholder for the panic and attraction projected on Black bodies in municipal space after the Watts rebellion. Two other photographs for the *66 Signs of Neon* appearing in the article were meant to interpolate whiteness and womanhood as the form of this artwork's address. In this respect, they stand today as surrogate subjects for the "audience of/ mascara and white coats waving," as well as for the "mixture of collectors, artists, dealers, curators, academics, amateurs, and of those who [now thought it] important for their social aplomb to be seen at such gatherings."[49] These connections telescope also to inform the wall relief by Edwards in the Shulman photograph of the hillside home designed by Richard Dorman—collapsing the spaces that separate the book collaboration in New York, the Watts assemblage artwork, and the private residence overlooking San Fernando Valley. The *Lynch Fragment* wall relief in the Dorman-designed home may have once served as a sign of progressive aesthetics and politics for its one-time residents. By dint of Shulman's image in the *Los Angeles Times*, in its photographic afterlife the artwork still manages to set into motion a redirection of "disquieting, dirty, or funky" content to belie the authoritative myth making of the "Home Section" daydream. Out of those emulsions the Edwards *Lynch Fragment* opens into the present as a disturbance, a sharp metal gleam in the field of vision, unbearable inasmuch as it upsets any fantasy of habitation that would disavow the coordinated hierarchies of residential location in Los Angeles. It discloses the historical uncanny ghosting any claim to an alleged city essence or ethos; it makes palpable the kind of hell deemed socially acceptable that some expressive spaces managed to keep concealed and out of sight.

10. [Oblique Shot: Moratorium]

Even though by mid-century Los Angeles had largely disowned its eastern and southern sections, home respectively to Chicanos and to African Americans, after the Watts uprising of 1965 those formerly excluded citizens now claimed their "right to the city"—to seek, that is, what Edward Soja has called "the fair and equitable distribution in space of socially valued resources and the opportunities to use them."[50] Assimilating Mexican Americans and politicized Chicanos alike found much to validate their brand of citizenship in the journalism of Rubén Salazar. After his assignment in Vietnam, he was for many years a *Los Angeles Times* staff reporter, later chief of its Mexico City bureau, and finally news director of KMEX, the Spanish-language television station in Los Angeles. During his tenure at the *Times*, as newswriter and guest columnist, he reported cultural stereotyping on television, specifically the damage it can cause to "the self-image of young impressionable Mexican-American minds" while endorsing prejudice among "young, impressionable Anglo minds."[51] He covered the 1969 Chicano Youth Liberation Conference held in Denver, where, most notably, Rodolfo (Corky) Gonzalez had outlined the manifesto of a cultural politics in his "Spiritual Plan of Aztlán."[52] Salazar addressed repression and its alienating effects in the barrio.[53] He wrote about *pachuco* folk heroes; about *bato locos* and their potential in organizational politics; about the need for jobs in unemployment-ridden ghettos and barrios; and about the lack of equal opportunities for education in the geographically overdetermined spatial layout of Los Angeles.[54] Born in Mexico and educated in the borderlands of El Paso, Salazar wrote about the bilingual experience; about growing Chicano nationalism; about border crossing and employment issues in the shift from agricultural to factory labor; and about the demands of Chicanos and Latino groups at UCLA concerning education, the entertainment industry, and communications media.[55] He spoke to the vicissitudes of the word "Mexican" as a maligned expression, and perhaps most notably he gave historical nuance to the name for those who so self-identified: "A Chicano is a Mexican-American with a non-Anglo image of himself."[56]

In the process, Salazar identified a new style of Chicano leadership that looked, now optimistically, now ambivalently, to antecedents in the Black Power movement: "The new breed of Mexican-American leaders, some anxious over strides Negroes are making with public monies which they consider should be going to Chicanos, are trying to emulate the more militant Negro leaders."[57] Salazar did not shy away from reporting on Black-Brown friction, but instead remained unflinching when comparing the ways in which Blacks and Chicanos were the subjects of racism. Finding it difficult to suppress resentment in their "scramble for better jobs, housing, and education," many Mexican Americans began to express feeling "short-shrifted" by all the antipoverty programs aimed at African Americans.[58] Whereas Chicanos were rapidly becoming the largest ethnic group in Southern California, it appeared to them as though African Americans were making greater strides.[59]

For Salazar, the ethos of Chicano identity—as conveyed to Mexican Americans and Anglos alike—was open to comparison with the African American civil rights movement; the social demands of the latter made it possible and desirable to articulate Brownness and other styles of positive selfhood in the forging of Chicano empowerment. Salazar reported on the turn away from "Spanish surname" identity to a self-confident ethnic pride in being of Mexican descent. This formed but one part of a broader cross-cultural identification and alliance that found symbolic and political partnerships in the burgeoning Chicano Art Movement. Antonio Bernal's 1968 mural at El Teatro Campesino's headquarters in Del Rey, California—canonical in the image archive of El Movimiento—featured historical figures from Mexico's revolution, including Emiliano Zapata and an *Adelita* (female insurgent), in line with Cesar Chavez waving the United Farm Workers' flag in a defiant stand, joined also by Martin Luther King Jr. and Malcolm X.

The everyday discrimination, desolate living conditions, and incidents of police brutality facing families and communities in South and East Los Angeles prompted Salazar to begin reporting on collective discontent and resistance. With the founding of the Chicano Moratorium Committee, an upsurge of organized protests—first against conscription and then against the Vietnam War, for a year's total of eighteen demonstrations in the Southwest—culminated in the National Chicano Moratorium held on August 29, 1970, in East LA's Belvedere Park. KMEX, where Salazar was now director, helped to promote the rally, for which an estimated twenty thousand peaceful protesters made their way from Belvedere Park, down Whittier Boulevard, to Laguna Park.[60] At first imperceptible to the demonstrators at large, panic at a nearby liquor store had led its proprietor to lock down the establishment, with rally patrons caught inside. Police arrived to form skirmish lines, and hostility rapidly escalated: Rocks and bottles hurled at law enforcement were met with tear-gas retaliation. The outbreak resulted in considerable property damage, four hundred arrests, and three fatalities. Most shocking was the death of Rubén Salazar, who in the Silver Dollar Café had sought refuge from the mounting violence being waged against the protesters outside. In the already disproportionate police offensive, Deputy Sheriff Thomas Wilson made Salazar's head the target of a tear-gas projectile; the journalist was killed instantly.[61]

11. [Group Portrait with LACMA]

Nearly four years after Salazar's death, his colleague at public television station KCET Edward Moreno was the one to cover *Los Four: Almaraz / de la Rocha / Luján / Romero* at the Los Angeles County Museum of Art. This milestone exhibition at the city's premier culture palace was the labor of Cecil Fergerson, a lively museum-world protagonist. James Tartan's 1974 documentary *Los Four* traces the days leading up to the exhibition and the group deliberations among the four members of the Chicano artist collective—Carlos Almaraz, Gilbert Sánchez Luján, Roberto de la Rocha, and Frank Romero—as they struggle with this unprecedented opportunity for legitimation within the art establishment. The opening scene finds the quartet around a kitchen table anticipating what will qualify as the first presentation of Chicano art in a major US museum. It is here, at Romero's house near downtown Los Angeles, "an informal meeting place for many local Chicano artists," that Los Four had instituted an alliance to meet and exhibit collectively. As a founding member, Romero describes in voiceover the close association he and Almaraz have shaped for more than twelve years—with the subsequent incorporation of Luján and de la Rocha—and how the group's iconography and ideas, when painting collectively, require the kind of exchange and compromise enacted now before the camera.

Romero had studied art at Otis Art Institute and California State University of Los Angeles (then called California State College), but it was the combined efforts of Los Four that brought Chicano street art to the attention of the Los Angeles mainstream community. Finding inspiration in everyday Mexican American working-class objects, folk imagery, and discarded items that they transformed into the raw material of assemblage art, Los Four's practice was one of *bricolage*, making-do.

They eked the most out of a bare minimum in sometimes flamboyant, unapologetically shabby, but always colorful and joyous domestic cadences of *rasquachismo*—an attitude more than an idea or a style. Tomás Ybarra-Frausto later summarized the poetics of *rasquachismo* as that which embraces "the worldview of the have-nots" even as it represents "a quality exemplified in objects and places."[62] For the LACMA exhibition, the group decided to contribute individually as well as collectively with the shared use of spray-can techniques, overlapping display, and a riotous accumulation of popular debris arranged into a pyramid altar.

In Tartan's film, the camera lingers on Romero as he wanders the streets of East LA, photographing vernacular displays of residential front yards. In voiceover he affirms:

> One of my private interests is collecting folk art in East Los Angeles, and I go out and drive, just to places I grew up around, park the car, walk the streets, talk to the people, and I'm basically involved in the kind of thing people with no art training do. . . . They decorate their gardens and what I find in East Los Angeles is a distinct Chicano style [cut to: a cactus plant and ornaments that include a bright yellow piggy bank atop a plaster cast elephant fronted by a plastic figurine of Daffy Duck], and I can only relate that to my own life experience the way I live: it's loose.
>
> What I'm saying is that these things had a strong influence on me as an individual and as an artist and I'm just now learning to reflect that input.[63]

The narrative curve follows the four artists moving materials from Romero's residence to the museum, installing the work on scaffolds in situ around the gallery assigned to them—"the back room," according to Romero's voiceover. The various scenes culminate with a KCET crew preparing to tape Moreno in an interview for his television magazine

Ahora!, a series intended to "increase awareness—inside and outside the Chicano community—of the problems, contributions and potential of the Mexican-Americas of Los Angeles."[64] Following the "five seconds" signal from the production team, Moreno intones the following in his graceful, accented English: "Cecil Fergerson is especial curator for this exhibition of Los Four. Cecil, how did the museum become interested in Los Four's art?" Moreno's gray Glen plaid suit and Fergerson's amber-orange tie and formal black shirt stand out against the bright pink pyramid constructed by Los Four. Fergerson punctuates: "For quite some time now, Mrs. Jane Livingston, curator of modern art, had been looking at a great deal of Chicano work, and works of other minority groups, such as Black, women's movement, and that sort of art concept." The Mexican journalist and the African American curator pause in front of the pyramid's stepped ledges packed with festive handcrafted articles: Mexican masks depicting humans, devils, and fantastic beasts; statuettes of saints; free-standing crucifixes; woodcut prints; church candles; paper flower bouquets; and *papel picado* streamers. Together with Los Four's individual works, all this must have struck some temperaments as a muddled assault on the institution's devotion to the alleged "purity" of modernist form . . . and such an attitude is captured by Tartan's camera at the opening-night events. The guests, a family affair comprising East Los Angeles and Hancock Park art patrons alike, mingle amid the Mexican music, food, and dancing, while a few dour faces—and a partial view of Frank Stella's *Hiragla Variation I* (1969), otherwise eclipsed—appear from time to time in the background.

If any advances were made in the LA museum world for people of color in the 1970s it was largely thanks to Fergerson's defiant efforts at LACMA. His affiliation had begun during the institution's earlier incarnation, part of the Los Angeles Museum of Natural History at Exposition Park, where Fergerson worked as a custodian. Promotions led him from janitor to exhibition preparator and, at the museum's eventual Wilshire Boulevard campus, a member of its curatorial staff in the division of modern and contemporary art. Throughout his LACMA career, Fergerson took the institution to task for its false assumptions, silences, and contradictions—kinder words for what amounted to structural racism. He was unambiguous in challenging the authority of a "white" institution whose aesthetic values were conclusive in determining art world economies of reward and prestige. With a reputation for being "irascible," he was also, in the elegant summation of a more recent *Times* feature, an "assemblage of enigmas and grace notes only the mind of God would have the wit and effrontery to propose."[65] Interviewed for that same article, Fergerson notes how his "rise in the hierarchy of the museum" coincided with changes there: "The curators went from snobbish sons of rich white people to guys who got outta college who weren't necessarily born with money. . . . [Curators] Maurice Tuchman, James Elliot . . . they all had a liberal kind of funkiness to them. Different from most of the white people that I met when I first got there and who would walk up and down the hallway all day long and wouldn't speak to you." In a profession that tended to draw from the gray and feeble, Fergerson had vitality and drive, and he soon fell in with the cultural elite connected to the Chouinard Art Institute and Ferus Gallery. Ed Ruscha recalls that "Cecil was not of the hierarchy, but everybody knew Cecil . . . he was the ambassador over there. Any artist who was working over there would always seek him out, [and] Cecil was right there to help them."[66] Together with Claude Booker, a museum shipping clerk, Fergerson had formed the Black Arts Council in 1968. In 1972 the council sponsored *Panorama of Black Artists*, a large group exhibition that marked the first museum showing for many of the fifty-one artists—Betye Saar, Noah Purifoy, David Hammons, and John Outterbridge, among them. Even though the works had to be installed in LACMA's small rental gallery in the lower recesses of the museum, it was a platform for a "sort of art concept" that Fergerson was able to extend, two years later, to include Chicano artists. And there is no overstating their indebtedness to Cecil's efforts.

The *rasquachismo* of Los Four's 1974 exhibition conveys an affinity with Cortez's *Festivals and Funerals* as a parallel Chicano performance of the joyfully abject—the poet's "pop bottle of tears," "torn suede shoes," and "donkey heat" in alignment now with the art collective's cactus paddles, spray paint, and pink pyramid, as though "from the basement smell of their budget." The labors of Fergerson and Salazar overlap into a portrait whose double exposures provide a transcultural glimpse into the function of minority journalists and curators working as agents of social change. By seizing opportunity within the institutional framework, they altered policy within the newspaper establishment, the museum world, and beyond.

12. [Landscape: Life in the Park with Debris]

"Astrobrite melon" is the commanding silk-screen color. Two fields of vibrant orange-pink divide the poster into upper and lower planes, one in a diagonal pattern, held together over an area of the underlying paper as though attached by two black strips that resemble electrical tape on which letters appear to spill. They reiterate the bannered moniker above, a high-pitched announcement—"PLUGZ"—broadcast in radioactive yellow typeface. A slanted inset over the cantaloupe backdrop features photographic material, the headshot of a male youth sporting a spiked coiffure, his eyes bulging, mouth open, and teeth firmly chomping on a spiral telephone cord. Over the purple and black dot pattern of yet another tilted bar below, the typeface in jukebox brush-script reads "Nuevo Wavo," transposing "new wave" into Spanish (plate 4). By 1978, the year artist Richard Duardo created this poster, The Plugz, a punk-inspired trio fronted by Tito Larriva (the poster's likely photograph subject), had gained much admiration among critics, peers, and fans alike as one of the most exciting outfits playing the Los Angeles club circuit. With its underground origins linked at first to short-lived venues like the Masque and Larchmont Hall, the scene gradually surfaced to include other locations: in Hollywood the Whisky a Go Go and the Starwood; in Chinatown Madame Wong's and the Hong Kong Cafe; and downtown Al's Bar. In 1980 the all-age performance venue the Vex began to operate in East LA as an extension of Self Help Graphics and Art, the community art center founded by a Franciscan nun, Sister Karen Boccalero.[67] Duardo, after graduating from UCLA in graphic design, had begun working in the early 1970s with several art collectives. One of these was Self Help, which served East Los Angeles's primarily Chicano and Mexicano community by offering print facilities so local artists could create silk-screened works like *Plugz/Nuevo Wavo*.[68]

Cultural as well as geographic distances separated the worlds of Hollywood and East LA, but if there was any band capable of bridging those gaps it was The Plugz—for example, when they headlined "East LA Night" at the Roxy on Sunset Boulevard, together with the Brat, Thee Undertakers, and Los Illegals.[69] Tito Larriva's oft-remarked charisma was matched by the calibrated musicianship of bandmates Chalo Quintana and Barry McBride (later replaced by Tony Marsico). Talking to *Times* writer Kristine McKenna, McBride summarized the sound of the band as "an amalgam of rhythm and blues, heavy metal, and traditional Spanish music," whereas McKenna herself described them as playing "hard driving punk with a melodic edge," with Larriva as the riveting exemplar of "elegance, humor, and conviction."[70] With his lyric minimalism Larriva skewered the media-driven "mindless contentment" looming over the new creative class of Los Angeles ("All of the normals want to be on TV"). He sang about desires and discontent, too, in the emergent "scene" of which he was a participant-witness, all of it taking a toll on everyday selfhood: "A gain a loss / No matter the cost."[71] With rare emotional tenor, their songs—recorded on two albums, *Electrify Me* (1979) and *Better Luck* (1981)—belie those US promises that do not distribute equally, especially if you are socially marked in the spatial disconnection of Los Angeles itself: "When things look closer / that's when they're furthest away." To the actual distances separating parts from the whole of the city—indeed, so often keeping the various scenes asunder—came the increasing price of oil throughout the crises of the 1970s. Duardo's silk screen includes the numbers intoned by Larriva and The Plugz in a secret-agent punk tune entitled "Gas Line," referring to price hikes at filling stations in Los Angeles from 1975 to 1979. At a time when fuel was still counted in cents per gallon—"55 to 61 / 61 to 84 / 84 to 90"—the song conveys a historical moment whose continuation was at best precarious: "We're all tapping gas . . . Don't light a match."

The posters for upcoming shows at venues throughout the city reflect a public culture that emerged in the late 1970s and early 1980s around nighttime concert settings. This culture satirized fantasies of the status quo, and Hollywood's image engineering was one of its particularly dependable targets.[72] By the early 1980s, there emerged in Los Angeles a phantom version of Hollywood that included the Groundlings Theatre's 1981 midnight skewering of children's television, *The Pee-wee Herman Show* (starring Paul Reubens in the title role, Tito Larriva as his friend Hammy, and actor-by-day nightclub-bouncer-by-night Laurence Fishburne as Cowboy Curtis). There was Peter Iver's cable-access delirium known as *New Wave Theater* that hosted bands such as The Plugz, the Suburban Lawns, the Blasters, the Circle Jerks, and Fear.[73] Its intrepid editing and gonzo variety-show format both aped and indulged in late-night kook philosophizing, the drone of advertising culture, and Southern California transcendentalism. The vernacular assemblage art that was punk fashion lampooned the glamour of Hollywood by pillaging secondhand stores for its own rough-and-tumble spectacle, unwittingly *rasquache* through and through, even as its manifold styles shared, as McKenna pointedly observes, a "quality of studied amateurishness."[74] If so much depended upon "How to Look Punk"—inasmuch as a "simple T-shirt, punk-style necktie, a few chains or safety pins, and jeans is getting it on"—corporeal expressiveness proved at best to be a form of nonconformist swagger linked to misfit pragmatism.[75] In this culture's patterns of looking and being seen, photocopied flyers, promotional shots for bands, and zines such as *Slash* and *Flipside* all captured a style that made it possible for idolaters to individuate and connect by way of insider distinctions that mapped you among the happy few. What Fred "Phast Phreddie" Patterson dubbed the underground rock elite of Los Angeles was as much involved in staging the nightmare aspect of Sunset Strip glamour—John Doe and Exene Cervenka's dissonant vocalizing to "Sex and Dying in High Society"—as it was committed to spoofing industry ennui and showbiz exceptionalism.[76] One need only consider the Circle Jerks (such trinkets of sentiment as "I've got the world up my ass") or, more darkly, the stream-of-consciousness lyrics to X's "Nausea"("like a candy bar wrapped up / For lunch that's all you get to taste / Poverty and spit / Poverty and spit") to see connections pointing back to the proto-punk poetics of Cortez and her critical dissociation from the beau monde and other elites in the kind of exuberance that can intone "No admittance No return Keep out / Cash only day of Shit."

Video maker and performance artist Ulysses Jenkins described the precariousness of racial and ethnic experience in the shadow of Hollywood. "What [it] represents, especially in my work, is the classic plantation mentality. Although people aren't necessarily enslaved by it, people enslave themselves to it because they're told how fantastic it is to help manifest these illusions for a corporate sponsor."[77] While artists and musicians scrutinized *that* Hollywood and its detrimental effects, the actual Hollywood district became, if not entirely a zone of social détente, then at least a place where "punk" as an identity in its broadest sense, and shorthand for LA's avant-garde, was prone to trump other (at times limiting) social and sexual identities. New modes of musical performance emerged from those initial inflections in an extended Hollywood field that included venues such as Club Lingerie, the Anti-Club, Cathay de Grande, China Club, and especially Club Lhasa. It comprised the heady high jinks of an avant-cabaret style, such that brassy chanteuse Magie Song of the Fibonaccis ("Fellini-circus-chamber-mobile-home-park-Muzak from hell") could vamp about interethnic sexual politics ("Disgusting Man") and confront audiences with radical cultural difference, as in the number "Rice Song," alternately growled and cooed in Korean.[78] There were also enactments of a "Third World video vision," combining the sounds of soul and art-rock with a political critique of US global ascendancy during the Reagan era.[79]

It's in this latter configuration that Jenkins's work comes into panoramic view. *Times* journalist Don Snowden wrote that Jenkins looked to combat "cultural stereotypes and the media saturation of modern society."[80] Earlier, the abjections enacted in Cortez's *Festivals and Funerals* had been meant to underline and redirect "visceral feelings about Black bodies fueled by sexual myths of Black women and men . . . as threatening creatures who have potential for sexual powers over whites, or as harmless, desexed underlings of a white culture."[81] For his 1978 art video *Mass of Images*—produced while completing an MFA at Otis Art Institute—Jenkins appears before a draped backdrop in a recording studio. A transparent mask forms a bubble covering his face, over which he wears large, tinted glasses.[82] From behind a pyramid of television sets, the artist swerves toward the camera in a wheelchair. He wears a bath or hospital robe, with a knitted scarf in an American flag design pulled around his neck, and he wields a sledgehammer. As captured by cameraman Bob Dale, Jenkins begins to recite a set of rhyming verses:

You're just a mass of images you've gotten to know
from years and years of TV shows.
The hurting thing, the hidden pain
was written and bitten into your vein.
I don't and I won't relate
and I think for some it's too late

Subsequent editing splices the single-take performance with jarring images from a variety of sources: D. W. Griffith's *Birth of a Nation*; *The Little Rascals*; Al Jolson in *The Jazz Singer*; vaudeville minstrel Bert Williams; and Laurel and Hardy in *Pardon Us*. Just as Jenkins prepares to lift the heavy implement and demolish the TV sets, there's a "break" in the performance and a burst of laughter, and the performer heckles "Oh, my Lord Jesus . . ." A gasp for breath; more laughter. "What the hell does *that* mean!?" Jenkins seamlessly transitions back "into character" and continues to recite verses again as he draws close to the camera for the final blackout. The deeper inference from that eruption—whether scripted or unscripted, a moot point—is the possibility of regaining composure and self-possession within the mass of images that work to contain Black bodies in representation.

In the early 1980s, Jenkins expanded cross-culturally in ways that were consistent with the public culture of those post-punk intersections of genre and social constituency. Life in the Park with Debris was a music-dance troupe formed when Jenkins, then working for a video-rental reproduction company in Hollywood, met guitarist Michael Delgado. Life in the Park's choreographed art-wave, jazz-inspired compositions originated in a "riff" the artist had presented to Delgado for a performance-art class Jenkins was teaching at California State University, Dominguez Hills. Jenkins added his vocals—part of the "Debris"—to Delgado's ensemble. The resulting sound also highlighted futuristic computer-blip coloring on synthesizer by VinZula Kara, a leading figure in the LA underground music scene who later collaborated with politically driven conceptualist Daniel J. Martinez.[83] In *Without Your Interpretation* (1983), Jenkins experimented with the emerging music video format, based on footage from a performance that took place on September 18, 1983, at the Art Dock in downtown Los Angeles (plate 5). The video features Life in the Park performing in the urban open air, an afternoon musical presentation intercut with Debris's twilight choreography staged with members of the Rudy Perez workshop.[84] To these were added scenes assembled from the news media in what Jenkins describes as "a critical examination of mid-80s American culture and global issues through musical performance." The video's reliance on multilayered content, at once documentary and experimental, connected to the aims of fellow makers such as Senga Nengudi who shared an interest in generating "an image tapestry of sound, movement and sculpture."[85] The opening sequence begins with Life in the Park's acoustic drifting, with tonal qualities referencing Jimi Hendrix ("Drifting" from *Cry of Love*), Pere Ubu ("One Less Worry" from *New Picnic Time*), and Tuxedomoon ("East/Jinx/ . . . /Music #1" from *Desire*)—musical gestures contemporaneous as well with ideas explored by the New York M-Base jazz collective. The video's opening footage transitions in a sequence—sliver of moon, planet earth, an aerial topographic view—that gives way to the 1983 downtown Los Angeles skyline and finally to the band in free-flowing preamble. Rapid edits show the Rudy Perez troupe as each dancer alternates shoulders and hands outstretched against a wall, evoking arrest or entrapment by law enforcement. Pendant flashlights illuminate the futurist totem face-paint designs of Patssi Valdez, founding member of the Chicano conceptual art collective Asco—to be sure, Jenkins was exceptional in his cross-cultural prescience and in foregrounding women of color in his multimedia works. Majestic landscapes, snowcapped mountains, pristine rivers and waterfalls: Intersecting scenes of natural beauty return to shots of Jenkins vocalizing at the microphone or kneeling over an East African xylophone, the singer clad in a gingham-print pantsuit, the Stars and Stripes forming a sash tied at his waist. "Somehow you feel, somehow you feel, what's going on. For our ancestors say, somehow you feel that they're not getting a fair share." The ensuing chain of images includes an Asian mother grieving a son killed in combat, Space Shuttle *Columbia* and Spacelab astronauts, a heart-replacement surgery, anchorman Charles Gibson in a financial news report, the civil war in El Salvador, Ronald Reagan and Gorbachev ("Still not talking/Starting to talk") during a disarmament summit—as Jenkins, in song, implores, "Don't let them push that button." Scenes of US pleasure economies (Venice Beach rollerbladers, a Miss America pageant) fluctuate with images of political protesters, law enforcement crowd control, and a stack of South African Krugerrands: "Let's scream and holler for the earthquake, what's going on?"

The piece was restaged that same year, as *Without Your Interpretation 2*, at Hollywood's Club Lhasa, "a popular alternative performance art venue." In Jenkins's description, the work was "directed at the insensitivity of middle-class attitudes towards the Third World. As a yuppie couple barbecued an evening's meal, chilling & drinking their wine, oblivious to everything . . . primal states of movement evolved into the robotic movements reflecting societies [*sic*] lack of concern." A TV set on the couple's picnic table functioned as "an 'omnipotent eye' looking back and forth on the screen watching them."[86] Tito Larriva of The Plugz had sung, in *Better Luck*'s track entitled "American," of US global interventions and the sinister side of naiveté: "American took the bait/American took the gun. . . . He watches he waits he takes/He watches he waits he takes." That same evening, as Life in the Park with Debris performed *Without Your Interpretation 2*, on the twilight of yet another US effort to gain ascendancy, Ronald Reagan sent troops to occupy the island of Grenada.

As Snowden has written, only "a handful of local outlets, ranging from museums to underground rock clubs, exhibit[ed] fine-art videos and Jenkins' political thrust and Third World perspective often encountered stiff opposition there."[87] *Los Angeles Times* writers from Salazar to McKenna and Snowden have been essential in making public "the creative scene that is seldom seen or written about," remarkable for a mainstream print publication.[88] City nightclubs and journalistic prose, like the inter-art relation of poetry and drawing, give way to each other as defiant locations for experimentation, commonality, and action. Geographer Edward Soja recalls that social space—human exchanges enacted over a concrete landscape—and such writing that submits place for legible view join to constitute the ground and consequence of an amalgamated process for mobilizing urban stories.[89] In visual and written arguments against a backdrop that connects the Vietnam War to the US occupation of Grenada, bodies in public prompt awareness of internal and external differences that make a subject distinguishable in evolving sequences of social crises and survival. Salazar, Cortez, Edwards, Los Four, Fergerson, Duardo, Larriva, and Jenkins: they telescope in time and the historical uncanny. Secretly familiar, their practices here collapse spaces of ethnicity, global geography, and working method. They ghost claims to an alleged city essence or ethos for Los Angeles by exposing what some versions prefer to keep concealed and out of sight.

13.

Newspaper photographs in the mediated sphere, printed matter that circulated among a few. Soundscapes "embedded with symphonic parts, doses of hard rock, a few volts worth of electronic effects and interesting stray elements such as the plaintive bullfight cry of a horn . . . drawing power from the insanity and beauty of individuals and society which feeds and kills them."[90] Fireworks display and rekindled debris: the connecting conduits contain an urban space whose cultural geography is insinuated between disparate media and art-historical actors evoked by circumstantial settings. It all obliges little narratives that cannot but mirror the structures they intended to describe about the contingency of institutions and the mediated sphere in terms of social life and art making. In *Secret Exhibition*, Rebecca Solnit tells of assemblage art's capacity to deal with disparity; it "proposed an order that was neither absolute nor eternal, but conditional and personal."[91] Solnit turns as well to William Seitz who saw in assemblage the means of metaphor to coalesce in objects the discontinuities of historic locations—something akin to the narrative distance covered by placing photographs side by side in an art-historical present.

From this place, the anxieties and desires of such group power expressed in public display coexist with affirmations that materialize in a deteriorated window frame. As abrupt pictures of a built environment and of a broader cultural formation, some photographs survive as prime real estate for rhetorical claims. They prompt arguments apt to reconfigure constellations of the past, recognizable only if we're able to step outside the categories we inherit between the stratosphere and ground level. This is the ether: billboard, skywriting, concrete and steel; newsprint display and the rubble of uprising; freeways, typographic lines and a chain of ink markings. A form of history that can account for Purifoy and Powell's assemblage in the *Times* photograph enacts something as well akin to the writing process as a problem, proposing an order "neither absolute nor eternal, but conditional and personal." Like the material evidence issued forth to look like a picture frame and flower vase, cultural accounts prove, time and again, to be only almost indistinguishable from what they meant to resemble of the past—our language in material fragments at odds with the ideal architecture of the narrative totality. In the pause of that method, little objects from a newspaper photograph throw everything into uneasy relief. That's when they reassemble the hierarchies attached to distraction and destruction, resemblance and remembrance, abjection and objection; the promises and pitfalls of rewriting the order—analogical rather than necessary, simultaneous rather than consecutive—all over again, and as though for the first time.

THREE

Mexico City: Art Stories with Roberto Bolaño

To the degree that narrative *bricolage* and juxtaposition are able to connect disparate spaces, I turn to Roberto Bolaño's 1998 novel *Los detectives salvajes*, published in Natasha Wimmer's English translation in 2007 as *The Savage Detectives*.[1] It aligns uniquely here with my aims to narrate arts scenes in 1990s Mexico City. In structure and storyline, Bolaño's writing can serve as a model for providing unity to episodic methods in art writing, so assembled as to join disparate time periods and metropolitan settings: progression and simultaneities that approximate the migrant condition, mass-media spectacle, high-speed communication technology, and other cultural encounters that are the matter of everyday life in today's transnational Americas.

Bolaño's sprawling three-part novel—described again and again as fractal or kaleidoscopic—presents visual enigmas or structures that appeal to the problem of interpretation, even as it enlivens, among many things, the artistic underground of Mexico City described through the lens of a band of young writers and bohemians, mostly poets; and in one important sense, the novel is about the dynamics of an emerging ethos related to the historic avant-gardes. A present-tense narrative in the mid-1970s splinters into networks of time future—intersections and nodal points that, before telescoping back to the scene of disruption, rotate suspended in staggered views of the twenty years awaiting, more and more proximate in time to that of the novel's material writing. But even this is disservice inasmuch as to describe the structure is to find oneself reaching in vain for what the method successfully defies. With Bolaño's novel as a discursive model, I suggest a few lines from a project whose logic interrelates factors that, during the 1990s in Mexico's capital, gave way to improvised practices and subcultures as they formed legitimate art scenes in dialogue with the official cultural apparatus, and representatives across the continuum lobbied for position within the purview of global art practices. With Bolaño, I experiment in the mediated sphere to convey visual stories about the dynamic between art practice, state and market initiatives, the production of a viewer in particular works, and the political emotion around social crises in Mexico and the upsurge of violence. This proximity to Bolaño allows alternate perspectives to animate the objects and actors of art in late capital, and to dissolve categories of knowledge that often view artistic practice and culture as separate activities, especially in light of the "neoliberal turn" and its economic and artistic effects at stake during those years. With the permission Bolaño grants in terms of narrative techniques, methods of layering and splintering that insinuate historical sweep, I include works relevant to that recent historic moment, the 1990s, regardless of what an international market has been able to accommodate, and I incorporate them into disconnected but possible episodes.

One way to tell this story is to begin at the enigmatic end of *The Savage Detectives*: "February 15: 'What's outside the window?'" The final pages of the book compose a sequence of visual puzzles that, in 1976, the bantam member of the Visceral Realist poets, seventeen-year-old Juan García Madero, registers in his journal. It points back to earlier passages about the single published work, also a visual poem, by the sole living representative of the 1920s Visceral Realist movement, Cesárea Tinajero, the obscure, mythic figure who drives the novel's quest narrative. The fugitive band of youths (poets Arturo Belano, Ulises Lima, García Madero, and Lupe), having escaped an encroaching threat in the final scene of part 1, are now on the road and on the run from the depraved gangster Alberto, Lupe's abusive former boyfriend and pimp.

Expectation looms heavily on the final pages, and to convey as much is already to oversimplify the arcs that lead to the visual dismount. In the novel's first part, viewpoint belongs to García Madero in journal entries that relate a sexual and cultural initiation among a widening network of friends, poets published and aspiring, the urban environment conducive to artistic alliance and criminality, all the life possibilities for the would-be writer discovering a sector of Mexico City's literary bohemia and, with it, the resulting sleeplessness of elective affinity. He writes: "and suddenly I realized that my horizons were expanding imperceptibly and my life was being very gradually enriched."[2]

In the outburst comprising the second section, an onslaught of written statements and spoken interviews, dated variously and moving forward in uneven increments from 1976 to 1996, conveys the wanderings of Arturo Belano and Ulises Lima in discursive patterns that enact a central theme: a life, obscure to objective fact, as being composed of present-tense commitments, but whose mark is never more than transitory, the meanings of human action and intimacy vanishing readily in the recollection of a person and in pursuit of something—literature, art—as though every life depended on it.

That final section circles back to García Madero's truncated journal narrative. It unites in the figure of Cesárea Tinajero a resolve to confirm in the present a survival from the past with a journey into the underside of a Mexico wherein criminality is complicit with law enforcement; the final confrontation and its resulting casualties are a perverse poetic justice. It's plausible as well that the visual poems occur to García Madero as suggested by something in Cesárea's notebooks, which he retrieved from her home in the Sonoran Desert after the altercation that is the novel's climax. On the road alone now with Lupe, García Madero considers again "the strict rectangle of the Impala's window" to record—"Bamuri, Pitiquito, Caborca, San Juan, Las Maravillas, Las Calenturas"[3]—the place names en route to who knows where.

"February 15: 'What's outside the window?'": In an essay that locates these diagrams within a cognitive poetics, Chilean scholar Ricardo Martínez suggests that the quadrilateral of broken lines could be a window "from which there emerges a blinding beam of light . . . a window that has just shattered . . . a window shot through and destroyed. A window forced open to give way to future windows and to give way to a poetry of the future."[4] In a series that begins with the partial view (insinuated point of a star) and the metonymic view (frame and object, a bedsheet, as though selfsame), there follows a form so unspecified, at once complete and incomplete, as to foreclose the concept of totality, unassailable object commensurate with the structure of history that has, until now, been sustained in the foregoing six hundred pages. Another Chilean scholar, Patricia Espinosa, suggests that "tension is to be found in a future that advances in the opposite direction to that of prevailing modernity, thereby making possible new experience of the present, which will end up being recovered, enriched by means of establishing a non-standardized relationship with the past."[5]

"February 15: 'What's outside the window?'": The shape weighs heavily as a self-reflexive end-stop, a pattern greater than García Madero or his journal, a void in which the present is emptied of a past and a future looms, inaccessible and virtual to the optimism of youth in 1977, but flickered in flashpoints for the reader in the middle temporalities and location of the novel—Mexico City, Barcelona, Luanda, Tel Aviv, the Arizona-Sonora borderlands—intervals that diverge, overlap, distend, and recede. What that final picture does and does not contain, what is in excess of the novel's frame even as it was present for Bolaño in composing the work in the late 1990s—a method that salvaged and reassembled from twenty years of unpublished writing—is the shape of time unhinged in a market economy of feuding novelists and publishers that the novel's structure gestures to delay or circumvent as historical inevitability. If we accept the description of the neoliberal project as a scenario of "complex, unevenly developing spatialities that are deeply constitutive rather than merely contingent aspects of the project of state authorized market transformation,"[6] *The Savage Detectives* performs a structural disintegration of the everyday frame as a result of that incomplete pattern of public management to which the world of the young poet García Madero is still immune.

"Mexicans Lost in Mexico": Another way to tell this story is to flash forward to an exhibition that gave these phenomena visibility in terms of art in Mexico, of a piece with Bolaño's novel, so transposed from its site of production as to position Mexico's capital on a par with the global art world's "metropolitan hubs." *Mexico City: An Exhibition About the*

Exchange Rates of Bodies and Values opened at New York's P.S. 1 Contemporary Art Center (now MoMA PS1) and was on display from June to September 2002. The curatorial script and the selection of artists aimed to articulate the fractures in Mexico's capital, including its extreme social contradictions, the uncertain status of its civic agencies, and the dysfunction of its sprawling built environment and urban activity. Curator Klaus Biesenbach framed the visual and conceptual territory of the exhibition by summoning natural disaster: the Mexico City earthquake of 1985 became the overarching image representative of "the tension between wealth and poverty, between progress, stagnation and improvisation, and between violence and civility that animates this vibrant city and makes the voices of its people—the artists, the politicians, the everyday masses—especially potent and enduringly combustible to draw a picture of our world, the world outside of the artificially protected bubble of First World–guaranteed wealth and security. Life is obviously dangerous in Mexico City. The body becomes a good to be protected, dealt with, or exchanged for other values."[7]

The most notorious contribution was the work of Teresa Margolles, also known for her participation in SEMEFO, an artist collective of the 1990s, whose acronym alludes to the national forensic medical agency. Independent of SEMEFO, Margolles had elsewhere made a display of the pierced tongue of a male teenager who had died a violent street death; encased for viewing in the gallery space, the tongue was acquired by Margolles from the family of the deceased in exchange for monies disbursed for a proper burial. Margolles's work at the New York installment of the *Mexico City* exhibition required viewers to sign a waiver before entering a room permeated by a gauze of mist, illuminated from above just enough to configure the looming bodily contours of other viewers within the environment; it could have suggested the sexualized steam of a public bath until one was reminded of the signed disclosure stating that the vapor had been derived from water used to cleanse the sometimes violently mutilated corpses of the city morgue—an après coup that all of a sudden prompted the room to be thick with the scent of latex and disinfectant (fig. 11). Biesenbach wrote:

> *Vaporization* (2002) . . . visualize[d] the physical memory of a last washing, but it also alludes to the notion of fading away or dissolving—the disappearance of the individual into the dense fog of a city populated by far over 20 million people. . . . In reality, as citizens of a tightly woven urban fabric, the water drained from the city morgue will eventually enter our water system, and may even show up as tap water. Even though Margolles appropriates the ancient rituals in honor of the dead, for many the work appears threatening, as death and the corpse have been determined by modern First World society as taboo.[8]

The formal habits of the kind of work represented in the P.S. 1 exhibition connected to aspects of what cultural critic Carlos Monsiváis identified as the magic compelling neoliberal economic policies as another form of millenarianism in Mexico; a series of "market Utopias" prompted mass migration to a "Utopia without documents." To make possible an effective civil society, Utopia could be defined as the autonomy of dreaming, a location

FIGURE 11. Teresa Margolles, *Vaporization*, 2002, installation, P.S. 1 MoMA exhibition *Mexico City: An Exhibition About the Exchange Rates of Bodies and Values*. Courtesy of the artist.

where the incentives for "action and . . . fantasy alike" inhabit the places containing the "oppressive inertia of everyday life."[9]

"February 15: 'What's outside the window?'": After 1988 artists and writers in Mexico began to affront the political economy, the predicament of urban overdevelopment or the effects of industrialism on the environment. This is the shorthand for the complex transformations that took place in Mexico, chiefly associated with the presidency of Carlos Salinas de Gortari and his immediate successor, Ernesto Zedillo. Although the former's executive legitimacy was negligible—given the overwhelming evidence of fraudulent elections that led to his investiture, a fact never lost to public feeling—Salinas launched a campaign of so-called moral renovation in government to obliterate corruption. It began with the shocking early-term incarceration of shady government and labor officials.[10] The print media were no longer subject to a government "monopoly on newsprint, which had been used to punish newspapers that were overly critical."[11] And there were heightened political expectations that the economic reforms of privatization and free trade would fulfill, as per the effects of NAFTA (effective January 1, 1994), the promise of a more fully transparent democratic electoral process.[12] Then on March 23, 1994, Luis Donaldo Colosio, presidential candidate of the Institutional Revolutionary Party, or PRI, and de facto successor to Salinas, was shot and mortally wounded during a campaign rally in Tijuana. The political crime and ensuing crises were felt in urgent ways in Mexico, insofar as political and symbolic investments in Mexico's democratic transition had been attached to the person of Colosio. It was so commonplace to speak of conspiracy hand in hand with the actual or symbolic breakdown of authority, that public feeling—raw with language and images where evidence was lacking—transmogrified from one story that confirmed or covered over another. Colosio's assassination appeared to forebode inevitability, and it produced apprehension in Mexico about potential widespread violence: A *New York Times* article later reported that "during the remainder of Mr. Salinas's administration, which ended on Nov. 30, 1994, his government was unable to convince the public that it had solved the murder, even though a lone shooter arrested at the scene had been convicted and sentenced."[13]

When the attorney general of Ernesto Zedillo's successive administration reopened the case, he promptly arrested "a second suspect and announced that there had been a conspiracy to kill Mr. Colosio that might be connected to Mr. Salinas's own government. A few years later, investigators pursuing the Colosio case questioned Mr. Salinas in his exile in Dublin. Although no charges were ever brought or proof given that there had been a conspiracy, let alone one attached to Mr. Salinas, many Mexicans still believe he was in some way involved in Mr. Colosio's death."[14] Meanwhile, Raúl Salinas, the former president's brother, waited out his sentence in a Mexico City jail on charges that he had engineered the September 1994 assassination of José Francisco Ruiz Massieu, secretary general of the PRI.

"Mexicans Lost in Mexico": As public feeling and popular imagination vilified Salinas, artist Carlos Aguirre turned to making sobering objects whose formal and critical equations managed to underpin the fragility of Mexico City's collective bonds. Signed before a notary public, then framed and placed on a pedestal for a 1994 installation at the Galería Metropolitana, were formalized agreements between the artist and a donor. In the contracts, Aguirre committed to producing an artwork with the human ashes of the cosigner. Through this pact, he established parallels between that which is legally binding and the physical body as a free-market token of exchange. Aguirre's 1995 exhibition *Images of Neoliberalism* comprised several mixed-media paintings and installations that submitted a possible link in Mexico between the surge of the finance economy and the unleashing of political crimes played out from above, to the detriment of those below official discourse, with a direct reference to impunity as the product of a vertical spatial relationship.[15] An untitled polyptych comprising six narrow, large-scale panels resting on the floor and tilted against the wall of one of the gallery spaces featured a heavily layered and dingy use of dark sepias and a gritty black hue that dripped down the panels. Cluttered with objects applied by various means to the surface—cables sustaining a block of wood, surgical scalpels, and a bare lightbulb, as well a series of stapled police-station mug shots obtained by the artist from an archive—a text inscribed on one side of the piece expressly called into question the hegemony of a global free-market economy. The installation ensemble served as a forceful commentary on the entangled links between social violence and environmental depletion. Recycling certain elements from previous works in an analogous formal ecology, the untitled central piece of this exhibition was a large sculptural form composed of a heavy wooden construction beam which had been hacked along its length and on its sides by eleven axes with their corresponding tree-branch handles jutting out. Suspended by cables from the steel beams of the gallery's ceiling, the entire mass hovered at eye level, and at a near 45-degree-angle tilt—a veritable sinking vessel or self-consuming vortex of "natural" and "constructed" forms.

In one part of the installation (plate 6) the viewer entered what seemed to be an empty room—even as, from above, three sets of thin metal strips jutted out like diving boards from each side of the wall where they had been fastened with clamps near the ceiling. A slaughterhouse spear separated each facing pair, held in place by the pressure created between the two metal strips. The fragility of the tension could be registered in the movement of the shadows projected by the gallery lights on the back wall; and any abrupt jolt may well have released the spear, sending it into a downward plummet. Underlining the potential danger to which viewers were subjected, Aguirre thematized the violent social reality of the moment as the weight and counterweight of Mexico's political gravity, going so far as to put the viewer's physical safety in potential danger, with axes and saw blades protruding from the walls and hanging from suspension wires above.

"February 15: 'What's outside the window?'": In his Mexico City work of the late 1980s and early 1990s, Miguel Ventura had been exposing the underside of empowered imaginations and sinister worldviews, in which bodies and language disintegrate as stable boundaries of the transnational self. US-born and of Puerto Rican descent, Ventura, before relocating to New York in 1992, produced a variegated, transitional series of canvases and works on paper that helped shape the course of his subsequent practice. Paring down his visual vocabulary by favoring smaller formats, and employing translucent scrims or kitschy pre-patterned fabrics, like gingham and floral prints, in place of canvas, many of these works focused almost entirely on bits of telegraphic or mutilated text, a miscellany of English, Spanish, German, or Cantonese transcription, treating it as a "decorative" component, regardless of how obscure or disconcerting its content. Others featured lifeless or fiendish-looking faces of men, women, and children in frontal renderings; the names of stimulants, depressants, and tranquilizers inscribed in floating capsules; scraps of hardcore gay pornography; or the chessboard background formed by pages torn from handbooks.

In 1995 Ventura went deeper into the dual fear of nonuniformity and sameness in the artist book entitled *Die Notizbücher der Mademoiselle Heidi Schreber / The Notebooks of Mademoiselle Heidi Schreber*[16] (fig. 12). Using Daniel Paul Schreber's 1884 case history *Memoirs of My Nervous Disorder* as a point of departure, and establishing a pseudo-organization called the New Interterritorial Language Committee (NILC) as an eerie underpinning, Ventura submitted a creepy artifact that was the compendium of a mind's self-image or society's psyche in the process of deterioration, with voices spewing out the raw sexual relishings and vehement doggerel of an ersatz, worldwide antiassimilationist vigilante group. (The book, incidentally—a Babel of German, Spanish, English, Chinese, Arabic, and Swahili—concludes with three appendices: an additional vocabulary in Chinese, a sizable list of medications, and a complete translation of all texts into Spanish and English.)

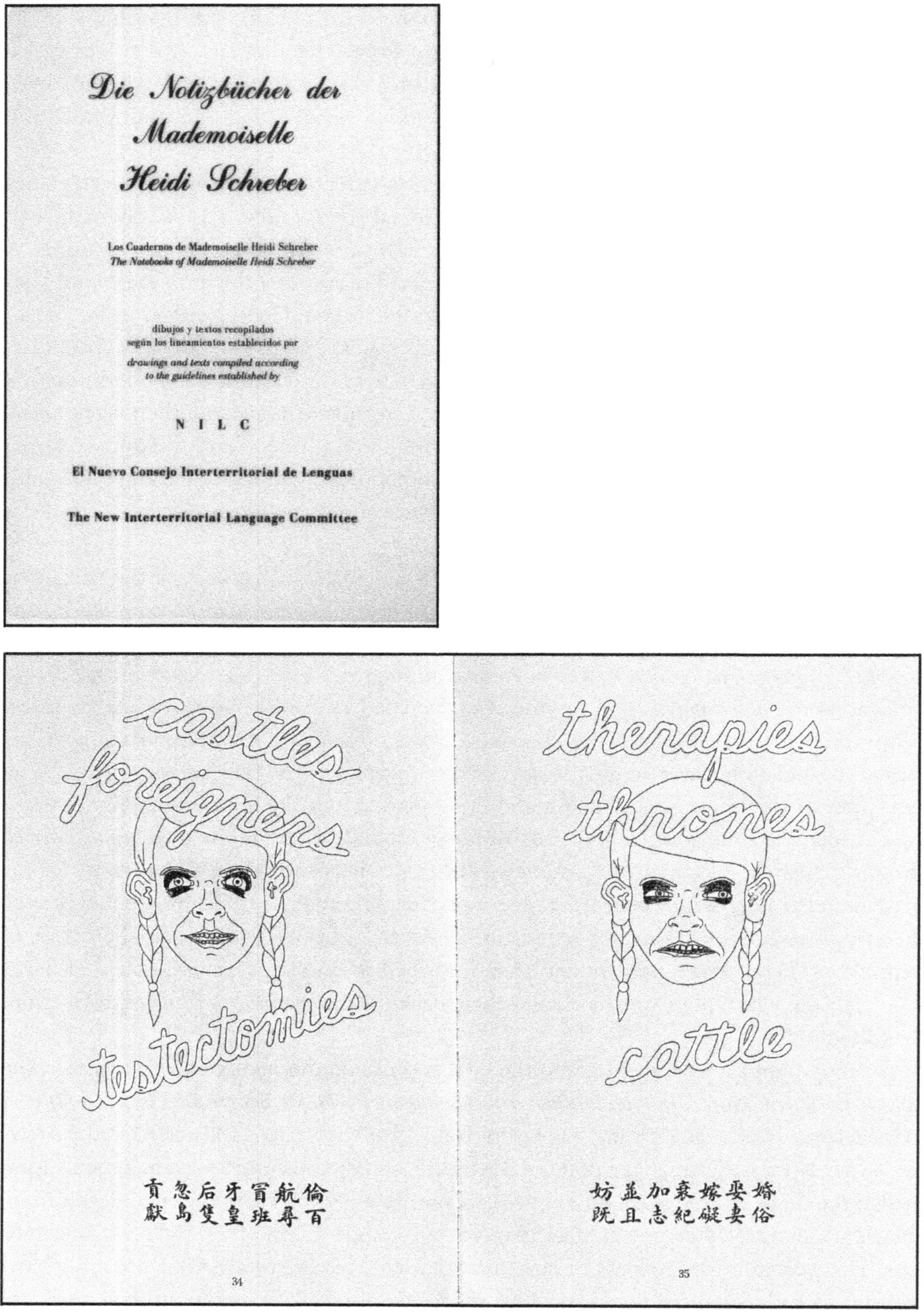

Figure 12. Miguel Ventura, *Die Notizbücher der Mademoiselle Heidi Schreber / The Notebooks of Mademoiselle Heidi Schreber*, 1995, artist's book: (a) cover; (b) interior pages. Courtesy of the author.

The translucent paper jacket and cream-colored wrappers endowed the book with the aura of a harmless primer, but for the progressive depictions of a face in-folding, multiplied by the automatism of repetition, morphed into a variety of gender-graftings, tongues and protuberances thrust in and out of ears, nostrils, and eye sockets, in turn becoming sinewy veins of cancerous growths spelling out manic rants or three-word slogans ("therapies/thrones/cattle; eggs/axes/maids"). The accompanying polyglot text throughout was a ceaseless assault on fixity and its self-contradictory phobia of all things hybrid—namely sex, species, and language:

> "Where are you, little mongrel rascals?" New Interterritorial Language Committee allows for greater harmony and coexistence
> between the bastardized hybrid elements and the pure elements of this new republic![17]

The asylum personas organized around Heidi Schreber, a stand-in for public feeling in relentless transmutation, spoke the decay and self-obliterating assurance of NILC's new ghetto-state and its punitive laws aiming to appeal to the viewer as a prospective interterritorial citizen. In a 1997 artist statement, Ventura wrote:

> The New Interterritorial Language Committee [had] aspirations [that were] closer to a multi-national corporation or association—with a mission to accomplish and a message to communicate on a global scale. Yet NILC's proposals—of a deadened and twisted political and social rhetoric inspired by texts from *Mein Kampf* to vocabulary from the Chinese Cultural Revolution combined with a naïve sense of joie de vivre—inevitably sabotage[d] any form of participation with this organization; NILC became a model of a dysfunctional organization which welcomes participants yet excludes them because of the nature of its own contradictory philosophies.
>
> Whoever advocates the simplification
> of the languages is considered an enemy!
> Whoever tries to stand still in this transformation goes against Nature![18]

*

"February 15: 'What's outside the window?'": Here's a 2001 scene coincident with the P.S. 1 exhibition and the Vicente Fox presidential administration. One of President Fox's high-ranking officials, Sari Bermúdez, head of the National Council of the Arts and Culture of Mexico, contributed to the P.S. 1 exhibition catalog with an official endorsement. A journalistic note ties this all together. In a coup of investigative reporting, Sara Silver of the *Financial Times* reminded her readers that

> On October 21 2001, [in] the historic castle glowing above Mexico City's Chapultepec Park . . . Mexico's elite feasted on lobster and filet mignon at the $10,000-per-plate launch of Fundación Vamos Mexico [the personal project of First Lady Marta Sahagún de Fox]. The Castillo de Chapultepec, from which Mexican patriots jumped to their deaths to avoid capture during the Mexican-American War, is a national monument normally unavailable for private parties. But Sari Bermudez, who was promoted from journalist to minister of culture after writing a flattering biography of Mrs. Fox, put the castle at her friend's disposal for the evening.[19]

Bermúdez, it should be noted, in her role as minister of culture, opened her acknowledgement in the P.S. 1 catalog with the following axiom: "In an era of globalization, no country is to be left out from the international settlement or a new worldwide arrangement."[20] (A generalized newspeak worthy of Ventura's Interterritorial Language Committee.)

Three years later, embroiled in a scandal further exposed by the *Financial Times*, Mrs. Fox, who had refused to seek alliances with established benevolent agencies for her Fundación Vamos México, was at pains to account for its financial statements, and there was evidence to suggest that the foundation's moneys were funding Mrs. Fox in her insinuated ambitions to run for the presidency in 2006.

Meanwhile, according to Silver, "none of [President Fox's fiscal and monetary] reforms ha[d] softened the grinding poverty that afflict[ed] half the population. Although Mr. Fox promised 7 per cent economic growth and one million new jobs each year during his term of office, per capita GDP ha[d] fallen in each of his three years in power. . . . The president claimed credit last year for lifting 700,000 Mexicans out of poverty. But economists say the statistical improvement [was] largely the result of a fall in the prices of the basic commodities that [made] up the basket of goods used to define poverty." The National Action Party administration had already lost its credibility and moral high ground "when [the Mexican journal] *Proceso* published documents that the Fox campaign had received millions of dollars from half a dozen Mexican companies despite laws that outlawed political donations."[21]

"Mexicans Lost in Mexico": To the degree that Margolles is able to coalesce political emotions for the viewer of *Vaporization*, the work activates what the philosopher of affect Alphonso Lingis meant when he wrote that "in the foreboding sense of a day imminent in which one will not be there, there stirs an imminent anxiety that senses that the place one occupies is empty of oneself."[22] But *Vaporization* served also as a counterpractice to the brazen privatizing of the public trust—at its limit point death, which arguably can or cannot be privatized. The work functioned moreover as the uneasy appeal to a procedure that—in the words of Mario Vargas Llosa, a writer not unfriendly to the neoliberal market—would "clean up the fundamentally dirty, immoral, corrupt activity that, unfortunately, has passed for politics" in Latin America.[23] Margolles decontaminated the residue of the morgue's cadavers as a perverse rehearsal for the eventual cleansing of "the neutral, dead system of symbolic community and exchange that . . . —as per Joan Copjec on film noir—had given way . . . to a world that crawls with private enjoyment and thus rots the old networks of communication."[24] Cuauhtémoc Medina calls that enjoyment a "mutual abuse" on the part of the globalized art market and on the part of the artists who embrace it in order to answer back.[25] The viewer of *Vaporization* was not so much confronted by a work in which she or he was a stand-in for the "disappearance of the individual into the dense fog of a city populated by far over 20 million people."[26] Rather, the viewer was asked to enter and leave it as part of a wider life and its range of reference when public feeling seeks confirmation in the social text. In 2002 alone it was calculated that Mexicans risking their lives to work in the United States died at a rate of one per day—a figure ghosted by the cadaver-rinse water transported by Margolles to New York's P.S. 1.[27]

Between a privatized Chapultepec Castle and the lower depths of the city morgue, and in direct affront to the political indemnity that is the historic grounds for the decay of public institutions, *Vaporization* betrayed civil munificence with the shadow outlines some artworks oblige the viewer briefly to inhabit.

Time and again in *The Savage Detectives*, voices intone accounts of the transient relation: "The term started, I met someone else, and I stopped thinking about him . . ." "At five in the morning we went our separate ways . . ." "See you soon I said, and then I never saw him again. . . ." "And I said: all I'm going to tell her is that her son isn't in Mexico anymore. . . ." ". . . because we're alone and we're lost . . ." "And that was the last time I saw her alive . . ." "A week later, we said goodbye, and I went with him to the station . . ." "The rest is just one sentence, one scene after another. I'll try to string them together."[28] In theme and structure, *Vaporization* and *The Savage Detectives* align with the historical consciousness of a present that views the past "only as an image which flashes up at the instant when it can be recognized and is never seen again."[29] The experience of departure, disappearance, and the fleeting social relation that is the premonition of demise adjoin to Benjamin's well-known formulation, whereby "to articulate the past historically [is] to seize hold of a memory as it flashes up at a moment of danger."[30] That menace is the subject as well of Aguirre's counterweights of axes and saw blades, Ventura's New Interterritorial Language Committee, Margolles's corpse evaporations—possible futures looming outside the window in García Madero's journals. I offer no tidy hypothesis that can unite these separate symbolic acts that epitomized Mexico City as a palpable experience of the State, and whose rapid transformations prompted cultural accounts to unsettle system expectations in light of subjectivities and social interaction, or perverse proxies as when Ventura's NILC threatens, "Whoever tries to stand still in this transformation goes against Nature." Bolaño makes it possible to stagger or overlay the reality of historical circumstance as being composed of so many loose ends, false starts, scrap remainders of experience or public opinion, the stuff of self-conscious gestures, cruel ironies, unsubstantiated exchange or contrasts, a frame through which to view the horizon of relations. This is writing that reaches uneasily for what Stephen Greenblatt called "the whole structure of production and consumption—the systemic organization of ordinary life and consciousness—that generates the pattern of boundary making and breaking, the oscillation between demarcated objects and monological totality."[31] A tall order, but one that reaches for the ordinary; the more unassuming aim of giving rhetorical and temporal form to uncontainable contingency of events and attitudes, an unpuzzling of incidents and practices capable of creating a contiguous space in discursive terms. With Bolaño, to resist the developmental account—intervals and arcs capable of connecting episodes around subjects and locations—is in hindsight to circumvent the outcome finally favored by the global art market and to cast doubt on any conclusive version. Storylines, in short, whereby "The rest is just one sentence, one scene after another. I'll try to string them together."[32]

FOUR

Family Resemblance in 1990s Mexico: Francis Alÿs, *The Fabiola Project*

I begin with nothing, a mere scrap of paper measuring 4×6 inches, its surface yellowed mildly over time (fig. 13). If you look closely, you can see the muted green lines and the topmost horizontal red bar of the paper neatly torn from a composition notebook or ledger of the kind sold at local stationery suppliers in Mexico.

Dominating the upper left corner of the arrangement's likeliest orientation is the diamond or chevron support for the celestial globe that features as the centerpiece of the Brazilian national flag, its five-pointed stars meant to evoke the night sky over Brazil, with the equatorial band and motto *ORDEM E PROGESSO*, order and progress. The lines of the diamond rest not on a field proper to a flag, but on marks depicting a circular surface, maybe a dinner plate, in view of the serrated knife that so rests on an edge as to cast a shadow and provide depth of perspective. Is the diamond a tiny pennant? A paper cocktail napkin? Is the dish rather the oversized lens of a magnifying glass, with what appears to be a short handle protruding from the lower curve? The signs further destabilize under the handwritten phrase in the uppermost left corner, a promissory note: "I will be back soon." At any rate, in the graphic logic of this drawing—a doodle, really—those elements give way to a cascade of objects below, rendered in fine-point pen. Edgy and agitated markings rendered in hairline strokes depict a series of items that include three packs of cigarettes—two hard packs, one soft, the foiled paper neatly torn away to create a convenient dispensing aperture, cigarette protruding. A beer bottle, its contents half consumed, is orbited by a mass-produced square-shaped glass ashtray with remains of recent smoking, as well as a saltshaker, a sugar dispenser, a small juice glass and straw or stir stick, and a pair

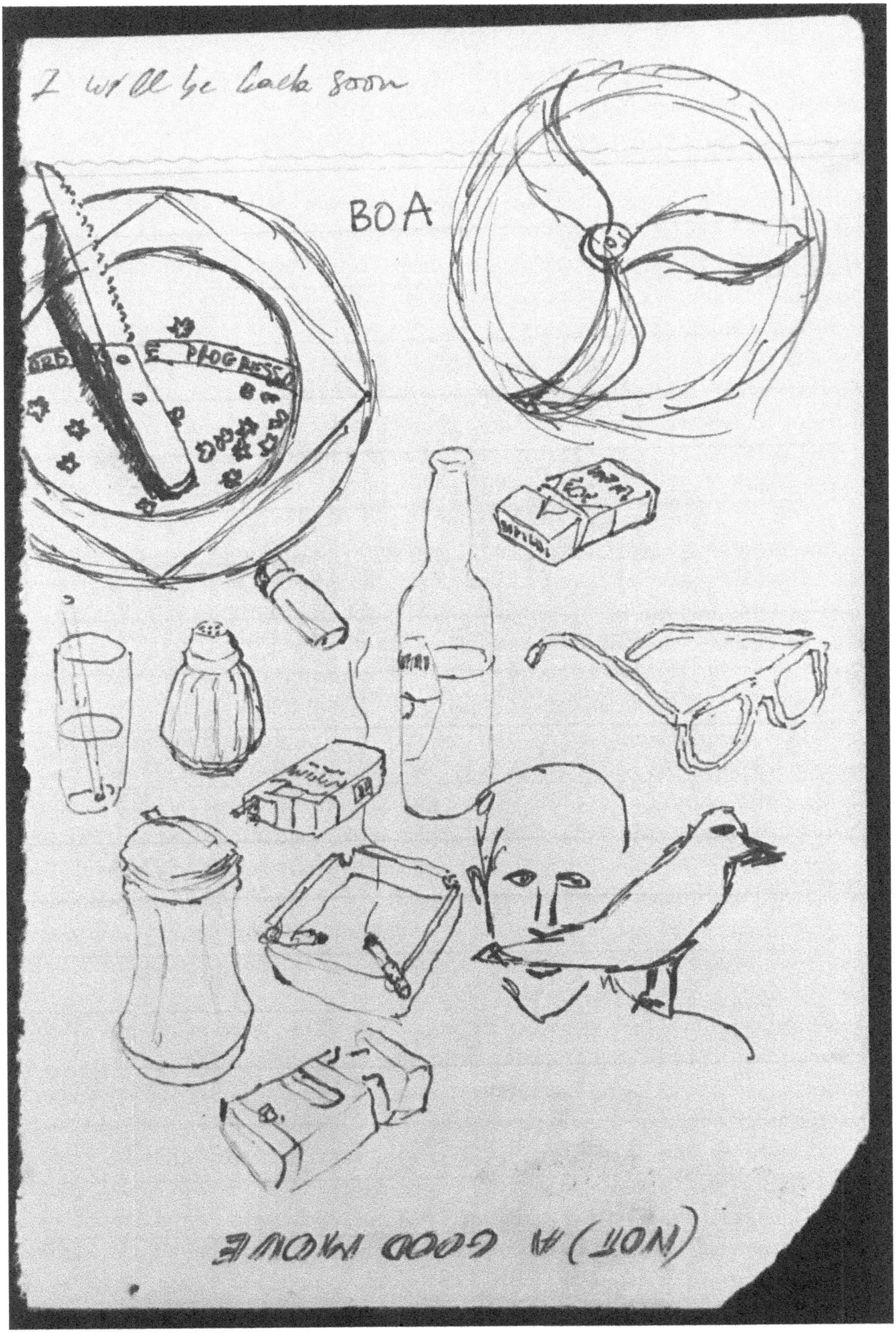

Figure 13. Francis Alÿs, untitled drawing, 1994. Private collection.

of eyeglass frames. Suspended as well in unspecified space, a few more irregular lines render the notation of a male figure, face slightly obscured by a sizable bird resting on a shoulder. Above, three propeller blades pertaining to a free-standing desk fan seem to emit or make hover in all-caps the word *BOA*, Portuguese for good—"nice," "cool"—that strikes a distinct contrast with the inverted phrase along the lower margin: "(NOT) A GOOD MOVE."

The Mexico City–based Belgian artist Francis Alÿs scrawled this composition while our attentions were otherwise caught up in conversation around the dining table at my apartment on calle Durango 127 in the Colonia Roma neighborhood. The year was either 1994 or 1995, but at any rate the flag motif was a possible allusion to Francis's forthcoming or current 1995 exhibition at the Galeria Camargo Vilaça in São Paulo.[1] Featured prominently in broader conversations were the excitements in Mexico around Brazil's contemporary art world—further confirming the current internationalization of Latin American art that had already in large measure by then been consolidated. I had arrived in Mexico in 1987 and had first worked on the editorial board of *Vuelta*, a monthly magazine of politics and the arts published by the poet Octavio Paz; then in 1990 I worked for the quarterly art journal *Artes de México*. In 1992 on a windfall, I was recommended by Robert Littman, then director of the Centro Cultural/Arte Contemporáneo in Mexico City, to serve as his proxy on the judging committee for the award exhibition *EcoArt 92* at Rio de Janeiro's Museu de Arte Moderna, held in conjunction with the Rio Earth Summit, a global conference on ecology.[2] One of the prizewinners was the Brazilian painter Daniel Senise, about whose work I later wrote for the artist's first museum exhibition in Mexico, at the Museo de Arte Contemporáneo de Monterrey (1994), and I featured an image of one of Senise's large-format canvases (*O beijo do elo perdido*, 1991) on the cover of the 1995 issue of *Mandorla: Nueva escritura de las Américas/Mandorla: New Writing from the Americas*, the annual, multilingual journal of poetry, poetics, translation, and visual arts I had founded in 1991 (fig. 14). Senise's canvas depicts what appear to be the calcified crania of two birds joined at the beak, the monumental form a connection or kiss telling of a "missing link" or abandoned attachment. Too, Francis Alÿs deployed bird forms in works he submitted to the 1993 group exhibition *Lesa natura*, for which Cuauhtémoc Medina and I cowrote the catalog essay on works by fourteen artists, including that of Francis, and later in *Untitled (Man with Bird)*, a 1998 oil and encaustic on wood.

International connections survive in the ink-and-paper composition by Alÿs—Mexico, Belgium, Brazil, and US *Latinidad*. It is tenuous supporting evidence for so much else that evanesces into the past, the reverse side to an image of the world before the emergence of high-speed digital delivery and storage systems, an exponentially expandable archive that endures, however more fragile than this tiny ledger tear sheet. I begin with a private notation—small memento from the past, perishable scrap of history—to contain the elements of memory, itself a kind of doodling, free-associative and produced out of conversations with pen and paper at hand. I want contrary things, what anthropologist Kathleen Stewart calls "ordinary affects," as well as a public narrative about innovative artists and alternative spaces—a society of alternate belonging around Mexico City's historic center in the late twentieth century.

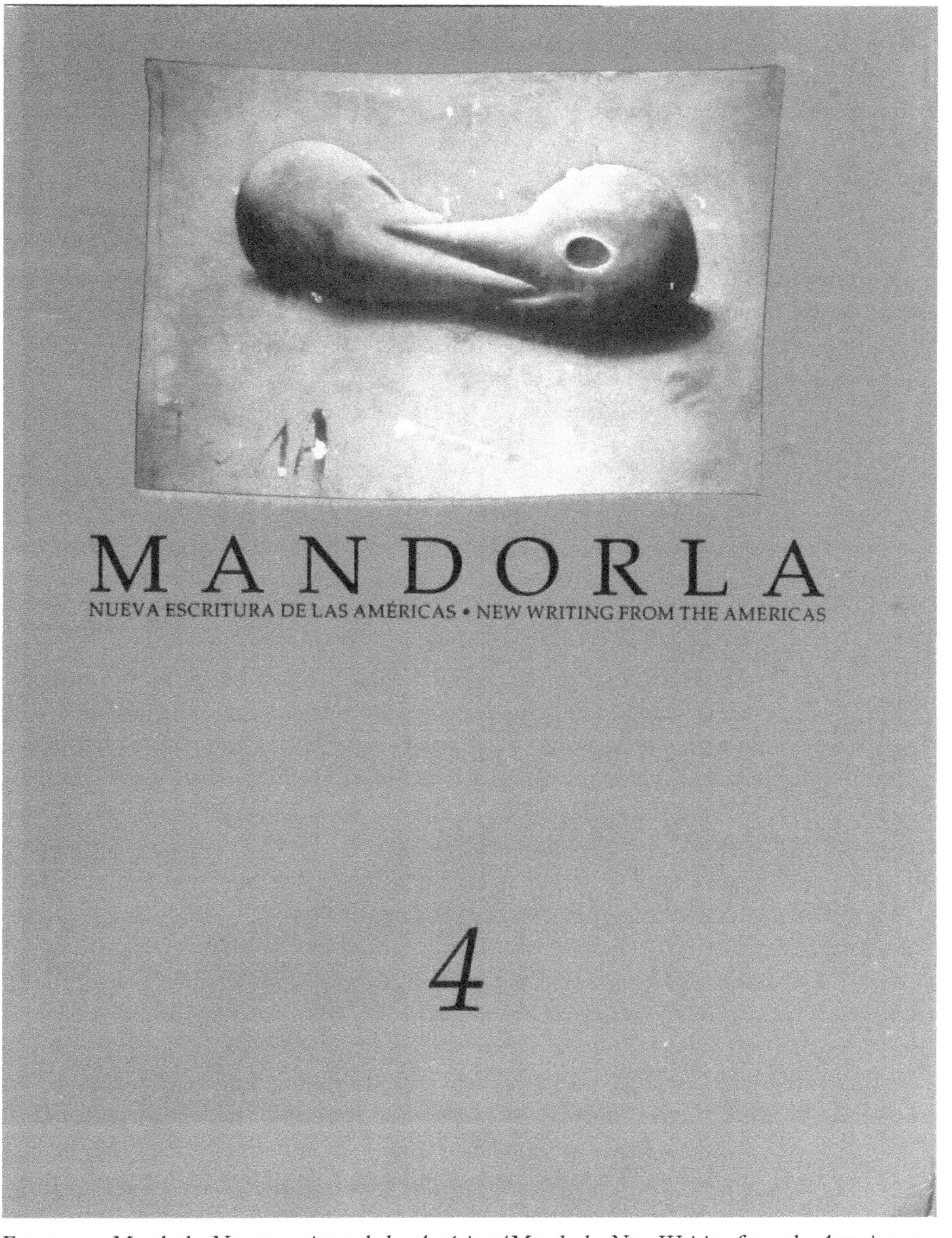

FIGURE 14. *Mandorla: Nueva escritura de las Américas/Mandorla: New Writing from the Americas* 4, 1995 (cover image: painting by Daniel Senise, *O beijo do elo perdido*, 1991).

Private notation and public narrative get blurred in this photograph (fig. 15) made around the year Francis Alÿs left on my table the little remnant of a dialogue. In the picture, together with Francis, whose elongated physique (on the right) is so crucial to his art of public interaction, are the historian Danna Levin and the art critic and curator Cuauhtémoc Medina, with me below completing the quartet. The occasion was one of any number of pretexts for sociability and carousal at the apartment of US artist Thomas Glassford on calle Licenciado Verdad in the historic center of Mexico City. Danna, Cuauhtémoc, and I—as well as philosopher Ernesto Priani and psychoanalyst Manuel Hernández—had been meeting from time to time as part of a quasi-secret society reading group called *La dalia negra* (the Black Dahlia). Our name derived from the infamous LA murder case, and our bibliography included crime texts both high and low: Michel Foucault's *I, Pierre Rivière, Having Slaughtered My Mother, My Sister, and My Brother . . . : A Case of Parricide in the 19th Century*; Thomas De Quincey's essay "On Murder Considered as One of the Fine Arts"; and true-crime accounts and pulp fiction, like Thomas Harris's *Red Dragon* from the Hannibal Lecter series. By 1993 I had published art reviews in magazines and Sunday supplements, and Cuauhtémoc invited me to coauthor the catalog essay for an exhibition that joined avant-garde art to the cause of ecology at the Museo de Arte Moderno, *Lesa natura: Reflexiones sobre ecología* (Marred nature: Reflections on ecology). For the catalog essay we framed the exhibition, which had been conceived "by poet Homero Aridjis and the young artist collective known as 'La Quiñonera,' curated by Carlos Ashida and Patrick Charpenel, supported by several official institutions and various independent [if not oppositional] organizations in the field of ecology in Mexico, and comprised of artists whose viewpoints and techniques [were] extremely varied." The exhibition, "hardly . . . unilateral or conclusive," included work by artists Francis Alÿs, Thomas Glassford, Silvia Gruner, Gabriel Orozco, La Quiñonera, and Pablo Vargas-Lugo, among others. These artists were able to insinuate visual grammars and many names still unfamiliar to institutional settings in Mexico in "an attempt to fracture" what many perceived as the "airtight vessel [through] which Mexican art" was officially legitimated.[3]

In the photograph with Francis, Cuauhtémoc dons a cartridge belt that is an early gourd piece by Thomas Glassford (fig. 15). A borderland native of Laredo, Texas, Glassford had arrived in Mexico in 1990, along with Texas Latina/o artists Ethel Shipton and Alejandro Díaz. The cartridge belt was an allusion to those worn by insurgents in Mexico's Revolutionary period (1910–20) and its depictions in post-Revolutionary visual culture. Contemporary parallels to that historic moment were inevitable and more than casual insomuch as they lent substance to the high-spiritedness; and murals like those by José Clemente Orozco were but a few blocks away from calle Licenciado Verdad at the former National Preparatory School, now the Museo de San Ildefonso.

Glassford's early sculptural works opposed elements in combinations that were sensuous but unsettling. Material clarity—gourds or *guajes*, steel, leather, vinyl, and rubber—gave way to sometimes-violent pleasures in viewing constituent parts and tactile surfaces subjected to perverse combinations of reason. Glassford's visual grammar addressed the indeterminacy of matter, the desire rehearsed in acts of embodiment, and the ambivalence prompted by a sexualized gaze.[4] By contrast, in other works, like his *Endless Column* of 1994,

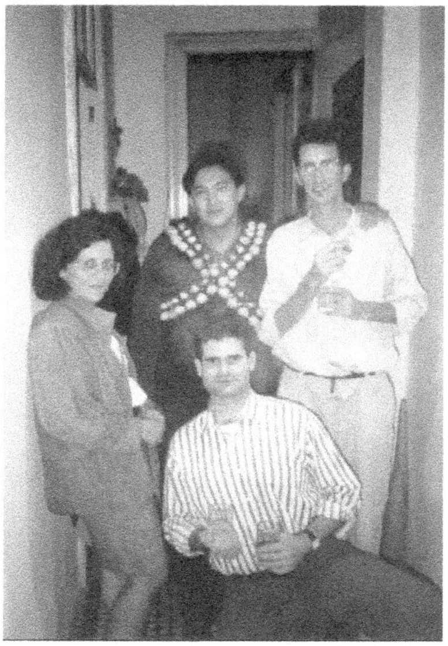

FIGURE 15. *Clockwise from left:* Danna Levin, Cuauhtémoc Medina, Francis Alÿs, and Roberto Tejada (*center*), ca. 1994. Photo courtesy of Adriana Konzevik.

he collapsed art-historical references to Brancusi with the social use of materials related to the lower body—American Standard bathroom ceramic in the shape of gourds (fig. 16).

In a 1992 installation entitled *Arteria* (Artery) at Curare: Espacio Crítico para las Artes, Glassford dissected the exhibition space into two discontinuous horizon lines—minimalist sequences of soft blue and deep red, so deflecting the respective hues onto the while walls of each gallery as to suggest an interconnected circulatory system. A series of rectangles of red enamel plates on steel rods contrasted with a blue row composed of wood blocks over each of which the artist had affixed a tile (plate 7). The materials and colors suspended the unity in a sort of optical congealing. For the blue horizon Glassford had used commercial bathroom tiles whose design was a *trompe l'oeil* of water drops and splashes as though beaded over the actual ceramic. The contrast activated an analogy between hydrophobicity—the absence of attraction or adhesion of water molecules to a surface—and corporeal anxieties about blood, saliva, and semen. The body and its fluids were charged with particular significance during years in which cases of HIV/AIDS had increased exponentially in Mexico.

Transposing design elements from class-specific social spaces—gymnasium, public bath, corporate office, or domestic interior—Glassford collapsed real-world settings, at once microscopic, corporeal, clinical, and systemic, and for which the gallery walls of Curare served as a placeholder.

Curare, a space for creative research in Colonia Roma, was founded in the summer of 1991 by a group of art historians and cultural theorists, largely led by the late Olivier Debroise, and it was a training ground for an eclectic circle of art writers and curators who were seeking new methodologies and networks of intellectual exchange.[5] Two years after Glassford's *Arteria*, Francis exhibited at Curare the first iteration of the ongoing and proliferating *Fabiola Project* (*Fabiola: Una investigación de Francis Alÿs en colaboración con*

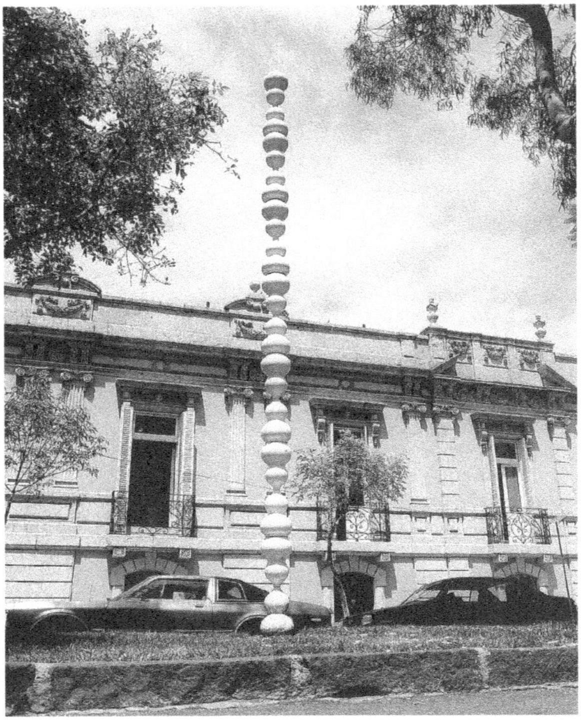

FIGURE 16. Thomas Glassford, *Endless Column*, 1994 (Avenida Álvaro Obregón, Colonia Roma). Courtesy of the artist.

Curare Espacio Crítico para las Artes) (fig. 17 and plate 8). Snapshots show Cuauhtémoc at a desk typing on the keyboard of an Apple Macintosh Classic, Debroise nearby reclining on a couch in the office-gallery, and the first Fabiolas assembled by Francis lining the walls. For an aerial view of the actors, objects, and circumstances that gave rise to the early downtown art formations in Mexico City (1987–92) there is no better narrative than the one related by Debroise in his essay "Entry and Exit: Internationalization of Mexican Art, 1987–1992," featured in the catalog to the 2007 exhibition *The Age of Discrepancies: Art and Visual Culture in Mexico, 1968–1997*, which he curated together with Cuauhtémoc and many of the researchers from Curare, a year before his premature death.

Debroise was himself a foreigner—born in Israel, educated in France. In that essay he reviews the constellation of forces that led to an "international Mexican underground." Set against the backdrop of rapid industrialization, increased neoliberal policies, and the deep-seated cultural and political apparatus of the Carlos Salinas de Gortari administration, there emerged at the margins a set of new cultural contests, one of which involved the arrival of foreign cultural actors. Within a brief timeframe a confluence occurred. More than thirty Cuban artists managed to obtain letters of invitation to depart from the island for Mexico (Juan Francisco Elso, José Bedia, Quisqueya Henríquez, and Consuelo Castañeda, among them). A band of British art school contrarians and associates found their

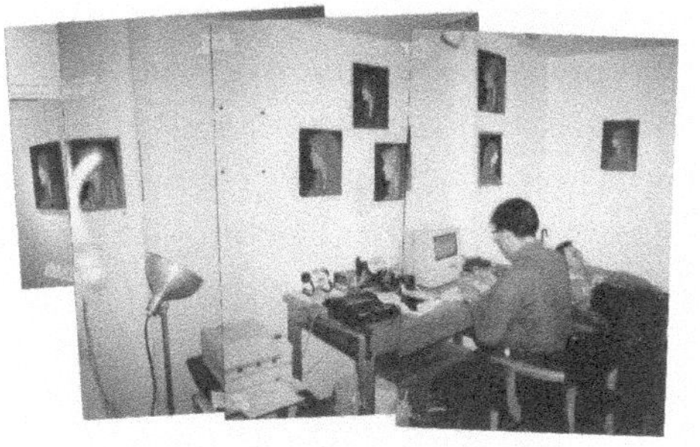

Figure 17. Unrecorded photographer, Francis Alÿs, *Fabiola* project at Curare: Espacio Crítico para las Artes, pictured with Cuauhtémoc Medina at desk and Olivier Debroise seated, 1993.

way from Thatcher's England to the chaos of Mexico's Federal District. Unconnected but each passing though at distinct moments were slightly more senior figures like Jimmie Durham and Michael Tracy. Debroise chronicles the appearance and interaction of these foreigners with Mexican artists like Gabriel Orozco, and others who had spent time abroad, including Silvia Gruner, María Guerra, the ubiquitous polymath Guillermo Santamarina. He relates the August 1986 opening of the adventurous Galería Arte Contemporáneo as well as improvised locations of display, like Salón dès Aztecas (which Aldo Flores ran out of his family's furniture shop) and La Quiñonera (otherwise known as the home of Néstor and Héctor Quiñonera).

It would be difficult to overestimate the importance of rentable real estate in the rough-hewn apartment buildings of Mexico City's historic downtown, many of them early modern constructions or *vecindades* nestled among the colonial buildings and preconquest ruins that comprise the urban grid, with its abundant evidence of previous political regimes and Revolution-era murals, together with the appeal of the populous avenues and overcrowded streets. The constant interchange of affordable housing from one artist to another led to a cluster of living situations on the calle Licenciado Verdad and the nearby Plaza Santa Catarina.

Lorna Scott Fox, a British writer, cultural journalist, and translator, had rented an apartment on the upper floor of the building on Licenciado Verdad, and in a nearby apartment lived the British photographer Ian Dryden, who recorded scenes from the social life of this moment, including a portrait of Lorna. Writers emerging onto the scene supported artist friends by writing copy for makeshift catalogs, articles for the press, reviews of exhibitions—labor often remunerated with the gift of an artwork—or by purchasing directly from the artist or commissioning a piece destined for home display. Not long after she had moved from her downtown apartment on Licenciado Verdad to a *vecindario* in Colonia Roma at calle San Luis Potosí 27, Lorna Scott Fox acquired a portable sculpture by Francis Alÿs—one of his earliest works (fig. 18). The untitled work provides a glimpse into the modesty of materials, the clarity of design and execution, and the poetics of the everyday that defined the work of Alÿs at the time, and to this day.

Francis painted a set of 40 linoleum rectangles on both sides so as to resemble a deck of playing cards for an unspecified game. The back of each card is rendered with deliberate marks, as in a paint-by-numbers pattern, depicting a bouquet of sundry flowers (in light pink, yellow, and aqua green). The floral design, over a chalk-blue background with cloud formation, suggests a kind of overly ornate arts-and-crafts wallpaper. The front of each card features a central symbol—a tea kettle on a stove burner, a house at a railroad crossing, a pack of smokes, an ashtray, and a smoldering cigarette. In relation to the suit-of-cup goblets on the upper right- and lower left-hand corners are the letters spelling out a series of comparable terms in English and Spanish: *límites/paciencia; maybe/maybe not*; *staying/leaving*. The bilingual references to understanding and endurance, on the borderline between decision and fate, activate a system of meanings about the incidents of transit and the instability of belonging. An archival snapshot shows the artist installing the work in Lorna's apartment, on the top shelf of a cluttered bookcase beside another shelving unit that blurs the division between the living room and kitchen space, with its blue-and-white speckled enamelware for cooking and a tequila shot glass nearby.

Together with the tile floor that served as a background for one of these documentation photographs, these elements are evidence of how interior domestic living inflected the materials, style, and treatment of works by an artist like Francis Alÿs. In these works, diminutive gestures are prone to have monumental consequences—of staying or leaving—free-standing but as unstable as a castle of cards.[6] I think of Lorna pausing at this work from time to time, with its image lessons in the day-to-day—house, tea kettle, cigarette—as being encounters randomly dealt but also occasions that contain—despite all precariousness to the contrary—the ability to transfigure.

Early works by British artist Melanie Smith also turned—in form and subject matter—to the question of home, habitat, architecture, and interior design. Smith had already taken over an apartment on the Plaza Santa Catarina left by artist couple Silvia Gruner (from Mexico) and Gustavo Pérez Monzón (from Cuba), who had moved to Licenciado Verdad around 1989. In works from 1990 and 1991, Melanie salvaged materials from the debris of buildings undergoing restoration or used other methods akin to urban archeology. In one untitled work—full disclosure: I own the piece—the artist assembled wood components from an interior cornice molding or some other decorative element from an abandoned interior—re-enchanted residues bespeaking a formerly more sumptuous past. The artist covered the wood in gesso and then stained the assembly in dark brown pigment. From the lower base and right side of the hollow volume protrudes a combination of elements: a rose-papered pegboard construction in the shape of a heart, and the pink tuft of a slightly weathered but still ostentatious tassel. The rose-patterned paper doubles back to Francis Alÿs's house of cards, and together—Francis and Melanie were a couple and shared the same apartment—the unrelated works speak of that past and its commitments to the shared energies and experience of a life when it involves the crafting of value, if even for a circle of friends. A household art in its twin sense, these works are talismans of affect and tributes to the labor of place making, an art whose form and content harmonize when displayed in the rented space of home. These works are so tied to the conditions of their manufacture and display as to be indivisible from that intimacy. The work of Alÿs and Smith connected, more distinctly now from the residential perspective, as it did with that of other artists, foreigners and national alike, through collecting practices, very often as a kind of city gleaning.

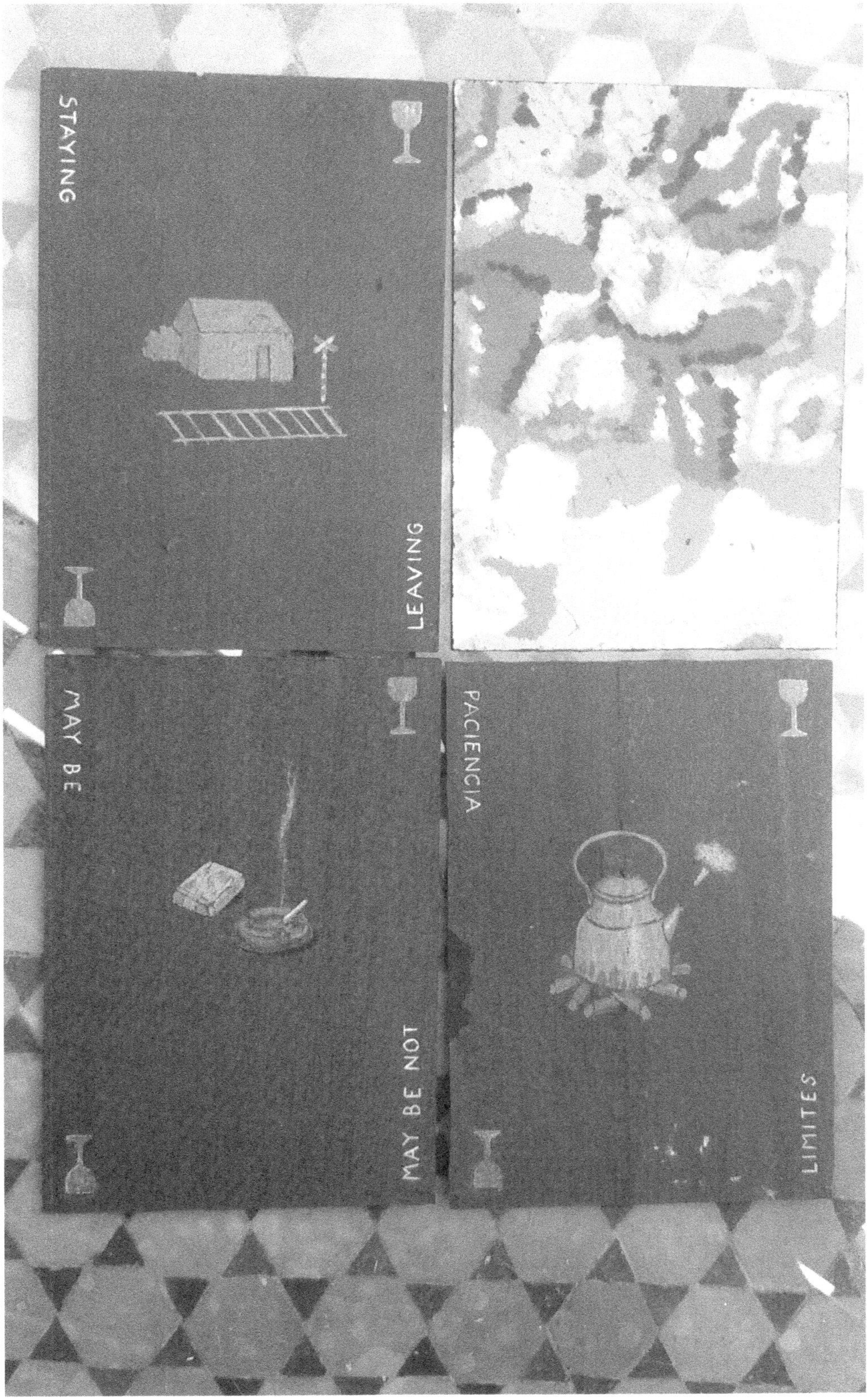

FIGURE 18. Francis Alÿs, untitled work, ca. 1991. Personal collection, courtesy of Lorna Scott Fox.

For example, from 1990 to 1992, Alÿs undertook a series of studies, maps, notes, and actions entitled *The Collector*, a form of street theater documented in collaboration with Felipe Sanabria. The artist paid tribute to Mexico's working class and to the vernacular genius in its forms of *bricolage*—the inventiveness obliged by making do.[7]

Holding a leash that dragged a "magnet sculpture with rubber wheels" in the shape of a makeshift toy, Alÿs walked the downtown streets of Mexico City, day or night, inhabiting a persona that was equal parts actual and fictional. He wrote, "For an indeterminate period of time, the magnetized collector takes a daily walk through the streets and gradually builds up a coat made of any metallic residue lying in its path. This process goes on until the collector is completely smothered by its trophies."[8] Similarly, from 1994 to 1996, British artist Melanie Smith turned to sites of exchange on the streets of downtown Mexico City. In a collecting practice restricted to the color orange, the artist scoured a profusion of mass-produced synthetic objects sold in a casual marketplace composed of street vendors and local retailers. The artist bought these items en masse and assembled the resulting accruals into an ultra-mix of wall-sculptures and photographs to create environments such as that insinuated by the title *Orange Lush* (plate 9). Smith upended any compulsory cause and effect between modes of production and the activities of consumption, between social contact and dislocated economies, or between sensual appeal and purchasing potential.

Purchasing potential was at stake for these artists, and not only for everyday means to bankroll the bohemian free time necessary to enable a practice. Debroise and Medina in the catalog for *The Age of Discrepancies* recall: "After she arrived in Mexico, Melanie Smith's first studio was located in an old building on the Plaza Santa Catarina. . . . On weekends, [she] and Francis Alÿs ran an informal restaurant serving brunch; designed to help make ends meet, it also provided a space for informal exhibitions and the exchange of information. Their multinational and polyglot circle was defined by immediate impressions and direct experience: artists and visitors wandering through the heart of the capital, gazing out over colonial church domes and Aztec ruins from rooftop patios, using their imagination to come and go anywhere."[9]

Even as these artists and writers had been attracting attention to the public spaces of Mexico City, it came as well with the ambivalence of curiosity, whose pleasures could never entirely camouflage anxieties about the public turmoil brewing beyond the refuge of this bohemian expatriate community. Recalling those years, the American poet Susan Briante, who also lived in Mexico at the time, wrote: "The passage of NAFTA and subsequent Peso Crisis were foundational to [an] understanding of the brutality of global capitalism. When you experience a national currency devaluation as we did in Mexico in 1994, you begin to understand the fragility of system."[10] As for *La dalia negra*, we more or less disbanded, but how could we *not* but have felt the uncanny in our midst looking back at our research into the literature of crime and criminality?

Recalling the vulnerable ties that bind the political to the personal around that particular historical juncture in his memoir essay "Homeland Insecurity," Thomas Glassford underscored the traditional structures of kinship and economy in contemporary Mexico, with its vestiges of colonial protocol and patronage systems: "Family life, social bonding through environment, education, and cliques are very prevalent. On any given Sunday afternoon one is expected to be having lunch and spending time with [one's] family. Inevitably, this same rigor . . . led many individuals living in Mexico to form their own family units [including those of us who were] foreigners living in Mexico City in the beginning of the 90s. . . . [A] group of artists, writers and historians arriving in Mexico from different locations . . . chose to live in the city's center, the historical, then downtrodden and rough but invigorating heart of the Centro." As for the nuclear family, Glassford notes that it was

> difficult to arrange renting contracts in Mexico without one. All contracts must be signed by a *fiador* [a resident cosigner] or a property owner [to] guarantee that the rent will be paid and rental property preserved. Obviously, some of us found this favor to ask difficult and arranging to rent out a floor in a building as an artist was not exactly the ideal for some of the proprietors (much less being a foreigner). Consequently, there were a couple of buildings in particular in the Centro, one being on the side street off the Zócalo, Licenciado Verdad, the other a few block further north on the Plaza Sta. Catarina where inevitably we found ourselves primarily ensconced after other artists had arranged previous relationships with the owners and established what in one case in particular, Sra. Susana [was] an extension [of] the family as well. While we would often share meals together, drink together and live in each other's spaces, we also began to organize exhibitions and projects because we hadn't found many other alternatives to show our work. Through this community of *extranjeros en el centro*, we began to have some influence within the cultural/social infrastructure of the city, sharing our homes/studios through parties, exhibitions, meals and other disorganized events. When we began to show our work along with other Mexican artists in more formal settings and galleries, we also became more entrenched as a separate movement due to our style of work and method, but primarily as a family unit.[11]

Foreignness, friendship, and foreboding: family refashioned in flights from everyday predicament into the sociability of art and the art of sociability. The disintegrating systems that led to the crises of 1994 included the collapse of the national currency; corruption and brutality of the state; the breakdown of authority and, with it, challenges to a narrow view of citizenship. However, none of this could have been anticipated by so modest a sculpture as a castle of cards, even as its meanings accrue over time in the historical viewpoint. Francis Alÿs made and installed this work in the home of Lorna Scott Fox in the years that led to the critical points for political and daily life in Mexican society, but the cozy metaphor of the house of cards alluded nonetheless to potential situations vulnerable to chance and the elements, prone to unpredictability and collapse. The modular work allowed for the enactments of the precariousness of play that remains precarious all the same. It made concrete possible collapse or disintegration while serving, importantly, as an object for household display meant to recall that work and play unite to reinforce the network of social relations.

That unassuming work telescopes from a snapshot in the past onto the walls of the Menil's Byzantine Chapel.[12] Around the time he made the untitled house of cards, Alÿs had already set into motion collecting practices that have now led to more than 450 reproductions amassed since 1992. They depict the fourth-century Roman Saint Fabiola, all of them copies of a lost original, an 1885 painting by French academic artist Jean-Jacques Henner. From the surplus of these reproductions that point to a prototype, each portrait remains a unique object, even as its maker remains unidentified and the assembly the result of that adhesive known as idea and design.

The Fabiola Project is the result of durational process, an evolving collection instigated by the act of sifting and sorting through flea markets, first by Alÿs himself, and then also by an expanding network of friends and other artists who have served as accomplices, stakeholders, and surrogate researchers in the project. Alÿs unleashed a concentric relationship between collector and collection. The lost original looms ever larger, its absence glimmering ever more forcefully in direct proportion to the increase in the number of objects that comprise the impossible completion of any infinite series. From the modest to the monumental, and always suggestive of an immensity, this particular collecting method reflects the insider-outsider perspective. *The Fabiola Project* is not neutral, in that it represents the foreign, the expatriated, the exiled—the amount of effort and time invested in collecting these vernacular images in Europe, Mexico, and elsewhere speaks of a drive that seeks a still point from so many objects dispersed over time and geography; to find a home for the infinite set.

Collectors are haunted by the infinite set to which assembly aspires impossibly. Collections betray the repetition compulsion whose fantasy is that of detaining or stopping time, as though the next object added to the series would guarantee completion. The sum insinuates a temporality that both centers and disseminates place as a need for certainty which, as Michel de Certeau reminds us, so frustrates our understanding of the past as to inflect the writing of history.[13] The uncertainty of the historical method itself: If the past is a reality that was once a living unity but no longer, then history is a viable form only in proportion to what it is able to relate. The writing of history is a continuum between the internal points of view about an action and the external ones. Historic truth remains obscured, always in the past, always in the distance between the place of enunciation, the statements about what was formerly lived experience and the function of language to speak what is absent, what is other to the present.[14] It's the fever Alÿs describes in a different project, *Sleepers IV*, as being one that "records the way dreaming might have a role in a possible rethinking of our conviviality."[15]

Feminist philosopher Elizabeth Grosz reminds us that family—namely descent—is not only a genetic concept, but also a durational one, "a way of accumulating the past in the present; to inherit something from a family is to live something of their past in my present; it is what I inherit as my living being body."[16] The proliferative effect of *The Fabiola Project* is about the kinship and difference established in foreignness and the private remnant to the public document. Allen Grossman wrote that exile and displacement make visible "the material contradiction of relationship."[17] And the art historian Georges Didi-Huberman: "Before an image, finally, we have to humbly recognize this fact: that it will probably outlive us, that before it we are the fragile element, the transient element, and that before us it is the element of the future, the element of permanence. The image often has more memory and more future than the being who contemplates it."[18] Following the lead of *The Fabiola Project*, I seek to enliven memory as prompted by photographs and remarks that friends have generously provided. They and so many others endure, in our former and future selves, family resemblances in the face of every Fabiola; energies and attitudes that emboldened us with a purpose to transform in art and writing as forcefully as is tenable in sociability and friendship. Fabiola is a monument to the little genealogies of conviviality and life, the aspirations of art and emergent community; an elegy to the household conversations lost to the public record: *límites/paciencia . . . staying/leaving . . . maybe / maybe not . . .*

FIVE

Diaspora Assemblage: "Held Together by Stardust"

Dispersions of form and discipline unsettle consensus about the modern, its authority over the past and future and the purity of time; its state of exception and ranks that often close in the service of assimilation. From another angle of lived particulars, an alternate belonging points first to Mexico City, where, in the late 1980s and '90s, I had fallen in with a lively, discerning cohort of artists and art historians, critics, curators, psychoanalysts, and poets; a band of nationals, exiles, and expatriates; a lifeworld out of place and on the margins of US-based art markets and institutions. Critic collectives like Curare: Espacio Crítico para las Artes, led by Olivier Debroise and Cuauhtémoc Medina, were sites for debating the emergent complicity and antagonisms among artistic group formations, global market forces and domestic commercial galleries, state and private museum cultures, regional and international systems of value, and pedagogies that linked Mexico to art schools and cultural institutions in Europe, the United States, and the Global South—a nexus that helped shape for me a diasporic Latinx understanding of the modern in its expanded field.

To align a poetics of history that comprises colonial violence, cultural misrecognition, and scenes of perverse hospitality, I've had to navigate the personal view and collective enterprise of art history and experimental writing, in matters that coalesce around the modern project and its vastness—a shorthand and placeholder for geographies and times that contest the authority of US American exceptionalism when faced with the unbearable intensity of the neighbor in uneven distributions of modern life.[1] These conjugations estrange the modern with divergent national-origin, racial, or ethnic experiences of the Latinx diaspora in knots untangled along a diagonal line . . .

In the 1990s, critic and curator Mari Carmen Ramírez identified the "conceptual crisis confronting the North American art museum as a result of the challenges that ethnic groups and new social movements" were posing to "self-centered exclusionary practices." She invoked the writings of Cuban anthropologist Fernando Ortiz and his concept of transculturation, "a dynamic whereby different cultural matrices have a reciprocal impact, though not from positions of equality, to produce a heterogeneous ensemble." Latin America and its diaspora in the United States "do not comprise one sole race, or *etnia*, but rather an amalgam of races, classes, and national heritages that elude any attempt at easy classification."[2] For me, that image of the heterogeneous ensemble recalls how the modern—its horizon of history, a promise, a latitude, a completion—gave way to a distressing standstill when I first viewed Cecilia Vicuña's *precarios*, those little assemblages the artist had made of wood, bone, thread, clay shards, matches, nails, shells, cardboard cutouts, stamps, feathers, rags, tiny containers of all kinds, twigs, and plastic debris (plate 10). With titles like *Cemetery*, *Guardian*, and *Tree of Life*, those small flagstones or altars were the findings of a fragile archeology—stand-ins for the accountability involved in all refiguring of patrimony, tiny markers that served as surrogates for the wreckage of the modern and its extractive drive. Defining these works, Vicuña recounts:

> [They] were not documented, they existed only for the memories of a few citizens.
> History, as a fabric of inclusion and exclusion, did not embrace them.
> (The history of the north excludes that of the south, and the history of the south excludes itself, embracing only the north's reflections.)
> In the void between the two, the precarious and its non-documentation established their non-place as another reality.[3]

Contained in that non-place, in that void separating north and south, is a "shared inheritance." Macarena Gómez-Barris calls this a site of memory within "the sweep of colonization and histories of social and ecological disappearance."[4] Between the modern and its discontent, in overt and furtive forms, other arguments emerge in a chorus of voices that, while working across boundaries and disciplines, account for hemispheric Latinx cultures by way of innuendo and sidelong conversation—undercutting, so to speak, from within the laws of exposition, unacknowledged proximities, and intervals given to resemble the diasporic.

A range of disciplinary formations and elective affinities between writers and artists challenges the assumed homogeneity of the modern archive, a configuration that includes inter-American cultural studies, US-Mexican borderland art, hemispheric cultural-policy studies, and art criticism during the Cold War period. From these various perspectives, historian and theorist Claire F. Fox proposes a hemispheric model to "rethink the meaning of disciplinary scholarship in general." She urges the field to look at artistic formations and "social, political, cultural, and economic developments in the Americas; migration, cultural production, and change in border areas; transnational cultural exchange within and among specific ethnic and racial groups; and comparative historical accounts of nation-state formation and national, regional, and ethnic identities."[5] Her study of US cultural policy in relation to Latin America during the Cold War uncovers a contrapuntal narrative involving the Organization of American States, Pan-American Union art initiatives, and the ambivalent attitudes of its Venezuelan curator and arts administrator José Gómez Sicre—"an anti-Stalinist fellow traveler; a homophobic homosexual; an exile without a generation; and a Latin American Latino." This complex archive reconfigures "significant transfer points of modernist aesthetics," insomuch as Fox uncovers an alternate mid-century-modern account shaped by US anticommunism, the visual arts as the site of diplomacy, and cultural citizenships on the move across the hemisphere, episodes that serve as antecedents of the modern for contemporary Latinx art practices.[6]

Another transfer point of modernist aesthetics can be found at the comparative juncture of visual and literary archives and in between the "strong modernisms" of Brazil and Mexico. Esther Gabara has theorized the narrow uses and abuses of the modern by situating colonization and colonial experience as central to an ethos that troubles the very function of modern art in Latin America, neither entirely the result of formal innovation nor solely of social reform. Rather, the modern is a function of an ethics enduring errant situations that so traverse places, not only nations, as to be constitutive of a people or community.[7] Gabara further expands the scope of the modern and its objects, which are not one, with forms of fiction that refute the system of free-market triumphalism that emerged throughout Latin America during repressive regimes of the 1960s and '70s, and again following the 1990s free-trade agreements. The hemispheric expansion of neoliberalism led multimedia book artist Ulises Carrión, for instance, to reconfigure "literature's liberation from narrative time," transforming materials into fictions composed of visual or sculptural dimensions that can be linked, in theory and practice, to Indigenous thought. As understood by Brazilian anthropologist Eduardo Viveiros de Castro, Amazonian concepts of somatic perspectivism underscore the "intimacy innate to fiction" and are akin to the avant-garde's "cutting, non-narrative time."[8]

For Chicana conceptual artist Celia Álvarez Muñoz, the modern bequeathed "two different worlds joined at the hip" along the colonial time zone of the Texas-Mexico borderlands.[9] Consequently, she inherited a variety of seemingly irresolvable antagonisms—between the empirical and theoretical; between personal history and information; between storytelling and statistics. For over fifty years, the Texas artist has turned to the modernist grid, and to the sameness and variation amplified by the photomechanical process, especially with her *Enlightenments* series (1980–83), a form of bookwork in the expanded field (plate 11). She subjects the language games of conceptual art to vernacular wisdom and wordplay, prompting visual tutorials about the world-bound relationships contained in accounts of upbringing. Her socially engaged art and ethics are scored in the key of insinuation, undertones that flout idolatry of the modern by accentuating material human circumstances and contingencies. Álvarez Muñoz has demonstrated that conceptual art's reliance on tautology is only a provisional escape from the culture concept; that systemic thought is often at the expense of lived experience; that reason's commitment to noncontradictory logic advances the dominant culture as universal. Her visual references to Marcel Duchamp, Donald Judd, Sol LeWitt, Andy Warhol, Claes Oldenburg, and John Baldessari at once enliven and deflate the modern and its hierarchies of value with little insurrections of irony and humor in the thought processes of English and Spanish. Universal reason gives way to that of intimacy in dislocation; and the future as a form of engineering so recedes as to inaugurate, in her photo-based work and installations, a diasporic alternate belonging.

Concepts of home, region, and belonging, and of homelessness, migration, and exile, are inseparable from the hierarchies wrought by the modern-industrial complex where global capital encourages nations to profit from human beings who wager life itself, leaving home behind in the hope of an everyday existence rid of the precariousness that economic injustice, wartime, and other social pressures dictate. The 2017 exhibition *Home—So Different, So Appealing*, co-curated by Chon Noriega, Mari Carmen Ramírez, and Pilar Tompkins Rivas, brought focus to Latinx and Latin American art since the 1950s, with painting, sculpture, installation, performance, photography, film/video, and public sculpture by Mexican-, Puerto Rican–, and Cuban-descendant US artists together with artists from Argentina, Colombia, Guatemala, Mexico, Venezuela, and Uruguay. In his essay for the catalog, Noriega builds on Heidegger's notion of dwelling to account for the twin acts of thinking and building, engaging the concept of home in what he calls a "matrix of places." The concept calls into question "the categories, frameworks, and processes by which home is made to appear natural, normative, and nation-bound." This matrix, he argues, becomes the "one true archive of modernity" to the extent that it serves as "the place where progress deposits its most telling artifacts and documents" in a form of history's wreckage. Thus, many of the artists he examines produce works that speak of inhabiting a home "but not a body," often existing "outside of language and without a place on the map." In his discussion of camera-based work by Perla de Leon, Jay Lynn Gomez, and Christina Fernandez, Noriega posits their images as encapsulating states of things "unsaid and unseen," with the purpose of viewing "home as central to a complex social reality that is hemispheric and global, not strictly local and national . . . and from the vantage point of what appears to be an absence, a dispossession . . . at the very core of our imaginings about home: immigrant labor." Noriega discusses the familiar strangeness of the home as a meeting place of "consumer culture, imperialism, network communications, ethnic segregation and assimilation, modern art, and family secrets." Artists from Latin America and its diaspora, as this exhibition and others demonstrate, have reconfigured the modern relation of an individual and the collective body to home, homelessness, nation, and migration; they make visible the shifting boundary between public and private spheres, between insider and outsider, and between citizen and stranger. Noriega grounds the modern as an unfinished practice, especially manifest by artists from the Latinx diaspora, who resist the modern as a certainty, much like the metaphor of home, which "offers no easy answer, but rather a hauntingly unspoken imperative upon which we dwell."[10]

Art critic and curator Rachel Weiss offers, too, a poetics of disarticulated dwelling in history, a haunting across different historical times and specificities of place. Her subject is the variability of the violent past, which subsists in the present as an imperative, with Walter Benjamin, to craft a telling proper to the "amplitude that information lacks."[11] The diasporic afterlife of Chile's Allende government survives in "postmemories" that tether the Pinochet regime to the present day, observed through the lens of filmmaker Patricio Guzmán. The past is seen as an inheritance lived belatedly—in diasporic time—even as it is mediated by the elegiac imagination, thus marking the refrains of individual trauma and collective memory. The past becomes a question for those who mourn victims, but also for archeologists and astronomers. In Guzmán's *Nostalgia for the Light* (2010), "time is unsteady, out of joint: the astronomer argues the present out of existence," and the "past acquires meaning by coming into relation with the present" through "a process of substitutions" wherein the "disarticulated strains of the tale [are] held together by stardust."[12] In the diasporic company of Guzmán, the precarious objects arranged as constellations by Vicuña achieve what Gómez-Barris views as work that "does not claim an authentic Indigenous past" but rather "resurfaces collective amnesia over buried histories of coloniality."[13]

For Weiss, the past "becomes, maybe, elastic with incipience." In elegies to the modern—to the art and social projects it promised—she affirms that, like the diasporic condition, the modern amounts to a series of "unsettling apprehensions." To write the modern from the position of the diasporic condition—"the place where knowing and not knowing intersect" within "the difficult truths of the past"—is to compel the "languages of fidelity to emancipatory promises" and the diasporic "languages of departure from them."[14] As with Vicuña, for me the non-place becomes a site for the idiom of departure that names a location remaindered from the exclusionary undercurrent of industrial and artistic development, the economy of accumulation, and homogenizing terms of encroachment. The non-place confirms a symptom. It encourages, too, a position for effectively eliding the modern, or the arena for articulating forms that are its refutation. Opposed to geopolitical and cultural grounds that separate localized dwelling from national narratives, a non-place gives way to the heterogeneous ensemble, aesthetic transfer points, a situational ethics, intimacies of dislocation, the matrix of places, and nonsequential fictions arranged to overturn the ongoing colonial residues of modern life.

SIX

Frameworks of Intelligibility: Latin American / Latinx Art

In his *Cheerleader* series of 2001–3, multimedia artist Luis Gispert employed a "mutable pop icon" long fetishized in US culture and media but in configurations that defy the laws of gravity (plate 12); suspension wires allowed some cheerleaders in typical outfits and rap-culture bling to levitate, often pointing to art-historical antecedents.[1] These large-format photographs understood what powers the circuitry of image making exerted in today's cultural economy, where economic and aesthetic values loop around each other through social and cultural sampling. Gispert's work examines social identities and their representation, as well as the material basis of subcultures when they become a visual commodity for art world consumption. They expose that image technology is to fashion as culture is to commerce. His multimedia practice uncovers points of agreement between iconography, style, and the system of contemporary art. Cuban American and Miami-based, Gispert's image can serve as a starting point to track the development of distinct but interconnected categories and conceptualizations in the history of art that relate geopolitical narratives and artistic geographies for Latin American–descendant experience in the United States.[2]

Walter Mignolo in *The Idea of Latin America* viewed the region neither as a bounded place, nor as a definite identity within a visual horizon, but rather as a "problem" or as a contested concept.[3] Similarly, the notion of a Latinx artistic geography has led intellectuals and artists interpellated by the designation to grapple with the inadequacy and contradiction of categories.

* * *

Historian Ramón Gutiérrez relates a narrative of Hispanic and Latino panethnicities originating with the "Spanish conquest of the Indigenous peoples of Mexico's north, which started in 1598," further developing with "the United States military's takeover of what became the American Southwest at the end of the Mexican War in 1848," and more recently with "the mass decolonization civil rights movement undertaken by radicalized minorities in the United States during the mid-1960s and early 1970s."[4] He argues that what is "new and distinct about panethnicities is that they can emerge not only from above through the actions of states and elites, but they also percolate upward from below, as acts of popular mobilization and consciousness in direct opposition to state actions."[5] For instance, a panethnicity was enforced among Indigenous peoples under the brutality of conquest, colonial subjugation, and the linguistic erasure of distinct cultures and ethnic affiliations executed using the Spanish plural noun *indios*.

Similarly, when the colonial settlers of the United States occupied the "Southwest as a conquering caste, they reacted to the ethnic geography much as the Spaniards had in 1598; they saw few cultural distinctions" and so organized racial and ethnic differences into "large panethnic groups."[6] As self-defined "Anglos" and "Anglo-Americans," they differentiated themselves from residents of the region who were all deemed "Mexican."

However, when gold was discovered in 1848 following the Mexican War, the wave of prospectors arriving in California included Spaniards, Chileans, Peruvians, Panamanians, and Mexicans. Anglo settlers "saw no apparent physical or cultural difference" between long-residing *Californios*, Mexicans, and the other ethnically diverse but Spanish-speaking groups. To "counter being stereotyped as a conquered population, to insist that they were unlike Mexican nationals, and to imagine membership in larger, liberatory spaces, californios began insisting that they were either *latinoamericanos*, or *hispanoamericanos* . . . calling themselves *latinos* as the shortened name for their hemispheric membership in *la raza latina* (the Latin race)."[7]

The art of Latin American–descendant peoples in the United States from the 1960s to the present also involves questions of panethnicity imposed by institutions from above and emerging from below through a vast complex legacy.

Gutiérrez notes that through the efforts of "Mexican Americans and Puerto Ricans" and other Latin American–descendent groups, a panethnicity emerged "from above through such things as the boundary-making national census (1980), or from below through interactions, commiseration, and mobilization."[8] With a few selected examples we can trace a little history of enabling terms and how certain authors have conceptualized the cultural particularism and the shifting place of enunciation for the evolving categories. Artists and writers have offered a diagnostic of cultural symptoms related to social space as a container of political strategies and aesthetic styles.

The Chicano art movement emerged as a process aligned with the United Farm Workers struggle, and it radicalized Mexican American life and culture with startling visual styles and a self-referential method, employed as early as 1967 in Delano, California, by Luis Valdez and El Teatro Campesino (fig. 19).

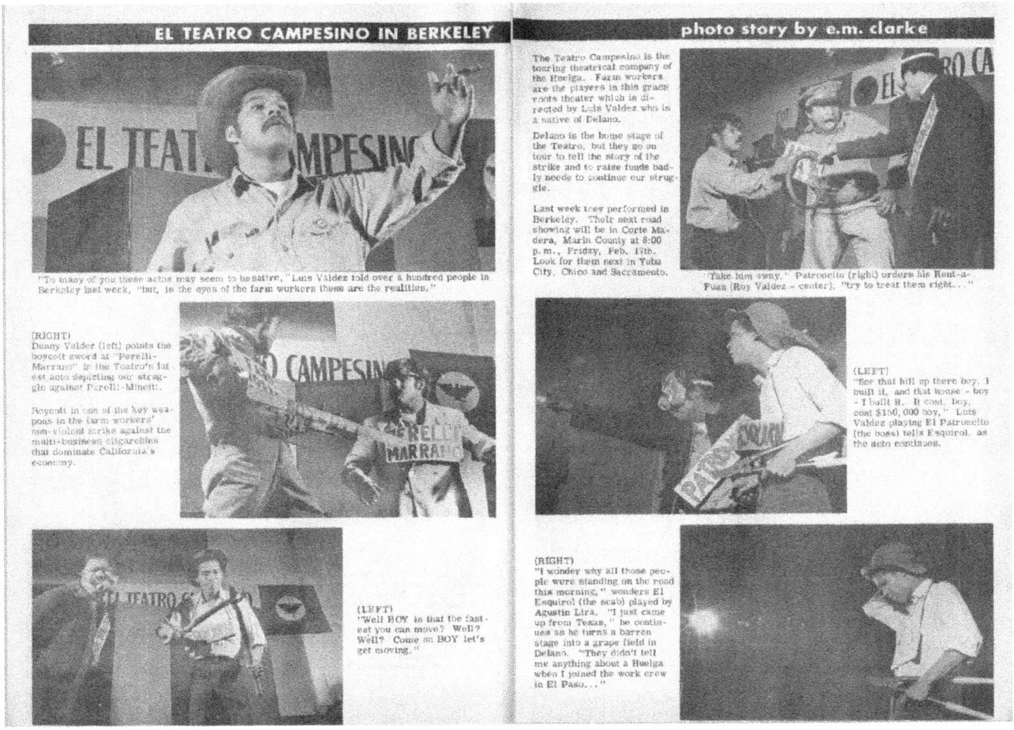

EL TEATRO CAMPESINO IN BERKELEY

photo story by e.m. clarke

"To many of you these actos may seem to be satire," Luis Valdez told over a hundred people in Berkeley last week, "but, in the eyes of the farm workers these are the realities."

The Teatro Campesino is the touring theatrical company of the Huelga. Farm workers are the players in this grass roots theater which is directed by Luis Valdez who is a native of Delano.

Delano is the home stage of the Teatro, but they go on tour to tell the story of the strike and to raise funds badly neede to continue our struggle.

Last week they performed in Berkeley. Their next road showing will be in Corte Madera, Marin County at 8:00 p.m., Friday, Feb. 17th. Look for them next in Yuba City, Chico and Sacramento.

"Take him away," Patroncito (right) orders his Rent-a-Fuzz (Roy Valdez - center), "try to treat them right..."

(RIGHT)
Danny Valdez (left) points the boycott sword at "Perelli-Marrano" in the Teatro's latest acto depicting our struggle against Perelli-Minetti.

Boycott is one of the key weapons in the farm workers' non-violent strike against the multi-business oligarchies that dominate California's economy.

(LEFT)
"See that hill up there boy, I built it, and that house - boy - I built it. It cost, boy, cost $150,000 boy," Luis Valdez playing El Patroncito (the boss) tells Esquirol, as the acto continues.

(LEFT)
"Well BOY is that the fastest you can move? Well? Well? Come on BOY let's get moving."

(RIGHT)
"I wonder why all those people were standing on the road this morning," wonders El Esquirol (the scab) played by Agustin Lira. "I just came up from Texas," he continues as he turns a barren stage into a grape field in Delano. "They didn't tell me anything about a Huelga when I joined the work crew in El Paso..."

Figure 19. "El Teatro Campesino in Berkeley," pages from *El Malcriado: UFW Voice of the Farm Workers*, no. 54, January 13, 1967.

Following Valdez, who joined the coordinated energy of labor movements to the self-reflective techniques of avant-garde theater, Mexican American farmworkers enhanced efforts to organize and advocate for change in labor practices by means of popular stagecraft. Whereas the UFW's boycott strategy was becoming "one of the key weapons in the farmworkers' nonviolent strike against the agribusiness oligarchies" that exerted power over California's economy, El Teatro Campesino was to coin a unique brand of carnival didacticism armed with a repertoire of cultural types and visual forms culled from Mexican and Chicano roadside vaudeville (*carpa*).[9] Its style resisted the temptations of piousness, even as it brought religious pageantry and banners of the Virgin of Guadalupe into play with reimagined preconquest rituals and a reversal of the kind of seventeenth-century theatrics designed by Counter-Reformation clergy to evangelize natives in Mexico—a revisionist project from below aimed to reverse the colonizing project from above.

Tomás Ybarra Frausto, connecting "the cultural expression of the farm workers' cause" to a "highly vocal and visible Chicano student movement" that emerged on campuses and in urban centers, further telescoped these formations to the "worldwide radicalization of youth" and "international liberation movements—especially the Cuban Revolution, the Black Power movement and varied domestic struggles. . . . Institutionalized racism was targeted as a key problem, and cultural affirmation functioned as an important basis for political organization."[10]

In the classic formulation affirmed by Rubén Salazar in a February 1970 *Los Angeles Times* column, "A Chicano is a Mexican-American with a non-Anglo image of himself. He resents being told Columbus 'discovered' America when the Chicano's ancestors, the Mayans and the Aztecs, founded highly sophisticated civilizations centuries before Spain financed the Italian explorer's trip to the 'New World.' . . . Why, ask some Mexican-Americans, can't we just call ourselves Americans? Chicanos are trying to explain why not." Salazar identified the white supremacy of American exceptionalism as well as the self-affirmative appellation of Chicano as an oppositional consciousness and counterargument. But in a wavering final gesture, Salazar concluded that "Chicanos, then, are merely fighting to become 'Americans.' Yes, but with a Chicano outlook."[11]

These snapshots tell of a dialectic that emerged in the mid-1980s, one Ybarra-Frausto identified in his essay "The Chicano Movement/The Movement of Chicano Art." From its inception as a category, Chicano art was unstable or a fluid name for encompassing diverse histories and aesthetics often in response to racist exclusions. Ybarra-Frausto viewed Chicano art as an aesthetic that "seeks to link lived reality to the imagination. Going against mainstream cultural traditions of art as escape and commodity."[12] A collective cultural project, workers, activists, artists and intellectuals mobilized to surmount "strategies of containment by struggling to achieve self-determination on both the social and aesthetic planes. It was the Chicano movement—through various political fronts, such as the farm workers' cause in California, urban civil-rights activities, the rural land-grant uprisings in New Mexico, the student and anti-war movements on college campuses, the labor struggles of workers without documentation, and the rise of feminism—that gave cogency to the cultural project."[13]

In a variety of media and other expressive forms of collective cause, artists opposed the mainstream art world to which, largely anyway, they had virtually no access. They refuted its exclusionary distinction between "fine art" and "folk art," and many worked to bring "practices of daily life and the lived environment" into a practice that operated in in keeping with everyday barrio life, where "art objects are embedded in a network of cultural sites, activities and events." In the now classic formulation of Ybarra-Frausto, this *rasquachismo* is "neither an idea nor a style, but more of a pervasive attitude or taste."

As an "underdog perspective" and "a stance rooted in resourcefulness and adaptability," it affirmed both the material and meaning of lived experience when "things are always on the verge of coming apart (the car, the job, the toilet), lives are held together with spit, grit and movidas . . . coping strategies one uses to gain time, to make options, to retain hope."[14] Ybarra-Frausto foregrounds resilience and resourcefulness as energies on the side of "syncretism, juxtaposition and integration," and as a "sensibility attuned to mixtures and confluence" where "communion is preferred over purity. Pulling through and making do are not guarantors of security, so things that are rasquache possess an ephemeral quality, a sense of temporality and impermanence—here today and gone tomorrow."[15]

This vernacular aestheticism was inseparable, in Ybarra-Frausto's view, from forms of internationalism which "entered this vocabulary via iconographic references to liberation struggles in Vietnam, Africa and Latin America, and motifs from cultures in those areas."[16] By the 1980s, however, Ybarra-Frausto saw receding the "utopian buoyancy that sustained a national Chicano art movement as more Chicanos" and Chicanas "enter the professional class and are affected by the social mobility," even as he also identified a "new agenda of struggle" that had surfaced. Given the demographic data marking the significant increase of Latin American diasporic peoples in the United States, the ongoing ethnic and racial discrimination against "Spanish-speaking groups," and the continuous waves of immigration from Central and South America, Ybarra-Frausto proposed that these "new cultural undercurrents among Chicanos" called "for an awareness of America as a continent and not a country. In the new typology an emergent axis of influence might lead," he specified, "from Los Angeles to Mexico City, then from there, to Bogotá, Lima, Buenos Aires, Managua, Barcelona, and back to the barrio. For artists, such new political and aesthetic filiations expand the field with hallucinatory possibilities."[17]

This emergent axis of influence summoned Chicano artists to view identity and culture as concepts that "are open-ended and [that] offer the possibility of making and remaking oneself from within a living, changing tradition." This cultural negotiation required a "to-ing and fro-ing between numerous aesthetic repertoires" and networks of association that included "mainstream galleries, museums and collections." Rasquache particularism, with its "temporality of impermanence," had a spatial counterpart in panethnicity and internationalism. In what Stuart Hall defined as a "framework of intelligibility,"[18] a rasquache perspective preferred juxtaposition, syncretism, and communion over purity. Reflecting the US Census Bureau's panethnicity from above, "Hispanic" appeared as the designation in such exhibitions as *Chulas Fronteras: An Exhibition of Contemporary Texas Hispanic Art* (curated by Benito Huerta, Midtown Art Center, Houston, 1986); and in the much-debated *Hispanic Art in the United States: Thirty Contemporary Painters and Sculptors* (curated by John Beardsley and Jane Livingston, Museum of Fine Arts Houston, 1987).

Even as the unfolding historical context emboldened certain orthodoxies in an "attempt to fracture the mainstream consensus with a defiant 'otherness,'" it also led to greater "recognition of new interconnections and filiations, especially with other Latino groups in the USA," as well as with allies in Mexico and elsewhere in Latin America. One can only imagine the horizon of elective affinities, "utopian buoyancy," and cross-cultural association that led Ybarra-Frausto in 1986 to the optimism of his underlying view. He wrote: "Confronting the dominant culture leads to recognition that Anglos' visions of Chicanos and Chicanos' visions of themselves support and to an extent reflect each other."[19]

A similar framework of intelligibility had been articulated by artists in statements like those of Rupert García, in a paper delivered earlier in 1983 at a convening at the University of Texas, San Antonio Research Center for the Arts and Humanities, and in a volume edited by Jacinto Quirarte, *The Hispanic American Aesthetic: Origins, Manifestations, and Significance*. García clarified: "Instead of the inadequate, illusive, reductive and historical label 'Hispanic American,' I will be using the composite term 'Chicano-Latino' throughout this paper because areas like the Mission District of San Francisco, California largely include people from or of the heritage of Central America, South America and the Caribbean. Furthermore, 'Hispanic American' emphasizes the Spanish speaking nature of the Chicano-Latino and therefore the 'Euro-Spanish-Anglo' character. This elitist and racist approach negates or ignores (perhaps both?) the Native American and Afro-American cultural and racial realities of the Chicano-Latino. When referring to cities having a large Chicano population like Oakland, Sacramento or Los Angeles, 'Chicano-Latino' means 'Chicano.'"[20] This position was consistent with García's art of the 1970s, which decried the war in Vietnam and US collusion in the social terrors of Latin America. He altered photographic portraits with bold screen-print technique, exceptional economy, and psychological impact to mobilize opinion; or to affirm a New Left internationalism in such icons as Black activist and political philosopher Angela Davis and Chilean president Salvador Allende, assassinated during the US-backed military coup of September 11, 1973.

The landmark 1990 exhibition *CARA: Chicano Art: Resistance and Affirmation* generated critical debates in advance of, during, and long after the three-year itinerary and national tour, from its opening on September 9, 1990, at UCLA's Wight Gallery to its closing on August 1, 1993, at the San Antonio Museum of Art, with iterations in the cities of Denver, Albuquerque, San Francisco, Fresno, Tucson, Washington DC, El Paso, and the Bronx (fig. 20). Alicia Gaspar de Alba's 1998 book-length study of the CARA exhibition, *Chicano Art: Inside/Outside the Master's House*, pursued multiple lines in its analysis, including the notable collective order of its curation, the public reception of *CARA*, the surrounding politics of representation, as well as a discussion of its panoramic sweep: 128 artworks; 54 mural images by 140 Chicano and 40 Chicana artists; its ten sections with corresponding visual interpretations; and a "Selected Timeline" beginning with "Pre-Columbian America and Aztlan 1345–1699."

The exhibition concluded on an open-ended note. In Gaspar de Alba's discussion, the final section, "Redefining American Art," presented Chicano art aspiring to impact the mainstream art world as a model for antiestablishment expressive practice. Her framework sought to "connect the rasquache, counter-Colón(ialist), alter-Native 'eye' of the CARA exhibition which literally looks back at me as I study it with the native 'I' of a Chicana" lesbian feminist." Thus, she viewed Chicana art as an "indigenous" art formed at the margins of US culture, even as it demands to be situated within the national-international mainstream in the history of Western art. She argues that another "way in which to contextualize CARA is as a text about life practices of an 'Other' American culture," which "is both indigenous and alien to the United States."[21] In this she articulated a frequent suspicion and, citing Coco Fusco, joined in rejecting the mainstream appropriation of subaltern cultures in the United States, an action that "has historically served as a substitute for ceding those people any real political or economic power."[22] She refutes the nativist ideology that held creative work by Americans from other cultures as not counting in the category of American art, but she declines any form of absorption into the establishment institution. Instead, she offers the conceptual model of cultural schizophrenia and the insider-outsider perspective as a way to foreground the contradictions of the *CARA* exhibition, eschewing the "melting pot mentality of the exhibition *Hispanic Art in the United States: Thirty Contemporary Painters and Sculptors*," where "racial and cultural differences were erased."[23]

For Gaspar de Alba, cultural schizophrenia is a positive term and alternative pathway for those who otherwise "saw assimilation into the Euro-American mainstream as the only road to equality," or who believed they would "find racial acceptance from Anglo society

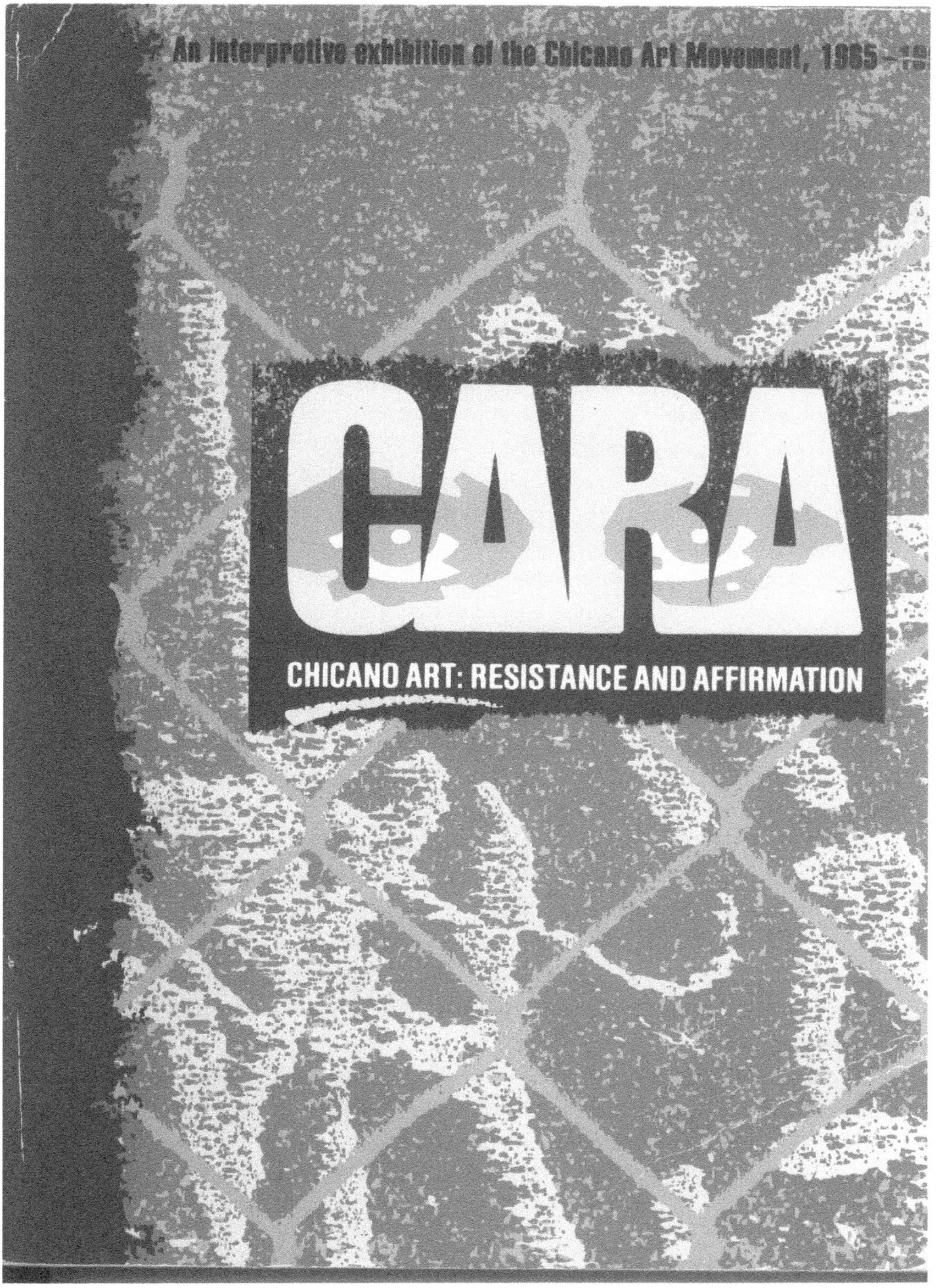

FIGURE 20. *CARA: Chicano Art: Resistance and Affirmation*, 1990 (catalog cover); exhibition logo designed by Willie Herrón and Patrice Roberts.

more readily if they claim Spanish ancestry." Rather, cultural schizophrenia, akin to *mestizaje*, functions as a value "in that it celebrates the racial and cultural mixing inherent in Chicano/a existence" and "the presence of mutually contradictory or antagonistic beliefs, social forms, and material traits in any group whose racial, religious, or social components are a hybrid of two or more cultures."[24]

Consider Judith Baca's 1976 mixed-media triptych *Las Tres Marías* (plate 13).[25] Baca's self-reflexive position aligned with that of Black lesbian intellectuals like poet Audre Lorde—whose classic essay "The Master's Tools Will Never Dismantle the Master's House" informs Gaspar de Alba's own queer person-of-color consciousness in assertions that "Difference must not merely be tolerated, but seen as a fund of necessary polarities between which our creativity can spark like a dialectic."[26] Cultural schizophrenia is another name for Chicana lesbian-feminist criticality, insomuch as it is able to locate works by artists of Mexican and Latin American descent within the US mainstream art world while never conceding to be entirely of it.

Parallel to the debates around *CARA*, cultural theorist and curator Chon A. Noriega turned to the transitory spatial medium of early 1990s installation art to rethink Latino contemporary identity and symbolic form. He offers an alternate history linking national and international arenas of description. In "Barricade of Ideas: Latino Culture, Site-Specific Installation, and the U.S. Art Museum" (1993), he looks to the writing of José Martí to reconceptualize identity as a spatial process staged "within, between, and against." For Noriega, by way of Martí, it was in terms of two empires (Spanish/US), while in the context of 1993, that one could think Latino identity and its expression as structures akin to installation art, insofar as identity is given to be conceived spatially, by means of artistic interventions that speak "within and to the institution of art." By activating the argument and prose style of Martí, Noriega suggests an alternate emergence for installation art—"an origin that grounds modernity and modern art within imperialism, rather than within a genealogy of aesthetic influences."[27]

Noriega foregrounds Martí's position as an elite criollo for whom race functioned on "levels other than that of color," namely as "cultural resource, class identification, and index of the nation (la raza)." The unresolved contradictions in Martí's *Nuestra América* (Our America)—the overemphasis on a mixed-race ideal (*mestizaje*) and the elision of the racial hierarchies that historically dehumanized Indigenous and Black lives—are the trick mirror that makes it possible for Martí to assert a "universal identity" and a pan-national narrative that "incarnates a particular set of bodies" and, in a form of political apotheosis, "produces communities-in-relation." This pan-national idealism beckoned a cultural negotiation not between the past and the present but between the present and the future—thus locating "the power of the idea over the object" while also understanding that the "object is evanescent in a way that the idea is not." Martí had affirmed: "Barricades of ideas are worth more than barricades of stone."[28]

If, in the reception of Latino art, critics had frequently written "about the contextual factors that make close visual analysis unnecessary—that make 'Latino' and 'art' irreducible terms," Noriega proposes a remapping of America, owing in part to Martí's program of *Nuestra América*, but one that follows a "genealogy of forms across multiple spaces." In this way, "another history emerges, one in which, for Latinos at least, the art installation owes as much to the baroque and its synthesis with the Indigenous practices and rituals of Our America as it does to the avant-garde and postmodern."[29]

Following this reformulation, in the work of installation artists like Amalia Mesa-Bains, Daniel J. Martinez, and Celia Álvarez Muñoz, Noriega views site specificity energizing the dynamic of inclusion and exclusion, for institutional overtures could serve as cover stories for all that heretofore had kept "various freedoms closed." The work of Martinez, Mesa-Bains, Muñoz, and many others asked "whether the underlying assumptions about cultural capital and racial difference" had changed; that is, whether admittance into legitimizing space was actually "congruent with the social" field.[30]

Noriega deploys a homophonic slip conveying the irresolvable gap between "*un Americano*" and the disdain or suspicion of American exceptionalism that views certain bodies and lifeworlds as being "un-American." He claims: "To date, Chicano, Puerto Rican, Cuban-American, and other Latino works of art are not considered part of 'American' art or of the U.S. national culture . . . and a more troubling trend has been the brokering of Latino artists into U.S. museums by way of exhibitions of Latin American art. What could otherwise be a provocative exploration of pan-national aesthetics, of Our America, becomes another form of the denial of citizenship." Noriega's challenge is to begin not with the "premise of cultural or racial otherness (that is, posit Latino art as a genre equivalent to its exclusion)," but to foreground an analysis of the media particulars. An emphasis on material format, while hardly a disavowal of "cultural and social determinants," preempts the vexed field of definition for the single focus on ethnicity. He adds, however, that "such subtleties are lost on many in the art world, where Chicanos, Puerto Ricans, Cubans, and other Latinos—despite their cultural differences from each other and aesthetic similarities with installation artists more generally—share a history of being excluded that is as persistent as it is unspoken."[31]

With an eye toward the unequal power relations that exist between and within cultures, Latino-identified artists uncover a desire "not for an essential truth, an underlying coherence, but rather [the need] to sustain contradictory images, shapes, languages, and frames of reference—all within the evanescent moment of the installation."[32] In short, Noriega deploys a media analogy in site-specific artworks as locations akin to those operative for Latinx identity in relation to US American exceptionalism and its frameworks for legibility.

More recently, scholars and curators have sought to place Chicano/Latino art "under the umbrella of art of the United States" as the corrective strategy to gain a more accurate picture of US American art. Curator E. Carmen Ramos, for instance, argues in her essay "The Latino Presence in American Art" and in the Smithsonian American Art Museum exhibition *Our America: The Latino Presence in American Art* that "the category of Latino art—and its multiple ethnic permutations and antecedents—could also stand for more than biculturalism," for more than hyphenated or hybrid cultural experience. Latino artists, she affirms, have "contested narrow definitions of American identity" insomuch as they reveal "the possibilities and tensions of expansionism, migration, and settlement."[33] By proposing "the messier and more challenging task of meaningful integration" into the US American canon, and historicizing artists like Luis Jiménez within the context, not of Chicano praxis, but of interactions with James Rosenquist, Andy Warhol, the 1971 Whitney Biennial, and Ivan Karp and his OK Harris Gallery nexus, Jiménez and his work—and by extension the objects and actions under the category of Latino art—"emerge not as an ethnic outsider embroiled in an intragroup conversation about identity but as a key participant in a national movement that inflects our historical past in a whole new way."[34]

A more recent Latinx aesthetic is concerned with the violent underside of the hemisphere's history. It is a work in progress currently enlivened by a generation of multiracial queer and gender-fluid artists and activists crafting pathways for discussing the X in Latinx art. Poet and scholar Alan Pelaez Lopez argues that "Latinx" is "not for everyone. Transgender and gender-nonconforming Latin Americans living in the United States have used the 'X' as a reminder that their bodies are still experiencing a colonization invested in disciplining them to fit a standard gender identity, gender presentation, sexual orientation, and a particular sexual performance." For Pelaez Lopez and for poet/performers like Jennif(f)er Tamayo the "x" is a scar that exposes four wounds that Pelaez Lopez nominates as being the legacies and histories of "settlement, anti-Blackness, femicides, and inarticulation."[35] By contesting the structures of power for which Latinx as a category is convenient, and by rejecting the contemporary corporate expediency of a Latinidad that is "fluid, placeless, and amorphous,"[36] Latinx artists are so situated as to animate the category and grapple with its contradictions, even as they critique the position of the United States in the geopolitical distributions of the present global nexus. They can suggest that Chicano/Latinx artists are especially poised to interrogate US ascendancy and resist the narrative seductions that deem the market the only legitimizing institution for art practice while rejecting group affiliations that underwrite or perpetuate forms of US American exceptionalism.

SEVEN

The Latin American Photobook in Context

"Once upon a time in the future."[1] With that fortunate turn of phrase, art historian Carol Armstrong deftly captures the untimely temporality of the photographic medium in its relationship to the book, and to the unique seductions of storytelling. In the narrative patterns that mobilize from page to page, photographic facts unite the "once upon a time" with the future, projected into the present viewing in an entanglement of contingent, evocative relations, not necessary or compulsory ones. Photography is inseparable from the history of the book, from experiences of reading and viewing, and from the sight and touch of mechanically produced page-dependent images and words, intended to generate social and cultural attitudes through media-specific effects. The photography book puts forward a description of a world in its particulars of time and place; of how that world could have been—can still be—otherwise. Proper to the theme of books and photography—and the union of the two in the photobook—the development of the medium in Latin America obliges a story about libraries, both institutional holdings and makeshift personal collections, as well as a much-remarked scene in a library that has served as an origin story for the history of the photographic medium.

The library as a critical site in the early development of the medium points back to an image by William Henry Fox Talbot, *A Scene in a Library*, plate 8 from his 1844 *The Pencil of Nature*, printed on salted paper from a calotype negative. Carol Armstrong provides a robust reading of Talbot's book *with* photographs and *about* the photographic process, and of this image in particular, in her 1998 study of British nineteenth-century photographers, *Scenes in a Library: Reading the Photograph in the Book, 1843–1875*. In her familiar account, Armstrong historicizes the "verbal framing of the photograph" to the degree that it has been naturalized or made invisible "in the [modern/contemporary] context of printed matter—newsprint, the magazine page, advertising copy, and science, travel, art, and other kinds of books."[2] She tells a story of "the nineteenth-century photograph in its textual surround" through the British photographers Talbot, Anna Atkins, Francis Firth, and Julia Margaret Cameron, claiming that the book "was not only the principal frame for the photograph, historically speaking, but also that it had something to do with the very being of the medium."[3] Talbot's *Scene in a Library* betrays the desire for camera technology to be the content of an older medium, the book. Armstrong relates the record-keeping function of the photograph through the frame of the book (its "narrative-tabular" method of "observation, experiment, and comparison"), and to the spaces that open out when the meaning of a photograph is at cross-purposes with that of the written word.

The contemporary photobook is an offspring of the liminal moment Armstrong describes, "when the photographically illustrated text was only just coming, hesitatingly, into being [insofar as the] early photographically illustrated book was not yet what it would become." She anticipates the modern fascination "both with the photograph's intransigence, its fundamental illegibility, its difference from and even hostility to what surrounded it—to the words that framed it—and with the effort required, early on, to harness it to the text and to the book, as well as the mixed feelings that accompanied that effort." Talbot's emphasis on the bookishness of *The Pencil of Nature* provides a distinction between a book that contains photographs (record-keeping; scientific inquiry) and a book that attains its denouement when a photograph works jointly with other photographs and attendant writing to create narratives that mirror the tropes of fiction: ghost stories, gothic tales, the detective novel, science fiction, or fantasy. In the text that accompanies *A Scene in a Library*, Talbot indulges in a speculative scene about an experiment with a prism emitting invisible rays from the light spectrum in a darkened room: "the camera would see plainly where the human eye would find nothing but darkness. . . . For what a dénouement we should have if we could suppose the secrets of the darkened chamber to be revealed by the testimony of the imprinted paper."[4] For Armstrong, "the text to *A Scene in a Library* is striking for the way it looks forward towards an experiment not yet realized, one that is to take place at an undetermined point in the future." "Once upon a time in the future" describes the space and time of the modern photobook, the evocation of scenes "coming, hesitantly, into being" but not yet what they promise to become—a romance that finds the inventorial function inadequate for books with images, the fictive preferable to the rational, and the speculative more desirable than the scientific.

The historical, geographic, and human realities of Latin America are critical to modernity and to its image histories. But only recent interest and scholarship has defined the field of the photobook in this region as distinct from the universal account. The intensive archival and ground-level research of Horacio Fernández, with input from a first-rate advisory committee, gave rise, in 2011, to *The Latin American Photobook* (published in Spanish and Portuguese editions, and in English by Aperture).

Fernández provides a panoramic view of the medium in Latin America, a twentieth-century story that is commensurate with the region's varied urbanizations, its modern social movements, its reconfigured relationships of the present to the past, and interconnected historical processes of politics, economics, and culture. The camera and its ripple effects were central to Latin American modernization, and to the processes that inaugurated new forms of human relations through joint technological and social advances, even as the modern project did not distribute its welfare equally within societies of the region. The Latin American setting I want to describe focuses on sites of exchange and dialogue, conversational junctures that gave way to energetic engagements with photography and to the vitality of photobooks. These developments were intentional and collective efforts that began in the late 1970s and early 1980s in Mexico City and emerged again in the years 2007 and 2010 in São Paulo.

The Coloquios Latinoamericanos de Fotografía were a series of public discussions and exhibition events, the first two held in Mexico City, in 1978 and then again in 1981, followed by editions including the 1984 Coloquio in Havana, Cuba.

The events were organized in a collaborative effort led by Mexican photographer Pedro Meyer of the Consejo Mexicano de Fotografía (Mexican Council of Photography). The Consejo's other members included photographers "Lázaro Blanco, Julieta Giménez Cacho, José Luis Neyra and Pablo Ortiz Monasterio." It also looked to "the advice of art critic Raquel Tibol and the support of government officials such as Víctor Flores Olea—also a photographer—and Juan José Bremer."[5] Emphasizing the importance of network exchanges, the Coloquios were meant to contribute to the debate about the cultural status of Latin America and the question of photography as a social tool, its place in fashioning forms of national selfhood, cultural and ethnic diversity, or regional singularity; in short, as part of the broader discourse whose shorthand is Latin Americanism.

Revelation, uprising, fiction: Looking back at the 1978 and 1981 Coloquios Latinoamericanos de Fotografía, a 2007 exhibition at the Centro de la Imagen in Mexico City, *Revelación, revuelta y ficción: Hecho en Latinoamérica*, aimed to sort through the debates, visual thematics, stress points, and imperatives for photography according to the call for work circulated by the Consejo Mexicano de Fotografía in the late 1970s (fig. 21). That *convocatoria*, or announcement, for the 1978 Coloquio expressed three defining tenets for the selection:

> a) That, bound to a time and place, photographers accept an accountability so as to interpret with images the beauty, conflict, triumph, defeat, and longing of their people.
> b) That photographers refine and affirm their awareness by conveying the reactions of man and society in crisis; that they aspire accordingly to produce an unambiguous and committed art.
> c) That sooner or later photographers must confront the need to analyze the emotional and ideological power of photographic work, independent of maker, so as to comprehend and define the ends, interests and aims that the medium serves.[6]

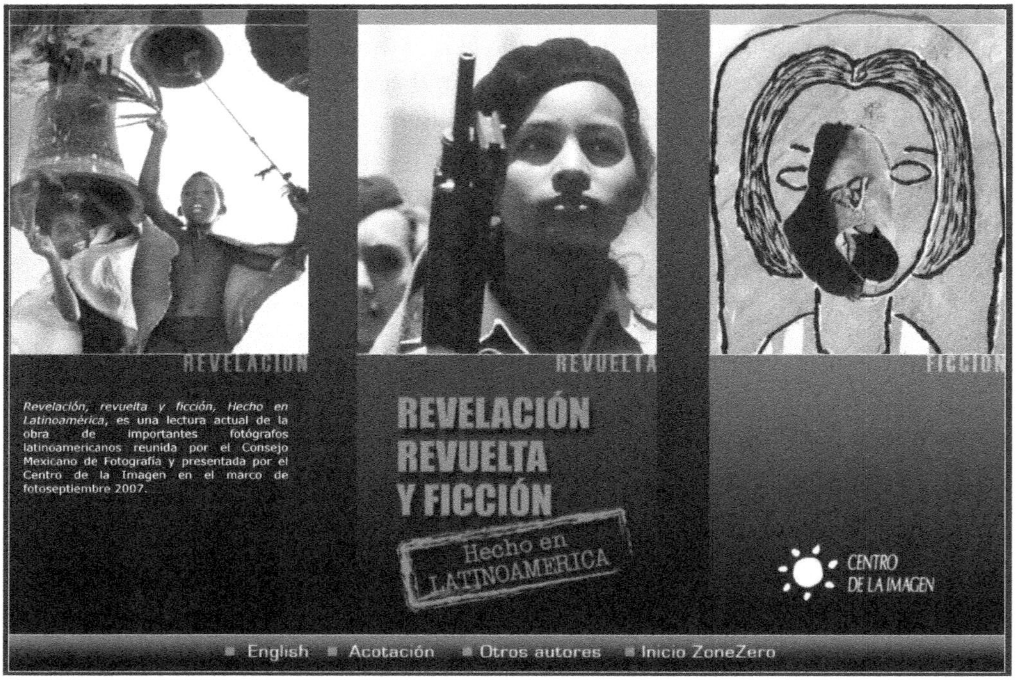

FIGURE 21. *Revelación, revuelta y ficción: Hecho en Latinoamérica*, digital exhibition, webpage, Centro de la Imagen. © 2007 ZoneZero, http://v1.zonezero.com/exposiciones/fotografos/revyficcion/index.php?idiom=ES.

In keeping with this photographic perspective and the foregrounding of other Latin American countries in the Coloquios, Brazil was represented by 150 photographers, whose images—1,217 of them—largely reflected the aesthetic counterpart to a brand of Latin American humanism of the 1960s and '70s, focusing on rural conditions, urban public space, the disenfranchised, or the subjects of police brutality. Many images portrayed the process of affirmation and defiance in the face of political oppression during the military rule, like photographs by Antonio Luiz Benck Vargas, Roberto Cecato, Evandro Teixeira, and Luiz Carlos Velho, among others. Brazilian photographer and critic Boris Kossoy served on the advisory board, which sought to prompt exchange between makers, critics, and researchers, and he was one of the invited photographers highlighted in the inaugural 1978 Coloquio.[7] Kossoy later recalled that "the Coloquio constituted an important frame for photography in Latin America, a watershed event amid the total lack of knowledge that reigned about neighboring countries' photographic production, and the beginning of a relationship at once artistic, academic, and political, that from that point forward was initiated."[8]

In this sense, the 1978 Coloquio Latinoamericano de Fotografía was consistent with an institutional discourse about the status of Latin America. Brazilian sociologist Darcy Ribeiro linked Brazil to Mexico in his foundational essay "A América Latina Existe?" (Does Latin America exist?). Ribeiro argued that Latin America existed only to the degree that there was continental continuity without a unified structure, a separate but associated coexistence remaindered from the colonial condition, an archipelago of islands with its perspective often turned elsewhere to world economic centers. Ribeiro argued, often in contrary claims, how the region's geography tended to isolate more than it was able to connect and that it was hardly homogeneous in terms of language and culture.[9]

Pedro Meyer's opening address at the second Coloquio, of 1981, outlined the ongoing terms of the context. He spoke of Latin America as a geography, history, and human process with a shared experience of systematic oppression and exploitation, in the form of internal and external aggression. He identified a Latin American iconography in photographic form, elements unique to a place of origin and to the social processes of its people. Citing critic Raquel Tibol, he spoke of a complex convulsive reality animated by hope, and he enumerated a series of arguments about the status of Latin American photography: "One must not forget that in contrast to Europe and the United States, Latin America has—on account of its sheer poverty and exploitation—become a setting for extreme social struggle, revolutions, and repressions; thus it contains the great seed of the future. Latin American photography finds itself necessarily connected to these realities, whether directly or indirectly, and it will have to reckon with itself and its eventual contribution as art, as testimony, as part of the culture of our times."[10]

Other forces in effect during the late 1970s and early 1980s, parallel to the first and second editions of the Latin American Photography Colloquium in Mexico, further energized the medium of photography as a social and national practice (fig. 22). In 1982, the year of the publication of the proceedings that served as a catalog to the *Hecho en Latinoamérica* exhibition, historian Alan Riding published an analysis in the pages of *The New York Times* that detailed another process taking place in Mexico: the Americanization of everyday life and the political economy, a low-intensity crisis of national identity. Riding describes the opening of Reino Aventura on the southern edge of Mexico City, an "amusement park on the wooded outskirts of Mexico City." Meant to provide a "form of leisure until now available only north of the border . . . Adventure Kingdom [was] the first such park to be built in Latin America." Though wildly popular, the theme park, unsurprisingly, "also touched off controversy. To leftists and nationalists, the park [symbolized] the steady 'Americanization' of Mexico's middle class." And it had been foreshadowed by the emergence in 1980 of Perisur, the largest shopping center in Latin America, built "in the image of Texas shopping malls." Not to be underestimated was the "cultural impact of television" in the form of "Superman cartoons or live broadcasts of American football games" with commercials for Kellogg's breakfast cereals and the Ford Mustang. These features conspired to transform values and forms of life insofar as they challenged the national sense of cultural sovereignty and self-determination; what Riding identified as a "bruised nationalist pride" joined, more importantly, to questions about the "impact of this trend on Mexico's political system."[11] The photography colloquia in Mexico—with their Latin Americanist aspirations—can be viewed therefore as a conversational counterforce to this predicament of culture and national identity.

One of the participating photographers, Pablo Ortiz Monasterio, played a definitive role in this respect. From 1980 to 1981, he had served as the editor for several photography

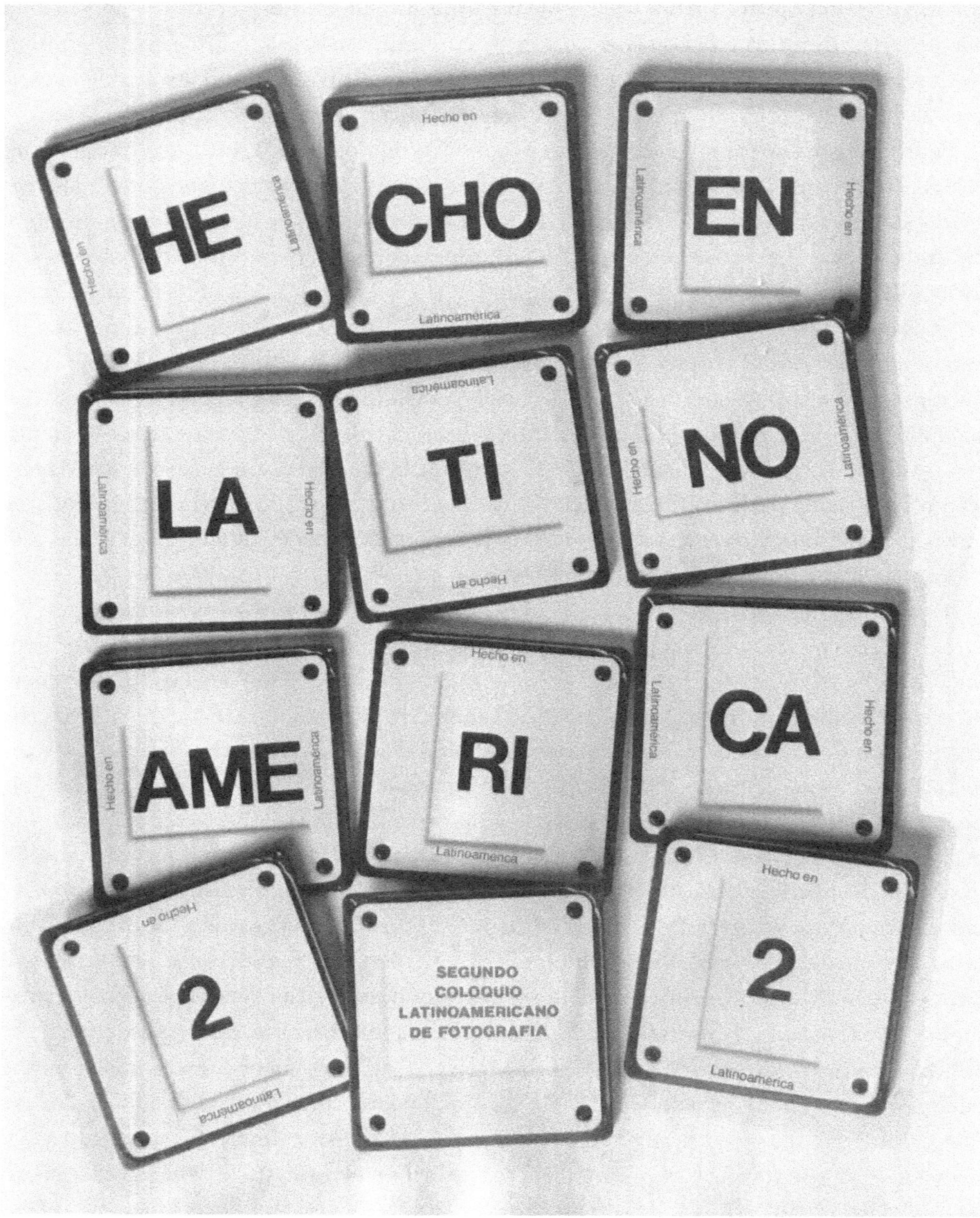

FIGURE 22. *Hecho en Latinoamérica: Segundo Coloquio Latinoamericano de Fotografía*, 1982, cover. INBA/SEP/Consejo Mexicano de Fotografía.

books published by the National Institute for Indigenous Peoples (Instituto Nacional Indigenista) and the National Endowment for Social Activities (Fondo Nacional para Actividades Sociales), producing books by Mariana Yampolsky, Graciela Iturbide, and Ortiz Monasterio himself, with respective prologues by such writers as Elena Poniatowska, Luis Barjau, and José Manuel Pintado. In 1984 Ortiz Monasterio went on to helm an even more ambitious enterprise. In August of that year, the Fondo de Cultura Económica—the partially state-funded and not-for-profit publishing house founded in 1934 by Mexican philosopher Daniel Cosío Villegas—launched a collection devoted to photography: Río de Luz (River of Light). In 1984–85, in a burst of activity, eleven titles were published, and from 1987 to 1991 another nine titles appeared under this imprint, the majority of them by Mexican contributors, a few by photographers from other countries in Latin America, and one by Iranian photographer Abbas, a Magnum photographer whose commitments to Mexico and its photographic worlds ran deep.

Each of the twenty Río de Luz books conformed to "a standard format of 275 × 205 centimeters"—in landscape or vertical orientation—and all were under the editorial care of Ortiz Monasterio, designed by Peggy Espinosa, with a print run of 3,000 and with "exceptionally high production values attained at the Imprenta Madero."[12] The covers featured soft metallic tones that made the series unmistakable, recognized in Mexico and abroad as the premier showcase of its time for photography in the Americas. In its near decade of existence, Río de Luz displayed the work of eminent Mexican and Latin American photographers whose aim was to complicate the social role of the medium in a region with specific cultural differences, but loosely bound by a common colonial history, issues of cultural contact, and a continuing process of political and cultural change. Ortiz Monasterio later attested to the "special effort" that was Latin America's investment in book production, for lack of a national market to sell photographs and for want of exhibitions with national reach. "To circulate our discourses, the book is very important. . . . We all understand, in terms of political education, how this nation is being influenced by other nations, [and that publishing] is an important project, not for short-term, but long-term results," which he equated with the US Farm Security Administration.[13]

Río de Luz managed to make dynamic the meanings of the photographic sequence in book format, and the series as a project possessed intentionality. It provided a rudimentary history of photography in Mexico that pointed back to early and mid-twentieth-century photographic antecedents, while offering a platform for contemporary photographers to register work and experiment in sequencing. As a unity, it involved a cultural constellation of novelists, poets, ethnographers, journalists, essayists, and art historians who wrote the introduction or afterword to each volume: Carlos Fuentes, Elena Poniatowska, Carlos Monsiváis, Guillermo Samperio, and Verónica Volkow, among the numerous contributors to the series.

Río de Luz activated a series of historical revisions and reappraisals, important for both the photographic record and for cultural memory (fig. 23). In 1986, the series published *Jefes, héroes y caudillos* (Commanders, heroes, and military leaders). The volume sought to craft a story at odds with what the Carlos Monsiváis called the "sequential and purposeful progression" of its anterior printed image source, the photography of Agustín Víctor Casasola.[14] Drawing from his own photographs and the repository of images by other photojournalists he had amassed in the period that spanned the Porfirio Díaz regime to the Mexican Revolution, Casasola published in 1921 a series of mass-produced photo albums. There, among its half-tone pages, was structured for Mexicans, still recovering from the brutality and bloodshed of the decade-long conflict, the social demise of the prior order

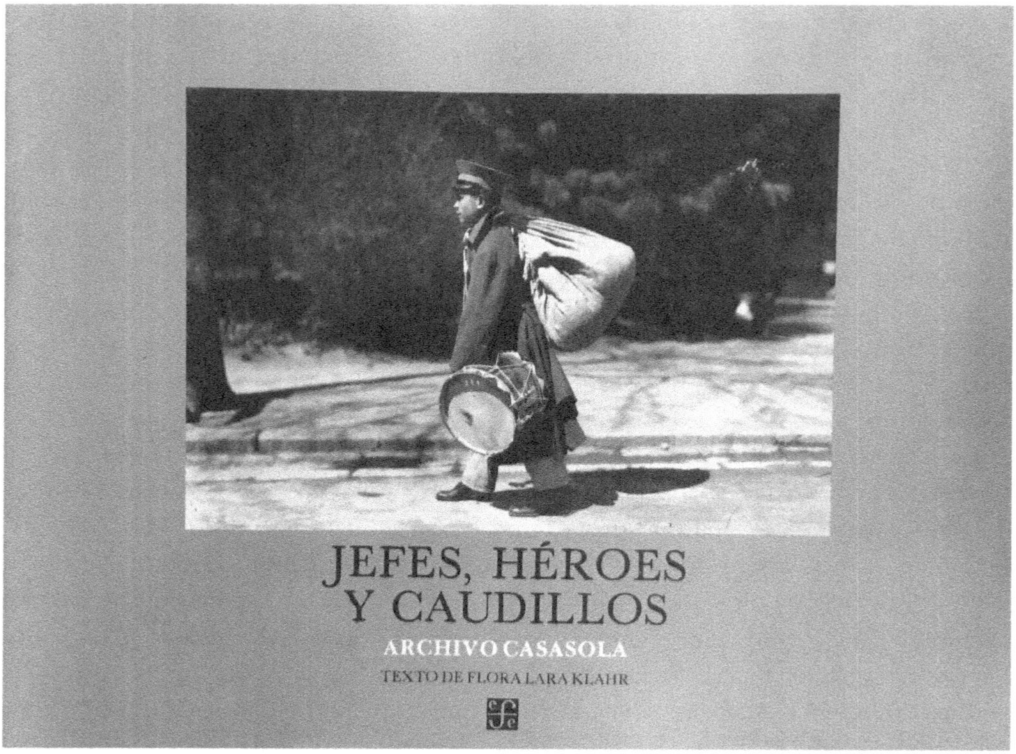

FIGURE 23. *Jefes, héroes y caudillos*, Fototeca del INAH, Archivo Casasola, Colección Río de Luz; text by Flora Lara Klahr, edited by Pablo Ortiz (Mexico City: Fondo de Cultura Económica, 1986), book cover.

and the "sequential and purposeful" progression of a society in restoration. These episodes included the non-reelection movement commanded by the affluent landowner from Coahuila, Francisco Madero, as well as his persecutions and exiles, and those endured by his supporters. A "purposeful progression" outlined in narrative form, the photo albums trace the parallel uprisings and armed rural mobilizations of Pascual Orozco, Francisco Villa, Emiliano Zapata, and Venustiano Carranza—in the tremendously complex, circuitous events of the Mexican Revolution—as well as the varied alliances and conflicting factions that finally gave way to the assault on the city of Juárez by a Maderista faction (against Madero's orders and led by Pascual Orozco) on May 10, 1911, and the resignation and flight of the dictator Porfirio Díaz on May 25. The means by which the following ten years are organized in the five-volume *Álbum histórico gráfico* (1921) is a chief example of how image technology could serve, a priori, to constitute the terminus of a teleology—the Revolution as an ongoing process in the making.

The Río de Luz edition of the Casasola archive made critical contrasts available to the present perspective disenchanted with the narrative of purposeful progression, preferring to make visible the strangeness of that history deeply rooted in the substance of Mexican society.[15] It served as well as a sly commentary on the continued cult of personality in presidential politics of the single-party system, controlled by the Institutional Revolutionary

Party, whose authority faced more and more challenges, and not only in state elections (as in the outcome of the 1983 ballots in the state of Chihuahua). Ortiz Monasterio structured the archive in cinematic terms—scenes attached to personalities and episodes—making no disguise of the ways in which images are prone to substitute for disconnected episodes that compose history from the public attachments of the past, lending narrative energy to the gaps, suppressions, and missing links in the historical record.

The Casasola commercial albums of the 1920s were a product of the alliance between photography and print capitalism, and they depicted succession and a display of human action in collective movement. Mexico's modern master of the photographic medium, Manuel Álvarez Bravo, developed, by contrast, a singular style during the 1930s and 1940s, through a method and technique that first applied the unspecified time of formalist or abstract compositions to frame the contradictions of Mexico's urban and rural life in social statements with metaphoric force about the dislocations of modern life, what Julien Levy called the "anti-graphic," or that which defies reason and the authority of cause and effect.[16] The photobook of 1945 entitled *Fotografías* was conceived as a rare object—115 copies, each containing "three original photographic copies," published to accompany a mid-career exhibition at the private foundation Sociedad de Arte Moderno. Horacio Fernández relates that "the catalog was entrusted to the artist and bibliophile Gabriel Fernández Ledesma, who created a classic and elegant—if somewhat conventional—layout," with texts by Álvarez Bravo himself, muralist Diego Rivera, poet Xavier Villarrutia, and cinematographer Gabriel Figueroa.[17] Unique to this 1945 edition, all photographs were printed vertically, even the images meant for horizontal display. But in everything else, the layout later served as the model Río de Luz adopted and developed in the 1980s: a single image on the right-hand page; a blank left page with a barely discernible caption; and abundant white space and the discreet positioning of the caption on the left-hand page. Discretion was both the method and subject matter for Álvarez Bravo's work, especially clear in many of his classic photographs that draw the viewer—and the very act of viewing—into the image. As observers attempt to decipher the cultural or formal elements depicted in certain pictures, observation itself comes under scrutiny: storefront windows rendered not only as intricate visual planes, but also as reflectors dividing society into those invested with purchasing power and the majority devoid of it. One of the later titles in the Río de Luz series, the 1989 publication *Mucho sol* (fig. 24), with a text by art historian Teresa del Conde, documents an aim to situate the canonical or classic images of the 1930s and 1940s within the ongoing opus of Álvarez Bravo's practice as a photographer and influential teacher in the 1980s. Pablo Ortiz Monasterio, one of Álvarez Bravo's disciples, produced photobooks that can be read allegorically, on one level, as the reckoning between the master and pupil, between classic modernist style and the contemporary pressures that compelled photographic practice.

A photojournalist by profession, Nacho López enhanced his practice with equal parts social concern, formal commitment, and narrative drive, testing the scope of Mexico City press photography of the 1950s. Within a prescribed information industry, his feature stories and pictorial essays advanced a dynamic that further galvanized the power of

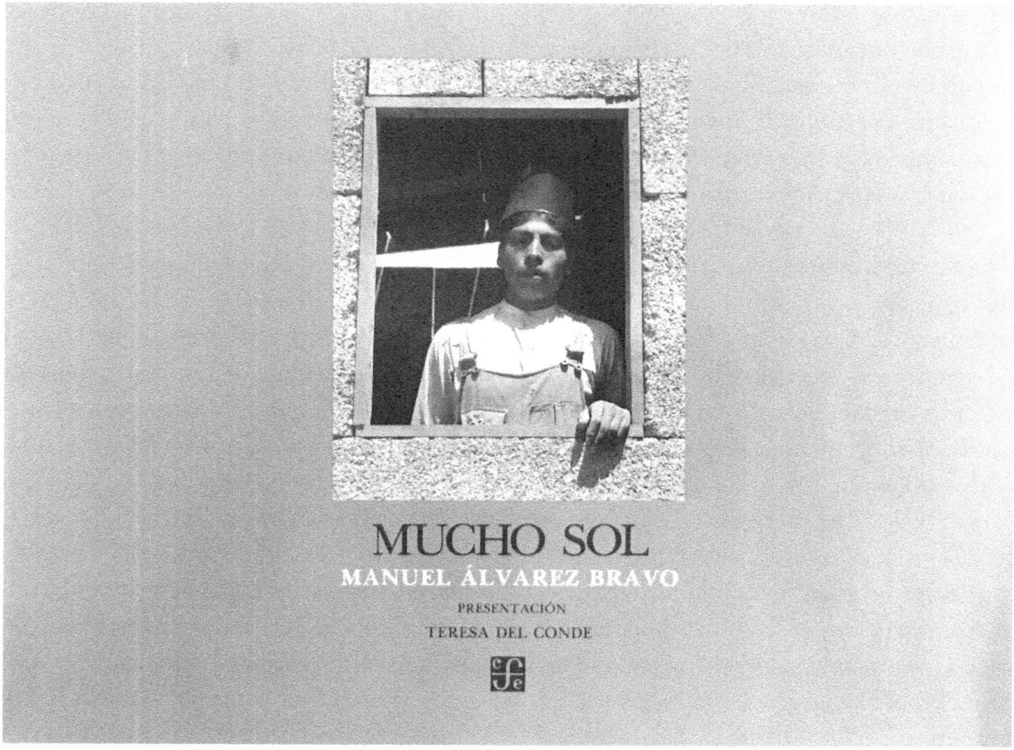

FIGURE 24. *Mucho sol*, photographs by Manuel Álvarez Bravo, introduction by Teresa del Conde, Colección Río de Luz (Mexico City, Fondo de Cultura Económica, 1989), book cover.

photomechanical images. López infused picture assignments for magazines with modernist objectivity and ethical resolve as gained from the example of art photographers like Álvarez Bravo, who were able to dodge the pitfall of representation that claims the common people as its source.

Counter to the assumption that newspaper cameramen in Mexico rarely strove for formal effects, López set himself the task to modify something beyond the immediate frame of the photographic act, and to test the narrative gaps of a chosen situation, made visible sometimes only in the final editing. López activated the relationship between specific photographic images and source meanings in the larger context of their publication history. The photographs provide evidence of the compliance and pressures in dealing with the information industries of the 1950s and the presidential cultures of Miguel Alemán (1946–52) and Adolfo Ruiz Cortines (1952–58). In the pages of widely distributed journals—*Rotofoto*, *Presente*, *Hoy*, *Mañana*, and *Siempre!*—López introduced social commentary, sometimes oblique, other times unambiguous. Subjects ranged from Indigenous peoples to entertainment celebrities, thereby confirming the national contradictions contained within the metropolis of the capital. López revealed the underside of the country's so-called miraculous modernization, even as he pointed to the blind spots in the visual discourse about national identity, rendering social polarizations caught between middle-class pathology and its idealization of the working class. He understood that the documentary or testimonial function of a photograph was never purely mechanical, and only effective to the degree that it could be structured into a creative—that is uncertain, or open—viewpoint.

In 1964, the journal *Artes de México* devoted an issue to "La Ciudad de México" (Mexico City) entirely composed of images by López and featuring the graphic design of artist Vicente Rojo, who recognized the thematic structure and layout of the magazine as being in aspirational dialogue with such publications as the Swiss journal *Du*. The bold patterning of photographs on the large-format pages was meant to perform the forces described by López in a literary fever dream he wrote to frame his work: "Yo, el ciudadano" (Citizen Self): "On the periphery, on the grid of chaos, the displaced. . . . Those who live beneath roofs of sheet metal and cardboard. Poverty is a faithful companion. And to the city dweller it gives freedom, like the lottery, to die of hunger."[18] It included percussive references as well to obituaries and the transitory fame of boxers and dance hall personalities, to churches and shantytowns: "The city is an eye of light that blinks in agony full of fog and hope. Its innocence and a necklace of pyrotechnics miscommunicate to men and women, or conditions their existence."[19] Twenty years later, in the second title of the Río de Luz series (fig. 25), López and editor Ortiz Monasterio rearranged the *Artes de México* edition. Divided into Days, Rituals, Afternoons, and Night, the photobook followed a day-in-a-life sequence, which, like city itself, may be apt to monumentalize even as it is unable to tell the whole story. "Yo, el ciudadano" gave narrative structure to the unequal conditions that determine the right of access to citizenship in the Mexican capital as a microcosm of the nation.

Early in her career Graciela Iturbide explored multiple exposures of the national, cultural, and emotional meanings that materialize in photographic images. Pressing against the dubious authority of her camera, she engaged a critical poetics about Mexico's ethnic, social, and sexual differences—engaging her subjects, Indigenous peoples and women in particular, to indulge in the self-reflexive, creative mutuality of performance that the camera compels. The images were visual evidence of the self- and mutually reflective meeting place between photographer and subject, without veiling the differences enacted in that encounter. Her ethnographic work included series made among the Indigenous peoples of Mexico—the Seri, Isthmus Zapotec, and Mixtec—as well as the religious folk pageantry of such pilgrimage sites as Chalma, and the urban polarities of Mexico City. One of the final books in the Río de Luz series was Iturbide's 1988 *Sueños de papel* (Paper dreams) (fig. 26).

Compared to the high production values of the series as a whole in its sixteen previous editions, the printing quality of *Sueños de papel* was demonstrably compromised by a decision to pitch the hues in sepia, and to outline the images tending to lighter tones with a design frame; and the excellent single images never entirely integrated into associative definition or continuity. Notwithstanding these shortcomings, in concurrent production was the work that became Iturbide's first definitive and career-making statement in photobook form, and its impact transformed assumptions about ethnographic photography

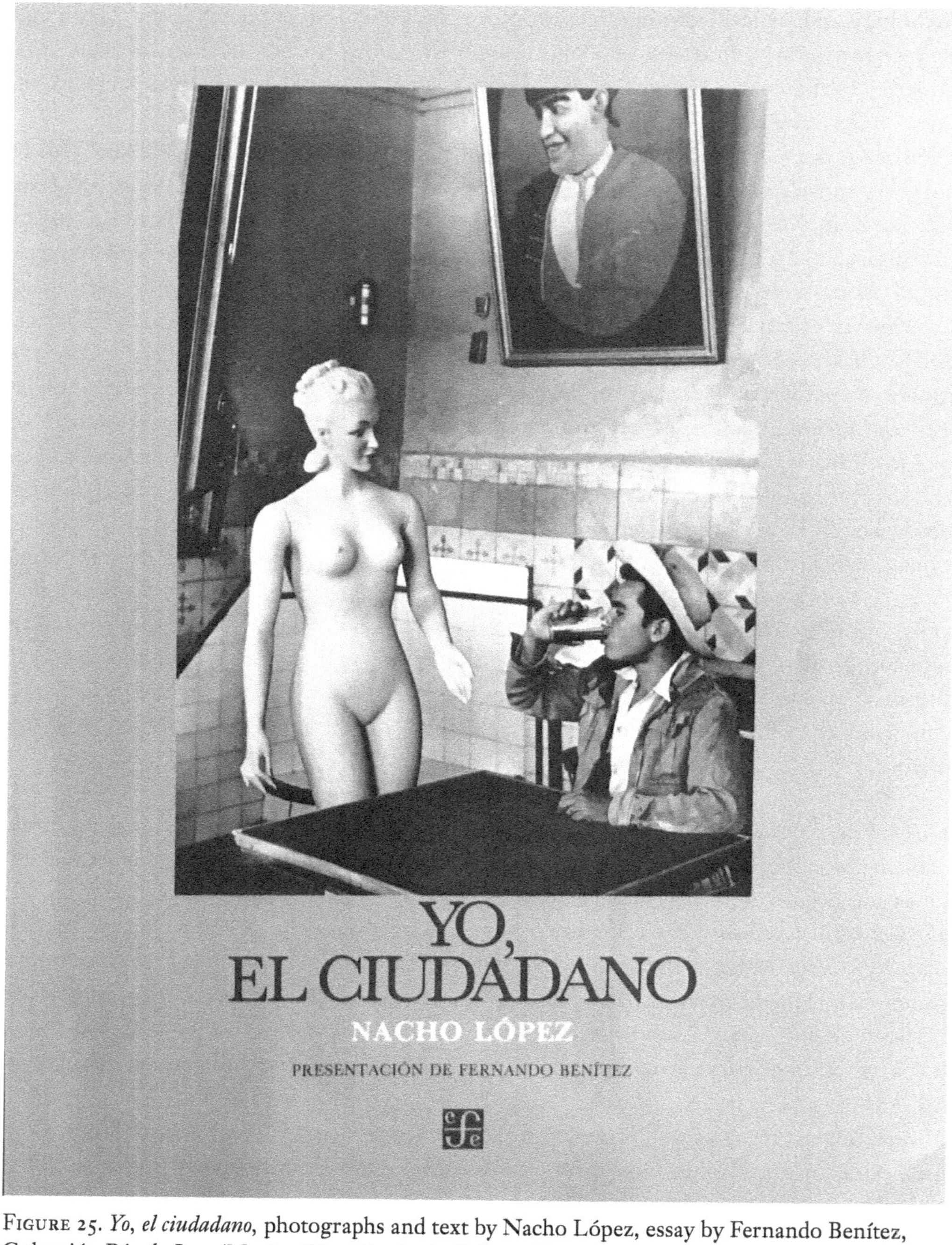

FIGURE 25. *Yo, el ciudadano*, photographs and text by Nacho López, essay by Fernando Benítez, Colección Río de Luz (Mexico City, Fondo de Cultura Económica, 1984), book cover.

and the narrative possibilities of the book. *Juchitán de las mujeres* appeared in 1989, after years Iturbide had spent living among a community in the Isthmus of Tehuantepec, accessed through her connection to the Oaxacan artist Francisco Toledo, some of whose relatives appear as photographic subjects. The cover image (fig. 27)—now one of Iturbide's

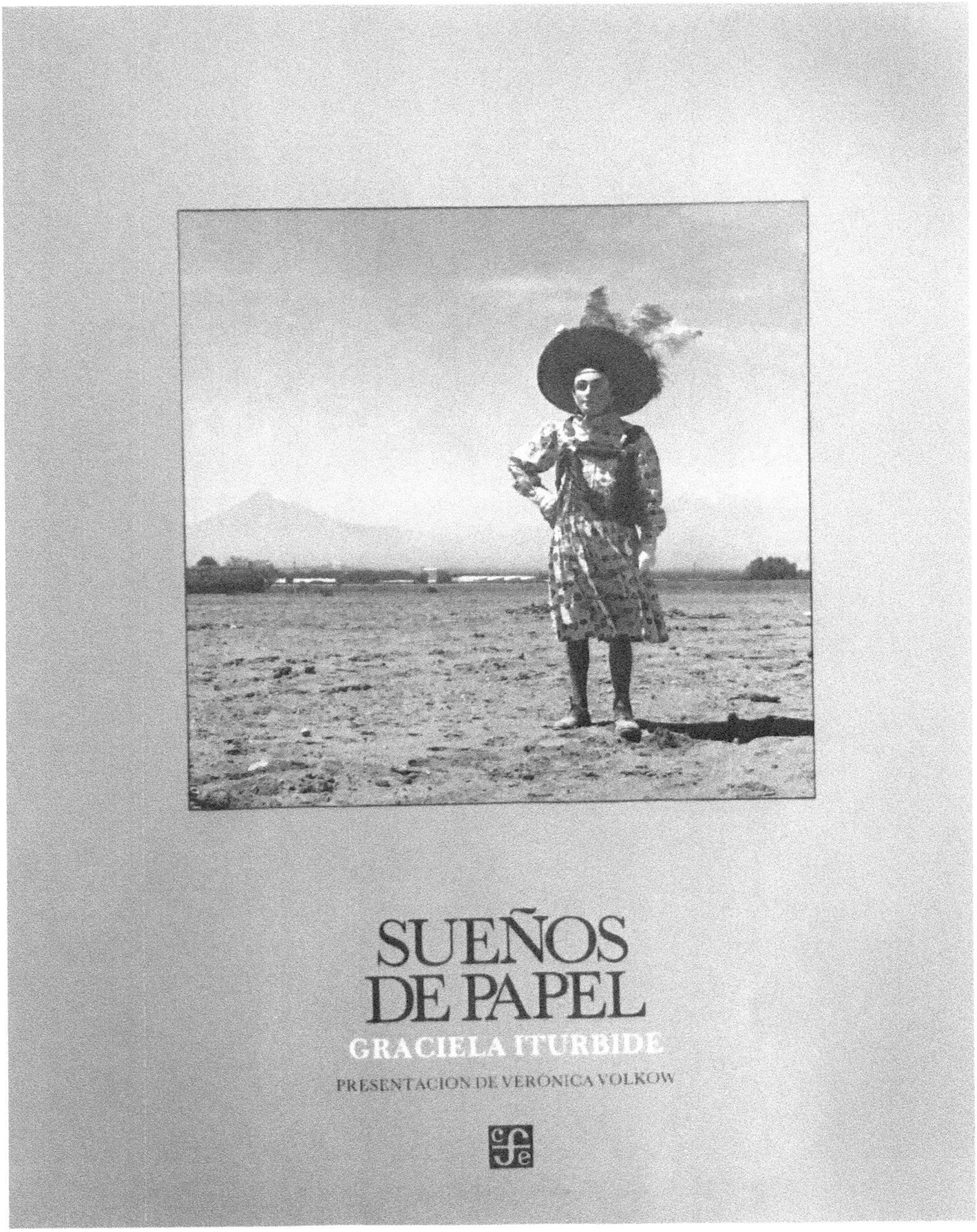

FIGURE 26. *Sueños de papel*, photographs by Graciela Iturbide, introduction by Verónica Volkow, Colección Río de Luz (Mexico City, Fondo de Cultura Económica, 1985), book cover.

most iconic—gives way to a title page and frontispiece in lava or blood red that flank the cover image appearing again, now designed to bleed off the right margin, rendering the progression off kilter. No captions accompany the images throughout the sequence, but *Nuestra señora de las iguanas* (Our Lady of the Iguanas)—its eventual title—depicts from

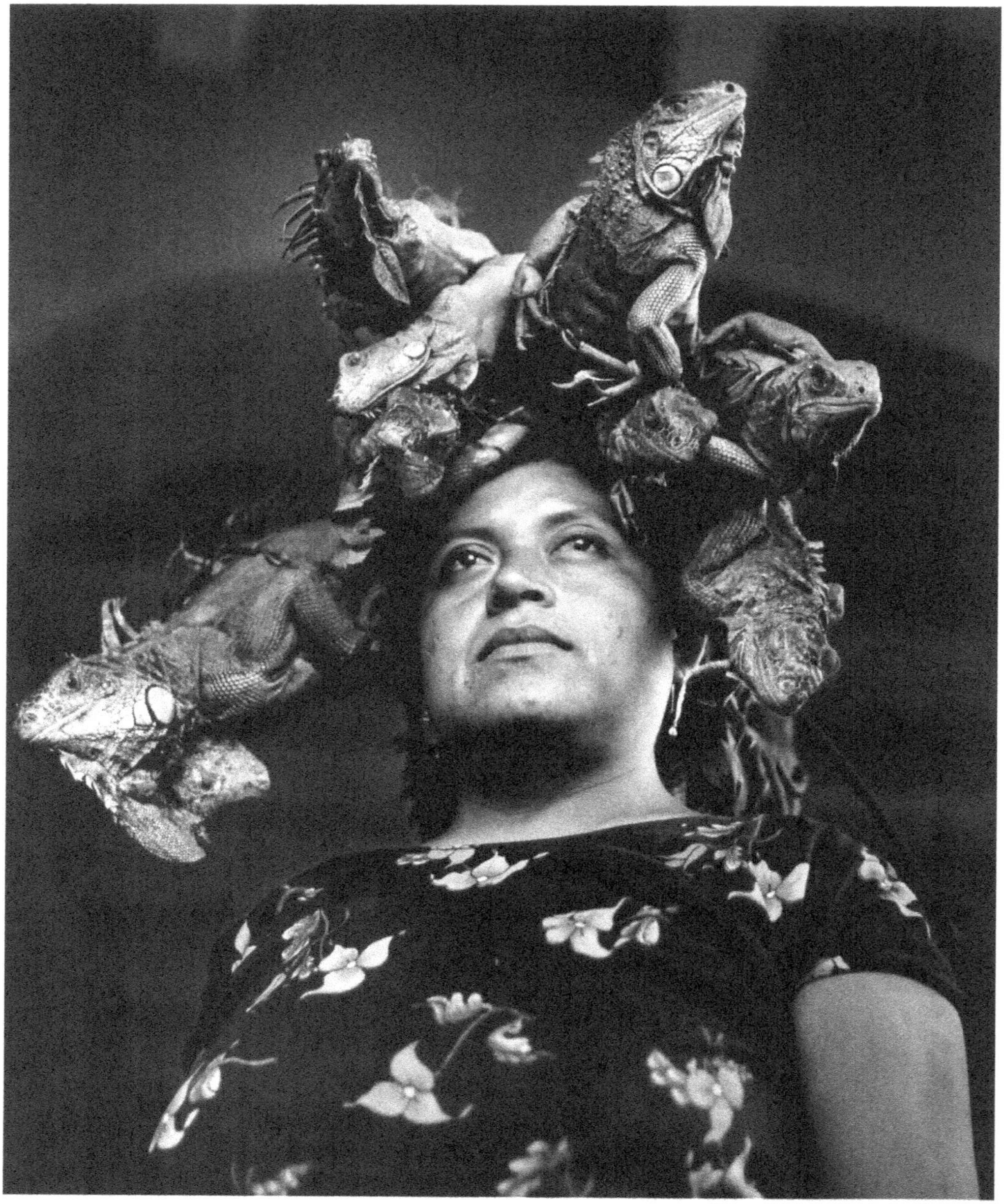

FIGURE 27. Graciela Iturbide, *Nuestra señora de las iguanas*, 1979, from *Juchitán de las mujeres* (Mexico City: Ediciones Toledo, 1989), cover and frontispiece image.

a low angle the arresting features of a woman in a floral-patterned blouse, her smooth bronze skin and inscrutable gaze in jarring relation to the radiating tangle of scaly heads of a wreath of iguanas that, with protruding jowls and dewlaps, crown the woman's now hieratic, now Medusa-like head. The image endures as an unflinching performance of fearlessness or forbearance, as much to do with precarious acts as with the hazards of representation.

Also sequenced by Ortiz Monasterio, the book that follows is as unflinching in tone as the expression of this opening scene and equally larger than life. With a graphic design by Bernardo Recamier, the large-font typography resembles that of storybooks, adding to the blur of registers offered by essayist Elena Poniatowska—"El hombre del pito dulce" (The man with the sweet penis)—a nearly unclassifiable amalgamation of ethnographic description, historical account, erotic folklore, and first-person fantasy that nevertheless conveys the everyday community episodes and other enactments where ceremonial practices and political organizing among inhabitants of the region are of a piece. Visual rhymes ensue between a veiled woman at a rally of the Coalición Obrera, Campesina, Estudiantil del Istmo (Coalition of Workers, Peasants, and Students of the Isthmus) and another woman, rushing away with a veiled child in arms. The gestures of defiance and flight depicted on these pages modify the violence suggested in the design elements that stain the margins of the title page, further complicated by a nearby photograph of a wind-rattled landscape of sand dunes and brittle branches devoid of human presence. Social commitments and ceremony unfold to describe the relations between women and men and third-sex *muxes* (fig. 28), as well between elders and children, in scenes both communal and domestic, sacred and profane, with the traces of coexisting modern life knowingly excluded from the frame. "I do not produce photographs to provide instruction about the Indigenous world or my country," Iturbide has said.[20] Prompting her subjects to be fellow storytellers in this fable of another world, in *Juchitán de las mujeres* Iturbide used the photobook form to choreograph descriptions partly dislocated from the subjects in order to mutually estrange the falsely unifying myth of the nation. Through book form, Iturbide formalized the ability to tell stories that are accountable neither to the literalism of anthropology, the realism effect of the photographic, nor to the political discourse of the cosmopolitan elite of a "society in crisis." Aligned with developments in the new anthropology of the 1980s and 1990s (for example, *Writing Culture: The Poetics and Politics of Ethnography* by James Clifford and George E. Marcus), Iturbide staged the so-called ethnographic photograph as a function of fantasy to the degree that camera-generated evidence is able to lay bare its mediated status.

Juchitán de las mujeres pioneered the possibilities of the photobook in 1980s Mexico, as did a 1985 volume in the Río de Luz series, *Dulce sudor amargo* (Sweet bitter sweat) by Brazilian photographer Miguel Rio Branco (fig. 29). Unprecedented for Mexico was its use of color photography in images the photographer had made around the seaport of Brazil's former colonial capital of Salvador da Bahia, where the photographer lived intermittently throughout the 1980s. A bold example of sequencing, the nearly eighty color photographs follow a horizontal pattern marked by measured movements of immediacy and afterglow. Together, they register the material complexity of daily life in Salvador as a partial view—partial as well in another sense, to color qualities in restrained or sharp accents that raise ethical and aesthetic questions about the medium itself.

Single images spill over to form narrative clusters, with an appeal first to the senses—the gold-orange folds of a curtain as flickered by the slant of a fading sun, the cadence of close quarters, or along the unshielded edges of the open sea. The tempo of color and

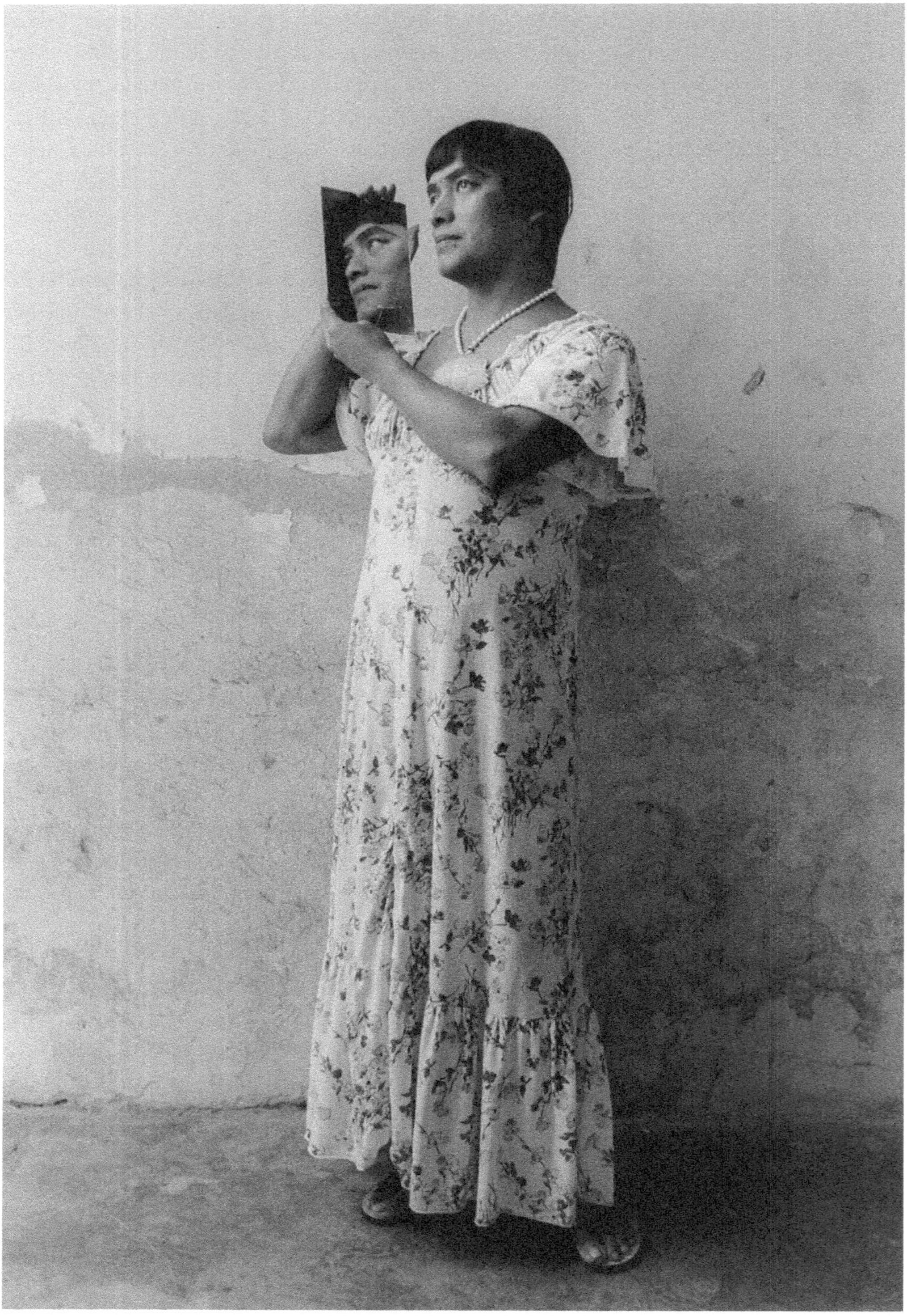

Figure 28. Graciela Iturbide, *Magnolia con espejo*, 1989, from *Juchitán de las mujeres* (Mexico City: Ediciones Toledo, 1989).

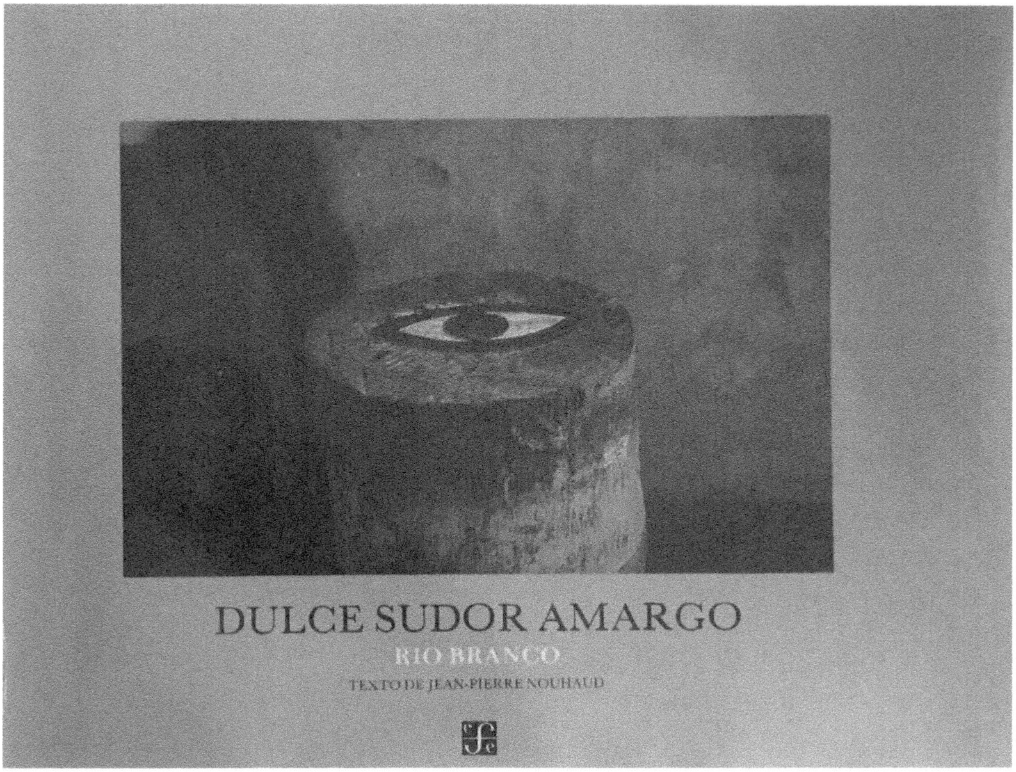

FIGURE 29. *Dulce sudor amargo*, photographs by Miguel Rio Branco, essay by Jean-Pierre Nouhaud, Colección Río de Luz (Mexico City, Fondo de Cultura Económica, 1985), book cover.

content from page to page replicates the confident strikes and the treacherous bearing of youth involved in capoeira. A counterpart to the physical prowess of everyday life, this syncretic form of self-defense and encoded violence, originated by African slaves, has endured a long history of repression and resistance that has survived to this day. A martial art often performed to percussive music, it is fused with elements that point to recreational sport, popular dance, and ritual observance. The view of a man shown face-down and apparently lifeless on the pavement, his ripped trousers exposing his buttocks and genitals—our eyes allowed to settle, instead, on the pink plastic bag over which he is sprawled—appears opposite a page that depicts a mangy dog. A group of images around the Pelourinho district of Salvador depicts vendors, drifters, and gamblers; this architectural complex is also home to sex workers, so many of whom are shown scarred with inflicted wounds. Rio Branco has called his photography a series of "monochromatic variations" on the realities of Salvador da Bahia, which complicate the language that would describe them solely in terms of "underdevelopment and low social indicators."[21]

The swells from blue to red, or from green to orange, enact a sort of structural motion of receding and advancing on both a formal and thematic level: a veritable choreography of ebb and flow, a passage from twilight to sundown, in chromatic ideas about alienation and self-determination, about codes between the sexes, and the social markers determined by the spectrum of skin. The unexpected turns create elliptical statements, or intricate relationships between tone and subject—the resulting clash and synthesis rich in reverberations of meaning, not the least of which are the scarcity of means and the hostility of the built environment.

Rio Branco has called this series a "parable of survival in distress; you can apply it anywhere you like in Brazil, even as a metaphor of the country as a whole."[22] Art critic Raquel Tibol described the publication of *Dulce sudor amargo* as a "triumph of color reproduction" in Mexico. Indeed, the four-color printing quality of the series was widely applauded as an achievement in state-of-the-art print technology for Mexico, a point of particular pride. Rio Branco, Tibol continued, had produced an "autonomous parallel discourse in the sequencing of the color photographs of marginalized men and women in the "zone of tolerance" (a term used in Mexico to designate the quasi-legal free zones for sex work). She wrote that Rio Branco's camera was attuned to the gentleness and violence gained not from encroachment but from lived experience, and she identified the book's complexity when "extreme brutality and extreme beauty" are impossible to unknot or disentangle.[23] The words are particularly foreboding: Tibol's review appeared in the September 7, 1985, issue of the political and cultural weekly *Proceso*.[24] Twelve days later, on September 19, a magnitude 8.1 earthquake would rattle Mexico and leave a devastating death toll and extreme visual brutality of its own.

Three decades after the Mexico City Coloquios Latinoamericanos de Fotografía, São Paulo became the locus for a series of public conversations that sought similarly to address the status and stakes of photography along a vertical geopolitical axis. With a first edition in 2007, the 2° Fórum Latino-Americano de Fotografia de São Paulo (2nd Latin American Photography Forum of São Paulo) took place from Wednesday to Sunday, October 20–24, 2010, with an audience composed of art-world professionals, emerging photographers, members of the creative and educated urban class, educators, students, and other stakeholders, who filled the auditorium of the Itaú Cultural, an arts center and exhibition space on the Avenida Paulista, the sponsoring agency and cultural office to one of Brazil's major banks. Like other events of its kind (Mois de la Photo, Paris; Fotoseptiembre, Mexico; and FotoFest, Houston), the Fórum included workshops and portfolio reviews for emerging photographers, and the opportunity to engage with personalities from the photography world, primarily from Latin America but also from Europe and the United States.

Iatã Cannabrava (who with Luis Weinstein organized and officiated the event) expressed the following by way of a general presentation to describe the unifying rubric of Fora de Casa, Fora do Eixo (Displaced, Askew):

> Following [the 2007 Fórum] Brazilian photography greatly intensified its network of relations with other countries in Latin America, generating a series of exchanges between artists, museums, curators, galleries, festivals, and conferences. The programming this year resulted largely from those discussions, and from the history of our own photographic output.

> With the expression Fora de Casa [Away from Home, Displaced] we address how, in such a brief time, our origins become destinies [the European diaspora is now a Latin American diaspora]. With Fora do Eixo [Askew, Off-Grid] we shift the focus of the debate to the realm of media and platforms. The previously well-defined borders between photography, cinema, and the visual arts become a common area.
>
> In that to and fro, we are constantly trying to define and redefine Latin American photography. Oftentimes we find ourselves affirming that such a thing does not even exist. . . . Is that nomenclature a merely geographic boundary or a concept, a form of representing the world shaped by intrinsic questions about (recent and unsettling) history in the region?[25]

Cannabrava's presentation and remarks throughout the 2° Fórum made implicit and explicit reference to the Mexico City Coloquios of 1978 and 1981 and to the language of network-building and relations made available through a willful casting of *redes* (networks)—a word accentuated in many of the conversations. The public panel discussion addressed themes that aligned with the Latin Americanist discourse of the Coloquios of the Consejo Mexicano de Fotografía. The 2010 Fórum in São Paulo paid homage to photographers who had participated in the Mexico City Coloquios (Claudia Andujar, Paolo Gasparini) while it expanded the role of image technologies and the possibilities of the Fórum's representational scope. Another important resemblance to the Mexico City Coloquios was the presence of US Latinos as being relevant to the discussion of Latin American photography. To the Coloquio's inclusion of Louis Carlos Bernal, Charles Biasiny-Rivera, Harry Gamboa Jr., and Robert C. Buitrón, the 2° Fórum featured Cuban American photographer Abelardo Morell. In short, the 2° Fórum Latino-Americano de Fotografia de São Paulo vied to place Brazil and São Paulo at the center of the debate about the status of photography for Latin America, presented and simultaneously translated in a productive slippage between Portuguese, Spanish, English and—in reference to the mélange of languages—what the organizers referred to as *portunhol selvagem*.

On the panel devoted to the *fotolivro*, the Spanish historian Horacio Fernández referred to the growing network of photographers, scholars, curators, and editors interested in the photobook, including British photographer Martin Parr, Argentine Marcelo Brodsky, Cannabrava, and Ortiz Monasterio. He classified the photobook as a unity that defies reducibility to any one of its distinguishable parts (photographic information, texts, design juxtapositions), the sum of which is always open-ended, dependent on no particular sequence of viewing or order, and in no way bound to habitual discursive reading or viewing practices.

Fernández spoke of the medium's thematic currency, hence its increased vulnerability to market forces, an idea he would echo in his 2011 publication *The Latin American Photobook*.[26] Regardless, he insisted, the photobook in Latin America, at least since 1920, has served as an "effective medium" for depicting and communicating realms of external and internal experience, decisive in terms of the region's modern urban photography, but also for documenting the social complexity of its folk forms.[27] From around the 1980s forward, however, the photobook has further defamiliarized the documentary register, with aesthetic, design-based, and sometimes post-medium image strategies. Thus photobooks are able still to alter and complicate the multiple canons in the histories of Latin American photography, usually by means of a few principles that distinguish the medium. First, the photobook foregrounds authorship in that it tends to privilege and make visible the conception of the photographer or maker who provides sequencing, order, design, and visual cues to the process of its making. Second, photobooks so energize from page to page as to show signs of behavior—a personality—inasmuch as the bound medium traffics in the open-ended idiosyncrasies proper to the book as a thought-form.

The photobook is something more than a mere collection of images. In the photobook, images and text are so structured as to produce a desire to translate design into intentionality and coherence. The subject matter of the photobook resides not in a single theme or visual content, but in the relationships activated in the manual multidirectional process of perusing, and the translation of concrete experience—place and memory—by means of photographic interplay on the page.[28] Photobooks—a relatively new field of research in Latin America—have brought certain foundational books out of obscurity to be part of the visual canon. This was the case of Claudia Andujar and George Love's *Amazônia* of 1978, about which even Brazilian photographers had been unaware. Even as the book had been censored by the dictatorship and did not circulate, both Andujar and her book were prominently featured at the 2010 São Paulo Fórum (plate 14).

For the philosophical sources to the contemporary photobook in Latin America one could reasonably turn to Argentine writer Jorge Luis Borges and his speculative fable "The Library of Babel" (1941), among others that ponder the arbitrary nature of alphabets, the remarkable status of copies, and the book as a reflection of geometrical space in that it can duplicate appearances in an inference of infinity. The art-ideology of book form foregrounds not only physical or material events but also a sequence of relationships set into motion between an object and its constituent materials, as between assembly and distribution. Venezuelan photographer Paolo Gasparini, a master of the book form, asserts that he "seeks to publish aesthetically successful books owing to an intelligent design in tune with the content of the images, which, quite apart from their being in good or bad taste, are works [in the service of] ideas and of ideas about art."[29]

The *nouveau roman* novelist and critic Michel Butor in his 1964 essay "Le livre comme objet" (The book as object) diagnosed the structure of the book and its effects as prompted by simultaneous exposure to our eyes of what they can or cannot grasp sequentially. For Butor, a key aspect of the book as object is its third axis of depth: "Just as the eye can grasp the whole line at a single glance, can very rapidly run down the page to see whether a certain word appears there, so with the help of an agile hand, it can leaf through the volume, making soundings here and there, taking samples, in order to identify a particular section rapidly." Added to the photobook's geometry of volume and depth is the effect of mobility and the simultaneous presentation of all the parts of the work: "a great mobility which most nearly approximates a simultaneous presentation of all parts of a work."[30] Overflowing at any given moment in the photobook is this juxtalinear translation. It requires the use of mixed metaphors to account for the intensity of font type; the silence of the white space; the pitch of sounds or intonation in the "color" or "timbre" that is the ensemble effect. The photobook form confirms the familiar quip by Jean-Luc Godard about the cinema, "A story should have a beginning, a middle and an end, but not necessarily in that order."

Butor wrote: "We are rediscovering the book as total object," and it applies especially to the photobook. An effect of the 2007 and 2010 São Paulo conversations at Itaú Cultural was a surge of photobook production, the logical extension an already robust camera culture in urban centers throughout the country. Private initiatives invested in cultural prestige, outreach, and the public trust, by means of collections management and programming, include the Instituto Moreira Salles (IMS), founded in 1990 by the late banker Walter Moreira Salles, who served as ambassador to the United States in the 1950s and as chairman of Unibanco. The IMS has published monographs on these photographers and others such as José Medeiros, Thomas Farkas, Chico Albuquerque, Alecio de Andrade, and Maureen Bisilliat. In addition to its literary journal, *Serrote*, the IMS launched *Zum: Revista de Fotografia* in 2011, a semiannual that brings high production values to the aim of situating Brazilian photography in an international context while providing the editorial space required to couple photo sequences to both short and mid-length articles on photography.

In tandem with a general increase in the publishing industry has been the appearance of lavishly produced photography books and monographs as epitomized by the imprint of Cosac Naify (founded in 1997 by Charles Cosac and Michael Naify). The publisher has aimed to recuperate and make available important aspects of Brazil's photographic history and to highlight contemporary image artists such as Miguel Rio Branco, Bob Wolfenson, Marcelo Krasilcic, Caio Reisewitz, Alair Gomes, Claudia Andujar, Cris Bierrenbach, Rosângela Rennó, Luiz Braga, Arthur Omar, and Marcia Xavier, to name only a handful of the more than 750 titles published to date, nearly one hundred of them photography-related.

The impact of the 2010 Fórum connects some of its participants to *CLAP! 10 × 10 Contemporary Latin American Photobooks, 2000–2016* on view at the MFA Houston's Hirsch Library in 2017 (fig. 30). As in previous editions of the format—*10 × 10 American* and *10 × 10 Japanese*—the organizers, Olga Yatskevich, Russet Lederman, and Matthew Carson, selected ten sets of individual or paired experts to in turn curate a selection of ten—in a few cases more than ten—photobooks produced in Latin America since the year 2000, the majority interestingly from the last six years: Brazil (28), Mexico (20), Venezuela (24), Argentina (24), Peru (11).

Featured among the expert selectors for *10 × 10* were participants in the 2010 São Paulo Fórum, including Iatã Cannabrava, Claudi Carrera Guillén, Luis Weinstein, and Ramón Reverté. Their selection for *10 × 10* is an important map or "initial atlas" for future "academic and critical exploration of the topic."[31]

I highlight three of these more recent titles from Brazil because they triangulate variations on the quest narrative by conceptual or literalist means. The technological turn that accelerated digital communication and transportation networks escalated—for some—the flow of national and corporate wealth, and the global movement for the traveling class and manufactured goods, complicating geographic identities and their cultural meanings. In her 2002 book *Aeroporto*, Claudia Jaguaribe deranged the visual language of advertising with analytic detachment to catalog the severe or inhospitable architecture from inside a

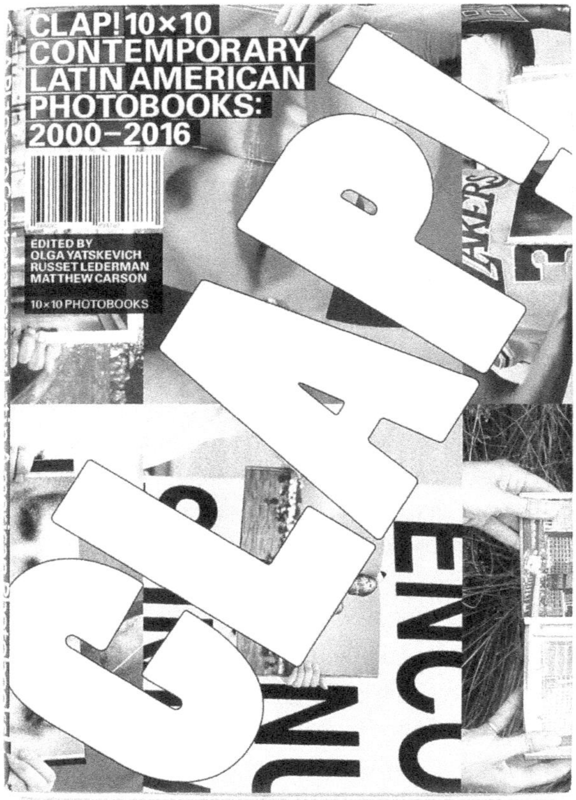

Figure 30. *CLAP! 10×10 Contemporary Latin American Photobooks, 2000–2016*, edited by Olga Yatskevich, Russet Lederman, and Matthew Carson, essays by Luis Weinstein and Joaquim Marçal F. de Andrade (New York: 10×10 Photobooks, 2017), book cover.

São Paulo airport—human figure blurred behind glass or the haze of timeless waiting—a space now abruptly devoid of any human presence (plate 15). These spaces of intermission trigger "chains of situations" at once "distant and anonymous" but equally "up close and magnified."[32] A new monumentality emerges in this transitional space-time suspended in the foreboding equation whose missing value is to be found between menacing jet engines and the icy portraits of flight attendants in unspecified space.

In *Hotel Tropical* (2013) João Castilho pursues a related but different side to the sameness and disconnection of commercial travel (plate 16). His self-published book gives shape to display configurations of photographs arranged on the page as charts of fading memory and emotion. The interior and exterior scenes at small hotels, painted in "improbable colors," manage to "escape the logic of globalization," according to Castilho, in that they "take flight from uniformity and architectural standardization."[33] The neon-like illuminations in red and green betray the undercurrent of desolation and solitude, the desperation of transitional spaces for those passing through or confined to a locality.

By contrast, in *Intergalático* (2014) Guilherme Gerais assembled drawings and diagrams, maps, and atlas illustrations, as well as black-and-white photographs from travels to Istanbul and Cappadocia in Turkey, Londrina (in the Paraná region of Brazil), and Prague. What appear to be cosmological charts to locations in the cosmos modify the photographic views of uninhabited expanses to make them double as documents to planetary exploration or survival hideouts on earth or in another galaxy, at any rate in the wake of catastrophic events or at the dawn of a future prehistory.

In the age of big data and with the increasing millions of still and moving images uploaded to social media platforms—the bulk of it generated in the past few years—the photobook can serve as a surrogate for concrete space, for place-making and place-keeping, making a provisional home to counter the sense of eviction from the present "technological sublime."[34] From the once upon a time in the future of a scene in a nineteenth-century library to the somewhere else in the here and now, these Brazilian photobook makers detain the flow of images to which we have grown accustomed, even as they identify the liminal locations of the present—hotels and airports and speculative whereabouts—spaces the photobook is a perfect stand-in for and a respite from those alienations.

Even a provisional anatomy allows views into the ways veteran and emerging photographers in Latin America have employed the book as a support or means to replicate the process of thinking with images in meaningful sequence, properly embodied but also embedded in a network that relates the part to a fugitive whole, using for this to great effect the missing narrative conjunctions or connectives that too readily provide reasons for deducing causes from effects; they proliferate a spatial practice in a combination of verbal scripts and image-oscillations from the factual and sensual world.

In rehearsing art and media histories between the Americas, between Mexico City and São Paulo for example, my commitments are to a cultural poetics able to convey historical processes and aesthetic values though conversations about camera culture in an inter-American context. By camera culture I mean the extended field of activity and energies around the practice of photography, broadly understood. Here and there, camera culture becomes shorthand for the multiple ways that the technical image can structure habits of being and viewing. It incorporates forms and processes animated by means—among them the photobook—that so mediate as to enable the redirection of attitudes about sensuous and social life.

EIGHT

Tropics of Broadband: Camera Culture and Experience in São Paulo

In rehearsing art and media histories, my commitments are to a cultural poetics of the Americas: a strategy and framework meant to convey historical processes and aesthetic values fashioned within a regional and inter-American context to test the notion of *latinidad*. Between 2010 and 2015 this led me to São Paulo and an immersion in the visual culture of contemporary Brazil, to the 2° Fórum Latino-Americano de Fotografia de São Paulo (2010), and to the work of the photographers who participated in this inter-American symposium on photography and media theory, focusing especially on Cia de Foto, an art collective whose practice gained attention for its unique postproduction blurring of the boundaries between documentary, photojournalism, and art photography.

I will return to the 2° Fórum Latino-Americano de Fotografia (2010) and to Cia de Foto, but not before offering a panoramic snapshot of the media and experience serving as the historical basis for this collective's work and which can provide a frame for its contemplation. Over the last several years, I've focused on São Paulo and its greater camera culture of the 2000s in order to draw art-historical links to earlier photographic practices in the hemisphere. By camera culture I mean the extended field of activity and energies around the practice of photography, broadly understood—camera-generated work and other platforms afforded by the new media—and, for my purposes, especially those that have emerged in relation to the megacity environment. Here and there, camera culture becomes shorthand for the multiple ways that the technical image can structure habits of being and viewing, and the degree to which it involves life forms and processes prompted by means of audiovisual imaging equipment that so mediates as to enable a redirection of attitudes about sensuous and social life, communication, and knowledge.

Contemporary Brazil provides a fruitful setting to test these phenomena. The recent upsurge of camera culture in urban centers throughout the country, especially São Paulo, is reflected in a multiplicity of factors and in the venues and spaces for the production, exhibition, and sale of early, modern, and contemporary photography. Even a brief account of recent programs and projects conveys an invigorated field. Private initiatives have invested in cultural prestige, outreach, and the public trust, by means of collections management and programming. The Instituto Moreira Salles (IMS), for example, was founded in 1990 by the late banker Walter Moreira Salles, who served as ambassador to the United States in the 1950s and as chairman of Unibanco. The IMS operates four cultural centers in Belo Horizonte, Rio de Janeiro, Poços de Caldas (Minas Gerais), and São Paulo, and it has featured a robust menu of events involving the visual arts, literature, and music, while it also oversees a major archive that comprises significant holdings in photography. The collection includes work by such makers as Marc Ferrez, Marcel Gautherot, and Alice Brill, to name but a few. The IMS houses over 550,000 plates and negatives in total, the varied cumulative effects of which have contributed to an ongoing redefinition of the national past and present-day selfhood. And it has published influential scholarship, including the excellent study by Natalia Brizuela, *Fotografia e império: Paisagens para um Brasil moderno* (Photography and empire: Landscapes for a modern Brazil), about early photography in the tropics, about the desires or drives that structured its representation, and about the historical record and the imaginary geography it made possible in books that feature significant image archives such as that of nineteenth-century cameraman Militão Augusto de Azevedo, the photographer to first assemble a comparative photo album on the city of São Paulo (1862–87), or that of mid-twentieth-century practitioner Geraldo de Barros, associated with Foto Cine Clube Bandeirante and traveling companion to the *concretista* movement, or that of contemporary image artists.[1] There is the Coleção Pirelli (Museu de Arte de São Paulo, MASP) that since 1991 has published annual or semiannual volumes drawn from the Pirelli photography collection. Beyond the print platform is the web-based journal *Icônica*, edited by historians and theorists Rubens Fernandes Junior, Mauricio Lissovsky, Cláudia Linhares Sanz, and Ronaldo Entler; the websites *desVirtual*, powered by Giselle Beiguelman; *Dobras Visuais* by Lívia Aquino; and *Galeria Experiência* by the eponymous collective (Davi Boarato, Juliana Nadin, Daniel Gutierrez, and Diego Lajst).[2]

The 2013 edition of the photo fair SP-Arte/Foto, founded in 2007, featured over two dozen national galleries representing both Brazilian and international photographers. With a domestic art market that has increased by the year—in 2012 it comprised 22 percent of all art sold in Brazil—and in concert with agencies like ApexBrasil (Brazilian Trade and Investment Promotion Agency) and Associação Brasileira de Arte Contemporânea, which advocate for the internationalization and commercial viability of Brazilian art—SP-Arte/Foto again took place in the exposition rooms of a luxury shopping mall located in the high-end Itaim Bibi neighborhood of São Paulo. The photographs on display and for sale included work by internationally known makers such as Sebastião Salgado, Vik Muniz, and others with increased visibility outside Brazil, such as Gustavo Lacerda, Claudia

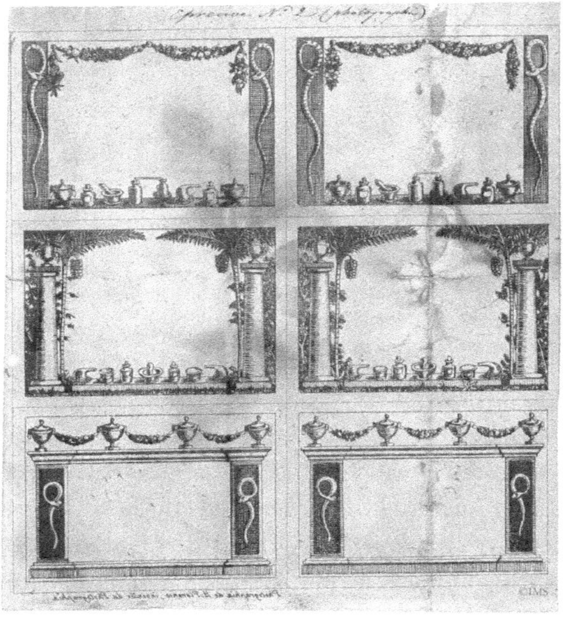

FIGURE 31. Hercule Florence, *Photographic copy of pharmacy labels obtained through direct contact with photosensitive paper under the action of sunlight*, ca. 1833. The lower left margin reads (in reverse): "Photography by H. Florence, inventor of photography." © Instituto Moreira Salles, São Paulo, Brazil.

Jaguaribe, and Cássio Vasconcellos. Necessarily a partial list, the foregoing is meant only to suggest the curve and intensity of production in terms of archives, book publishing, periodicals, websites, art fairs: multiplatform photography-related practices in Brazil, with a view to São Paulo in particular.

Far-reaching as well in historical and geographic scope, Brazil's photographic culture has a distinction that I believe has a bearing on contemporary practice, a critical origin story indebted to research that first came to light in the early 1970s. Boris Kossoy, in his parallel practice as scholar and photographer, provided an account of the papers and publications in the family archive pertaining to French-born naturalist and mapmaker Hercule Florence, who had settled near São Paulo in the 1830s after a four-year journey into the interior of Brazil as a painter on the Langsdorff expedition. Observing the phenomenon that fabric fades when exposed to light, and limited to the resources available to him in Brazil, Florence experimented with the camera obscura in the hope of permanently fixing an image. Kossoy describes the technical conditions and chemical results that led, perhaps, to Florence's unsuccessful *invention* of photography in 1832, even as he began using the word *photographie* to describe a kind of contact print designed for use as pharmacy labels (fig. 31), but that gave way to an unambiguous if "isolated *discovery* of photography in Brazil."[3]

Kossoy tells of the "pre-Daguerreian experiments" that Florence undertook in São Carlos Villa (today Campinas) and of the existing evidence and historical data comprising manuscripts and photographs. Florence had written:

> By placing a paper that has been wetted in the camera obscura, by a solution of silver nitrate, the objects on it are reproduced, but with the inconvenience that the parts that should be clear become dark and vice versa. From this it can be seen that, if because of the inconvenience in question, my investigations still held poor results, it is none the less true that I have obtained lines, forms and contours, harmonious between themselves, without the help of the human hand.[4]

Kossoy relates:

> Since there was only one printing press in the province of Sao Paulo, [Florence] found himself faced with the necessity of inventing his own printing process, for which he carried out a great deal of research, making continual improvements—he christened the process *poligraphie*. Next, still working on the printing process, one day he came up with the idea of utilizing sunlight for this purpose, thereby discovering the photographic process, which he called *photographie*, a term that naturally occurred to him as early as 1832.[5]

Accounts of the simultaneous "invention" of photographies, as Geoffrey Batchen has argued in his study *Burning with Desire*, serve to counter the commonsense notion that invention is necessarily an unvarying steady progression or tangible beginning and endpoint. All this provides site-specific meaning and nuance to Douglas Crimp's famous assertion that "if photography was invented in 1839, it was only discovered in the 1960s and 1970s—photography, that is, as an essence, photography itself."[6]

Kossoy provides some narrative sweep and geographic association, in that parallel to publishing his findings on Florence in the 1970s was his participation in the concurrent Coloquios de Fotografía Latinoamerica, discussed in previous pages.[7] Kossoy's own body of photographic work from the early 1970s can be read as an argument about the status of isolation, and as a wager to legitimize work eccentric to that of "objective" photography's alleged transparent perspective, or that was not predicated solely on serving as a mirror to developing-world realisms. For example, his series *Viagem pelo fantástico* (Travels in the fantastic) includes the *Portrait do Senhor Américo* (1973) and *Memórias do Senhor Américo* (1973), in which a plaster figurine of a large-headed finely dressed dandy confuses scale to puncture the naturalism and sobriety of the photographic scene (fig. 32).

In *Fotografia e império*, Natalia Brizuela categorizes the generic conceits of nineteenth-century photography, especially as relevant to Brazil, whereby the amateur photographer was associated with portraiture and the traveler or expedition photographer with landscape. She writes:

> The perfect conceptual and epistemological home for photography in the nineteenth century . . . was the tropics, and it was in the Brazilian Empire, more than in any other national territory, that photography served as a fundamental element in the project of the modern nation. The tropics as a real and imaginary zone, on the one hand, and as a

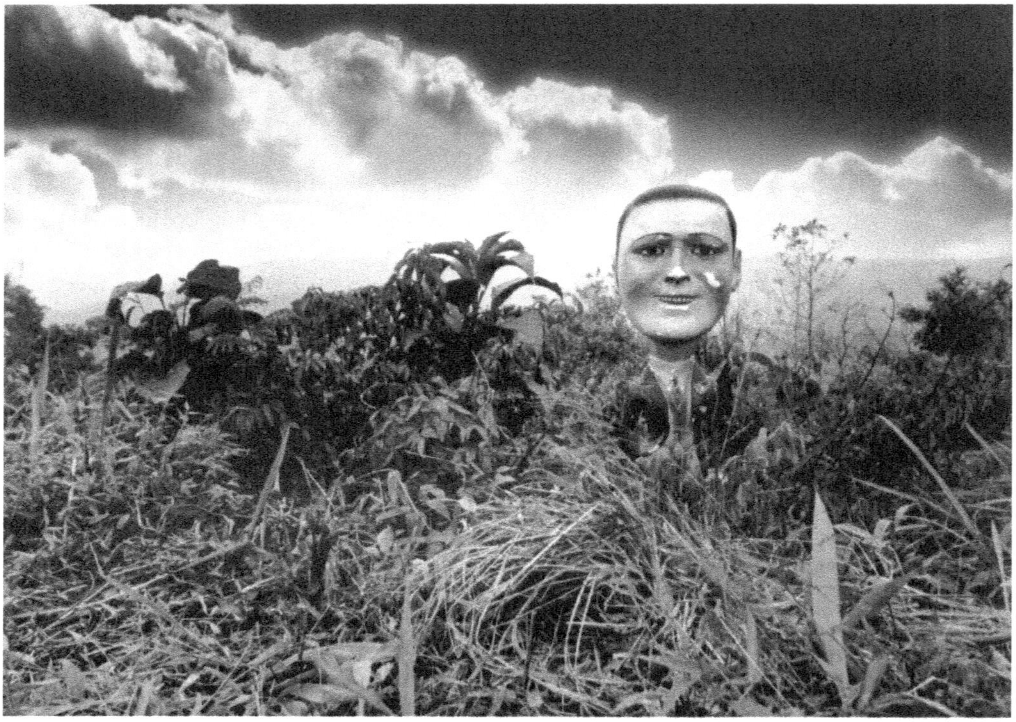

FIGURE 32. Boris Kossoy, *Portrait do Senhor Américo* from the series *Viagem pelo fantástico*, Itapecerica da Serra, São Paulo, 1973.

> technique promoted by Emperor D. Pedro II, on the other. . . . The modern rationalization of space left the subject an orphan, outside the protection of a magical and archaic nature. . . . Photography appears not only as a technique of accumulation and acquisition, but as a perfect technique for guaranteeing loss.[8]

With the nineteenth century at the forefront of his photographic research, Kossoy sought to disassociate the aims of the medium, as per the imperatives of the Latin American Coloquios, from the immovable solemnity in the rationalization of social space, enhancing nature and remnants of colonial built environment with visual quips about the status of the medium's accountability to literalism, preferring instead to prompt fictional worlds for a "society in crisis." Kossoy evoked the extended field of surrealist practice that values the ongoing potential of play as an alternate structuring device to that of indictment or negative critique, preferring happily instead to tell the lie about the metaphysics of depth. Roger Caillois wrote that play "can consist not only of deploying actions or submitting to one's fate in an imaginary milieu, but of becoming an illusory character oneself, and of so behaving . . . the subject makes believe or makes others believe that he is someone other than himself."[9] An apocryphal traveler of the here and now on one sideline of the camera is further doubled in the placeholder or stand-in for cultural uniformity performed by the effigy of Américo—as though caught between a figurative immobility and a future deferred (*outros tempos*) by the violence of the present. The paralysis of the plaster-cast Américo flies in the face of the Latin American cultural class, with its access to symbolic resources, as being invisible to itself, or immune from scrutiny, or not so distinct from the "external [that is, foreign] architectonic vision" that Ribeiro rejected as being that which "unifies and confuses our nations as variants of one pattern of people."[10]

Featured in various capacities at the 2° Fórum Latino-Americano de Fotografia de São Paulo were members of the photography collective Cia de Foto: as consultants, as panelists, as editorial advisers to a photography journal, and as co-curators, together with cultural promoter and gallery owner Edu Brandão, of the exhibition *Histórias de mapas, piratas e tesouros* (Histories of maps, pirates, and treasures), on display in the lower floors of the Itaú Cultural.

The four-minute film *Caixa de sapatos* (Shoebox) from 2008 serves as a collective autoethnography of the urban class to which the members of CIA belong. Commissioned by curator Eder Chiodetto, the work was first displayed that year as part of the Clube de Colecionadores do Museu de Arte Moderna de São Paulo (Collector's Circle of the Museum of Modern Art of São Paulo). In *Caixa de sapatos*, the staggered sequence of still images, video footage, and musical soundscape render the camera so self-reflexive as to fashion a many-sided, misleading subjectivity that dismantles the family structure, even as it tells a parallel narrative about the place of image technology in developmental accounts at once technological, genealogical, and social (plates 17–18).

An image of waking is delayed thirty-eight seconds into the four-minute film. In advance of that moment, the opening bars of the film's soundscape, and a strobe-like advance of still images, cast a form of audible broadening into fitful sightedness. As though from the hollow recesses of immeasurable space sound the quizzical electronic notes that stretch out in first ascent, sound pursued as by a dispersal of droplets or chimes in the immensity of the spheres—a little fanfare. As the musical horizon swells, a series of seventeen photographic images, in durations lasting but a fraction of a second, give way to sequential movement before fading to black. A child's tiny figure turns away from the camera that follows him down an asphalt ramp to the nominal open spaces of an apartment complex playground squeezed between the buildings of this São Paulo neighborhood. The rapid frames continue to flicker, and the boy, now in the intrepid undress of domestic space, already testing parental concerns about household objects latent with potential harm as he defies the line dividing playtime from danger, swaps his clothes for a clear plastic pouch or slip case worn over his head, physically puffing himself up into various gestures—and fogging the inside of his helmet in the process—as though to confuse the heroics of an astronaut with the antics of a pint-sized jester. A gap in time elapses to find the boy now holding two ring-shaped food snacks (*biscoto de polvinho*) extracted from the bag in front of him and that, over his eyes, are transformed into corrective lenses; and then the picture fades to black.

These flashes comprise the film's first ten seconds. That scene irrupts in successive relation to a sequence of seventeen photographs depicting the same child now in the ritual preparations for bedtime, brushing his teeth at the bathroom mirror, an adult, presumably his father, appearing beside him, fleetingly, the boy now propped on a bed dressing in pale blue pajamas, in his father's lap, seated and pressed against the floor and wall, eyes staring directly at the camera. Then a short video sequence follows, the camera nestled intimately next to the boy's tiny body sound asleep, the rustle of breathing sustained for the duration of a few seconds, then several cuts: an image of the same child outdoors in profile against the wall; now the image of another child, a girl, as though teetering unaccompanied on a pathway in the expanse of what appears to be Parque Buenos Aires in the Higienópolis neighborhood of São Paulo; the frames bridge back to the boy now behind the sliding glass doors of a shower stall, now on the toilet behind the shower door, a phantom; now asleep and nestled beside his golden retriever. The still frames reanimate into video again with the boy rising sluggishly from the slumber of the former footage. As the film returns again to a sequence of still images, there appears an adult man, presumably next of kin or close friend but nevertheless a newcomer to this circular scene, holding the child in an embrace upon entering the family habitat, an apartment—and then there is heard off-screen the clicking of a camera shutter.

The lurching still-image frames of the remaining three-and-a-half-minute succession repeatedly crisscross with fleeting video footage, an editing process that unleashes the unease and latent potential of a staggered view; that is, in animate and inanimate frames is described the patent and less visible domains of a household, or two, or three, in that it proliferates into various interior spaces inhabited by the metropolitan class embodied in the human subjects on either sides of the camera. Corrective lenses, the shutter clicking, the matter of sleep and waking, the banality of everyday routine countered with the graphic display of the intimate and sexually explicit—the alleged family slide show or home movie explodes and redoubles. To describe the identities and relations depicted in this four-minute film—whose spouse, whose child, what familial, legal, or other group bond between the adults, amid the overlapping connection and intimacies linking grown-ups and children and household animals—becomes futile and largely misses the point. At those moments when the film appears on the brink of attributing a narrative or kinship connection, the pattern of rapid succession again so overwhelms the viewer as to foreground the medium's materiality and, at various points throughout the four minutes, to stress the difference the film establishes between sight (associated with distance and depth) and sound (the sense of connection it provides), all of it unfolding a multiplicity of vision.

The São Paulo–based photography collective Cia de Foto had been active since 2003. Founding members Pio Figueiroa and Rafael Jacinto recount the origins of Cia de Foto and their meeting at the editorial offices where they were both employed, one of the multiple publications issued by the Grupo Folha, one of Brazil's largest media conglomerates, the finance magazine *Valor econômico* (whose first issue was published in May 2000). Confined by the conventions of newsroom staff photography and expressing a need for the time and place to discuss photography as a site of conversation, as opposed to the daily grind and competitiveness of the corporate workplace, the two photographers abandoned print journalism altogether, sacrificing job security for a place in which to discuss the status of the image, to indulge in theoretical readings and technical research, but also to generate an independent salary. Not long afterward, in 2004, Jõao Kehl, who had served until then as an assistant, officially joined the collective; and finally in 2007, Carol Lopes was enlisted in the team as a digital archivist and postproduction image specialist. The working method of the collective could double at times as an agency, and it pursued both commercial photography assignments and collective art projects undertaken at their headquarters, a two-story space on Rua Amaro Cavalheiro, 318, Pinheiros, São Paulo, outfitted with a common workspace with computer terminals, digital printers, a professional studio, and at any given moment a variable team of assistants and staff. In a 2011 televised interview, Pio Figueiroa noted that "there is no annihilation of the individual in the system of a collective practice; on the contrary, there is a realization of potential insofar as the group status is negotiated all the time . . . and there is no way of erasing the self in this collective process because no one will answer for doing what it is I do."[11]

It should come as no surprise that *Caixa de sapatos* emerged from an overlapping method. Over a period of several months, members of CIA produced thousands of images relative to self-imposed prompts and constraints. They mined the technical possibilities afforded by the Canon EOS-type SLR (single-lens reflex) digital cameras of the kind that began to appear in the early to mid-2000s. These group self-assignments pushed each member to experiment with approaches to framing, lighting design, color contrast, depth of field, stop-action structure, exposure control, and other options made available with digital high-dynamic range, but in a photographic language whose content was restricted, as per the agreement, to the most immediate and everyday.

The majority of the resulting pictures underwent a process of elimination in a collective editing: hence most were never made public, even as a substantial body of images began to form an archive of images uploaded to a Flickr account that doubled as a kind of public light box. The Flickr collecting process resembled that of a shoebox in which family snapshots and portraits are kept in makeshift or permanent storage, eventually providing a title to this work in progress. How to re-enchant or estrange the commonplaces of documentary? As individual cameramen and as a collective, Cia de Foto had been expressing dissatisfaction with photojournalism that had internalized the imperatives—like those of the *convocatoria* to the Mexico City and Havana Coloquios—of a compulsory, and thus calcified, social commitment in the form of the perfectly rendered print, oftentimes a specifically masculine, heroic expansiveness of vision that aspired to invoke such makers as Sebastião Salgado, whose classic images Cia de Foto nevertheless held in highest esteem. The challenge, as they perceived it now, was to make photographs out of nothing but the most mundane, "*da vida só*," not directed "*ao outro*," to some perceived alterity reflective of the national ethos, a social other mediated from a distance.

Discussions about subject matter led Cia de Foto to move away from the depiction of situations outside the most immediate realm of experience, especially after the 2006 work *911 Prestes Maia*, where the collective experimented with nondocumentary, improvisational, and performative strategies in portraying the inhabitants of the Prestes Maia building in downtown São Paulo who were menaced with imminent eviction (fig. 33). Also in line with previous works, Cia de Foto had begun to experiment with synchronized image capture: using the capabilities of the digital camera to record the exact millisecond of the shutter's click. The three photographers (Rafael Jacinto, Pio Figueiroa, and João Kehl)

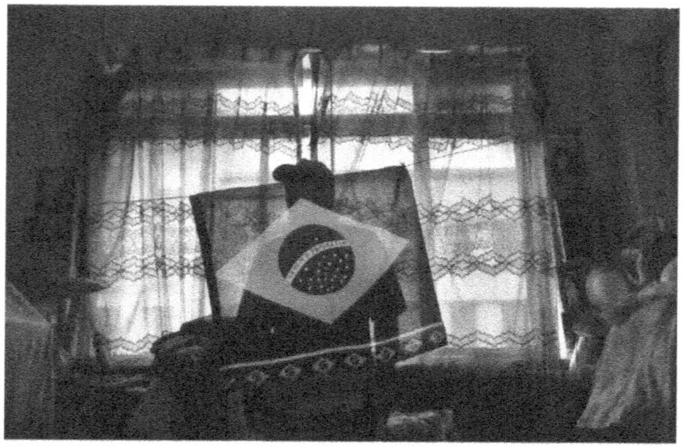

Figure 33. Cia de Foto, from *911 (Avenida Prestes Maia)*, 2006, color digital image. Courtesy of the artists.

ventured separately to document the politicians running for mayoral office in 2008 (Marta Suplicy, Geraldo Alckmin, and Gilberto Kassab). The results were triptychs that depicted the three different candidates in their campaign efforts at a precise moment of enacted political time. After the first round of voting left Kassab and Suplicy as the contenders in the runoff election on October 26, 2008, the photographers of Cia de Foto employed the same synchronic technique to document a day in each photographer's respective life, beginning with frames of early morning rituals (waking, urinating, showering) and culminating in the evening with a convening of photographers, spouses, children, lovers, and friends for supper at Figueiroa's apartment home.

How to re-enchant, estrange, or make critical the clichés of the family snapshot? With the growing *Caixa* archive on Flickr, and a commission deadline to meet, the collective sought the film editing expertise of Alex Carvalho, who pieced together sequences that fused images from the Flickr archive, pictures and video footage from the day in the life of that election season, distributed among the collective for rounds of commentary, until the final sequence was arrived at by way of consensus—even as the roaming of the city streets over the day's duration was to be virtually eliminated in the final edit. The fact of having such an "external" editor necessarily led to creative confusions and further complicated the question of authorship; and the additional constituent of a musical score—composed by DJ Guab in response to the image sequences—persuaded editor and artists to let actual relations recede in favor of formal ones, confounding the differences between kith and kin. Activated as a result for the viewer, then, in this unchained network of analogies is the coalesced desire to make relations legible with a reluctance to so disclose; and suspended as such, the work defies the logic of cause and effect when the necessary disorder of the shoebox archive becomes an elusive narrative sequence.

Caixa de sapatos unleashes three simultaneous times and temporalities: (1) the synchronicity of three cameras in the spatial sweep of interior and (a largely elided) exterior space; (2) the life span that is the duration of a day; and (3) the time of the memory archive encapsulated by photographs made prior or posterior to this election-time slice of life. Together, these temporalities in strobe or delayed sequence, or in the real duration of video footage, enact accelerated processes of displacement and abridgment, stretched or condensed into patterns of transient recognition, in an image style ranging from a kind of digital chiaroscuro to a bold saturated color scale shimmering in metallic liquids or blurs—all as though to interrogate or wonder: What assembly is required to constitute the "time" of the family? With so much crisscrossing between the daily life of childhood and the bedroom secrets of the adults, the film submits both a visual reference to and a refutation of the taboo keeping separate the world of grown-up sex acts and that of the child's curiosities. The film possesses a clarity and carefulness to keep description commensurate with an entire social life the frames evoke, all hanging on that wonderfully evocative title, a shoebox: at once a family album, an archive, that which collapses the everyday, the cardboard container of a manufactured product repurposed in an ancestral wager to outdistance the effects of history, with its inclination to raze and make level. At an important midpoint section, two children at a kitchen table interact with an iPhone—something routine and emptied of amazement—as the girl scoops some fruit into her mouth with a fork, and the boy addresses no one in particular, fixated on the smartphone video game: "A nave 'ta chegando, 'ta chegando" (The spaceship's landing, it's landing). In the film's four-minute duration is a constructed composite of adult subjectivity that examines the life forms activated by the camera and touch screen applications in the domain of the household, submitting an analogy that relates parturition, parenting, and child's play with image engineering, conflating biological reproduction with technical or electronic reproduction. The overlapping of childhood and technology through the editing process and discontinuous time signatures effects a deconstruction of the family as an exclusively or obligatorily conjugal or heterosexual institution—and so the frames give birth to another style of domestic affiliation. If, as Armando Silva has proposed, the "bourgeois family as a centered, blood-bonded structure of father, mother and children is ceding its place to other forms of collective survival," then *Caixa de sapatos* submits that authorship is to image making what the child is to the new family structure; that is, "the new family hero: the child, the natural survivor of the crisis and its very expression" confounds the certainties of so-called natural law of patrimony, be it biological, national, or cultural.[12]

This method reflects the demands of a new image economy foreseen by media and communication theorist Vilém Flusser, an exile from Nazi Germany who, from 1941 to 1972, worked as a researcher at various institutions in São Paulo, where his impact and legacy have been lasting, and over the years members of Cia de Foto, in interviews and public settings, have made direct references to Flusser's writings. Two of his works are relevant to *Caixa de sapatos*: the 1983 study, written in Portuguese, *Pós-história: Vinte instantâneos e um modo de usar* (Post-History: Twenty snapshots and a user's manual); and the 1988 essay published in German as "Die Stahl als Wellental in der Bilderflut" ("The City as Wave-Trough in the Image Flood"). In "The City," Flusser sees systems of relations allowing subjects to experience manifold subjectivity in the space he designates as the *Stahl*, even as this city is both a built environment of steel and concrete, avenues and skyscrapers, and a parallel place, an inhabited "field of flection," enlivened by the two-way audiovisual communication media. Flusser viewed the city being as much a practice of description or topography of place as the physical features of its arrangement, where each human subject enters into a knot of relations, becoming at once a channel of and for information in a web of spatial encounters. For Flusser, the city multiplies into an organizational unit, spatial system, a locality wherein subjects espouse and swap provisional identities in an energetic masquerade, both subject and system a work in process, with a view to the undertaking that is a kind of utopian forecast whose desires and attitudes feed back into the image of a city as the interface of communication networks and electronic media. In this intersubjective field of flections, input and output blur the customary division between the private and public inasmuch as the city is performed as a dance of masks rather than as argued in the town square. In this "playing field"—a net of representations where, one assumes, industry and labor are also likely subsumed—everything becomes divisible and calculable, even as relations and processes further elude description.[13]

This is all to say that a city may be apt to monumentalize even as it is unable to tell the whole story. Inasmuch as every partial account produces its own record from the available cultural patrimony, the family album is the localized subdivision or subset of the order whereby certain image sets structure the conditions of possibility for a national photographic history. National self-knowledge has an underside. *Caixa de sapatos* can be viewed in oblique relation to the image economy commensurate with the general emergence of high-speed audiovisual technologies, and the overwhelming production in Brazil to which such interface has given birth in terms of nineteenth-century archives, book publishing, periodicals, and websites, all the multiplatform camera-related practices that give way to varying levels of valuation, cultural prestige, and monetary value. As per the rubric of the 2º Fórum of 2010—Fora de Casa and Fora do Eixo—the film submits a twin eviction of household and history. The uncertain patrimony that is the twofold founding of photography in Brazil, by Hercule Florence in 1832, remaining latent in the historical record until its belated rediscovery in the 1970s by Kossoy, is formally and thematically equal to the uncertain authorship—both a biological and symbolic paternity—that is the strobe effect of *Caixa de sapatos*. Kossoy's reconfiguration of Florence and the nineteenth-century record is an enabling description that disturbs or belies the linear evolutionary storyline of what counts as true for photography in Brazil or elsewhere. In this respect, *Caixa de sapatos* performs the discontinuous and accidental histories that compose its lineage—untimely circumstances, simultaneous discoveries, and belated emergences that suggest the network of analogies that link the early experiments of Florence with the technical image to the discursive context of the photographic Latin Americanism of the 1970s. In the context of the second São Paulo Fórum on which its members served as consultants, Cia de Foto's cooperative process can be viewed as homologous with the attitudes of the 1978 Consejo Mexicano de Fotografía in seeking interpersonal and symbolic patterns of relations more significant than the individual. This is consistent as well with the discourse of diversification and unification inherent to the Latin Americanisms of Darcy Ribeiro and the Mexico City coloquios, frames of reference about the political and cultural identity of photography, asking the thematic and compositional question: On what grounds is unity founded?

The ever-changing subjectivity of *Caixa de sapatos* doubles back to the figure of Américo in Kossoy's *Viagem pelo fantástico*, in that it betrays the illusionism that is the optical centering of the single-point viewer or any certain self-sameness. To this end, Cia de Foto draws lines from the dissolution of the self in its collective working method to the denaturalized place that is the dismantled family structure. I read the unambiguous foregrounding of flesh in *Caixa de sapatos*—the carnality of sex and the matter of bodily functions—as a part of a larger lament for the loss of the analog, even as it welcomes that which makes palpable a world—in the language of Flusser—when it is calculable but no longer describable. The film's method is meant to stagger—in its double sense: to open up spatial and temporal intervals, and to amaze or astound. It examines the role of a culturally idealized object—the camera—as it shapes the bonds of kinship and sociability in relation to the contingencies of childhood. That overvaluation of the camera between group members has sexual overtones, made visible both thematically and structurally, and it suggests a series of visual accords and disagreements, effects that are affects mostly exchanged between men in bonds that link the individual to the collective formation, a tacit romance in excess of self, family, group membership, societal frame, or national imaginary. In *Caixa de sapatos*, the gestural hesitation of still images, video footage, and musical soundscape elongate and condense as a collapsing of places and times. It can be viewed as part of a larger debate about the practices and permissions of concomitant households in a global city and the role of camera-generated images in both enabling and estranging sites of group-specific private life. Fora de Casa. Fora do Eixo. Flusser wrote: "This is the new urbanism, when we no longer recognize our trusted home or our political opinion, nor our schools of profundity and learning."[14] *Caixa de sapatos* allows us to look at media and experience as something akin to, or coterminous with, society to the degree that it is a name for phenomena that rehearse the terms of photography in culture, coincident or lasting long enough—the duration of a frame in a four-minute film—to suggest the polymorphous temporalities enlivened by means of the technical image: a model of history adequate to present-day urban imaginaries.

NINE

Printed Matters and Pop Art in América

From Brazilian woodcuts to Chicano visual culture, a diverse array of artistic tendencies can be found in the printed works made in the Americas during the 1960s. Ambivalent about certain forms of avant-gardism and opposed to US political and cultural supremacy, artists from São Paulo to San Francisco turned to figuration and the anatomy of language as means for redirecting pop art innovation. The story begins in Mexico City, where in January 1962, the poets Margaret Randall and Sergio Mondragón published the first issue of *El corno emplumado / The Plumed Horn*, a bilingual literary-arts magazine (plate 19).[1] By 1967 Randall and Mondragón, who founded the journal in their mid-twenties, had published twenty issues of *El corno emplumado*, and the perfect-bound quarterly had gained a reputation as one of the most influential cultural documents of its time.

El corno emplumado featured avant-garde poetry and contemporary art and was international and multimedia in scope. Original and translated poetry appeared together with line-drawing illustrations and cultural and political news items. Artworks eventually featured on the cover of each issue. The aim was to capture contemporary thought by highlighting artistic experimentation: critical analyses of US foreign policy joined views of inter-American society and its politics through poetic and artistic expression. This cosmopolitan perspective tracked changes following the Cuban Revolution, and activated a network of artists and institutions in what Harris Feinsod has described as an "expression of geopolitical desire, a vision of an alternate world order."[2]

The first four issues of *El corno emplumado* (January–October 1962) coincided with a symposium held at the Museum of Modern Art (MoMA) in New York on the emergent attributes and values of pop art, featuring curators and critics Peter Selz, Henry Geldzahler, Hilton Kramer, Dore Ashton, Leo Steinberg, and poet Stanley Kunitz. That roundtable, transcribed in the April 1963 issue of *Arts Magazine*, rehearsed a public debate about pop art's relationship to the avant-garde and mass media: the "pervasive, persistent, and compulsive" qualities of the popular press, urban billboards, and television.[3] Some participants judged pop art iconography to be a mere visual transposing, at odds with aesthetic transformation; or rather that its style indicated the "new role of subject matter, after almost a century of formalist indoctrination."[4]

The MoMA symposium defined what would become mainstream exchanges about this influential tendency in contemporary US art in light of a mounting national and international scene of political restlessness and social dissent. In Mexico City, *El corno emplumado*, too, was at the center of artistic and political debates. As a small-scale enterprise that survived on both private and public patronage, it made sly reference to mass media and capitalist consumer culture and made room for pop art expressions in spaces marginal to such hegemonic institutions as MoMA. The magazine's particular Pop sensibility combined anti-imperialist outrage over US warfare in Southeast Asia and involvement in Latin America, as well as frustration with the authority of the US art world in the hemisphere.

El corno emplumado's unlikely contribution to an expanded history of Pop in the Americas can be seen in the idiosyncratic back matter of the first issue and includes illustrations by Latin American artists containing elements derived from comic strips, commercial window displays, and commercial design. Even as they solicited paid advertising, the editors ironized Madison Avenue aspirations, and poet Anselm Hollo recalled that Randall and Mondragón made ends meet by translating US comic strips into Spanish.[5] The back pages of the first issue included conventional mid-century magazine ads promoting Lenox dinnerware ("*Nuevas . . . Diferentes . . . Resistentes . . .*") and Gerber baby food (fig. 34). In the fourth issue, however, an advertisement for the Mexican chain of supermarkets Gigante S.A. doubled as a pop art poem lampooning the totalizing nature of alleged consumer satisfaction (fig. 35). It offered in cascading typography household items: "• quail/ • food/ • cars/ • turtles/ • tortillas/ • books/ • dry cleaning/ • instant keys/ *in a word*, EVERYTHING."[6] The poker-faced ad copy with its absurdist sequence may have been inspired by an advertisement that German-born Mexican artist Mathias Goeritz had conceived in early December 1961. With eleven other artist ringleaders (and a real-life hen) Goeritz organized an act of anti-art mischief called Los Hartos (The Fed-ups). Goeritz referenced this media phenomenon in his ad designed for the third issue of *El corno emplumado*, which matched self-promoting copy with an attack on the quintessential US commodity fetish (fig. 36): "MATHIAS GOERITZ | is FED UP but | DRINK Coca-Cola."[7] Disavowing Dadaism with an earnest quasi-ethical or spiritual call, Goeritz's contribution to Pop revealed deep ambivalence about innovation, which he and his weary crowd of artists were eager to call fraud.[8] *El corno emplumado*'s anti-imperialist standpoint was so fused with crafty derisions of capitalist consumer expectations that it made irreverence on a conceptual order compatible with action in the streets—an apt description of Pop in the Americas.[9]

The journal also helped launch the multiform career of Mexican artist Felipe Ehrenberg (1943–2017), whose lifelong commitments blurred the categories of Pop, Fluxus, and

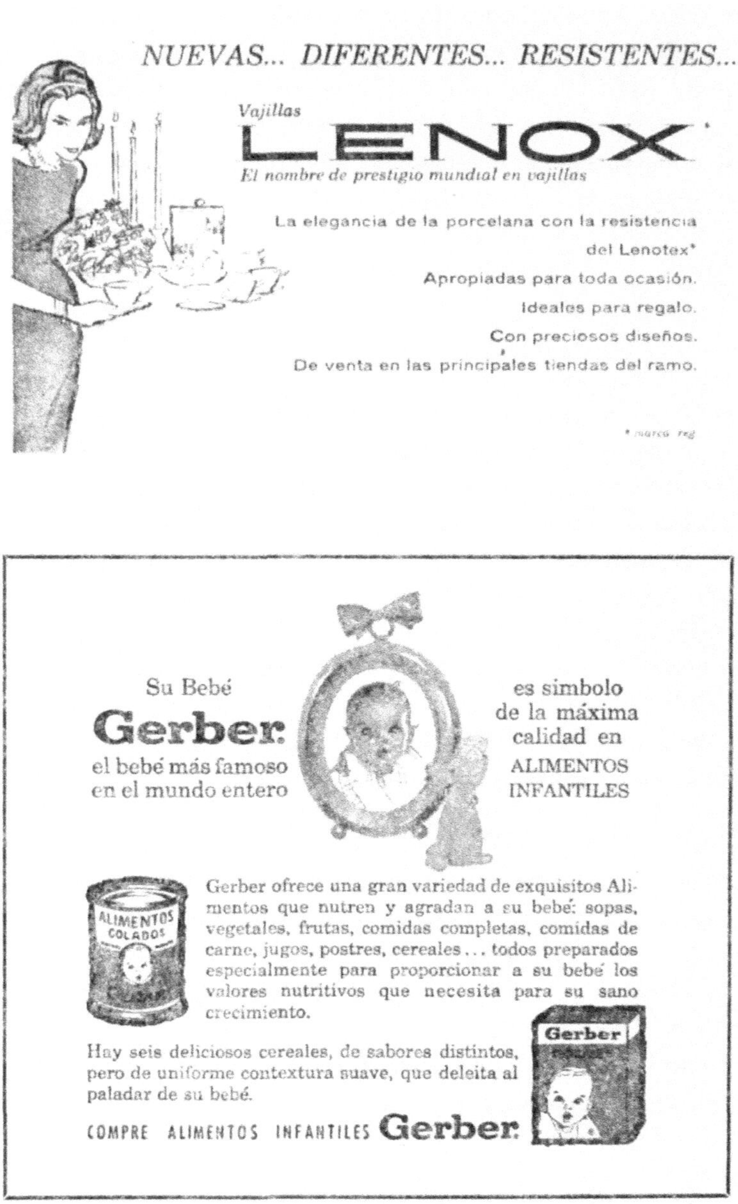

FIGURE 34. *El corno emplumado* 1, edited by Margaret Randall and Sergio Mondragón, Lenox and Gerber Baby Food advertisements, 1962. Courtesy of Margaret Randall.

conceptual art. Ehrenberg's work encompassed actions and happenings with the art collective Grupo Proceso Pentágono (Pentagon Process Group); advocacy on behalf of Chicana and Chicano artists from California during the early 1970s; and book arts, namely Beau Geste Press, which he founded in Devon, England, with fellow artist and spouse Martha Hellion ("Our Press is not a business, it's a way of life.").[10] His contributions to *El*

LA TIENDA DE DESCUENTO MAS GRANDE
DE LATINOAMERICA

G I G A N T E, S. A.

- codornices
- alimentos
- coches
- tortugas
- tortillas
- libros
- tintorería
- llaves al minuto

en una palabra, T O D O

Miguel Angel 170, esq. San Antonio, Mixcoac, México, D. F.
y nueva sucursal, Calz. de la Viga y Ermita Ixtapalapa.

166

FIGURE 35. *El corno emplumado* 4, edited by Margaret Randall and Sergio Mondragón, Gigante supermarket advertisement, 1962. Courtesy of Margaret Randall.

corno emplumado included mixed-media works on paper for two covers (issues 22 and 23) and a series of drawings (issues 19, 20, 22, and 23) that skewered art-historical classicism with a visual economy akin to that of the political cartoon and Dada collage, and with no small dose of Pop audacity and deadpan.

Ehrenberg's interest in cliché led him to deflate the solemnity of such art-historical antecedents as Diego Velázquez, El Greco, and Francisco Goya. With this Pop-inspired attitude, Ehrenberg produced a quasi-cartoon self-portrait in issue 19. The artist's crowned head and mustachioed face appear in a drawing within the drawing, as though emanating from an egg-shaped aura—a personhood reduced to an office-stamp number, 857334. Below, a body double, whose head and shoulders are concealed by the overlay, sits with hands pressed together, resting over a legend that makes pop art reference to commercial patents and intellectual property: "I reserve the right to withhold all premiums or referrals received by my person in addition to any monies thereby obtained through sales."[11]

In such sardonic, self-reflexivity quips, Ehrenberg was not averse to metaphor, a quality Dore Ashton lamented as crucially missing in Pop aesthetics. To Henry Geldzahler's claim that pop art was "instant art history, art history made so aware of itself that it leaps to get ahead of art," therefore "immediately contemporary," Ehrenberg added an element of ambiguity. The cover image of *El corno emplumado* 22 contained a vertical comic strip or jigsaw puzzle featuring a motif in probable allusion to Raphael's *Portrait of a Young Man with an Apple* (ca. 1505). In Ehrenberg's rendition, however, the apple is displaced onto the lower frames in the form of a giant red disk that overwhelms the subject, signaled by an arrow and legend identifying the shape as *alba* (dawn). Above, a caption reads: "With dawn

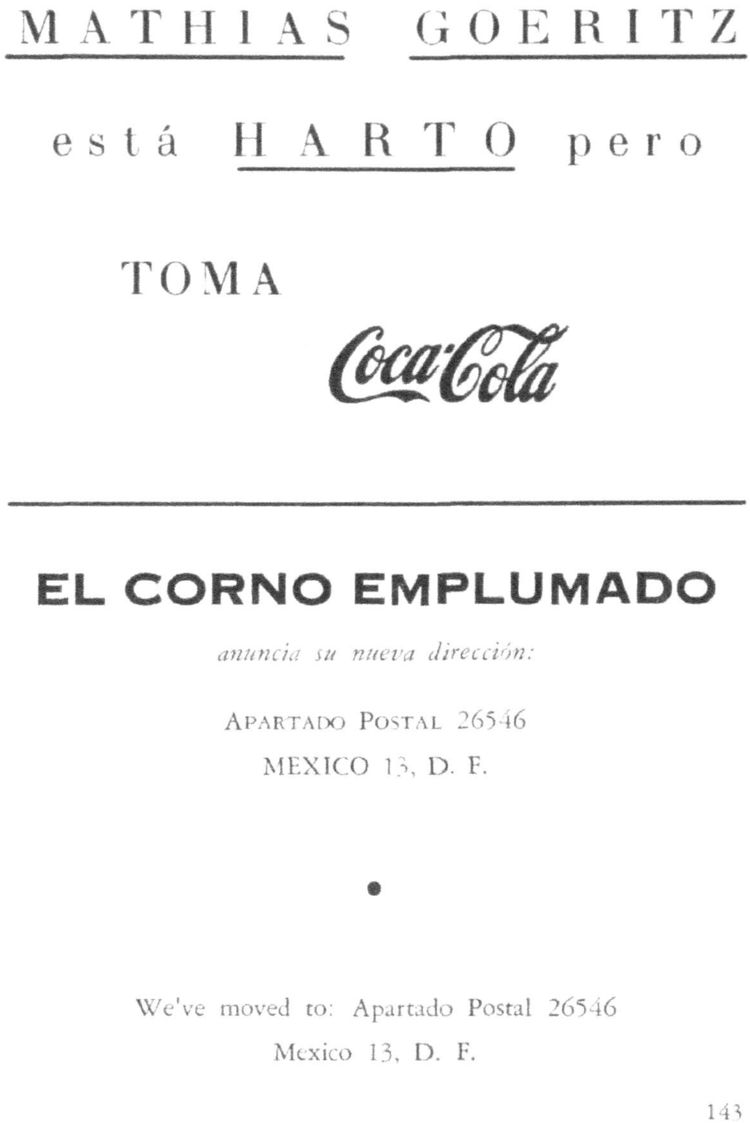

FIGURE 36. *El corno emplumado* 3, edited by Margaret Randall and Sergio Mondragón, Mathias Goeritz, Coca-Cola advertisement, 1962. Courtesy of Margaret Randall.

transformed/I closed my/eyes and saw/the moon."[12] The high-minded punchlines of this brand of old master conceptual comedy are in keeping with what Ashton identified in pop art as an "antidote to idealism."[13] Ideological euphoria was rendered uncertain in his cover art for *El corno emplumado* 23, whose pages showcased a selection of poetry from revolutionary Cuba. Layered onto a saturated background of blue, white, and red, comprising the chevron and stripes of the Cuban flag, are seven male heads in a pyramid formation. The insurgents, with the disheveled hair and scruffy beards associated with the Revolution, lack facial features; but they appear superimposed onto another shape—by turns yellow, red, white—suggesting a human heart or a deformed dove of peace.[14]

El corno emplumado united linotype commercial printing, the graphic arts, small-scale forms of figuration, advertisements with a Pop sensibility, and reports of art and protest in the Americas. In 1968, two years after the above-mentioned contributions to *El corno emplumado*, Ehrenberg made a shadow-box work entitled *Arte conceptual* (Conceptual art), where various elements combine to make axiomatic claims about the relationship of popular commercial amusements to sexed perception and estrangement, and about the status of artworks (plate 20). The composition activates the viewing process with a series of red instructional arrows that point to the back view of a Venus de Milo silhouette. Her inset figure is rendered as though seated on a ledge, looking out the window of an airplane; this scene, in turn, gives way to another, a low-rise industrial building sited on a desolate landscape. This midway aesthetic—a sideshow replete with visual uproar meant to beckon a male-identified drive in the form of the desire for a trophy, the art-historical female nude—is further confirmed at the bottom of the frame by a row of identical faces. Patterned in high contrast red and black, the faces are unspecified regarding sex but betray a stunned expression of disbelief or disaffection.

In a similar work, *Caja no. 25495* (Box no. 25495) (1968), Ehrenberg applies his familiar iconography of arrows and discs, now gray and black, over sober fields of solid red, yellow, and slate blue (fig. 37). Boxed areas and shelf formations provide surface and depth, and a stenciled figure 25495 refers back to comparable number-stamp motifs in Ehrenberg's earlier self-portrait drawings. There is a playful disjunction between the two- and three-dimensionality of this work, as well as between the diagrammatic dancers clad in leotards—placeholders for unfettered expression—and the boxed-in allusions to freight delivery and office management. The box once contained marbles that clattered, hidden from view, when it was held or moved by viewers or art handlers.[15] Ehrenberg suggests that mainstream pop art's celebration of consumer culture is a contradiction in terms for societies, like Mexico, where individuals are likely to be subsumed within the jumbles of bureaucracy.

These paintings further underscore the degree to which Ehrenberg's contributions to *El corno emplumado* presented earlier art-historical periods as perverse forms of symbolic capital and conspicuous consumption—the print-culture version of Geldzahler's "instant art history." Ehrenberg's drawings and cover artwork coupled figurative expression, conceptual art discursiveness, and popular media to confirm the primacy of printed matter. With a quarterly circulation of 3,000, *El corno emplumado*—a craft object by mass-produced standards, but ambitious in its international scope—was the ideal support for less monumental forms of experimentation in Latin America.

There emerged a kind of Pop print culture at the margins of the style's hegemonic domains and the lower rungs of its media hierarchies. In Brazil, Antônio Henrique Amaral's portfolio *O meu e o seu: Impressões de nosso tempo* (Mine and yours: Impressions of our time) (1967) employed elements derived from popular printmaking and the information media, housed in a tightly fitted metal folder or cover encasing the work as though to suggest a classified institutional dossier.[16]

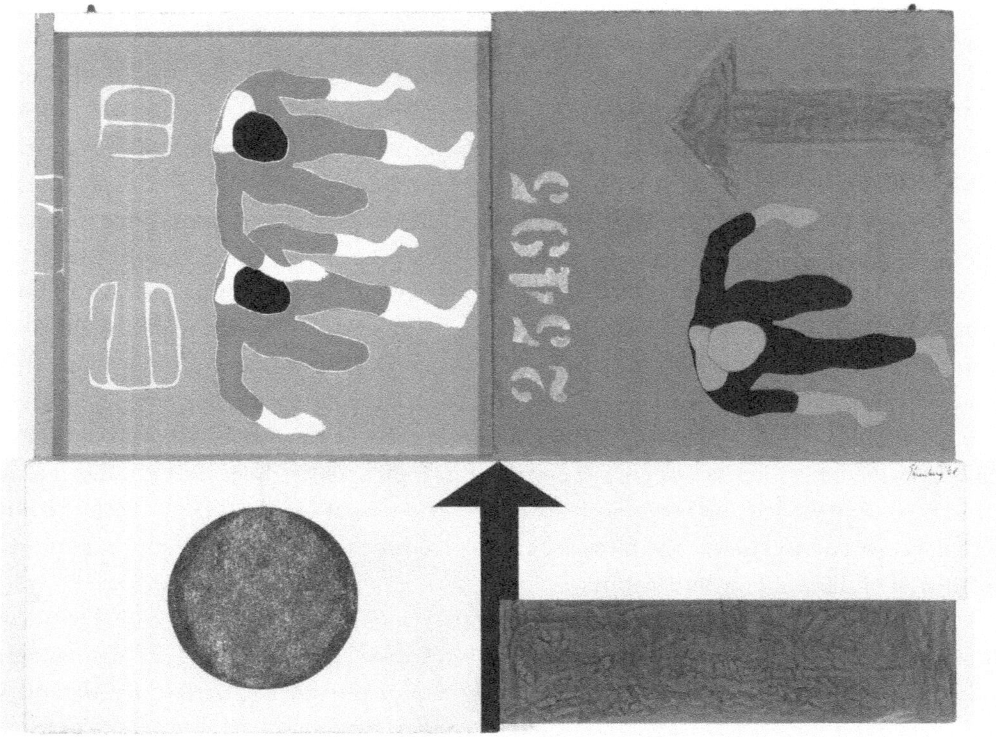

FIGURE 37. Felipe Ehrenberg, *Caja no. 25495*, 1968, acrylic, glitter, and sandpaper. Museo Universitario de Arte Contemporáneo, MUAC, Mexico City (DiGAV-UNAM), photo by Oswaldo Ruiz, courtesy of MUAC.

Seven woodcut prints comprise a sequence of bold compositions critical of contemporary Brazilian society, mass-media distractions, and the violent political authoritarianism of the military dictatorship. Referencing the broadside tradition known as *literatura de cordel* (string literature), but with subject matter that speaks to sexual depravity and violence, Amaral's portfolio offers a grotesque comic-strip iconography at odds with the US monopoly on popular cultural forms.

For example, solid shades of aqua blue and pink lend volume to an axis that serves as the central shape of *O idolatrado* (The idolized) (1967).[17] A microphone monument, crowned by a quartet of hands in the act of providing applause ("CLAC! CLAC!"), is seen grafted onto a pair of feet firmly planted on a column sustained by an audience of onlookers (plate 21). The crowd below appears overwhelmed by the elongated faces that flank the sides of the print, each face in possession of three mouths; each mouth in turn with protruding teeth and tongue. Telescoping cone-shaped megaphone speakers blare strains of a rock-n-roll anthem whose lyrics "YÊ, YÊ, YÊ" ("YEAH, YEAH, YEAH") are at once shorthand for the idolatry of a specific cultural import and a stand-in for stadium forms of authority.

In *Personagem contemporâneo* (Contemporary character) (1967), Amaral employed folklore and experimental figurative distortions that display what Frederico Morais identified as pop art's coterminous democratization of subject matter and of resources and media (plate 22).[18] In the print, mouth motifs shape the cranium of a figure surrounded by disembodied hands and feet. The female subject waves banners for *paz* (peace) and *prosperidade* (prosperity), below which the place names Korea and Vietnam are supported by feet protruding from the lower frame. The figure's visible gastric tract contains the dates 1914 and 1939, the inaugural dates of World War I and World War II, leading to the final function of her digestive system: A question mark in the form of feces is meant to interrogate related modes of consumption and waste.

Premier Brazilian art critic Mário Pedrosa associated a disaffection with US models of mass culture not only as a return of the repressed in the form of folk vernacular, but also as the most profound upheaval of the disenfranchised. In "Gewgaws and Pop Art," Pedrosa casts doubt on Roy Lichtenstein's contributions to contemporary art in Brazil, instead highlighting "an obscure 'cultural subset' emerg[ing] explosively from the urban environment of those artists who call into question the cultural whole from which—with fascinating invention—comes the North American Pop artist and exercises his activities. These are the Black uprisings."[19] Pedrosa identified specific social bodies within the everyday particulars that US pop art had aspired to present.

El Movimiento (the Chicano Movement) emerged concurrent to these uprisings, first within the United Farm Workers struggle and various student-led movements on campuses in California, then in the urban barrios of the Southwest. The poet Jayne Cortez wrote of the August 1965 uprisings in Watts: "Black people were tired of the contradictions, the inequalities, the mounting violations, police brutality, unemployment, lack of opportunity, lack of respect, and the amount of sacrifices made as a consequence of white domination."[20] El Movimiento radicalized Mexican American life and culture with startling visual styles and reached critical mass at the antiwar rally of the Chicano Moratorium in Los Angeles on August 29, 1970. For many Chicano and Chicana artists of the late 1960s and early 1970s, there were no arbitrary separations between "everyday life, art, politics, history" or direct action.[21]

At the foreground of this art and activism was Rupert García, whose poster art decried anti-Black racism, the war in Vietnam, and United States collusion in the social terrors of Latin America. Concurrent with Amaral and Ehrenberg, the Bay Area–based García addressed questions of folkways, sexuality, and race that Pedrosa had in mind when he identified the failure of mainstream Pop artists to address the human sensual and social life that US society had repressed as "cultural subsets." These socially and racially disenfranchised subjects organized politically to emerge "explosively from the urban environment." In an early collagraph, *Black Man and Flag* (1967), red and black values compose a vertically suspended American flag (plate 23). To the black and white stripes García added a star field substituted with a red-hued effigy, the bust of an unspecified civil rights or Black liberation leader.

The print intensified the imperative for the inclusion of Blackness in the national imagination, symbolically promised by the red, white, and blue. García's flag-portrait diagnosed attitudes that journalist Ruben Salazar would describe in his 1969–70 series of articles for the *Los Angeles Times* on Black and Brown relations in California. García's image of a

Black man on the national flag speaks of a moment prior to what Salazar identified as "growing distrust" on the part of young Chicanos "to form a new coalition . . . this time with the Blacks . . . until they, the Chicanos, find their own identity in their own way."[22] García's work preempts and refutes this idea. Consistent with Salazar in another article, he understood the partial view of ethno-nationalist representation and that, insomuch as Anglos had failed in coalition efforts, a "Black and Brown rift [could] only help those interested in slowing down the civil rights struggle."[23]

An internationalist in the turbulent period of a "worldwide Anti-Imperialist upsurge," García was reluctant to consider Chicano identity apart from either allied social struggles or the broadest cultural archive of modernism, and he imbued his poster art at once with cosmopolitan and anticolonial perspectives.[24] In *Decay Dance* (1969), solid areas of red, blue, and pink compose the background, buckled wide-brim hat, and partial but unequivocal face of the Quaker Oats logo (plate 24). Below, in silver ink laid over yellow paper, floats a ghostly image of the Mona Lisa, so distorted and in high contrast as to resemble the face of Marcel Duchamp's 1919 readymade *L.H.O.O.Q.* García, an avid student of Mexican history, philosophy, and culture, was also an early conversant in the surrealist canon, the existentialism of Jean-Paul Sartre, the poetry of Octavio Paz, and the photography of Manuel Álvarez Bravo. García's practice was the result of a surrealist analogy that combined two unlikely constituents: the art ontologies laid bare by Duchamp and the "social-economic-racial dimension of protest" exemplified in the writings of Martin Luther King. The result was what García described as a "socio-aesthetic machine" that inverted the visual grammar of pop art to contest art-historical relations in which whiteness monopolized the category of universal artist "dealing with the conditions of humanity in a post-industrialized context."[25]

Axiomatic homologies or disjunctions between visual signs and applied language informed the practice of other Chicano and Chicana artists. Some, like Mel Casas and Judith Baca, increased the critical level of pop art meanings derived from mass culture commodities, fashion magazines, comic strips, or commercial design by adding cognitive dissonance of the kind generally associated with conceptual art. In *Humanscape 62: Brownies of the Southwest* (1970), Casas gleefully took aim at the blatant racism in a derogatory term for Mexican-descendant peoples, the social capital of the Girl Scouts of America, and the Frito-Lay company mascot known as the "Frito Bandito," a Mexican bandit stereotype (plate 25). He countered the pop art photorealism of advertising and commercial packaging with folk figuration, even as he suggested cross-cultural links between pre-Conquest iconography (Quetzalcoatl, the green "plumed serpent," the skull of Tezcatlipoca) and native peoples of the American Southwest and Mexico. By contrast, Judith Baca's mixed-media triptych *Las Tres Marías* (1976), with its back-embossed upholstered panels, visually transforms the viewer's self-reflection in the front central mirror, therein gendered and racialized according to the terms composing the side panels, two finely rendered naturalist depictions on paper of Chicana expression (plate 13).

Viewer features reflected in the mirror—regardless of sex, age, or ethnicity—are equated and contrasted, on the left with the figure of a butch Chicana homegirl, and on the right with the 1940s *huisa* (*güisa* or *weesa*), the high femme model of Mexican American beauty.

Returning to the visual references in *Decay Dance*, García subverts the Quaker Oats logo's paternalism and wholesomeness with the quintessential art-historical representation of femininity in La Giaconda. By mongrelizing these two Euro-ethnic icons, and by enacting the wordplay of the print's title, García satirizes Cold War idealizations, both gendered and racialized, about the US household, mirrored in the market forces that drive art history. With economy of design, he charges against a strand of modernism that had failed to recognize as avant-garde the contributions made by artists from the Latin American diaspora, while suggesting also that—insomuch as it served as the dominant style for certain art world elites—mainstream Pop's idiom was already fated to flicker out or otherwise decline into decadence.

Margaret Randall and Sergio Mondragón described the hemispheric and aesthetic aspirations of *El corno emplumado* as a "moving totality," which I rehearse by linking Mexico City, New York, São Paulo, Los Angeles, and San Francisco in the late 1960s.[26] Mário Pedrosa encountered a "heteroclite repertory of resources and objects" that were not the "types" exemplified by the cultural supremacy of the United States or by its commercial products.[27] They were instead atypical examples that corroborate the idea that pop art in the Americas thrived surreptitiously, in the margins—in the footnotes and back pages, so to speak—in printed matter that encompassed literary journals, magazine advertisements, illustrations, comic strips, woodcut-print composites, social-protest posters, and in a body of writing proper to that archive. A brand of print-culture Pop subsisted in the pages of a poetry journal, in a limited-edition print sequence, and in the public promise of silkscreens conceived as though from a "socio-aesthetic machine." These examples remain at odds with the omnipresence of more mainstream media and principles of taste. They activated regional information-media references, unexpected anti-art iconographies, and alternate distribution networks, central to movements of social critique and particular to experiences of contrary consciousness in the Americas.

TEN

Center of Gravity: José Clemente Orozco

Center of gravity: proportion

Center of gravity: form

Center of gravity: color

Center of gravity: tone

Center of gravity: character

Center of gravity: meaning

—JOSÉ CLEMENTE OROZCO, *Notebooks*, 1931–1934[1]

Central to the mural cycle José Clemente Orozco completed at the New School in New York City by mid-January 1931—swiftly, in "forty-six and a half days"—is the rather slow-measured undertaking of human assembly, which obtains visual appearance in circular or semicircular formation.[2] The facing tableaux of *Call to Revolution and Table of Universal Brotherhood* enliven arrangements that synchronize, stagger, and blur the meanings of this uniquely immersive work in what was designed as a place of interaction, once a dining hall, now a lecture room, a modest 31.75 by 32 feet. Energizing the sleek geometries of the interior space designed by architect Joseph Urban, the overall effect of the fresco derives from a jolting choreography of cadmium yellows and reds, tawny orange, and a grim shade of sienna that predominates, as though together these colors meant to suggest, in sobering values prone to caution, a new-day optimism. Understated elements of green suggest an exit—a threshold, a window frame, a proscenium floor behind a tiny stage curtain—outward from the web of events for which there really is no leave-taking. Alvin Johnson, inaugural director of the New School, remarked that the depiction squarely "refuses to stay in the walls." As for the bodies configured therein, as well as my own, the viewer's, now idle, now poised for action, appearances here interrelate particular scenes and personas back into the general state of world affairs.

Nestled between the south-facing windows is a disproportionate rectangular surface commanding attention, an unwieldy volume in the hues of natural wood (plate 26). In order for the men depicted in *Table of Universal Brotherhood* to be rendered distinct, faces racially and psychologically legible, Orozco depicted each figure in off-kilter perspective, bodies elongated and aslant in relation to the center of gravity. Each facial expression conveys indeterminate degrees of solemnity or weariness, displeasure or expectation. Alvin Johnson remarked: "You see the Nordic, the Chinese, the Jew, the American Indian, the East Indian, the African Negro and American Negro cooperating in the enterprise of writing reality upon the blank pages of the book of peace." In what languages—it is tempting to speculate—did Orozco imagine the eventual covenants? Writers have pointed to these men of all races, as men all the same, contemplative in their presumed authority as agents of social change. Orozco's figuration in the cycle employs and departs from the naturalistic to span the jaggedly rendered or distorted. "Though he spoke slightingly of folk art," fellow artist and friend Jean Charlot reminds us, "Orozco could not fail to commune, in village chapels, with the tragic mood of the many *bultos* and *santos*—statues carved out of a beam by the local carpenter."[3] This folk figuration is mirrored in the depiction of women elsewhere in the cycle, notably in the *Homecoming of the Worker of the New Day*. And in an adjacent scene of foreshadowing: But for a single man bearing a rifle, there sits a village government of women, with children in their charge, convened in a circle, some with eyes open, most with eyes closed; heads covered in blue or black veils; one or two donning revolutionary *sombreros* (fig. 38). The consortium, expectant, as though waiting to care for the wounded, or to plot an insurrection, provides a correlate to the administrative table fraternity. In the disarticulated plane above the *campesinas* is the portrait of Mexican revolutionary leader Felipe Carrillo Puerto, a Maya temple from his native Yucatán in the backdrop, his eyes cast to a future that is our knowledge of his execution by firing squad at the hands of rebel forces aligned with Adolfo de la Huerta. A spectacle of crimson pennants leads the eye to a stadium portrait of Vladimir Lenin towering over the rank and file. Charging into the day, a throng of combatants is outfitted with helmets bearing red stars; the stabbing blades of their bayonets indicate an advancing menace. They form a kind of rear guard to the row of Red Army officials, with hammers firmly grasped in hand, and Stalin serving as just another affiliate either in the multiethnic "international family of communism" or in what amounts to a composite mirror of vulnerability to doctrine, to the cult of personality, and to the dehumanizing servitude of militarism.[4]

Orozco's intellectual appetite had found in New York a counterpart to Mexico City *veladas*, artistic salons, in the Delphic Circle that gathered at the lower Fifth Avenue apartment of Greek poet Eva Sikelianos and American journalist Alma Reed.

As related by Orozco in his autobiography, gatherings could give way to Sikelianos reciting passages from *The Dedication*, her epic poem translated into English by Reed; meetings with the patriarch of New York's Greek Orthodox Church; lectures on comparative religion; or, on some nights, a kind of a literary workshop, as when suggestions were offered to alter the "grandiose rhythms by Van Noppen, a Dutch poet."[5] Patrons included followers of Mahatma Gandhi, including the poet Sarojini Naidu—two figures depicted on the east wall of the mural cycle. "Though much was made of him," wrote Jean Charlot, "Orozco remained odd man in this choice stable of poets and mystics."[6]

His concern was with questions of the common good, universal values promised in art and industry, and the dubious prospect of a world heritage in light of social organizations repeatedly built on human trafficking and the oppression of peasants and

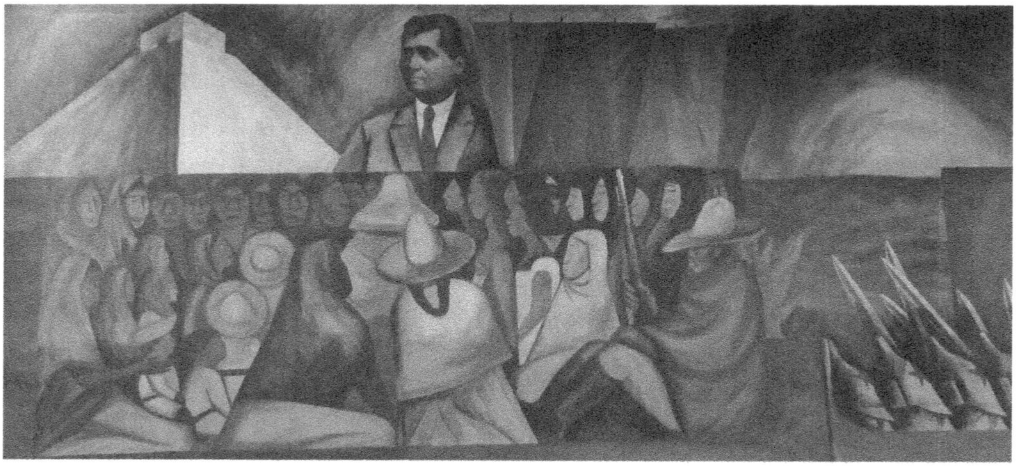

FIGURE 38. José Clemente Orozco, *Call to Revolution and Table of Universal Brotherhood*, 1930–31, mural, The New School, detail (Mexican revolutionary leader Felipe Carrillo Puerto and Maya temple). Artists Rights Society (ARS), New York.

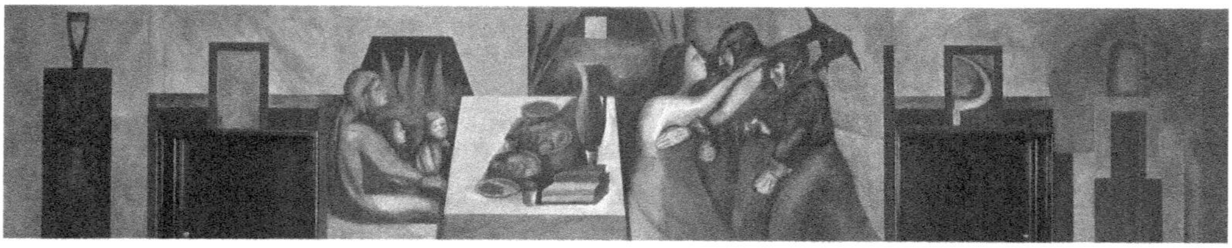

FIGURE 39. José Clemente Orozco, *Call to Revolution and Table of Universal Brotherhood*, 1930–31, mural, "Homecoming of the Worker of the New Day," The New School. Artists Rights Society (ARS), New York.

laborers. Orozco's assistant on the murals, Lois Wilcox, described the "great rhythms" that emanate from the scenes of slavery, the figuration "stylized for the purpose of forcing the eyes of the beholder to feel the abstract beauty of design."[7] Those effects oblige viewers to reckon as well with exploitative labor when rendered invisible by social design: cruciform mallets and pickaxe; a geometrical structure that suggests a factory and chimney in low-angle perspective; a triangle formed by shovel and pick intersecting at the handles. The corner elements in the mural are not merely ornamental. They further stage a conflict of violence and justice; they stand as proxies for those other tools of language, science, and art; and they mediate between events and drives that necessitate enacting laws of universal kinship.

Orozco, the ironist . . . Disinclined to identify with one belief or another, or to flatten into a palliative storyline the transformation processes of history, he gave free reign to human passion and grandeur in monumental form. *Call to Revolution* gives way, in the end, to a homecoming (fig. 39): a hearth, a mother, two children, a kitchen table; a temporal leap, then another woman, or a future version of the same figure, welcoming two workers—or are they rather her offspring, now laboring adults? Orozco, the dramatist . . . Like

Nietzsche, for whom history is the spectacle by which "to think one thing with another," Orozco mistrusted "unity of plan" as much as the mechanistic life. He favored instead the distance effects that make bearable the shock of the here and now, especially when brutal intrusions beyond the law turn our homes into likely places of eviction. You can hear his command: Do you want humanity at the service of justice, or justice at the service of humanity?[8]

ELEVEN

White Stone, Bramble, Gravity, Chance: Miguel Angel Ríos

Diverse kinds of artists have found in the moving image a means to make sense of regional experience while engaging the relation of digital film to other processes in the globalizing world. In a series of video-installation films produced over the last decade, veteran multimedia artist Miguel Angel Ríos has worked with sharp pictorial force to suggest historical urgency by first mobilizing, then capturing and editing live actions that are monumental in scale. In their durational economy, these films, typically five minutes in length, invite and resist while giving shape to the metaphorical possibilities they consign. In 2003, at Los Angeles Contemporary Exhibitions, Ríos installed the first iteration of *A Morir ('til Death)* (2003), a film on which Mexican cinematographer Rafael Ortega served as camera director. The death match and demise of the title plays out in black-and-white loops and three-channel floor-to-ceiling video projections, the visual glide and acoustic drone of spinning toy tops released onto thick lines of a floor grid in unspecified space. These shapes orbit in and out of alternating frames, into a crowd now converging, then colliding in sharp clacks of arrested movements, one or two of them capitulating finally to the law of inertia. Curatorial signage and reviews spoke of the "simplicity of form and color, and the grace of the black tops spinning out of control," but also of the ground-level angle shots that rendered these *trompos*, or Mexican folk-toys, "both ominous and startlingly human," as though committed to "edging each other out of the picture" in a visual and aural "dynamics of competition, invasion, aggression, and territorialism."[1]

In this immersive digital cinema made for museum display, Ríos has coined an elusive narrative form that nonetheless maintains compositional clarity relative to the outcome

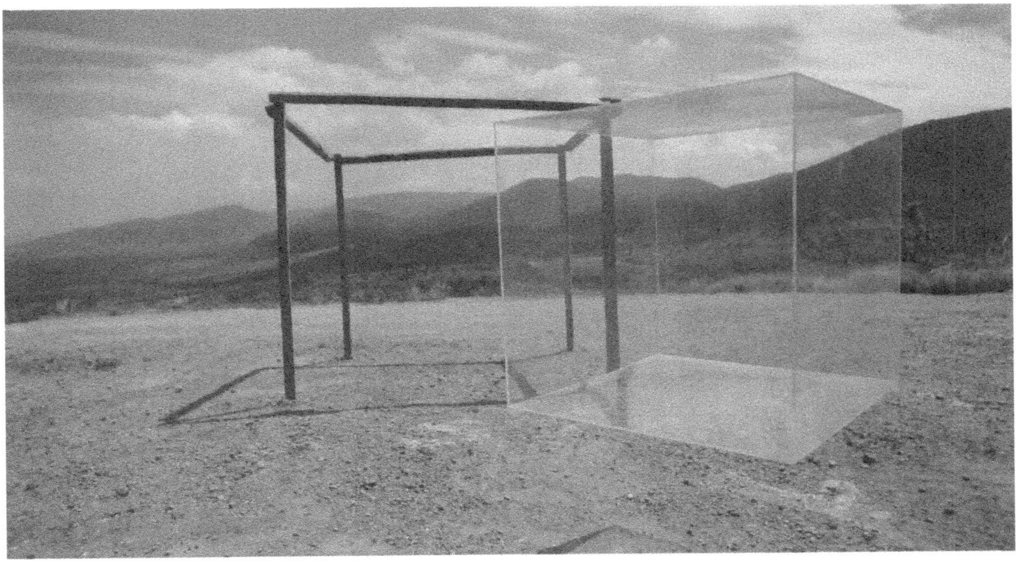

FIGURE 40. Miguel Angel Ríos, *The Ghost of Modernity*, 2012, 3'11", video with sound, one-channel wall projection (still). Courtesy of Miguel Angel Ríos & Sicardi | Ayers | Bacino. © 2025 Miguel Angel Ríos.

each video positions a viewer to anticipate. His subsequent lens-based works have featured an emphatic central trope or figure energized into rhythmic patterning and imagery that enhance the discontinuous flux of sense experience. The anthropomorphic whirling tops of *A Morir ('til Death)* connect to homologous movements that a white-suited dancer performs in *Crudo* (2008, also titled *White Suit*). Appearing from stage-set shadows in a ritualistic dance of cultural self-assertion, the male subject swings slabs of raw meat from two rope cords; he remains undistracted from his syncopated footwork evocative of *malambo*, an Argentine gaucho folk dance.[2] Against the white of his attire, the man's bronze complexion recedes and surfaces again from the surrounding dark. Menacing dogs emerge in a circle to assault the dancer's limbs, still in the throes of heavy dance steps, an ever more vigorous sequence adequate to the violence of this canine attack.

Dogs come into view again in *Landlocked* (2015), a line of them burrowing holes through the side of an embankment in a desperate fit of escape. In yet another series of related single-channel works, a hilltop enactment points to the residuum of a cultural past in connection to its latter-day architectural uncanny (fig. 40). *The Ghost of Modernity (Untitled)* (2012) features a cluster of preindustrial wooden-framed shelters around which hovers a Plexiglas cube serving as the former's purified ideal form, a haunted object severed from its manufactured status.[3] The camera follows the floating transparent cube motif in *The Ghost of Modernity (Lixiviados)* (2012), whose subtitle, *lixiviados* or leachates, is a term meaning water that has seeped through solid waste, as in landfills, where it poses a serious threat to freshwater sources. The setting here—a massive trash heap—is now stage to a spectacle of cube-form corrugated metal shanty homes crashing down in freefall from an unseen source beyond the frame.

Human subjects in transit; the cultural particulars dividing sheer residence from mere shelter; authority secured by technical means; and the social engineering attained at the expense of other animal species—these concerns of the artist look back at the anthropocentric focus that propelled some versions of early twentieth-century modernism, certainly that of Latin America, epitomized in the visionary agenda Joaquín Torres-García outlined as Constructivist Universalism. Torres-García took seriously the geographic contingency and localized histories that determine attitudes and action from one's position on the globe. He wrote in 1942 of an ethos in which "art cannot be separated from the human problem." For Torres-García art and life were not "different kinds of knowledge and principles, incoherent and random, but rather something mature, unified: a *structure*. Something integral, based on a main idea, on harmonious conjunction."[4] Extending the argument to suit the political realities of the present and his own time-based dynamics, Ríos sets into motion metaphors of earth, maps, and deracination, the violent underbelly subsisting in games and other cultural forms, and of warfare by means of architectural occupation in the cartographic expanse. For many years dividing his time between Mexico and New York City, and thereby having to navigate the insider-outsider status a global art world transfigures into marketable assets, Ríos has sought to analogize the structure of authority and connectedness that exists between nations, corporations, and individuals in the global flows defining present-day conditions and processes.

In recent single-channel video projections, Ríos continues to develop along these lines.[5] *Piedras blancas* (2014) begins with an extreme low-angle shot of a sun-drenched sky and cloud forms, the sound of whirring insects giving way to the click and rumble of a cascade of orbs traversing the frame of the camera, first nestled below, then level with the ground (fig. 41). The ensuing five-minute sequence follows the onrush of these all-white objects, some streaked with earth—hollow cement spheres seven to eight inches in diameter and totaling up to 3,500 in number—as they sweep over, hurl forward, and tumble down a network of mountainside striations. Many lenses energize the momentum and pulse in a kinetic pattern of forward and reverse tracking sequences, handheld shots, aerial perspectives, and ground-level placements of the recording equipment. Ríos and his production crew, with Carlos Adán Cárdenas as director of photography, used three GoPro cameras, two Canon C100s, and a Canon 5D Mark III.[6] In stampede flight, the spheres charge down enhanced water-drainage furrows, here and there a sphere suddenly shattering in the frame or striking the camera, the dash a downward knockabout ending in a repository for detention or ultimate demise.

Knowledge about the preparation behind the shooting of this digital work competes appreciably with one's real-time experience of viewing. It comes as no surprise to learn that the manufacturing process of those 3,500 cement spheres involved three months of collaborative labor; that the film production of the repeated sequence lasted eighteen weeks; or that each take comprised a time-intensive process of repainting and drying the multitudinous spheres, their transfer en masse and synchronized release, as well as the strategic placement of cameras along the craggy hill of Tepoztlán, Morelos, a location fifty miles south of Mexico City. Even as the projected video submits a scene for associations to

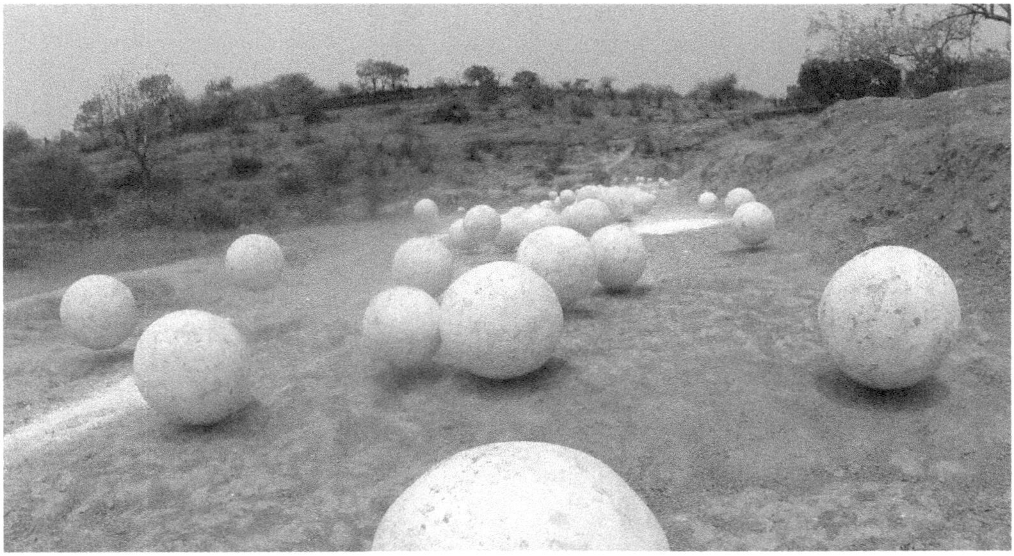

Figure 41. Miguel Angel Ríos, *Piedras blancas*, 2014, 4'52", video with sound, one channel wall projection (still). Courtesy of Miguel Angel Ríos & Sicardi | Ayers | Bacino. © 2025 Miguel Angel Ríos.

do with migration, collective flight, or asylum seeking, it remains impossible to suspend awareness of the painstaking real-life labor involved in the undertaking.

A 2014 series of untitled drawings that Ríos made in tandem with the film production documents the artist's conception, development, and design of the work. One pencil drawing in storyboard form describes the "frontal attack" of one take. Thousands of "stones" are to speed toward the camera, striking it in order to blur the image, with an additional note as to the importance of filming on a cloudless day so as to successfully capture the effect of particles bursting from the shattered spheres.[7]

Another drawing comprises a full page of text:

> The 2014 project *Piedras blancas* (white stones) explores the performance of objects and matter choreographed in the natural landscape. Undefined as to what they are made of, these solid and heavy white balls rapidly roll down from the side of a mountain.
>
> Their paths are determined by the existing trails in the landscape, channels eroded by streams of water created by the rain. The intervention of an unknown element, deployed into the natural conditions of the desert mountain landscape and responding through gravity and chance, lead to an inevitable search for metaphors.
>
> Are these rolling stones the supply of drugs coming from the South into the North across the U.S.-Mexico border? Are we witnessing some kind of game, or is it a catastrophe in the making? Are the inclines of the paths the effect of economic globalization on underprivileged populations? Do these white stones represent people caught in a migrating frenzy?
>
> These questions may never be answered, yet there is a haunting sense of urgency in the poetic juxtaposition of motion and matter. As white stones proliferate throughout the

landscape and begin to mount, the viewer is placed in an all too familiar situation: that of witnessing the rapid unfolding of events (often catastrophic) that remain elusive, beyond comprehension.

A bifurcating channel in yet another untitled pencil-and-ink composition draws attention to the ground as a surrogate body: "Furrows in the earth resemble veins through which toxic substances flow."[8]

There is at the halfway mark of *Piedras blancas* a fleeting ground-level close-up of thorns from a *huizache* plant set against the receding white spheres and the hazy mountain range in the background. An invasive species whose medicinal uses in Mexico date to preconquest times, the huizache is invested in some Amerindian folklore accounts with powers "to avoid the evil eye," especially when its thorns are worn pinned to one's clothes.[9] Its profusion serves as the material base for a series of camera choreographies enacted in the video *Endless* (2015). Production assistants Victor Labastida Moctezuma, Ignacio Rivera Flores, Israel Bustos Flores, Lorenzo Rivera Flores, Adrián Rivera Flores, and Ramiro Rivera Flores expended countless labor hours with the purpose of transfiguring massive quantities of the bramble stalks into barricades measuring eighty to one hundred feet in length and consisting of modular parts, both inert and in motion (fig. 42).[10] Beginning with aerial tracking as per the cinematic convention of representing a city from a helicopter's viewpoint, the camerawork in *Endless* sweeps above, over, and through these huizache blockades to the ponderous audio swell of Franz Schubert's *Ave Maria*. The various lenses employed proceed along parallel lines formed by contiguous barbed walls, on the bias as well, and through the minimalist bramble canyon; camera movements now receding or zooming in to penetrate the tightly entwined ramparts in oceanic surge, ending on a curtain-drop gesture of a smaller huizache bundle lowered into the depth of the barricades, followed by a fade to black. There is no beyond or other side to the looping video imagery enclosure.

Between the onrush staged in *Piedras blancas* and the shifting obstacles animated in *Endless* are suggested the new temporalities of migration that Ruben Andersson has described in pressing ethnographic accounts. In Andersson's narrative analysis, speed and stasis together compose the time of migration, the economically engineered durations that link "cross-border movement and waiting." Technologies of control, working steadily to outpace the action of migrants and asylum seekers, ever amplify the velocity of "real-time intelligence," for which lens-based surveillance systems are decisive in geopolitical locations like the Mediterranean coast of the European Union or the US-Mexico divide, a place "monitored by drones and shielded by barriers." Present-day capitalist nations double as security states and so profit from the willingness of human beings to wager life itself in the name of a promise; the hope of an everyday existence rid of the precariousness that economic injustice, wartime, and other social terrors dictate. States fund border agencies and outsource defense companies to run detention centers where indeterminate waiting makes palpable "state time" as distinct from "subjective time." In this scenario, a "quest for speed is intimately tied up with the concept of risk," and the temporal modalities of risk in turn define a "time-space compression" that further motivates "large investments

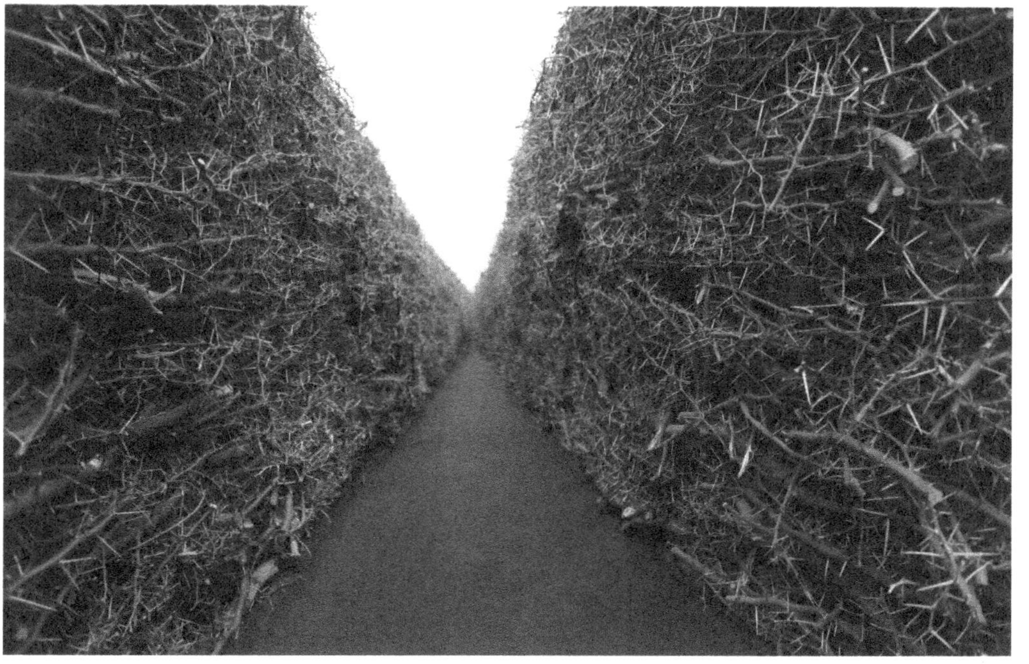

FIGURE 42. Miguel Angel Ríos, *Endless*, 2014, 6'33", video with sound, one-channel wall projection (still), courtesy of Miguel Angel Ríos & Sicardi | Ayers | Bacino. © 2025 Miguel Angel Ríos.

in new information sharing systems" that make border zones an "information channel, communicating up, sideways, and down in a chain of signals." In the time-space regime of globalization, "the possibilities of anticipation, interception, and deferral opened up by compression and speed have led to precisely the opposite reality for those who are targeted: a world of slowness and stasis."[11]

Relevant to these video projections by Miguel Angel Ríos, and to medium-specificity itself, is the biopolitical economy of high-speed communication as it relates to corporate and state interests in territory, security, and population management. Market forces and visualization technologies work jointly to monetize bodies driven to migration and border detention, facts that should be kept in mind as one seeks to understand the current material and social meanings of the digital medium. In her important writings, media theorist Yvonne Spielmann grapples with the image status of video as it differs from film and photography. The electronic, video, or *digital* film image, she writes, comprises "a constantly moving flow of signals . . . that differ from the spatial-temporal unity of a 'tableau' or 'frame' image" of analog media, insofar as the former prevail as "flexible, unstable, incoherent, and non-fixed forms."[12] In this respect the video medium goes hand in hand with the expectations, delays, compression, and speed endemic to the global fluctuation of bodies and goods.

Loosened from the codes of classical cinema but attuned to the inherent narrative potential of moving images, some digital film works designed for gallery projection have been critical in defining the capacity of video to apprehend, enact, or abbreviate aspects of the human enterprise in the flux of history. A synthesis of energies drives camera works of this kind to animate concerns about the picture-value of an image sequence, the containable duration of the short-form, aspects of presentational design, and the interplay of descriptive or self-reflective modes for video installation. Latin American film artists and video makers have played a significant role in developing these questions of form and media, offering accounts that speak to the singularity of place in the globalized world and to the electronically mediated image-time of contemporary conditions. Ríos and others have designed visual structures to convey the uneven experience of modernity while relating the present to the past in the arenas of politics, economics, and culture. *Piedras blancas* and *Endless* thematize the flux of migrant temporalities by equating global processes to the "passages between frames and frame positions" of electronically recorded imagery.[13] In these digital film projections, pictorial values are activated toward self-reflective ends. The time-space compression of the migrant speed and confinement economy has a material correlative in the hundreds of labor hours transformed, in pre- and postproduction processes, into five-minute art objects.

These camera-based works subject spectacular impulse to documentary demands by designing and recording monumental actions for the sake of the camera, but with formal elegance and a metaphoric force suggestive of human emergency and geopolitical experiences that persist outside the darkened confines of the curtained gallery space or partitioned area of the museum. Formally attuned to worldwide rearrangements and escalations, and by means of extended metaphors about displacement, Miguel Angel Ríos applies pressure to media technology and wrests subject matter out of gestures whose physical magnitude is commensurate with comprehensive reach.

TWELVE

The Capture of Cuauhtémoc: David Alfaro Siqueiros, Leo Matiz, and Javier de la Garza

In 1986, the Bank of Mexico issued the $50,000 peso note with a portrait of the last Aztec emperor in quarter profile, his facial expression an indeterminate cipher of equanimity and disapproval. That same year Javier de la Garza offered his own tribute, a timely addition to the repertoire of ideas and attitudes contained in iconographic survivals and revivals dealing with the image of Cuauhtémoc (plate 27). In an archive certifying the uncanny return of the repressed appearing at certain inflection points in Mexico's historical process, the figure of Cuauhtémoc has served expressive and political purposes. Even as a symbol of resistance for nineteenth-century *criollo* elites, postrevolutionary artists, and regional social movements, the use of Cuauhtémoc as an image also betrayed ambivalence about Indigenous autonomy within the national narrative. Discontinuous lines connect the discourses of *indigenismo* and *mestizofilia* in nineteenth-century integrationist policies to artworks in the twentieth century. Cuauhtémoc has had a persuasive afterlife in such works as Ramón López Velarde's 1921 poem "La suave patria" ("unparalleled hero at the pinnacle of art.//Anachronistically, absurdly") and Carlos Pellicer's 1924 "Oda a Cuauhtémoc" ("Oh solemn and tragic leader of men!/Oh sweet, ferocious Cuauhtémoc!") and in impassioned discourses resurrecting proof or refutations of the hero's alleged remains, excavated at Ixcateopan in 1949, the subject of recurring political controversy for decades thereafter.[1]

In a 1946 photograph, Orson Welles, David Alfaro Siqueiros, Rita Hayworth, and Angelica Arenal de Siqueiros are posed in descending order, eyes fixed upward in amazement, surrounded by otherworldly gargantuan figures comprising *Cuauhtémoc Against the Myth* (1944). Siqueiros painted this site-specific mural in the Mexico City home of the Arenal family on Avenida Sonora 9, meant to double as the future site of the Center for Modern Realist Art, although he later relocated the work to the Tecpan de Tlatelolco. A search to identify the photographer takes me down a different path, a detour leading to the Colombian cameraman Leo Matiz, who lived in Mexico from 1940 to 1950 and worked with Siqueiros to produce what the painter referred to as "photographic sketches." For Siqueiros the camera-generated image served as an optical diagram appropriate for composing, apt "to unravel, insurmountably until now, the phenomena of volume, space, the movement of volume in space, and [to affix] the largest and smallest elements that make up the human drama."[2] To that end Matiz photographed a seminude Siqueiros, his back splayed against a tree as in the martyrdom of St. Sebastian or as the subject of a present-day lynching. But there is more: Startling and intimate are the nudes of the attractive boxer Víctor Arrevillaga, who offers his body in full display, outdoors and in the studio, to the worshiping lens of Matiz's camera (fig. 43). The fighter's smooth brown skin and athletic build are so posed as to alternately suggest torture, glory, supplication, and surrender. Matiz's photographs of Arrevillaga served as the departure point for Siqueiros to paint the semi-abstracted figures and emblematic gestures of *Cuauhtémoc Against the Myth*, *Our Image* (1947), and *King Cuauhtémoc* (1950). Whatever else they reveal, these photographs of Arrevillaga, made by Matiz for Siqueiros, suggest triangulated scenes at once electrifying, secretive, and sadomasochistic; at any rate, an episode among others in the latent history of muralism's homoerotic imagination.

Carlos Monsiváis defined machismo in the art and culture of the Mexican Revolution as "the bloody display of recklessness and cruelty," and as a monopoly on images of dignity. In early photographs, homosexuals were portrayed as delinquents behind bars in the Belén prison, and Indigenous peoples were treated as a form of spectacle. These depictions rendered them as subhuman and a threat to genuine patriots who performed the only permissible "exalted version of the human."[3] A national commitment to exclusionary forms of masculine identity lingered as latent and manifest formations in the political arena, in media depictions, and in everyday discourse, despite the so-called sexual liberation movements of the 1960s and 1970s, reactivated in debates that specified *mexicanidad* in the 1980s. Such attitudes went hand in hand with what Federico Navarrete termed a "relentless pigmentocracy, that is, a racial, social, and cultural stratification based on skin color. The whitest 'mestizos' with a more Western culture occupy the highest positions on this value scale, and the darkest or most Indian, the lowest. This discrimination is economic and classist, a reflection of the brutal inequality of our society, while at the same time racial, since it feeds on social and cultural prejudices against the least white groups inherent in mestizaje."[4]

Javier de la Garza revived the image of the "solemn and tragic leader of men" in a painting that improvises in the keys of fantasy and unrestrained enjoyment in *Cuauhtémoc (The Capture of Cuauhtémoc: "Take your dagger, open my veins, let me bleed, etc. etc.")* (1986).

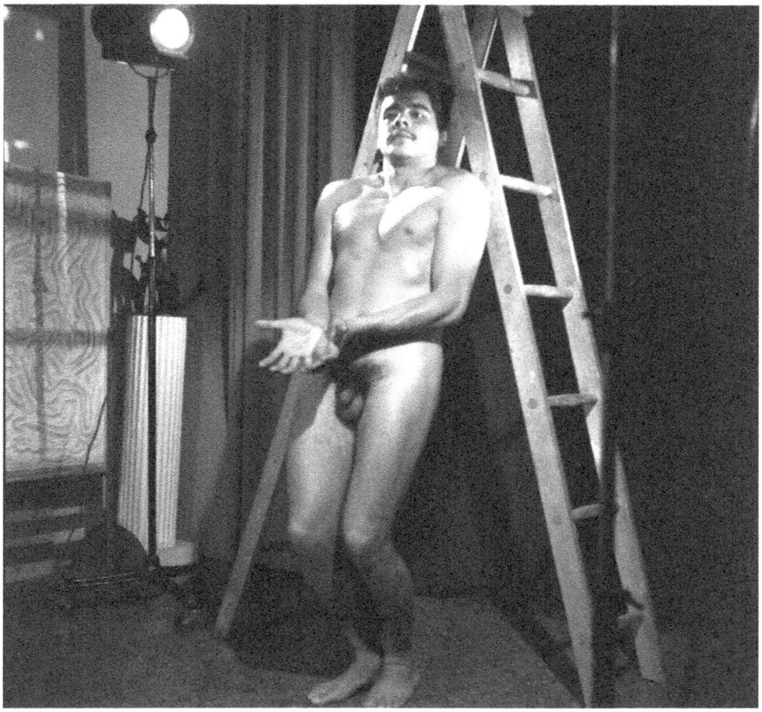

FIGURE 43. Leo Matiz, "Nuestra imagen actual," study for David Alfaro Siqueiros of boxer Víctor Arrevillaga, 1945, photograph.

The bronze and muscular seminude physique of this modern-day Cuauhtémoc poses in nearly full figure quarter profile. Brushstrokes enhance the virile contours of his upper arms, chest, abdomen, and buttocks, a body further deified in relation to the backdrop over which towers the "leader of men," an idyllic lakeside landscape. Cuauhtémoc's feather headdress and metal helmet, adorned with precious stones, feature prominently in colors that rebuff decorum or solemnity in favor of scandalous greens, reds, and blues. These elements work in tandem with material details—black velvet, trimming, and paper flower appliques—as decoys to distract the beholder from the loincloth, in colors of the Mexican flag, so draped as to suggest a well-endowed hero. High melodrama prevails in the full title of the painting, a lyric lamenting romantic deceit from the torch song "Amor gitano," made popular in 1967 by the Cuban chanteuse and international gay icon Guadalupe Victoria Yolí Raymond, La Lupe. Javier de la Garza prompts viewers to perform at once a desire for and an identification with the voluptuous Cuauhtémoc; his crimson lips and facial expression give away sorrow and the irresistible grandeur of masculine vulnerability. "Quiero desangrarme hasta que me muera."

The artist once described his process of recycling images in order to "expose a fiction, a search for a lost identity in the symbols which have permeated mass media"—the calendar art of Jesús Helguera, for example—while wondering whether such uncanny returns are inclined "to make an impression"[5] De la Garza fashions a self-contained world so that Cuauhtémoc can serve as another kind of currency ("El Banco de México pagará cincuenta mil pesos a la vista al portador"). In the painting the matter of masculinity, a form of camouflage, disentangles from the ideologies of Mexican modernity by staging for certain viewers a same-sex seduction, and by providing a field of meaning for the Indigenous male body, at once the subject of complex articulations and the object of desire in a grammar of pigment and mixed media.

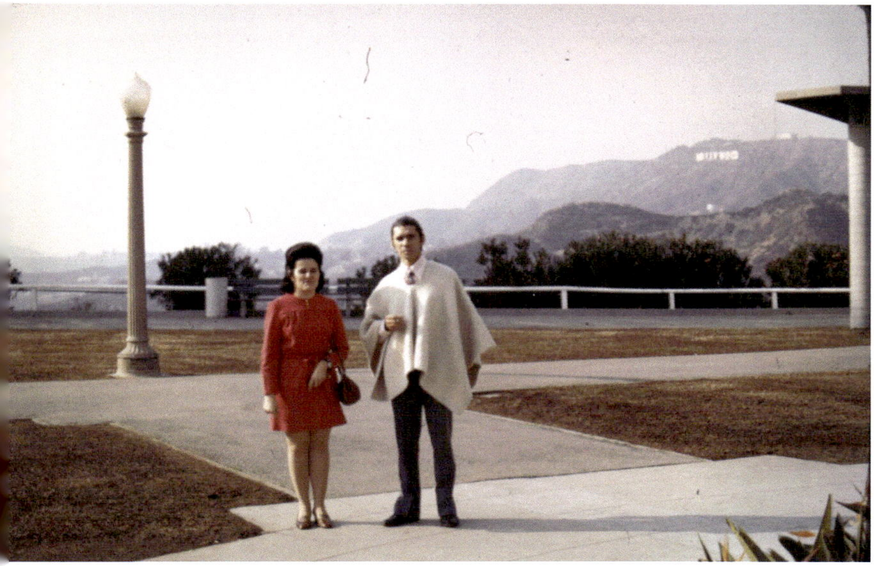

1. Eduardo Tejada, *Couple in Griffith Park* (Rafael and Berta Tejada), ca. 1971, Ektachrome slide.

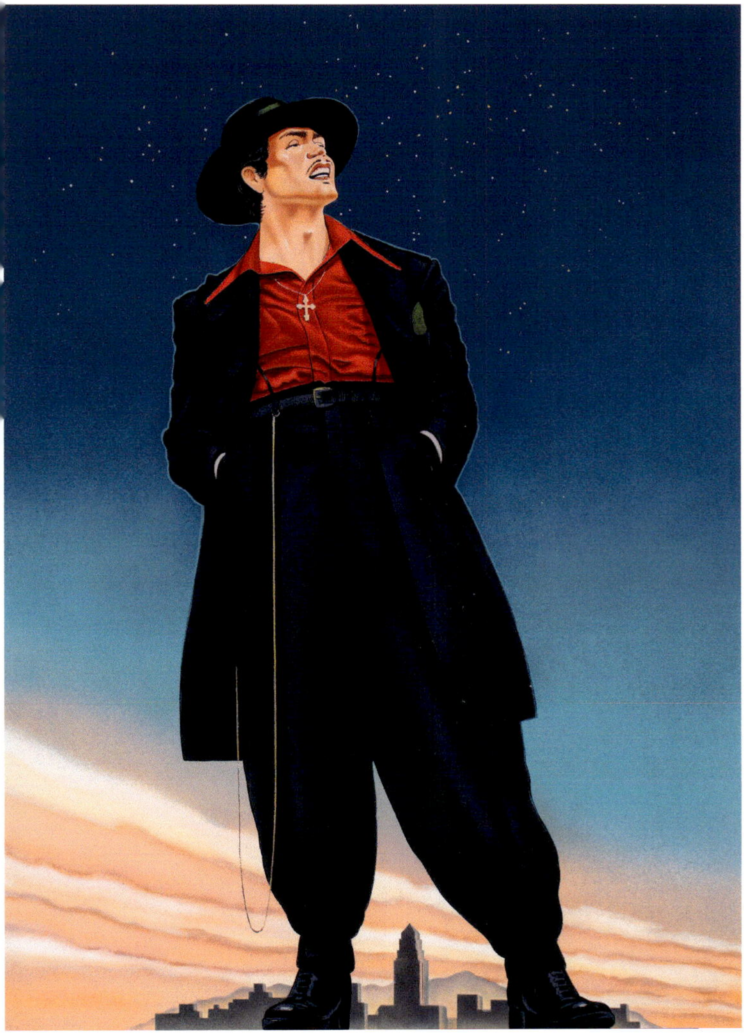

2. Ignacio Gomez, *Zoot Suit: A New American Play by Luis Valdez*, 1978, poster. © Ignacio Gomez, artist.

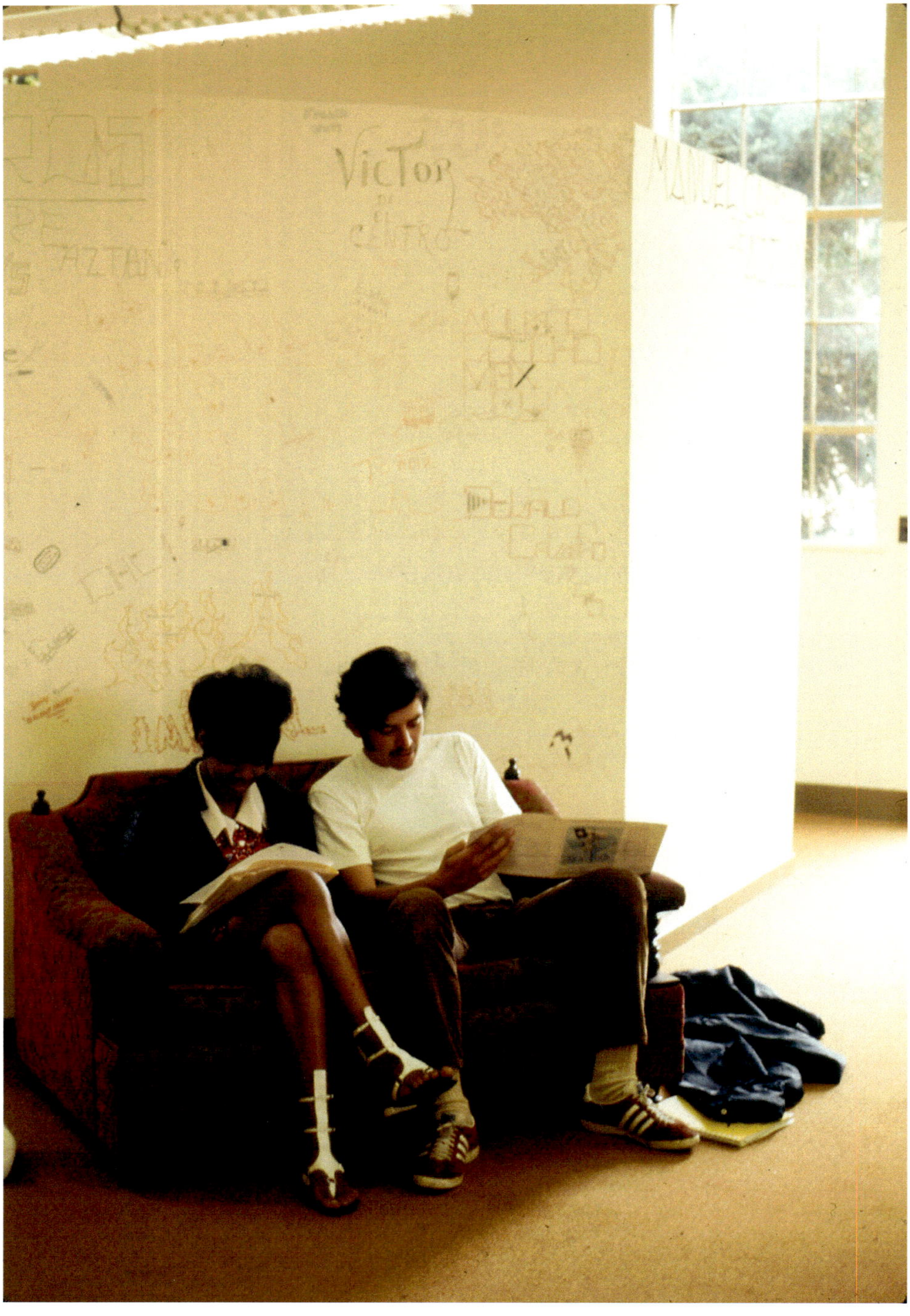

3. Oscar Castillo, *California Polytechnic University, San Luis Obispo*, early 1970s, color slide. Courtesy University of California, Los Angeles Chicano Studies Research Center.

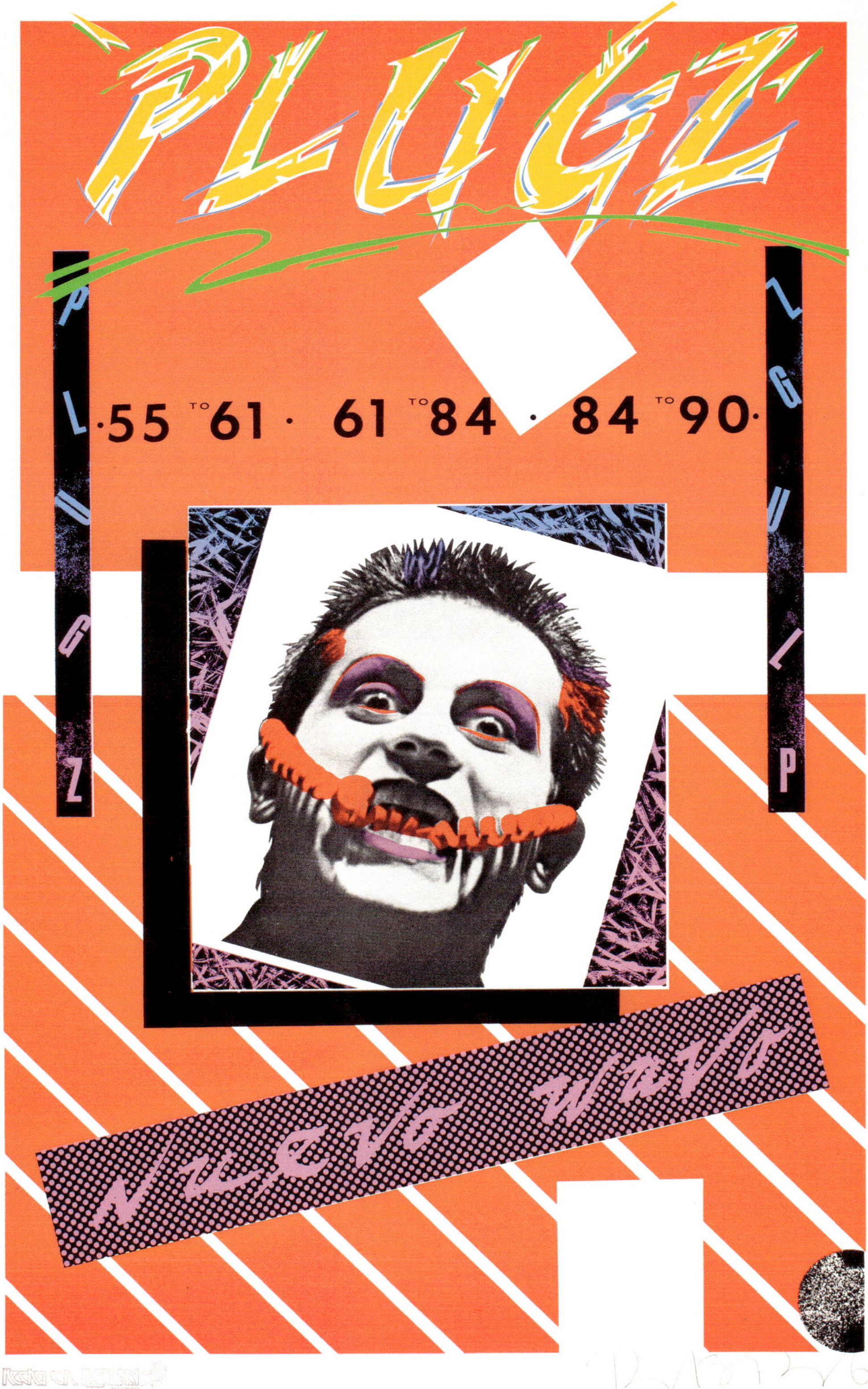

4. Richard Duardo, *Plugz/Nuevo Wavo*, 1978, poster, Richard Duardo Collection, California Ethnic and Multicultural Archives, Department of Special Collections, Davidson Library, University of California, Santa Barbara.

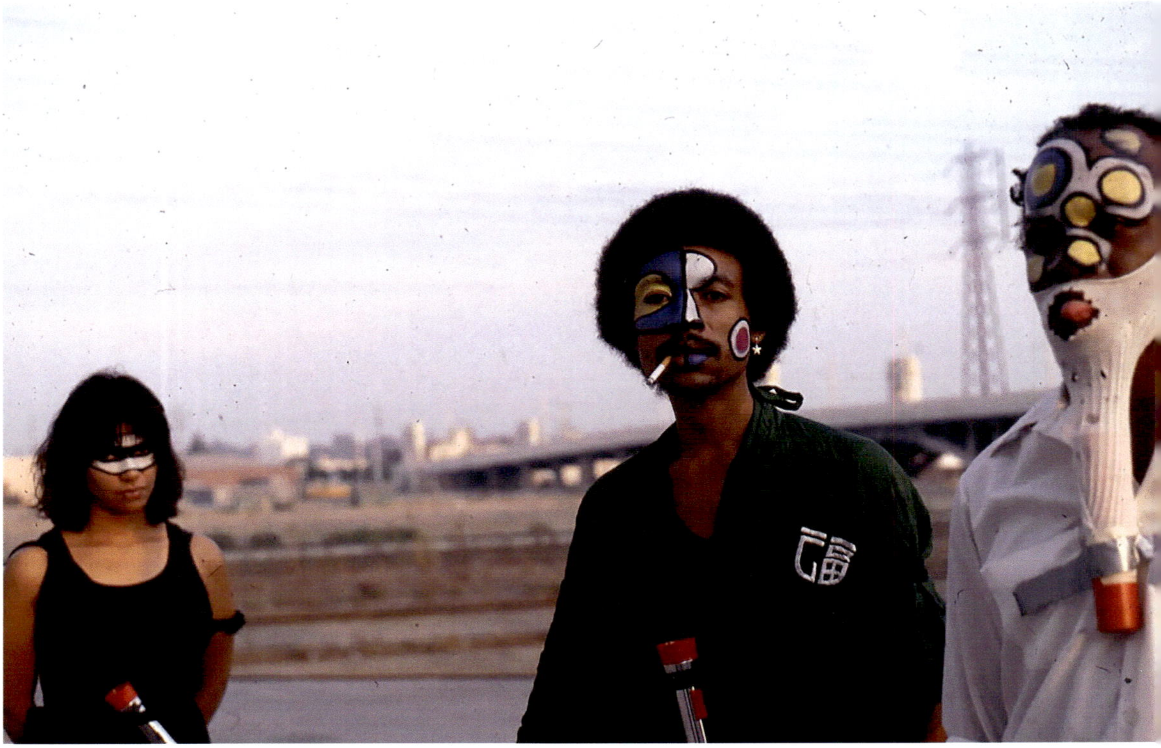

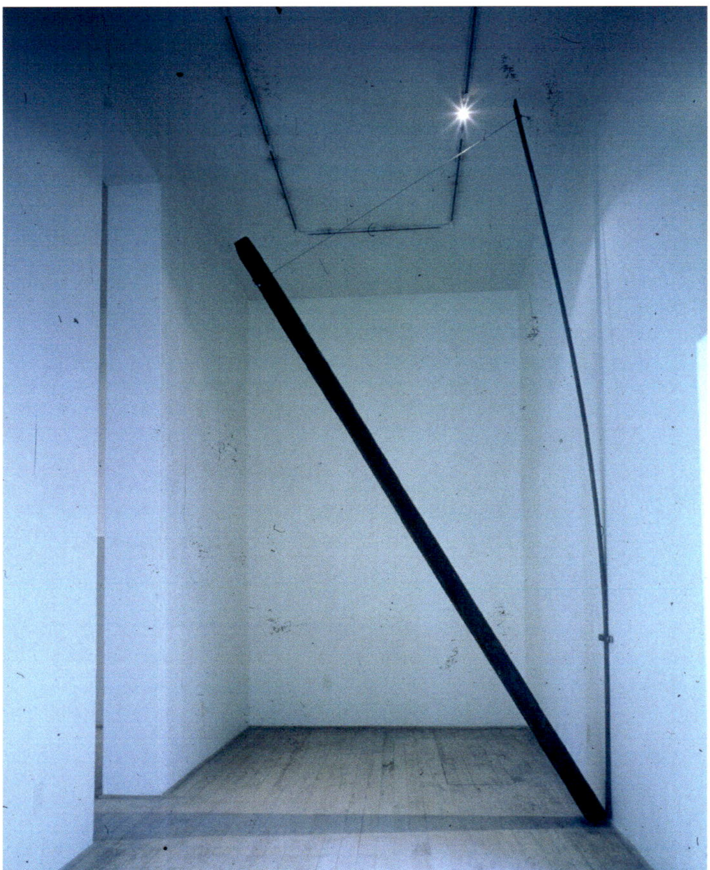

5. Ulysses Jenkins, *Without Your Interpretation*, 1984, rehearsal documentation, video (rehearsal photo Ulysses Jenkins, *New York Times*), color print, 3½ × 5 in. (8.9 × 12.7 cm). Courtesy of the artist.

6. Carlos Aguirre, *Images of Neoliberalism, The Three Powers*, 1995. Courtesy of Galería Nina Menocal and the artist.

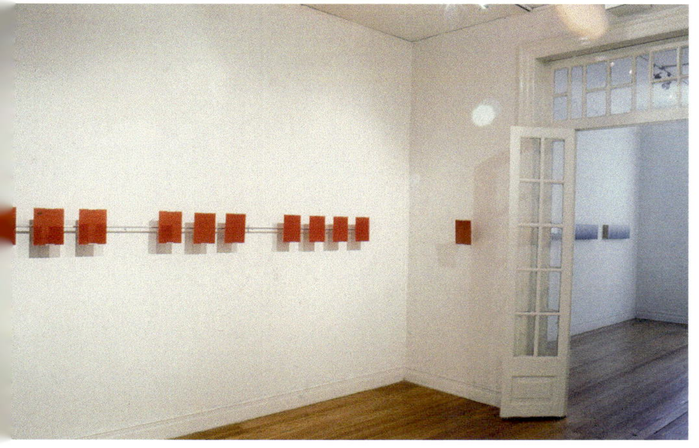

7. Thomas Glassford, *Arteria*, installation at Curare: Espacio Crítico para las Artes, Mexico City, 1992. Photo courtesy of the artist.

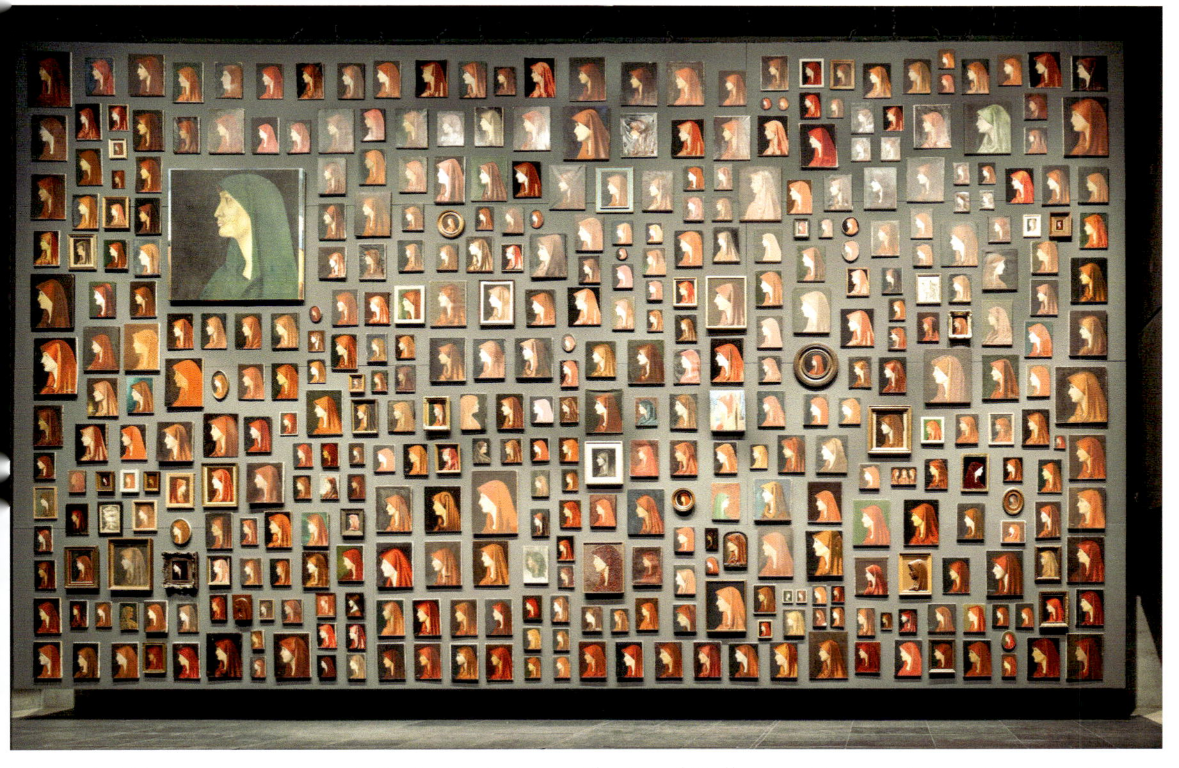

8. Francis Alÿs, installation view of *The Fabiola Project* at The Menil Collection, Houston, Texas, Byzantine Fresco Chapel, 2016–18. Photo by Paul Hester, courtesy of Menil Archives, The Menil Collection, Houston, Texas.

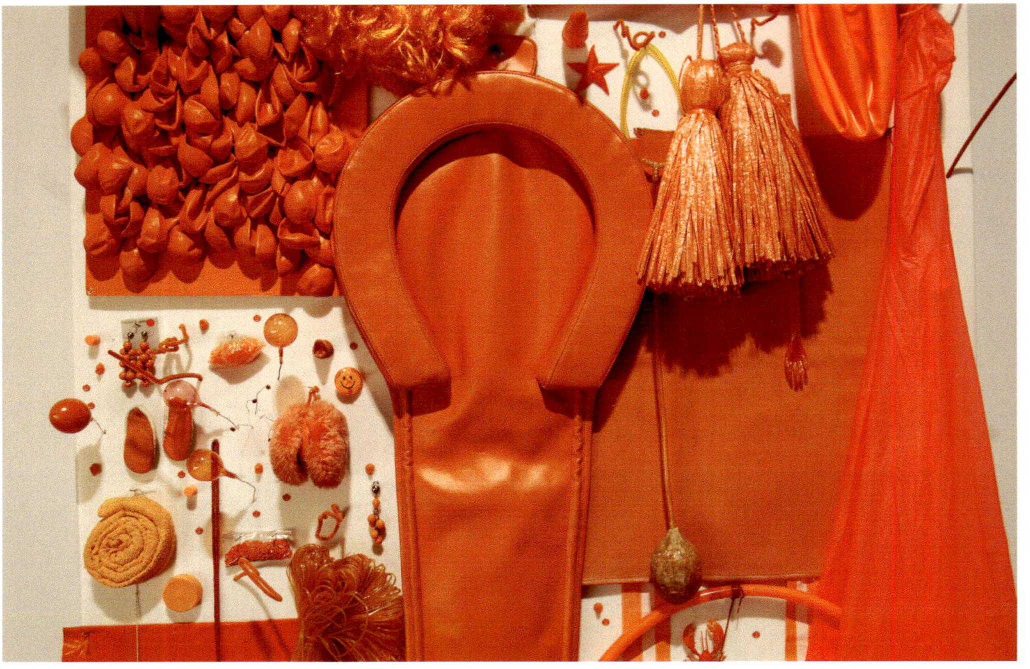

9. Melanie Smith, *Orange Lush 1*, 1994, plastic objects on foam and plywood, 8' × 4' × 10", MIT List Visual Arts Center, 2009.

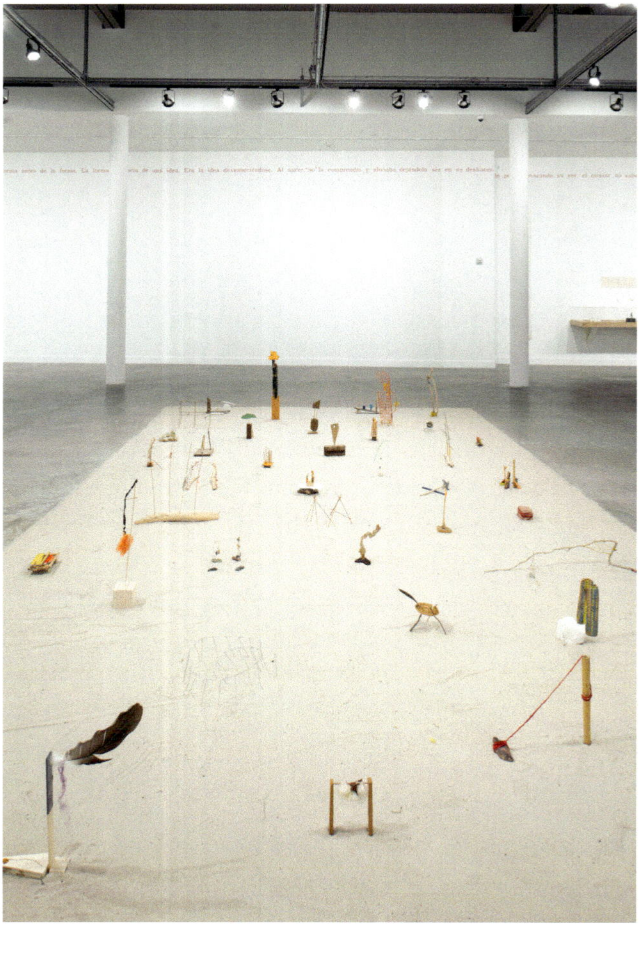

10. Cecilia Vicuña, *Pueblo de altares*, 1990/2019, site-specific installation of found-object sculptures, stones, shells, glass, wood, plastic, thread, debris; installation view, "Cecilia Vicuña: About to Happen," Museum of Contemporary Art North Miami (MOCA NOMI), 2019, photo by Daniel Bock, courtesy of the artist and MOCA NOMI. © 2025 Cecilia Vicuña/Artists Rights Society (ARS), New York. Courtesy of the artist and Lehmann Maupin, New York, Hong Kong, Seoul, and London.

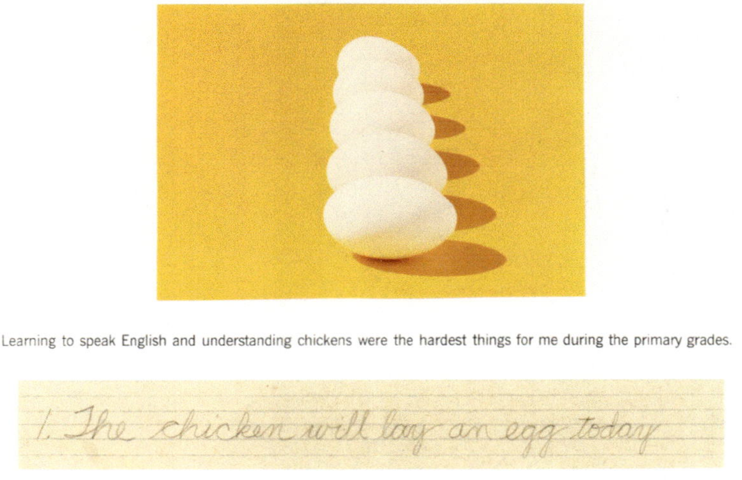

11. Celia Álvarez Muñoz, *Enlightenment #4, Which Came First?*, 1982, five color photographs, letterpress on rag paper, & graphite in curly maple box. Photo by Daniel Lang. Courtesy of Museum of Contemporary Art San Diego (MCASD) and Radius Books.

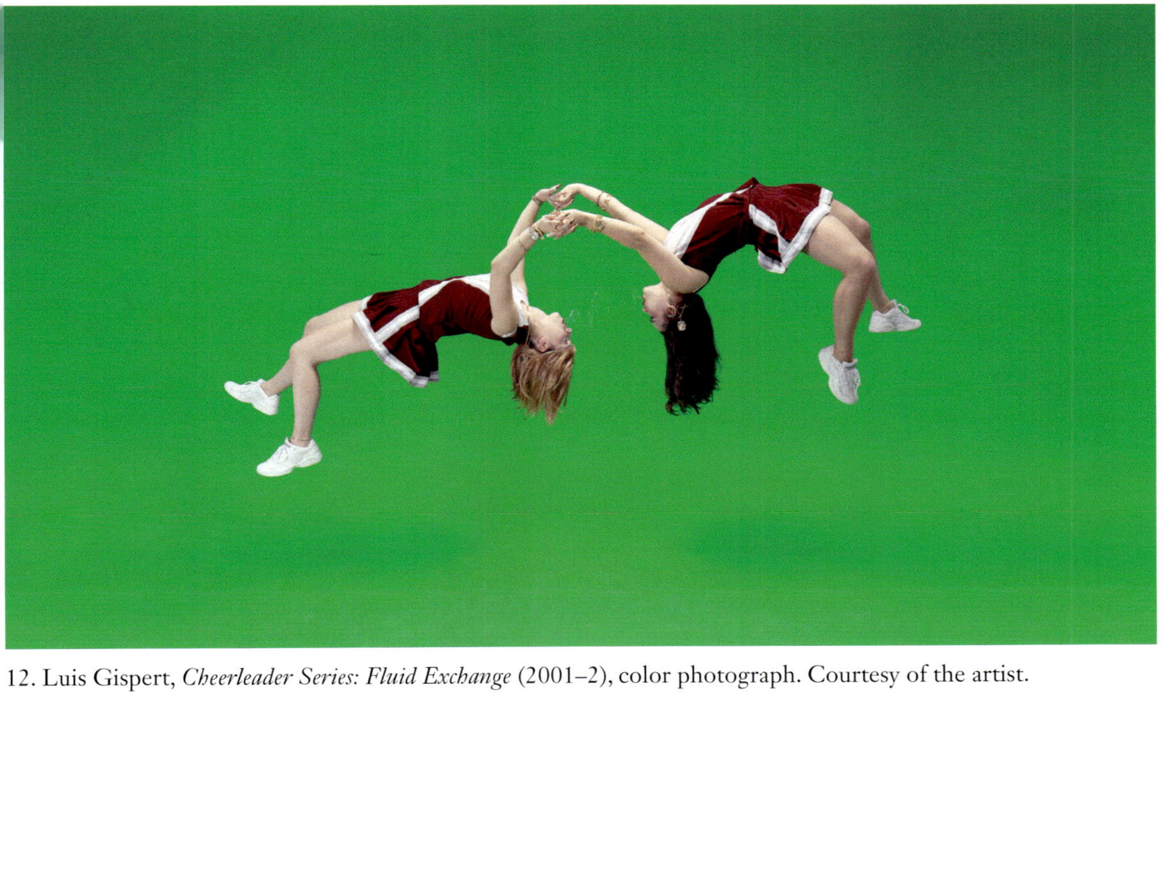

12. Luis Gispert, *Cheerleader Series: Fluid Exchange* (2001–2), color photograph. Courtesy of the artist.

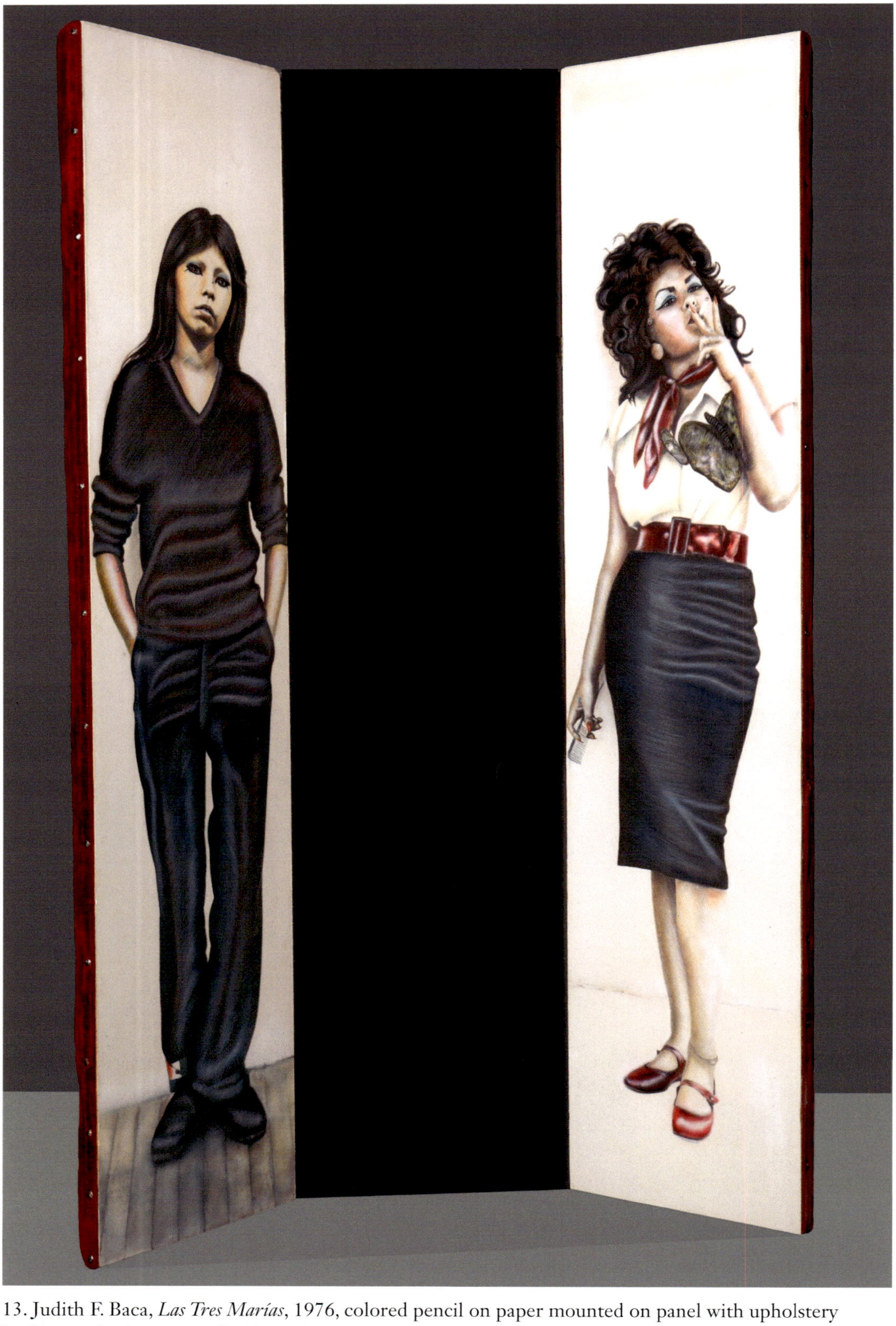

13. Judith F. Baca, *Las Tres Marías*, 1976, colored pencil on paper mounted on panel with upholstery backing and mirror, overall: 68¼ × 50¼ × 2¼ in. (173.4 × 127.6 × 5.7 cm). Smithsonian American Art Museum, SAAM-1998.162A-C_3, museum purchase made possible by William T. Evans, 1998.162A-C, Image courtesy of SPARC Archives, SPARCinLA.org. © 1976, Judith F. Baca.

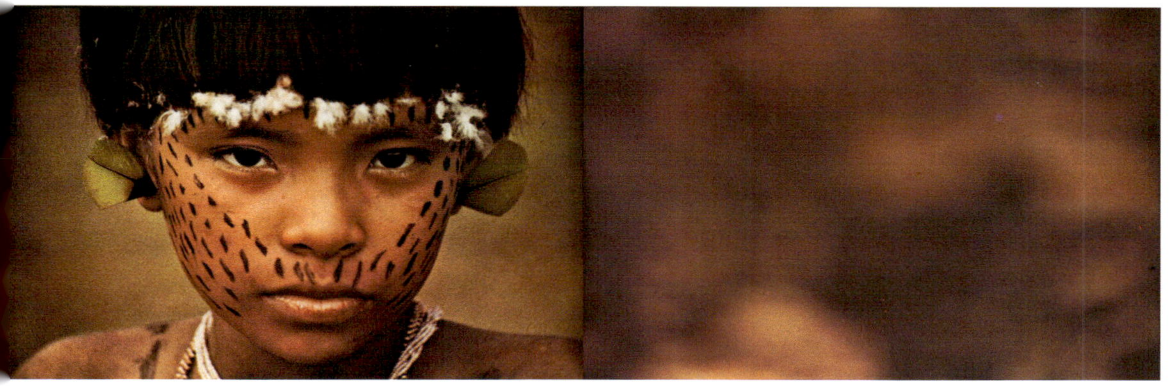

14. Claudia Andujar and George Love, *Amazônia*, Praxis, 1978, interior pages. Courtesy of Galeria Vermelho.

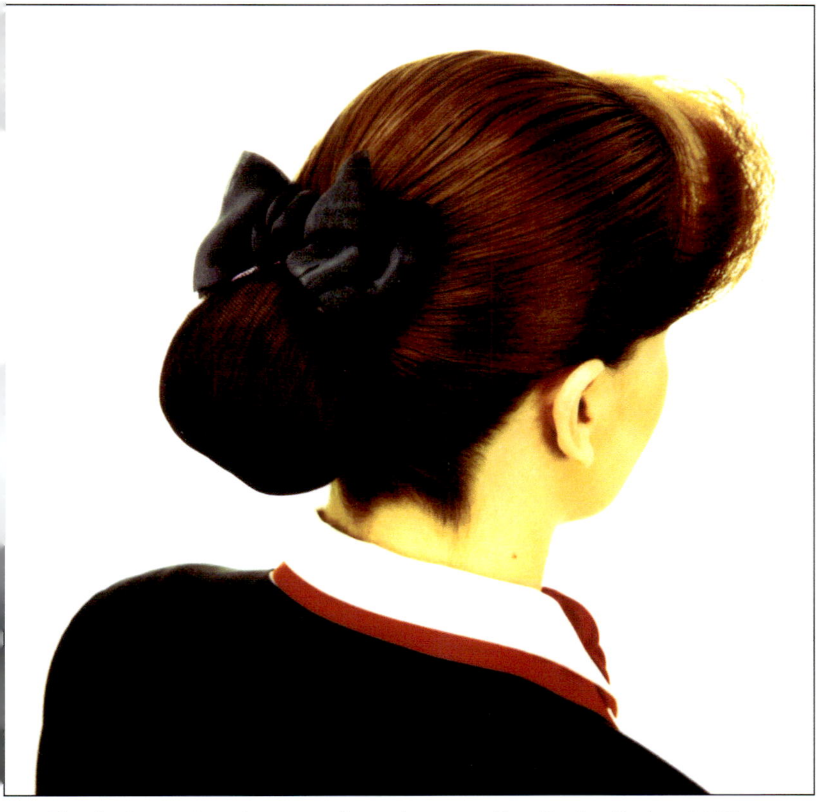

15. Claudia Jaguaribe, *Aeromoça*, from *Aeroporto* (São Paulo: Codex, 2002), interior page. Courtesy of Galeria Vermelho.

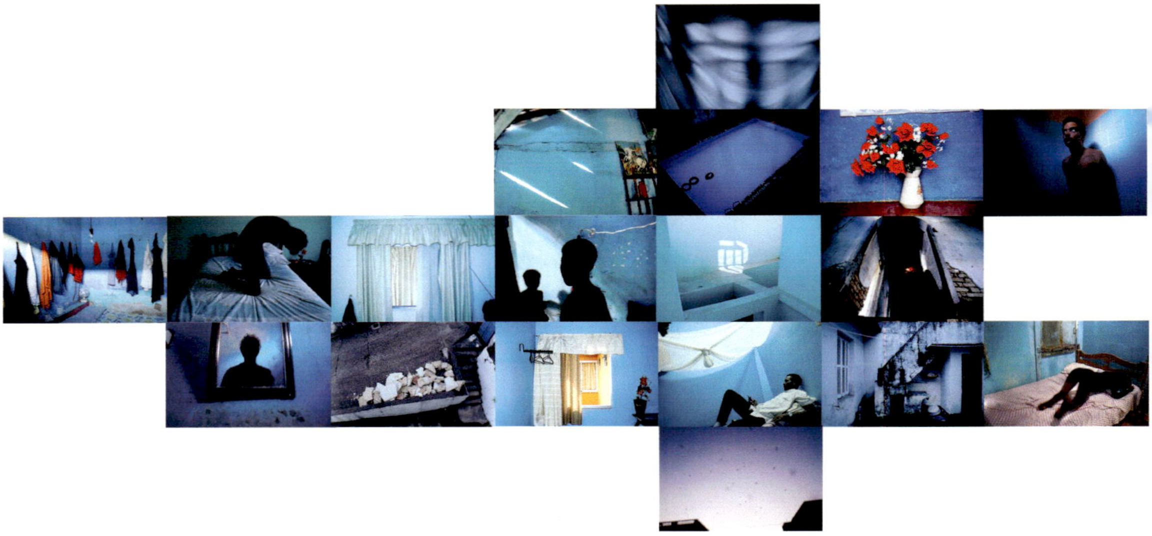

16. João Castilho, *Hotel Tropical*, 2014, artist's edition, interior pages. Courtesy of the artist.

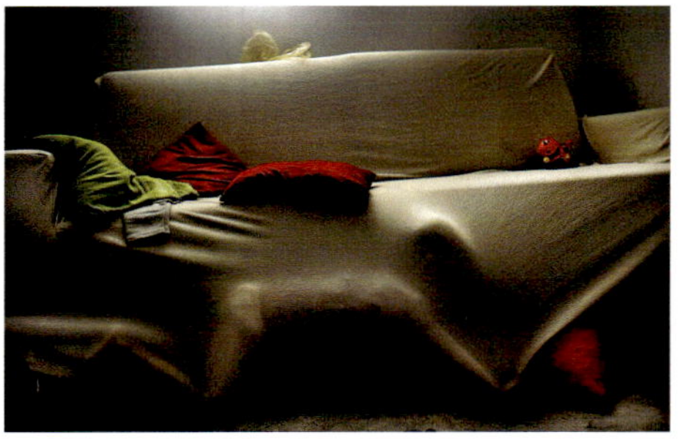

17. Cia de Foto, *Caixa de sapatos* (video film still), 2008, video (Alex Carvalho), sound (Guab). Courtesy of the artists.

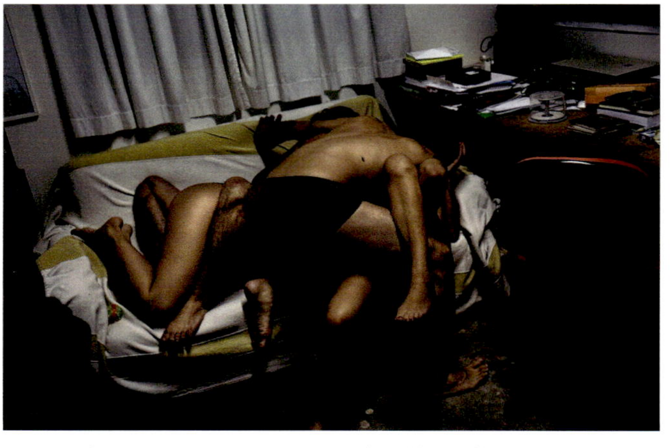

18. Cia de Foto, *Caixa de sapatos* (video film still), 2008, video (Alex Carvalho), sound (Guab). Courtesy of the artists.

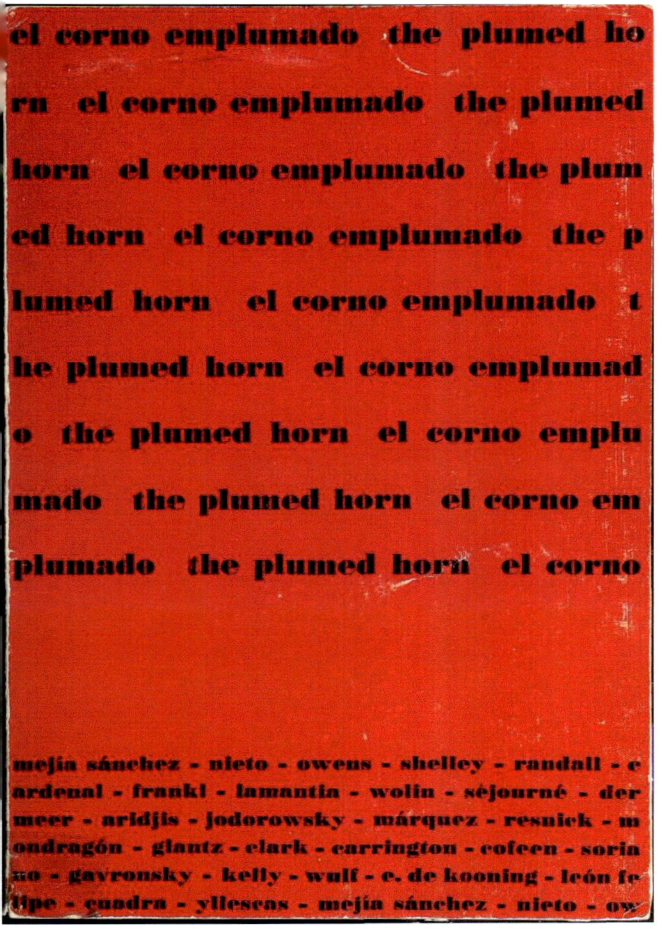

19. *El corno emplumado* 1, edited by Margaret Randall and Sergio Mondragón, 1962, cover. Courtesy of Margaret Randall.

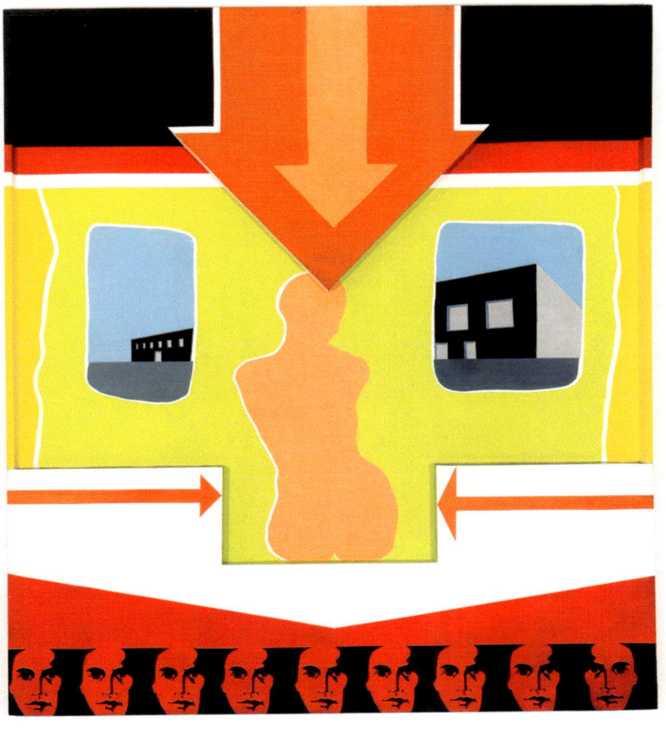

20. Felipe Ehrenberg, *Arte conceptual*, 1968, acrylic on wood board (200 × 180 × 5.5 cm), Museo Universitario de Arte Contemporáneo, MUAC, Mexico City (DiGAV-UNAM), photo by Oswaldo Ruiz. Courtesy of MUAC.

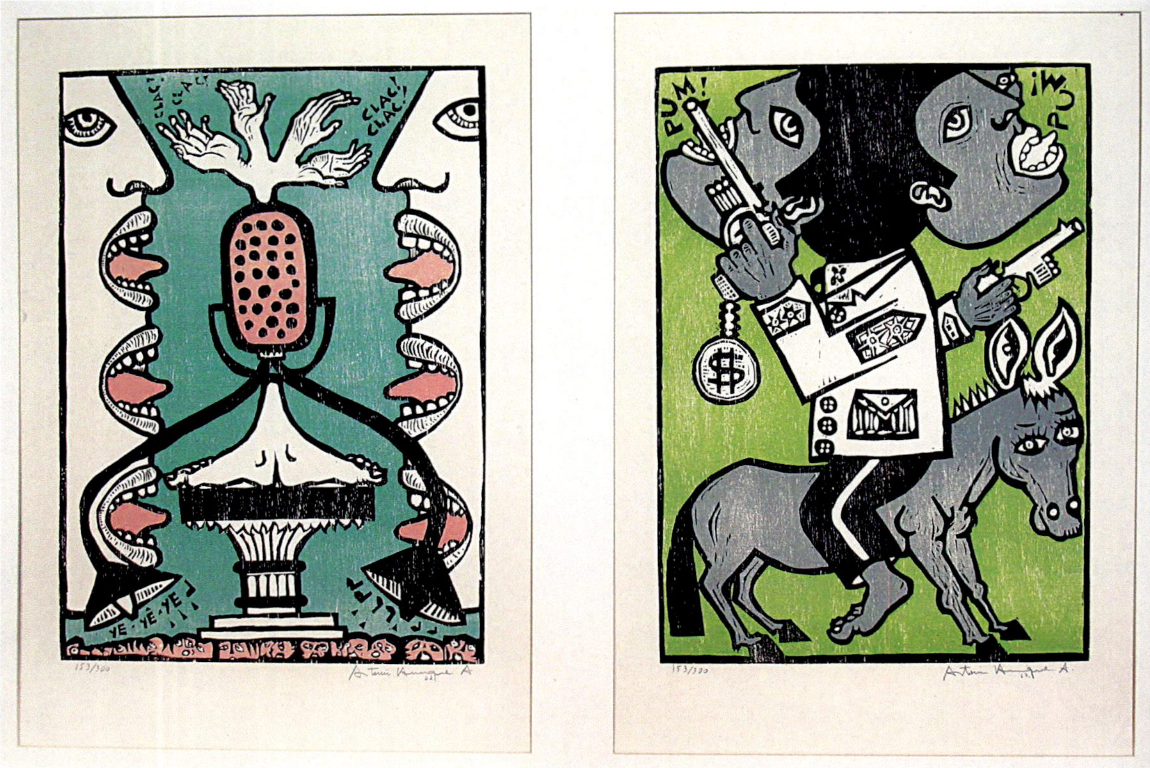

21. Antônio Henrique Amaral, *O idolatrado* and *Passatempo século xx* from *O meu e o seu: impressõe*, from *O meu e o seu: Impressões de nosso tempo*, 1967, print series. © Instituto Antonio Henrique Amaral.

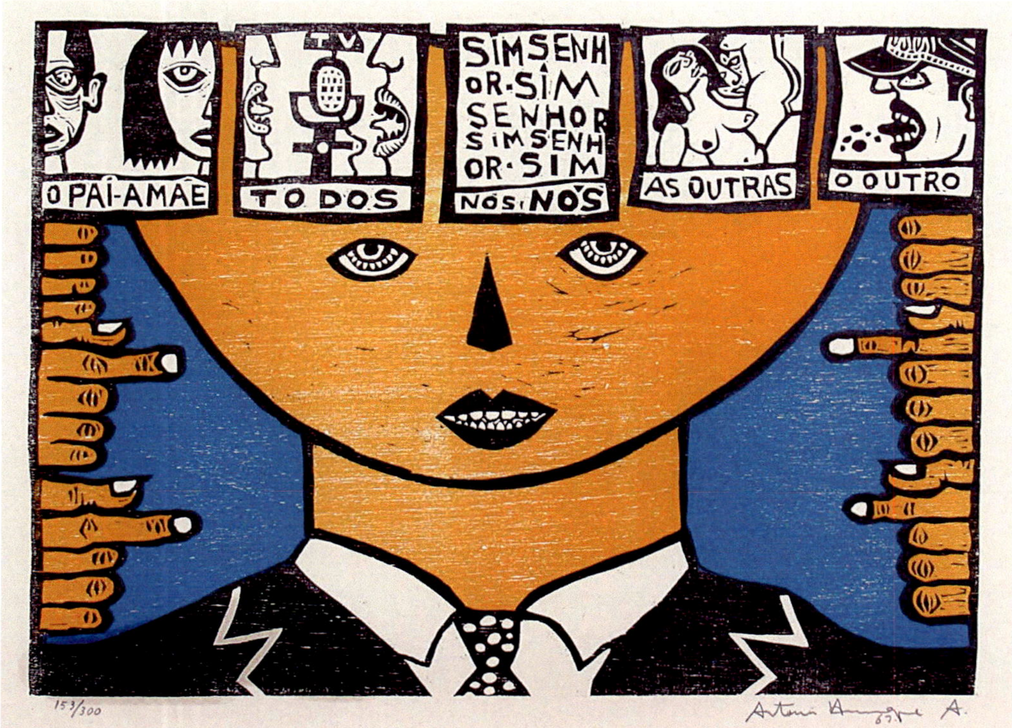

22. Antônio Henrique Amaral, *Personagem contemporâneo*, from *O meu e o seu: Impressões de nosso tempo*, 1967, print series. © Instituto Antonio Henrique Amaral.

23. Rupert García, *Black Man and Flag*, 1967, silkscreen. Courtesy of Rena Bransten Gallery, San Francisco, CA © Rupert Garcia.

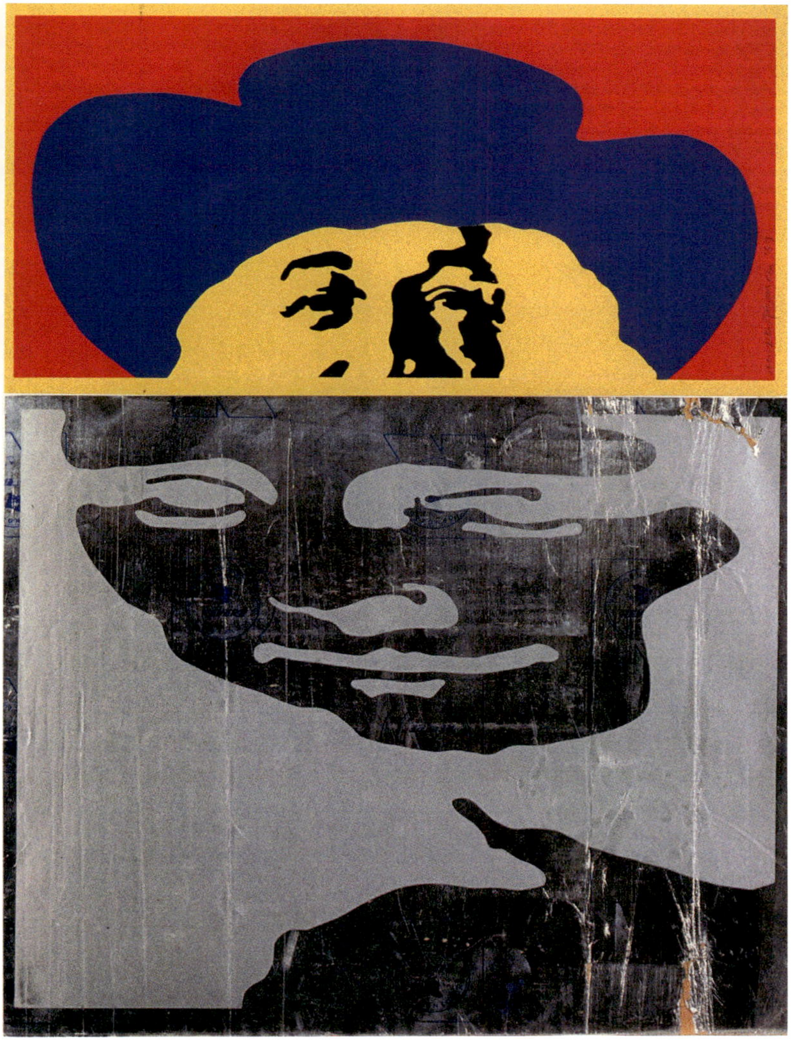

24. Rupert García, *Decay Dance*, 1969, silkscreen. Courtesy of Rena Bransten Gallery, San Francisco, CA © Rupert Garcia.

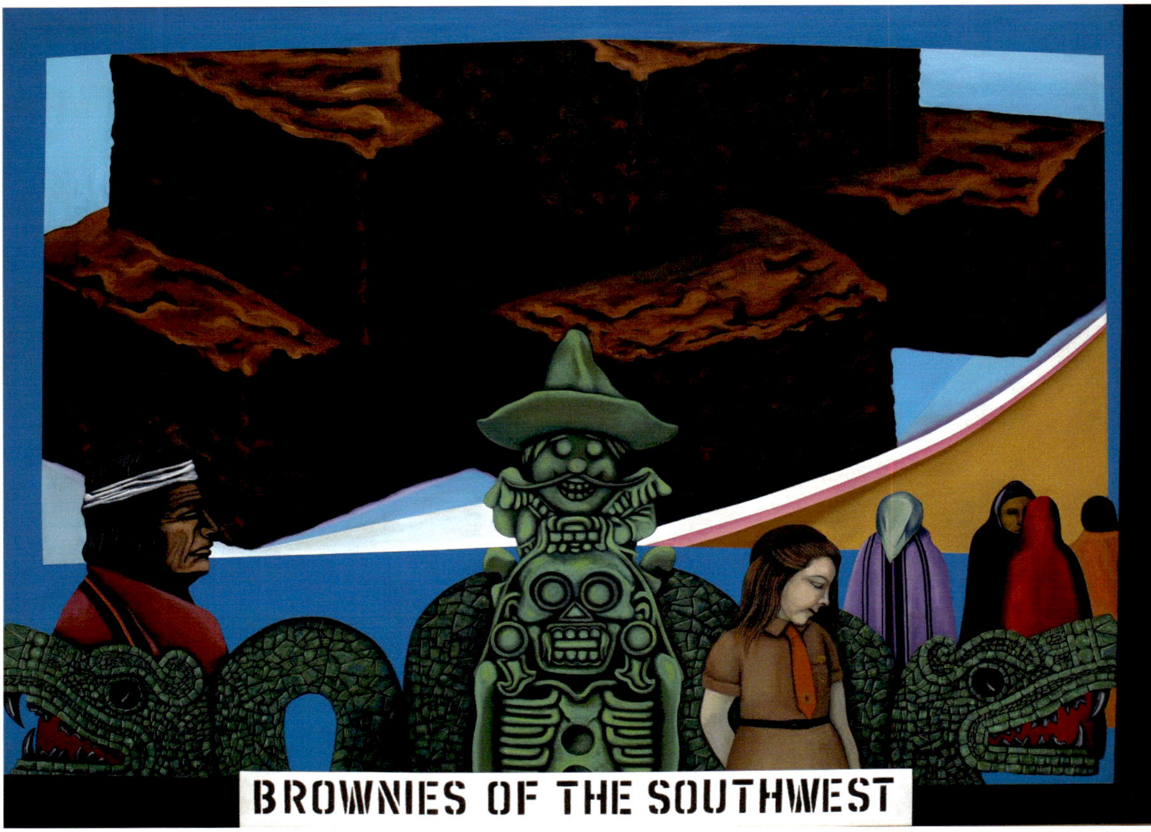

25. Melesio Casas, *Humanscape 62, Brownies of the Southwest*, 1970, acrylic on canvas, 73 × 97 in. (185.4 × 246.4 cm). Smithsonian American Art Museum, Museum purchase through the Luisita L. and Franz H. Denghausen Endowment, 2012.37 © 1970, The Mel Casas Family Trust.

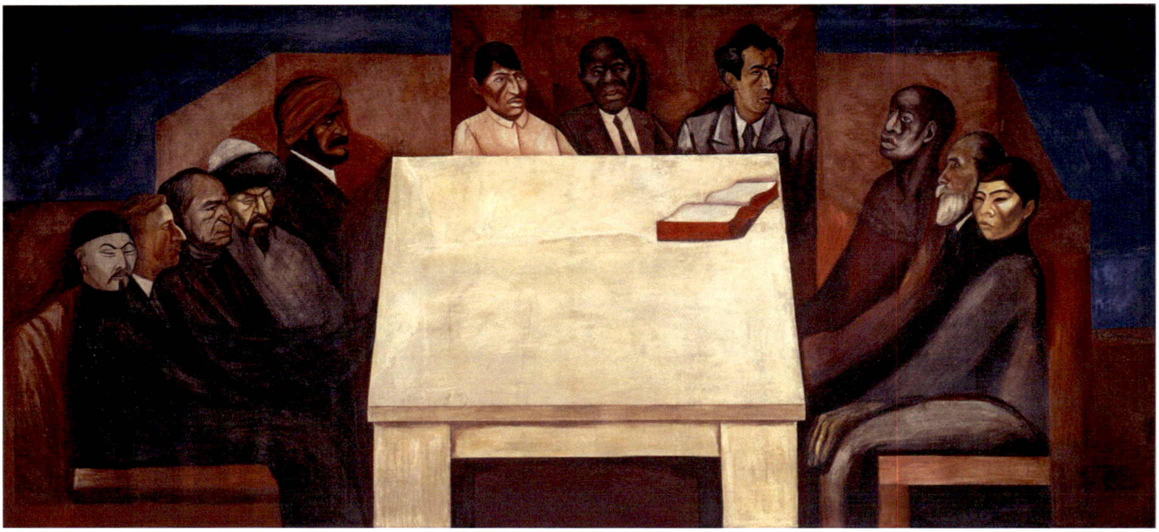

26. José Clemente Orozco, *Call to Revolution and Table of Universal Brotherhood*, 1930–31, The New School, mural. Artists Rights Society (ARS), New York.

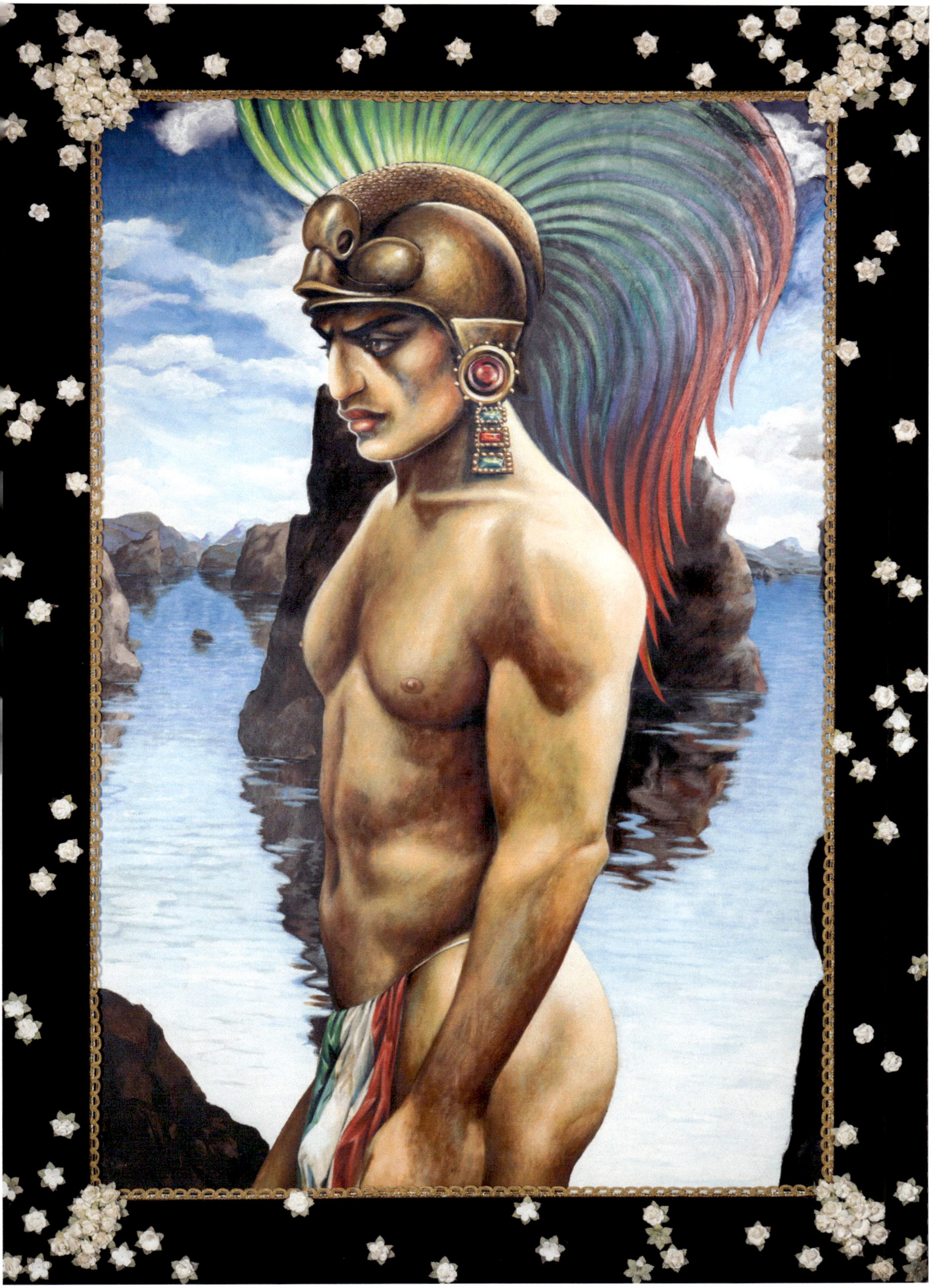

27. Javier de la Garza, *Cuauhtémoc (Captura de Cuauhtémoc, "Toma tu puñal, hábreme* [*sic*] *las venas, déjame desangrar, etc. etc."* / *The Capture of Cuauhtémoc: "Take your dagger, open my veins, let me bleed, etc. etc."*), 1986, acrylic and oil on canvas, passementerie, velvet, paper, and plastic flowers on wood, 222 × 155.5 cm, Museo Universitario de Arte Contemporáneo, MUAC, Mexico City (DiGAV-UNAM). Photo by Francisco Kochen. Courtesy of MUAC.

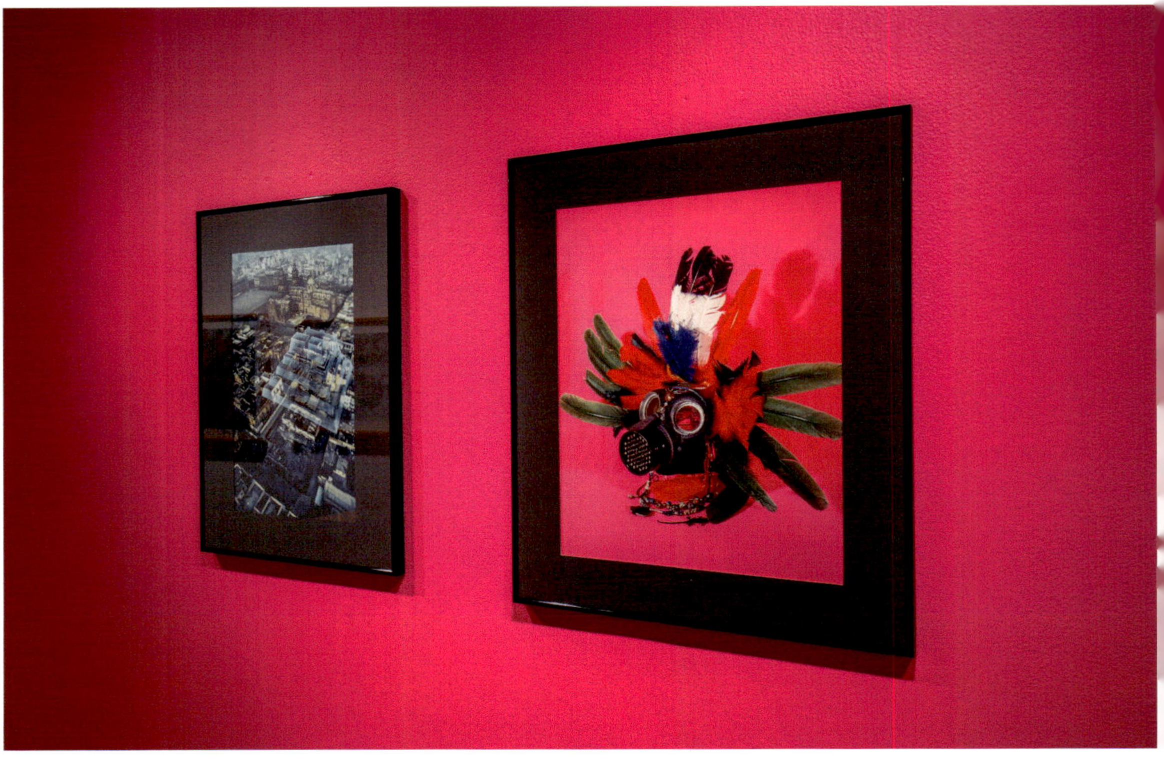

28. Celia Álvarez Muñoz, *Petrocoatl*, 1992, cibachrome, installation photo by Alex Barber. Courtesy of Art League Houston.

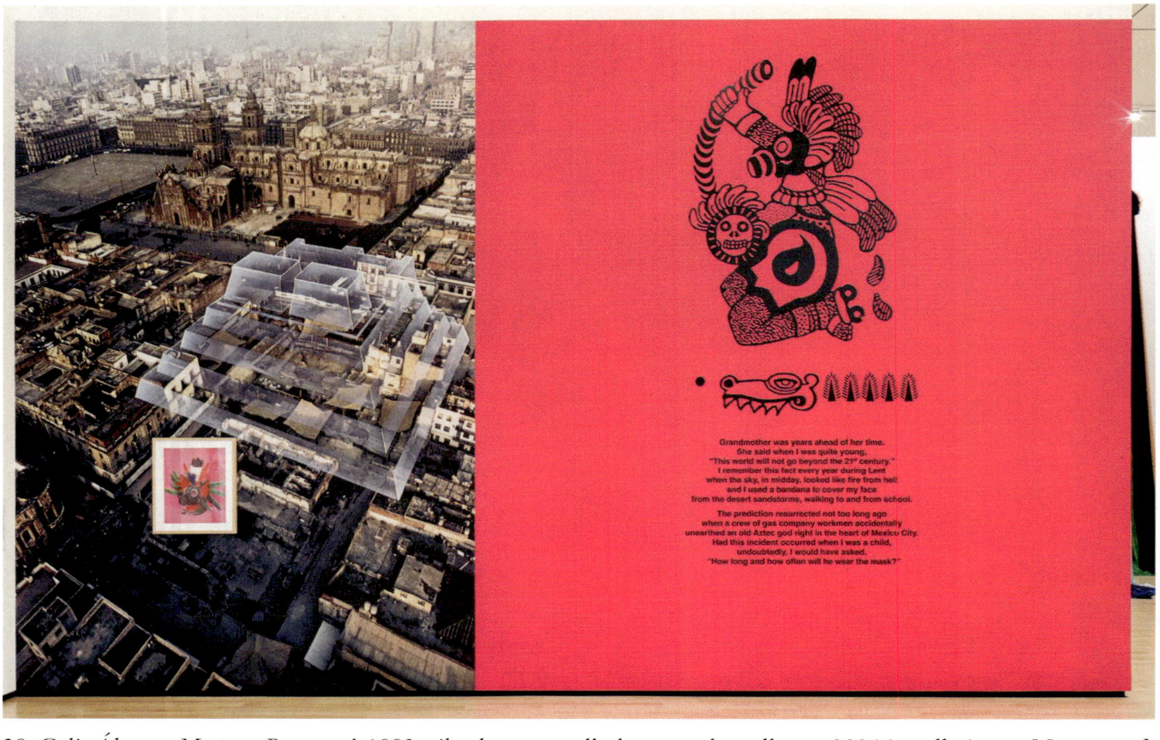

29. Celia Álvarez Muñoz, *Petrocoatl*, 1992, cibachrome, wall photograph, wall text, 2024 installation at Museum of Contemporary Art San Diego (MCASD). Photo by Daniel Lang. Courtesy of Museum of Contemporary Art San Diego and Radius Books.

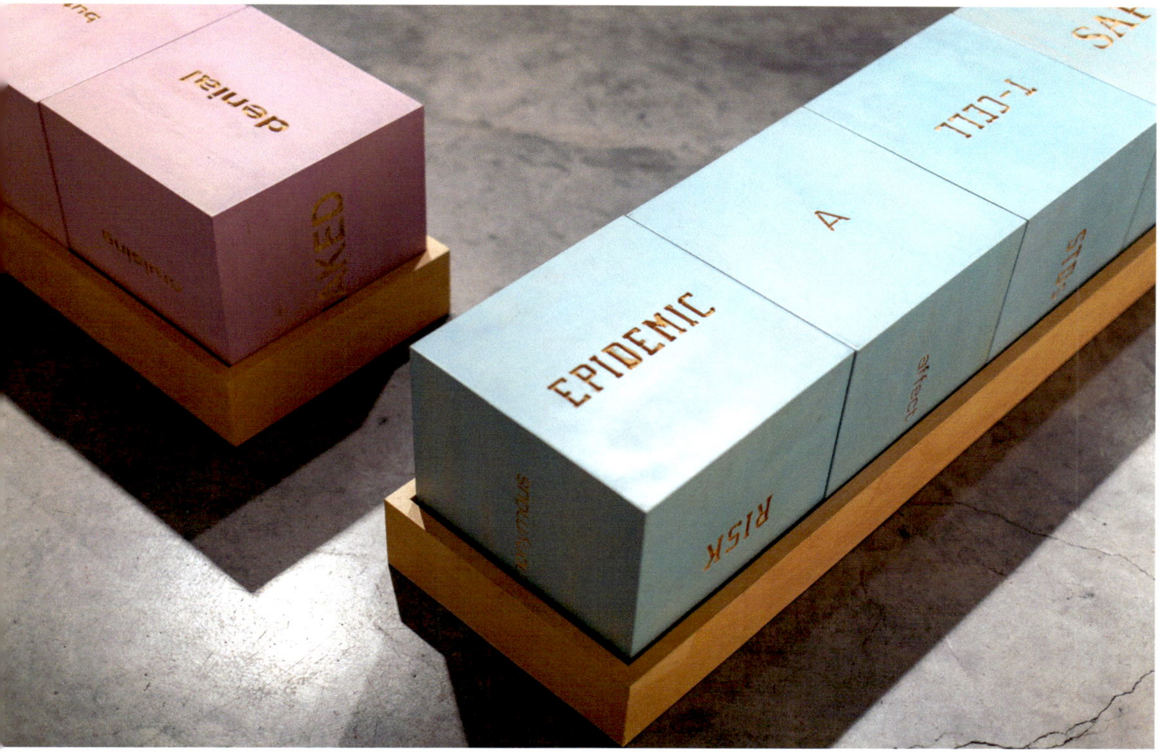

30. Celia Álvarez Muñoz, *A Brand New Ball Game*, 1994, Capp Street Projects, 2020, installation at Art League Houston. Photo by Alex Barber. Courtesy of Art League Houston.

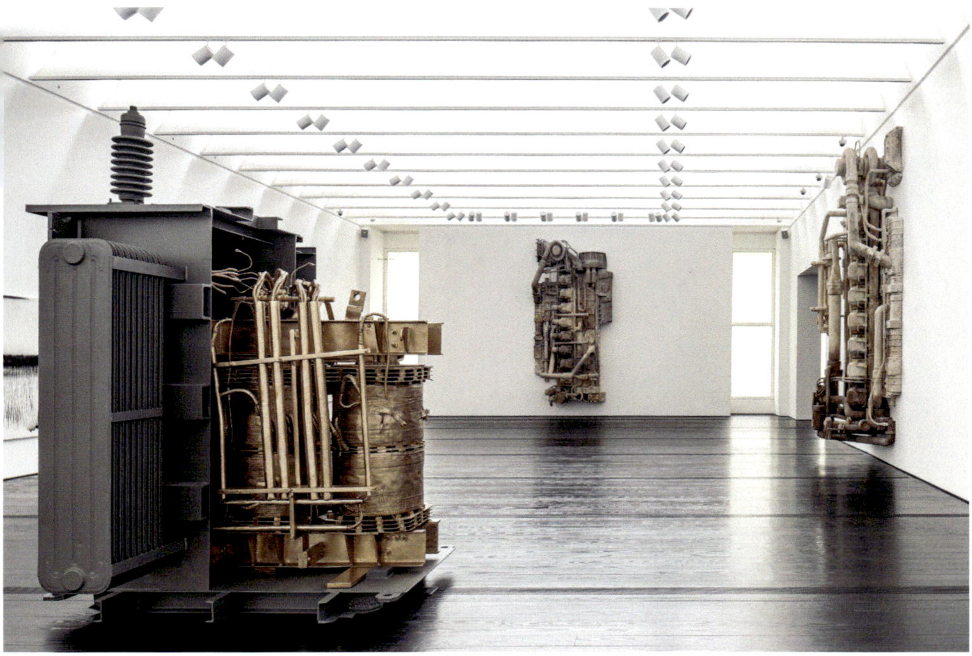

31. Allora & Calzadilla, *Specters of Noon* (installation view), 2020, The Menil Collection, *Blackout* (*center*), power transformer, bronze, electricity, vocalists, 120½ × 85½ × 78¾ inches (306.1 × 217.2 ×200 cm); and *Manifest*, bat and bird guano, side A: 180 × 84 × 42.5 in. (449.6 × 213.4 ×97.8 cm), side B: 180 × 82 × 39 in. (449.6 × 208.3 × 99.1 cm), commissioned by Leslie and Brad Bucher for exhibition at the Menil Collection. Photo by Paul Hester. Courtesy of Lisson Gallery, New York and London © Allora & Calzadilla.

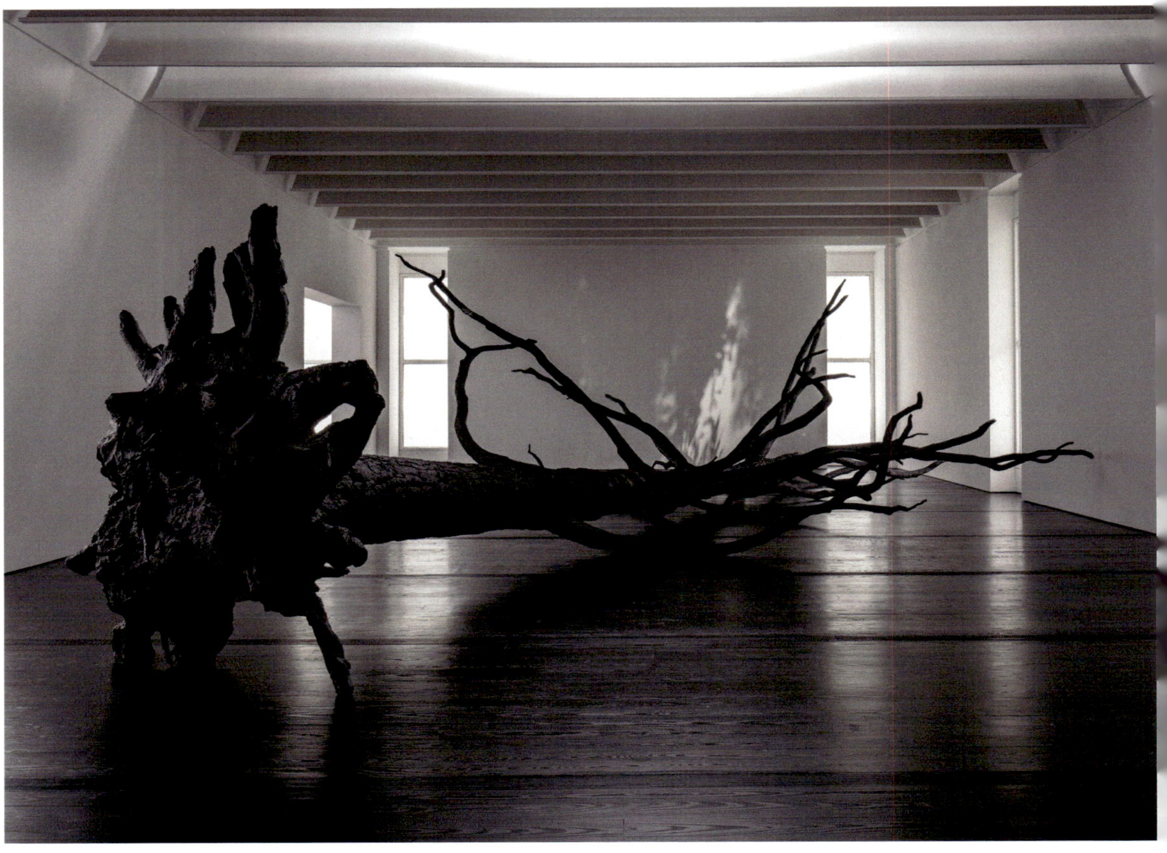

32. Allora & Calzadilla, *Penumbra* (installation view), 2020, digital projection with sound, dimensions variable, courtesy Gladstone Gallery, New York and Brussels; and *Entelechy*, 2020, coal, vocalists, 171¼ × 3743/16 × 581¼ in. (434.9 × 950.5 × 1476.4 cm). Photo by Paul Hester. Courtesy of Galerie Chantal Crousel, Paris, and Lisson Gallery, New York and London. © Allora & Calzadilla.

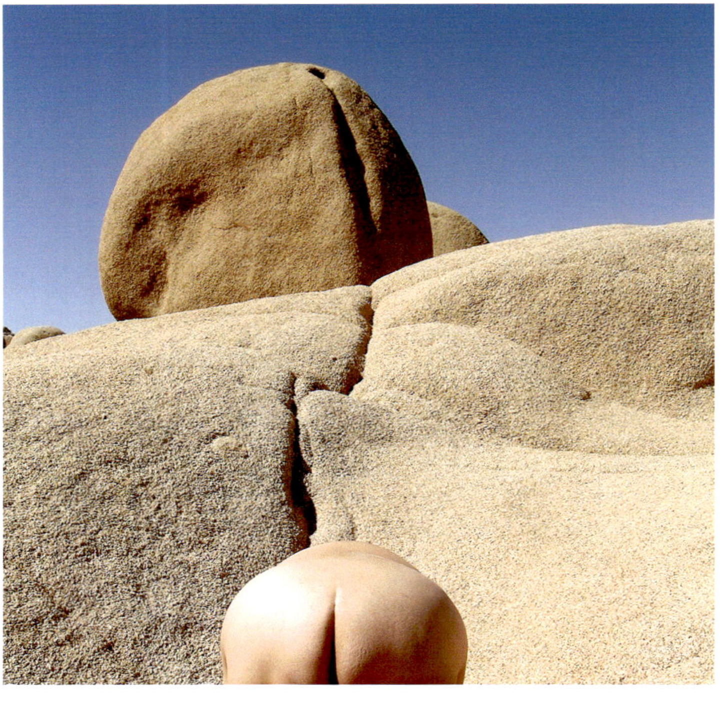

33. Laura Aguilar, *Grounded, Untitled*, 2007. Courtesy of UCLA Chicano Studies Research Center. © Laura Aguilar Trust LLC.

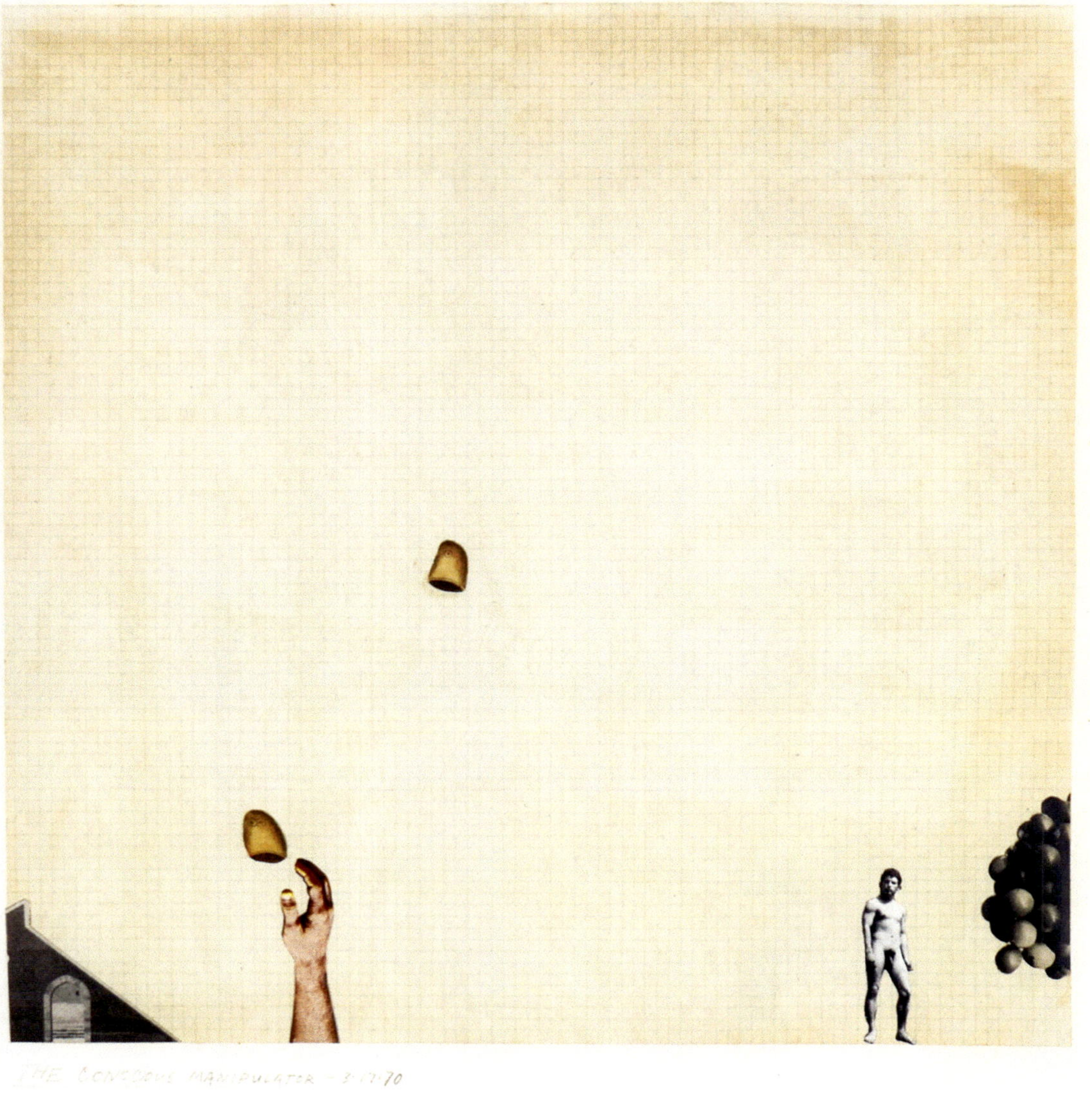

34. Carlos Almaraz, *The Conscious Manipulator*, 1970, mixed-media collage on paper, 14 × 10 in. (35.6 × 26.7 cm). Collection of Elsa Flores and The Estate of Carlos Almaraz Carlos Almaraz.

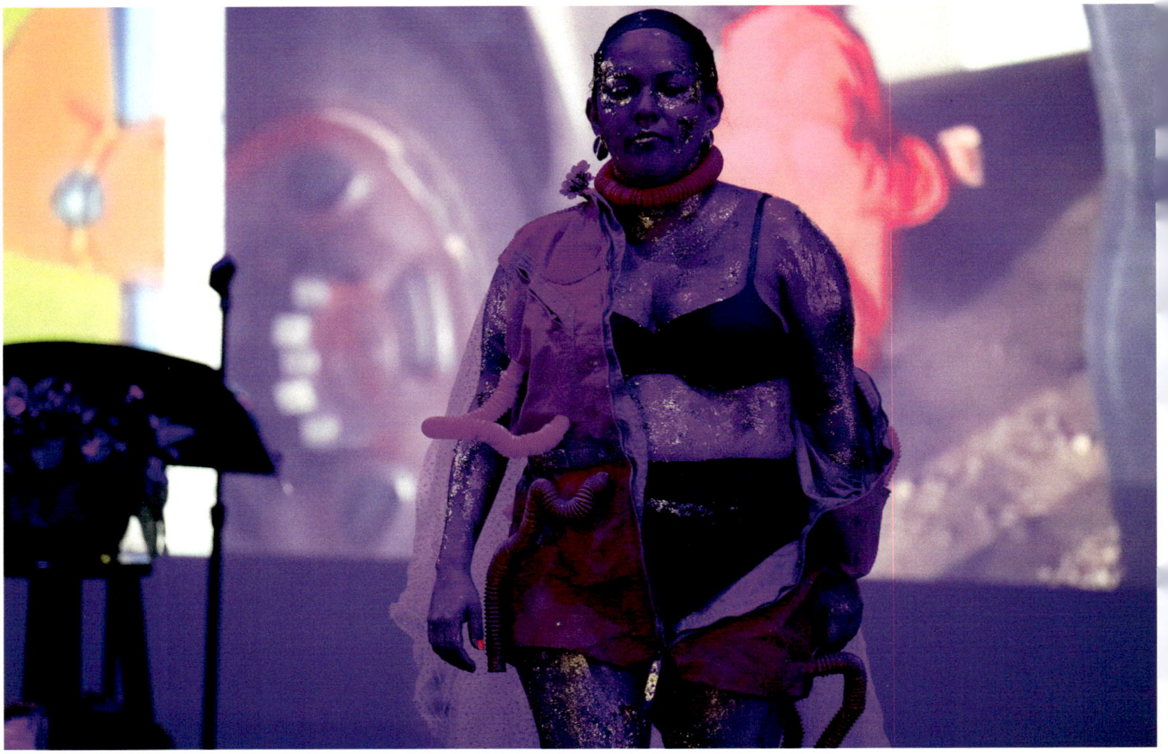

35. Jennif(f)er Tamayo, *LA QUEERADORA (Borderline)*, CounterCurrent 19, Houston, Texas, April 2019, performance. Courtesy of Cynthia Woods Mitchell Center for the Arts, Houston, Texas.

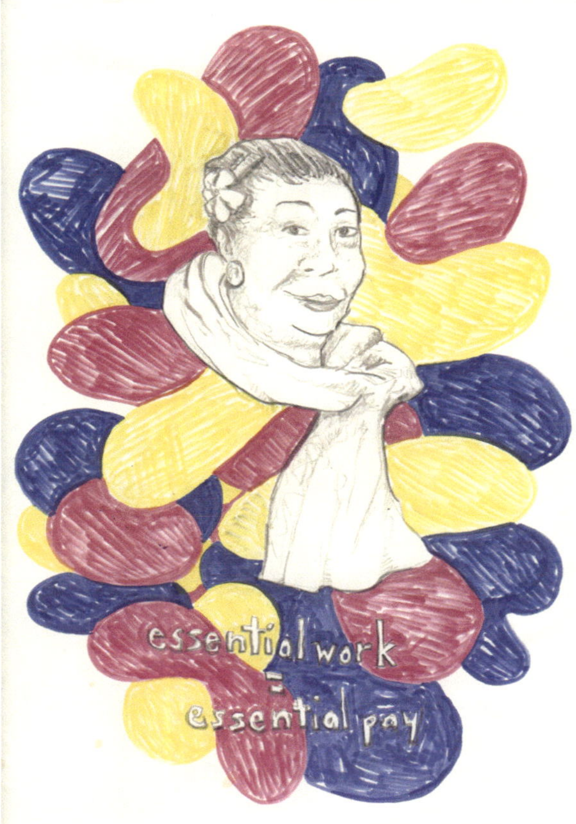

36. Jesús Macarena-Ávila, *Germscapes: Essential Worker (Lorena Borjas, 1960–2020)*, 2020, mixed media on paper. Courtesy of the artist.

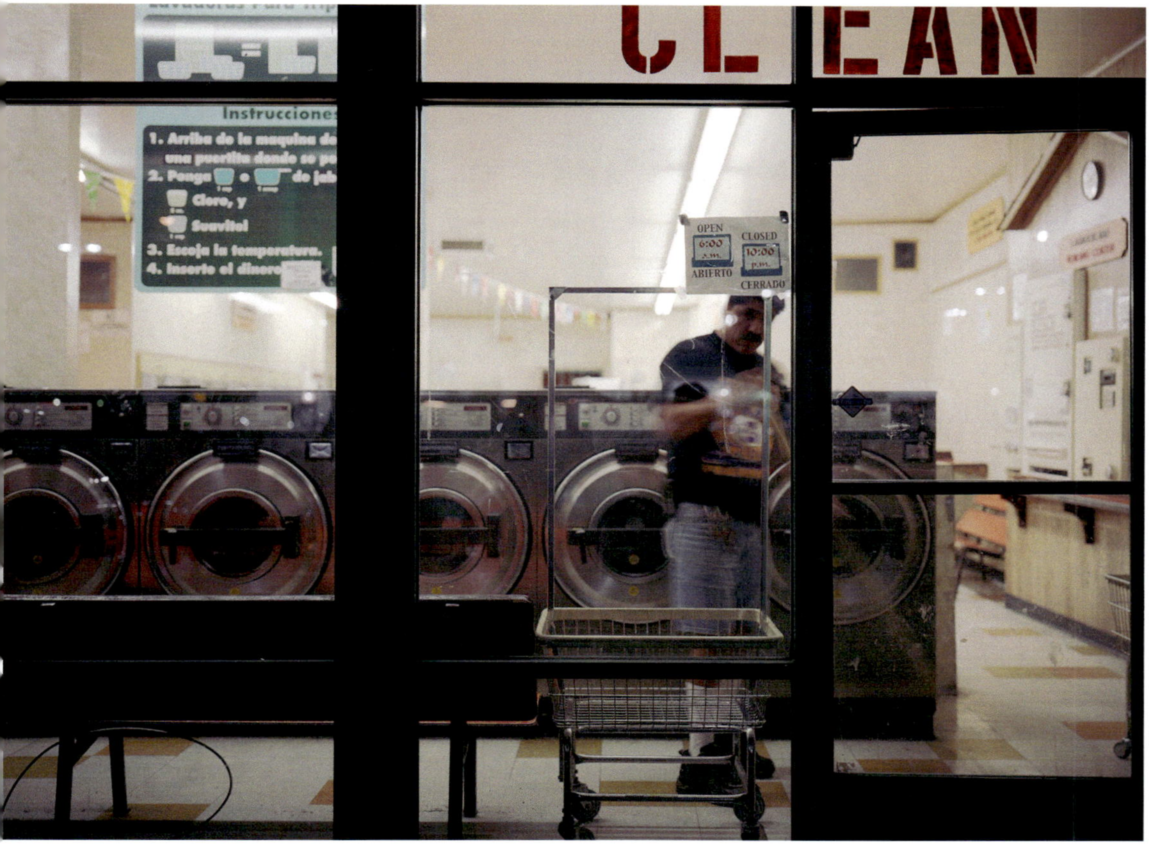

37. Christina Fernandez, *Lavandería 6*, 2002, C-print. Courtesy of Christina Fernandez and Gallery Luisotti.

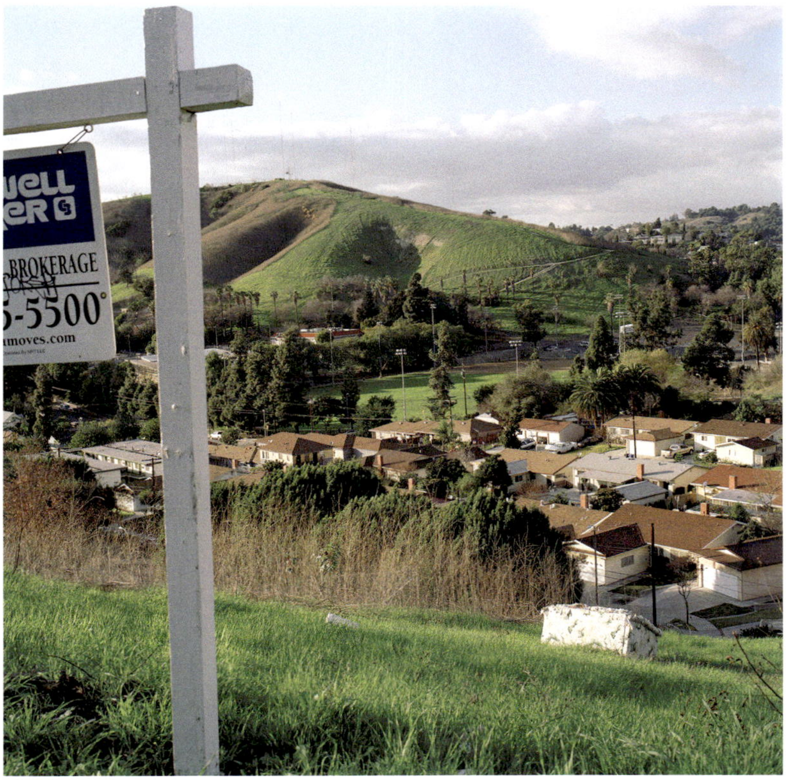

38. Christina Fernandez, *Sereno (Coldwell II)*, 2009, C-print. Courtesy of Christina Fernandez and Gallery Luisotti.

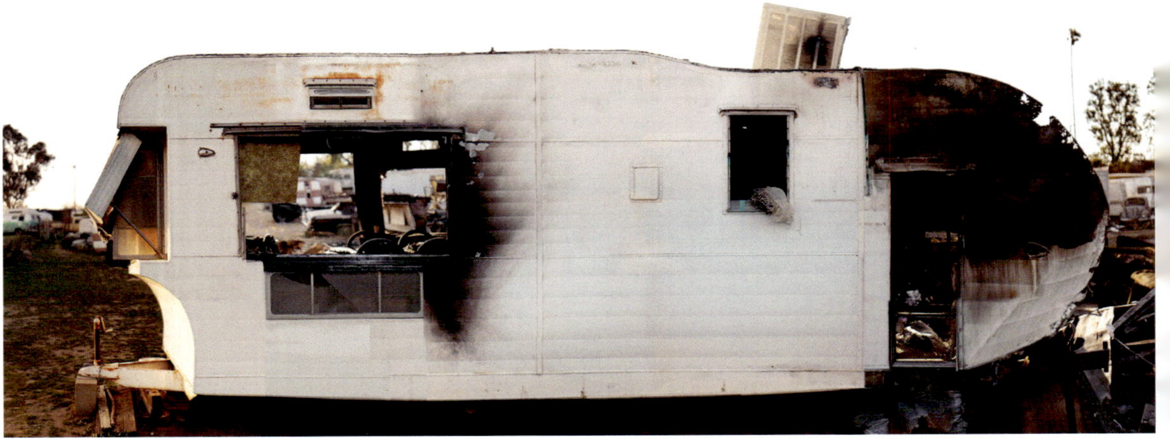

39. Christina Fernandez, *American Trailer,* 2018, C-print. Courtesy of Christina Fernandez and Gallery Luisotti.

THIRTEEN

Celia Álvarez Muñoz: "Ideas Are the Drivers"

In a body of work that now spans four decades, the multimedia art of Celia Álvarez Muñoz has never ceased to challenge and captivate, mediating commitments to both material dexterity and conceptual correlation. Formally innovative, uniquely sharp-witted, and emotionally absorbing, all together her photographs, book works, installations, and public art commissions comprise an inimitable corpus. Álvarez Muñoz has been unrelenting in her artistic scrutiny of modern life—its histories, locations, through lines—and of social contradictions on the borderlands between the United States and Mexico. Unimpressed with solemnity, abjection, or cynicism as displayed in some tendencies of the international avant-garde, and undaunted by postmodern decorum, her evolving series of works have preferred instead to kindle moods born of deep-seated curiosity, wily intelligence, and kindly humor. In her multimedia practices that marshal a cunning reassessment of value, Álvarez Muñoz avails herself of an ample bicultural heritage at once tangible and intangible. This archive includes preconquest iconography, Catholic religious imagery, life stories, family lore, popular expressions, working-class inventiveness, place-specific landmarks, commercial artifacts, media language ingenuity, sometimes alluding to vintage photographs, postcards, and other printed matter. These particulars relate by reassembling the personal experience of a cultural totality with the express aim of both confirming and defying avant-garde aspirations that hold the uncommon and exceptional as ideal forms of communication, all the while code-switching between Spanish and English, between locations in the Southwest United States and the neighboring cultures of Mexico, as well as between "folk culture" and "mass culture."

* * *

The writer Robert Craig Bunch in a 2012 interview with the artist inquired about the conceptualism of her practice inasmuch as the work insists also "on such a high level of craft." Álvarez Muñoz allowed that "ideas are the drivers." She reflected: "I favor following and unraveling and embellishing them, pulling them as far apart as I can to almost a breaking point. Irony is an excellent tool, too. That's the gig with fine-tuning. I love finely crafted stuff and have deep respect for materials and tools.[1] In her unmistakable brand of ironizing that stretches the congruity of an idea between the bewilderment of lived experience, a heritage-world's connection to place, and the particulars of perception, Álvarez Muñoz mines the implicit cultural and geographic biases of the art establishment, and the space between recorded fact and narrative fantasy, evoking memory-language and everyday life in US American consumer society. In this regard her contributions bear a family resemblance to those of fellow makers acclaimed by the contemporary mainstream. Her corpus has had an impact as influential and groundbreaking certainly as that of Jenny Holzer and Barbara Kruger, whose works she was early to notice on the alternate pathways of her own practice.[2] Consider Holzer's *Inflammatory Essays* (1979–82) or *Truisms* (1984); and Kruger's *I shop therefore I am* (1987) or *Untitled (It's a small world but not if you have to clean it)* (1990). Álvarez Muñoz eschewed the fiction of an ethnically or racially unmarked position represented in the disembodied countersubject of 1980s and 1990s feminism, with its own presumption of a universal voice betraying a corporate or technological unconscious. Contrary to the inflammatory mode of expected style of critical inquiry, Álvarez Muñoz has exercised the spell of fascination, ever prepared to unsettle a social scene of supremacy and make it foreign to itself.

Similar to Kruger—who in 1966 was employed with Condé Nast, working in the design department at *Mademoiselle* magazine in New York—but earlier, Álvarez Muñoz began her career as a graphic designer in El Paso, Texas.[3] A line drawing with copy produced in 1961 for the White House Department Store encapsulates the verbal and visual dynamic of advertising that in one way or another underpinned her later art practice (fig. 44). The half-page vertical newspaper notice, targeted to aspiring young women, regular patrons of the store's Jr. Circle, Mezzanine, features the season's fashion items as donned by three variously scaled figures in beehive and bobbed hairstyles, capri pants and pedal pushers, pleated culottes, and a "scoop- neck blouse, solid white, or pepper-cuffed white crop top, each [$]5.98." Álvarez Muñoz renders the trim gray-scale figures in skin tones that suggest a light shade of brown, and gendered commercial posturings that sociologist Erving Goffman later described as advertising's "hyper-ritualization" of types: "all the occasions and senses in which the ideal is not exhibited having been cut away," and often reconfigured by means of "mockery, and other forms of unseriousness."[4]

Álvarez Muñoz further lampooned the conventions of the universal by weaponizing the second stanza of "What Are Little Boys Made Of?," the traditional nursery rhyme that served as early schooling in attributions of binary gender roles. ("What are little girls made of? / Sugar and spice, and all that's nice.")[5] With a sardonic interrogative, *Sugar 'n Spice?*, followed by the bilingual quip *Qué Nice!*, Álvarez Muñoz employed the working-class function of the *vacilada*, a Mexican and Mexican American verbal tactic of everyday interaction

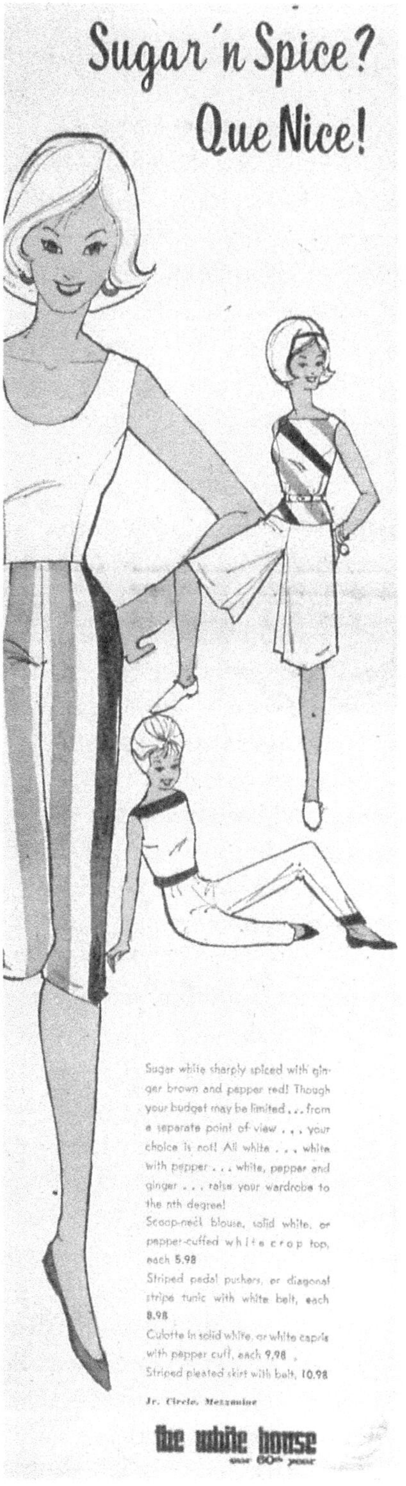

Figure 44. Celia Álvarez Muñoz, "Sugar and Spice," advertisement for the White House Department Store, El Paso, Texas, 1961.

given to reversing the social, sexual, and racial hierarchies with a playfulness that deflates the power relation of any pretense to solemnity or aggrandizement.[6] Working alongside the copywriter, the artist lent ethnically inflected visual ironies to ad copy describing the outfit pattern as being "Sugar white sharply spiced with ginger brown and pepper red!"[7] Devoid of belligerence, the image-text derided the advertisement's goal by conventionalizing conventions in the mechanism of hype.[8] It fired a skeptical wink at El Paso readers for whom the standard language of advertising was either culturally unpersuasive or unwelcoming. Art historian Kobena Mercer identifies the vernacular as that "entangled space in which 'popular' and 'official' worldviews are constantly antagonized."[9] With startling critical vitality, and as prefigured in the advertisement, Álvarez Muñoz aligned with the popular to eventually deflate official understandings of conceptual art. This process staged covert but no less theoretical insurrections of the kind expressed in the vacilada of *Sugar 'n Spice? Qué Nice!*

Consider the writing of Sol LeWitt in "Paragraphs on Conceptual Art" (1967) and "Sentences on Conceptual Art" (1969). LeWitt characterized the art he had in mind as being "usually free from the dependence on the skill of the artist as a craftsman." He held that the "objective of the artist who is concerned with conceptual art" is to beget work that is "mentally interesting to the spectator," rigorous to the extent that it remains "emotionally dry." He quickly added that there is "no reason to suppose, however, that the conceptual artist is out to bore the viewer. It is only the expectation of an emotional kick, to which one conditioned to expressionist art is accustomed, that would deter the viewer from perceiving this art."[10] Even as emotion and expression had been abstracted in general from literalist art, and from LeWitt's method in particular, he later asserted that conceptual artists—akin to "mystics rather than rationalists"—were well prepared to "leap to conclusions that logic cannot reach," and that these noncontradictory judgments "lead to new experience."[11]

While LeWitt had claimed that to "work with a plan that is preset is one way of avoiding subjectivity," his ambivalence about the first-person viewpoint and the question of narrative deepened with his contribution to the conceptual iteration of the artist's book, a work entitled *Autobiography* (1980).[12] Consistent with conceptualism's matter-of-factness, LeWitt's book contains 1,116 black-and-white photographs distributed into grids of nine square pictures on 126 unnumbered 10¼ × 10¼-inch pages (fig. 45). The inventory is an exhaustive documentation of the objects most visibly composing the immediate environment of the artist's studio on Hester Street in Manhattan. Rows of images depict books, records, artworks, electrical outlets, tools, clocks, kitchen utensils, file folders, a television, a record player, and other electronic devices. Most prominently, the cover features family pictures and memorabilia and objects belonging to the artist's father, Doctor A. LeWitt. Nevertheless, the publisher's jacket blurb for *Autobiography* insisted that "every reference is the same size with no object in [LeWitt's] space more important than another."[13]

Álvarez Muñoz inherited this variety of seemingly irresolvable antagonisms—between the empirical and the theoretical, between personal history and information, between storytelling and statistics—to the extent that conceptual art conferred the status of common

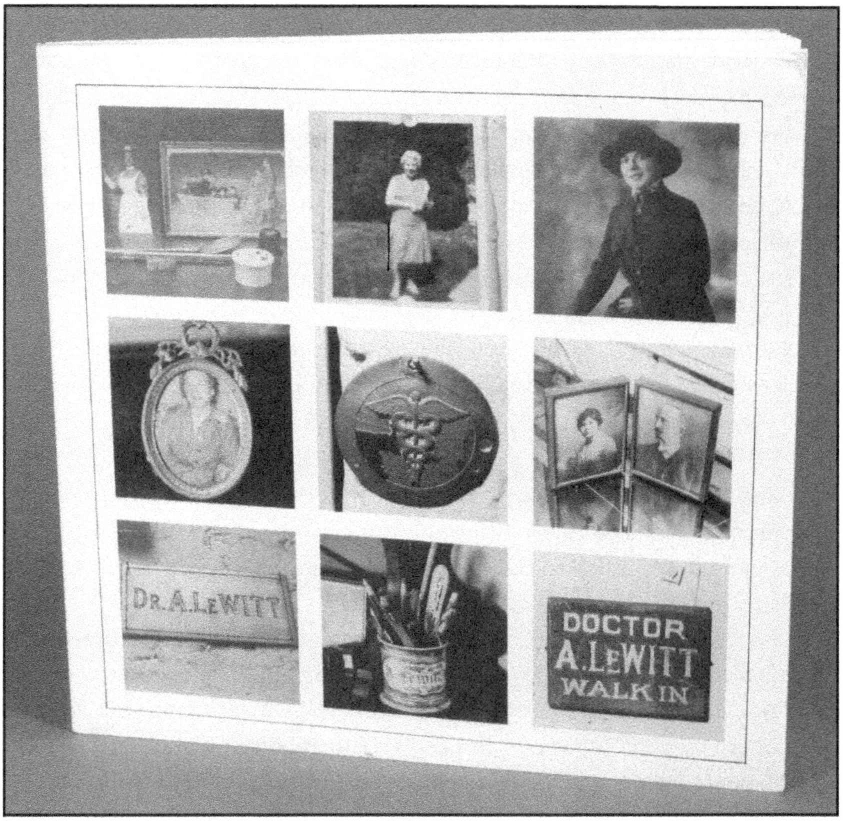

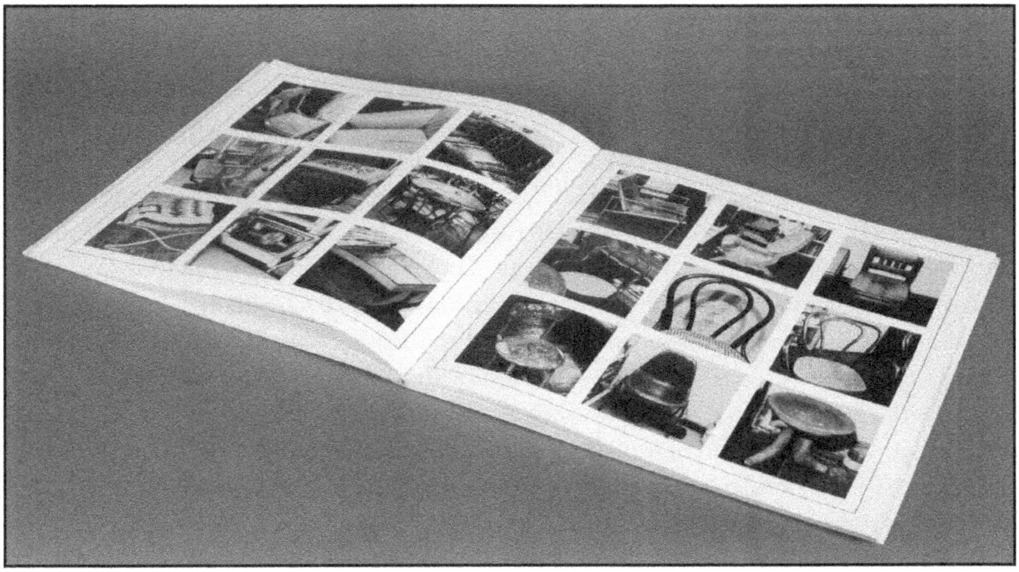

FIGURE 45. Sol LeWitt, *Autobiography* (New York City: Multiples, 1980), artist's book: (a) cover; (b) interior pages. © 2025 The LeWitt Estate/Artists Rights Society (ARS), New York.

sense to purity of method. Emerging in the early 1980s, the Texas artist turned as well to the modernist grid, and to the sameness and variation amplified by the photomechanical process, especially with her *Enlightenments* series (1980–83), a form of bookwork in the expanded field. She subjected the language games of conceptual art to vernacular wisdom and wordplay, prompting visual tutorials about the world-bound relationships contained in accounts of upbringing.[14] Since then her socially engaged art and ethics have been scored in the key of insinuation, undertones that flout the assumptions of conceptual art, and of the avant-garde more generally, by accentuating the human circumstance and its contingencies. Álvarez Muñoz has demonstrated that tautology is no match for the culture concept; that systemic thought is often at the expense of lived experience; that reason's commitment to noncontradictory logic advances the dominant culture as universal; and that all knowledge is relentlessly accident-prone.

In the context of numerous events in 1992, organized internationally to celebrate the dubious fifth centenary of the "Discovery of America"—but also the Native American counter-quincentenary that led to the Quito Declaration and to a summit held by the Indigenous Alliance of the Americas on "Five Hundred Years of Resistance"—Álvarez Muñoz produced a work for an exhibition at the Mexican Museum in San Francisco entitled *The Chicano Codices: Encountering Art of the Americas* (fig. 46).[15] According to guest curator Marcos Sánchez-Tranquilino, the exhibition's aim was "to reinstate the Indigenous art form of the codex as a contemporary Chicano artistic medium while symbolically gathering the dispersed and destroyed pre-Hispanic picture books of the Americas."[16] Alongside works by Amalia Mesa-Bains, Barbara Carrasco, Celia Herrera Rodriguez, Delilah Montoya, Gronk, Harry Gamboa Jr., Kathy Vargas, and Willie Herrón, among others, Álvarez Muñoz created an installation that manifested her well-established practice of combining wall drawings, narrative texts, and photographic prints.

In *Petrocoatl, Aztec God del Fin del Mundo* (1992) the artist provided visual centering in the polychrome sketch of an imaginary Aztec god, Petrocoatl, loosely configured to resemble depictions in the *Borbonicus Codex*, "a colorful pictographic religious document that may be the only authentic Aztec book in existence," featuring images of the gods in full regalia, among them Ehecatl, Tonatiuh, Xipe Totec, Huitzilopochtli, and Tlaloc.[17] Petrocoatl was drawn in solid volumes highlighting his deep-brown skin, in a kneeling position (fig. 47). His attributes included a green-and-red-feathered ritual cape and headdress, as well as a shield with a front-facing skull design and an apron with a black oil drop referencing the petroleum industry. Covering Petrocoatl's entire head and face was a protective gas mask, equipped with a respirator, as though the deity were prepared or preparing for chemical, biological, radiological, or nuclear disaster. To his right was a black vinyl sans-serif wall text relating the following parable in a voice that registered the adult recollection of a childhood reverie:

> Grandmother was years ahead of her time.
> She said when I was quite young,
> "This world will not reach the year 2000."

I remembered this fact every year during Lent
when the sky in midday looked like fire from hell,
and I used a bandana to cover my face
from the desert sandstorms walking to and from school.

The prediction resurrected not too long ago
when a crew of gas company workmen accidentally
unearthed an old Aztec god right in the heart of Mexico City.
Had this incident occurred when I was a child,
undoubtedly, I would have asked, "How long
and how often will he wear the mask?

Suspended to the left of the Petrocoatl drawing were two framed photographs: One pictured an actual object, a feathered gas mask and respirator, enshrined against a fiery pink background; the other was a page appropriated from a 1980 issue of *National Geographic* dedicated to "the Aztecs." The magazine page depicts a "ghost of the past," a semitransparent rendering of the Great Temple looming "over its ruins in an aerial photograph of downtown Mexico City" (plates 28–29).[18] Álvarez Muñoz's ensemble work related the devastations of conquest and colonization to folkways in the measure of cosmological time, and to the ancestral-future preservations of human life. Uncannily, given COVID-19 and our present-day health crisis of pandemic proportions, a grandmother's prediction meets the eternal return of catastrophic history and the persistence of colonialism. The artist's view of "mutuality and interdependence" between geological epoch, family descent, and potential planetary destruction resonates today with contemporary activism like that of Indigenous Action. In "Rethinking the Apocalypse: An Indigenous Anti-Futurist Manifesto" (2020), the authors—"dreamers dreamt by our ancestors"—pose the life-or-death question on which futures depend: "Why can we imagine the ending of the world, yet not the ending of colonialism?"[19]

The relationship of an elder (grandparent, mother, father, aunt, or uncle) to the figure of a child (or former self) serves as a leitmotif in many works by Álvarez Muñoz. The dynamic applies also to projects that explore the practical application, collective process, and affective possibilities of art making. In her role as teacher and facilitator she has inspired at least two generations of artists. The Chicago-based Chicanx artist Jesús Macarena Ávila tells of his studies at the School of the Art Institute of Chicago, which he resumed in 1992, after a period in Mexico where he had visited La Escuela Nacional de Artes Plásticas in Mexico City while enrolled in art courses at a university in San Luis Potosí. He writes of the impact Álvarez Muñoz had on his own development as an artist and on Chicago's Latinx cultural community. He relates that, in an artist talk he attended, "Álvarez Muñoz liked to provoke critical thinking through the interrogation of alternate history." She surveyed her influences and her "early conceptualization of bookmaking. Then came the 'chickens' [*Enlightenments* #4]," and other powerful life accounts crafted "into very witty, humorous visual statements. . . . I was just comprehending the pedagogical aspects of [her] practice . . . learning that her personal storytelling was the real 'power.'" Macarena Ávila further describes her *Postales* series as a "code-switched, deconstructed Norman Rockwell

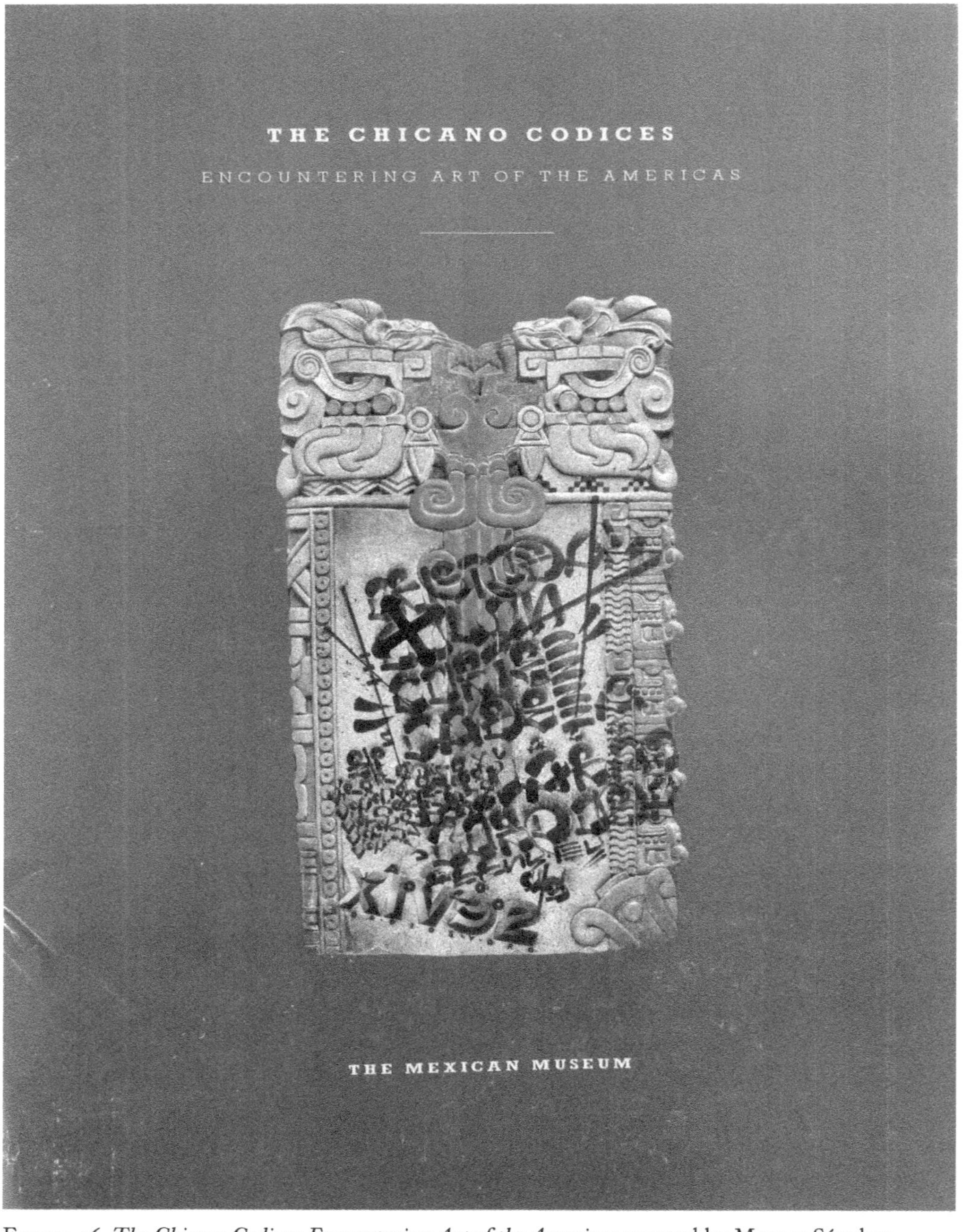

FIGURE 46. *The Chicano Codices: Encountering Art of the Americas*, curated by Marcos Sánchez-Tranquilino, The Mexican Museum, San Francisco, 1992, catalog cover featuring work by Charles "Chaz" Bojórquez, *Codex Bojórquez Año Loco XIV92 por Dios y Oro*, 1992, acrylic on wood, 69 × 41 × 5¾".

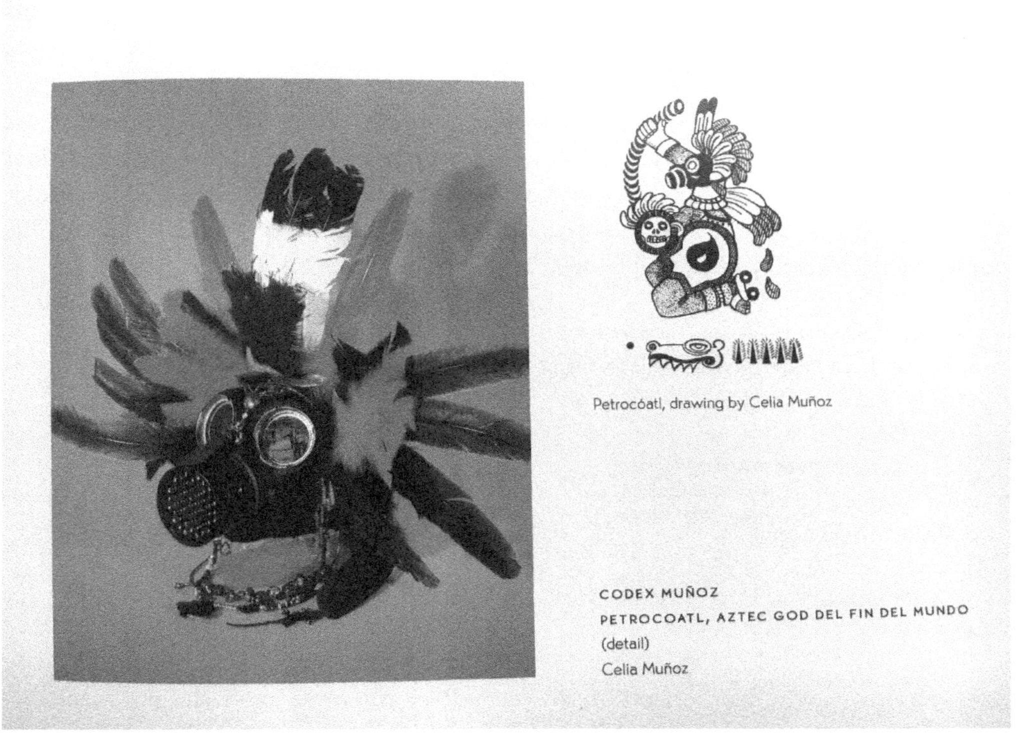

FIGURE 47. Celia Álvarez Muñoz, *Petrocoatl, Aztec God del Fin del Mundo*, 1992, in *The Chicano Codices*, The Mexican Museum, 1992, interior pages.

sensibility on what is the 'status quo.' It was questioning, where does the 'other' fit in this particular story?—I was trying to acknowledge within my young formation of thoughts, not understanding that I found 'home' from this edge."[20]

Issues of cultural transmission, societal estrangement, and belonging were the subjects also of a project Álvarez Muñoz presented at Capp Street Project in San Francisco two years after *The Chicano Codices* exhibition. *A Brand New Ball Game* (1994) provided the occasion for the artist to work with a community of Black and Latinx LGBTQ+ youth whose participation served as the conceptual grid linking the installation to socialization, sexuality, and gender identity (plate 30). A game-room environment in the exhibition space consisted of a large-scale floor-level chessboard and pieces, a pyramidal video chess game, and wooden blocks resembling oversized rows of dice, each die's six faces marked with a chance lexicon of discrete words or phrases—all in shades of light pink, blue, and lavender. Related to these works, and in advance of the exhibition, Álvarez Muñoz held a series of writing workshops with the queer youth of color using prompts to generate an ensemble process that liberated deeply personal experience into an experiment of collective feeling. This was the topic for writing assignments that led to creative disruptions in language.[21] Some of these experiments—working papers and negatives for wall text—were "condensations of the students' letters of testimony." Álvarez Muñoz speaks of these exercises as word clusters and sentences that delved "to the core. I've kept [them] for the right moment.//They are heartfelt.//We all went through an awakening process."[22] Consistent with the conversational workshop technique, where craft and concept interface, the resulting texts named the unities and disunities of personhood as becoming, of anxious horizons and forthcoming pathways. The writing foregrounded collective occasions where the fixity of an individual can give way to entanglements of a self with others, life brimming in the safety of elected home:

married forever t r i c k horny partner
SHY LICK LOVES NAKED HE'S OLD
MADE THAT YOUR SHE'S
NEW CAN DRAG silence
drag queen butch camp
queer femme c l o s e t
pride dyke denial gay
diva out fear rag
ACT DO BE MY A
ALL IN NOT OF AT

Using the typographical effects of concrete poetry, the word compositions evoked discrepancies that may or may not exist between lasting intimacy ("married forever"), casual sex ("t r i c k"), the flux of queer desire (SHY LICK LOVES NAKED), the constraint of closeted survivals ("NEW CAN DRAG silence"), as well as the multigendered emotions of self-determination and foreboding in the social field ("diva out fear rag"). These visual poems pointed to a political horizon of possible inclusion wherein protections await as afforded by the law ("ACT DO BE MY A/ALL IN NOT OF AT"). In this respect, Álvarez Muñoz's 1994 work telescopes from the past to coincide with contemporary collectives similarly devoted to community strategies, criticality, and self-examination as an emancipatory act, a "personal and intimate pedagogy that is not based on the individual, but on difference," and "the enjoyment and management of freedom."[23] At any rate these are the present-day techniques activated, among others, by the Network of Empathic Pedagogies (Red de Pedagogías Empáticas), a constellation of artists and institutions from Mexico, Costa Rica, Colombia, Chile, Brazil, Spain, Norway, and Poland. Today, *A Brand New Ball Game* further refracts in light of the US Supreme Court interpretation of the historic Civil Rights Act of 1964, determined as being applicable "to sexual orientation and gender identity," thereby protecting "LGBTQ employees from workplace discrimination nationwide."[24] (Regrettably, the cruel ironies that sever that none-too-distant past from our political present can hardly be overstated.)

Given to startling narrative insight and audacious design structure, Álvarez Muñoz mobilizes material systems of experience for a viewer to puzzle over, while aligning her practice with legacies proper to art history. Her work draws uniquely from high-modernist conceptual and minimalist art, and from the postmodern afterlives of these tendencies in art of the 1980s and 1990s, as well as from Mexican American language games and a self-reflective appreciation of the folk imagination as the unacknowledged pedigree of avant-garde invention. Grounded in the cultural world of the US-Mexico borderlands, Álvarez Muñoz infuses conceptual art's tautological self-containment with the accountability of human attachments, vitality, folkways, and the touch-trace of the handmade, material forms that reflect and activate human connections lived outside the encroachments of totality. Her method is kin to the "pathos of nearness," the narrative style of thought—the anecdote—that Walter Benjamin likened to a "street insurgence," a measure of the world "adequate and comprehensible to human life."[25] Her art unites cultural ideas to the actuality of matter; the changing status of the object to forms of social life; and the unruly relation of autobiography, fable, and family lore to conceptual orderings of experience.

"There's all kinds of lures that we can conjure," she affirms as though exhaled with a sigh. "You can pull a thought in many directions."[26]

FOURTEEN

Allora & Calzadilla: Wonderstruck on the Edge of Decline

To endure in daylight, as though the sun moved slowly or not at all, was deemed a sin, a sickness; the work of devils made the hours intolerable.

Inclined to relate the imagination by means of its material cause or correlative, Roger Caillois, the French sociologist of the sacred and onetime surrealist, crafted a brief account of noon and its connection to suffering in the ailment early described by the monastic writer John Cassian the Roman. So afflicted, Cassian came "to feel an overwhelming revulsion for his life, for his monastery and companions. He is overcome with insuperable laziness. Daily work repels him; even reading fills him with disgust. He is weary and hungry, with a kind of morbid need to sleep as the sixth hour is drawing near—the fearful hour of noon. At that time he keeps on watching the sun, judging that its decline toward the horizon is too slow."[1] This inner commotion, Caillois continues, will betray the symptoms that structure the history of acedia. Condensed into prose at once mineral and opaque, Caillois's "The Noon Complex" telescopes from fourth-century Christian moral theology to 1936 in sentences that speak to the social distress of a there-and-then burdened with its own particular "psychological hypotension."

Caillois describes acedia as "a sense of apathy toward life, the dull anxiety of a frustrated heart and an intellect confused by irrationality," an agitation that emerges "when the heavy, burning slumber of nature (with light's star at its zenith and in that state of fullness on the edge of decline) gives man at the same time the justification, illustration and exaltation of life's letting go into its opposite." In the year prior to the essay's appearance in the October 1936 issue of the journal *Minotaure*, Caillois had helmed "the antifascist intellectual group Contre-Attaque" and thereafter signed a manifesto denouncing Spanish fascism.[2] May elections in France had favored the Popular Front, even as the summer gave way to newsreel images of Hitler's 1936 Olympic Games, General Franco's Nationalist assault on the Republican government, and the outbreak of civil war in Spain. With Europe thrown into conflict, the historical present loomed as though foreign to itself, a "fullness on the edge of decline," a war of light and darkness that summoned the language of substance and shadow. Whatever misery or dissipation the experience of noon once enabled—forbearance of mind and body in the relentless exposure to sunlight; fortitude to face the unending hours of day—the spell it once cast had dissolved into the fear and loathing of midnight; that is, into another kind of disturbance. If life was now letting go into its opposite, how was one to resist the inclination to surrender—"What's the use?"[3]

Noon owed its prestige to its function of dividing day into equal parts—the soundless peal of transition. "At noon, it would seem that life takes a pause, organic matter returns to an inorganic state, and everything blazes pointlessly and without ardor in a futile desire for luxury and display." It was the hour of shadows disappearing, a rift that gave way to the apparition of ghosts, the coalescing of a soul to its body's shadow, the hour of "rise and decline." The ailments it produced—"heatstroke, sunstroke, cerebral fever"—were the persuasive proof that demons did exist, "the moment when the forces of life and light yield to the powers of death and darkness." Caillois recalls that ancient Greece had not attached "moral qualities to light and darkness," that midnight had long been the counterpart to daytime's hour for ghosts, but that with Christianity came a decline of noon's authority, insomuch as demons, the enemies of light and integrity, now wandered "under the cover of darkness." For Caillois the "noon complex" served as the unsuspecting analogy and moral fable for political vulnerabilities so troubling the present hours as to encourage consciousness and action—antithesis of inclinations to the inanimate or apathetic state. Caillois foreboded also the emerging war machine imagination and its prospect of terror, when "the dead make their appearance—*they who cast no shadow.*" So, noon returned as a metaphor to counter the sensation, akin to acedia, wherein the "will to live withdraws somewhere unknown, as if absorbed by thirsty sands." Caillois appealed to the biological basis of the death drive, citing Freud to claim that "nervous life in general" tends toward "abatement, invariance and the suppression of 'internal tension produced by excitations.'" If noonday was prone to lull the individual into false consciousness, it was equally inclined to suspend or unify the pull of "paroxysm and resignation" in order to cut the losses of history to allow for a pathway akin to discernment.[4] With references to Caillois and a constellation of related cultural allusions, artists Jennifer Allora and Guillermo Calzadilla enliven a space of encounter for material and metaphoric stagings, in a present-day poetics of distress and astonishment.

On gallery walls, Allora & Calzadilla cast a flash sensorium whose conceptual and sonic designs are meant to encompass and collapse a span of centuries into a short-lived duration activated each day at solar noon. Informing the laser projection *Specters of Noon* (2020) was an archive composed of fourth-century mystical writing by early Christian ascetics, whose language often attested to extreme physical and spiritual states of dejection. For Evagrius Ponticus, noon's acedia "instilled the idea that love has disappeared from among the brothers and there is no one to console him."[5] A related daylight burden led Amma Theodora, "probably a fourth-century monastic of Lower Egypt," to avow that she was "ill and not strong enough to perform" her sequence of prayers.[6] Allora & Calzadilla link these testimonies to the semantic and psychological range of esoteric knowledge that drove the solar imagination of twentieth-century surrealism, with its purchase on the primacy of intuition and its wager on a speculative horizon beyond the confines of the present, as when Roger Caillois rehearsed acedia in the pages of *Minotaure*, or as registered in writings by André Breton ("Break of Day"/"Pointe du jour"), Georges Bataille ("The Solar Anus"/"L'anus solaire"), René Magritte ("Surrealism in Broad Daylight"/"Le Surréalisme en plein soleil"), and Aimé Césaire ("The Great Noon"/"Le grand midi"). The latent archive as sensorium meant to evoke a gnosis of all that a moment is able to contain of feelings associated with *accidie*, or acedia: dejection, boredom, ennui, listlessness, disdain, hubris, and the contempt of neighbors and environs, an entire repertoire condensed into fugitive moods and flashpoints that translate and distend, even as they are meant to ward off the fears of day and the phantoms of night.

The references further compound in relation to the fleeting images projected by means of a laser light module, recalling that the word *laser* itself performs a condensation as the acronym for "light amplification by stimulated emission of radiation."[7] The video footage depicts an army of tropical carpenter ants (*Camponotus leonardi*), found in the jungles of Taiwan and Thailand and studied for the remarkable nature of their host relation to a parasitical fungus (*Ophiocordyceps pseudolloydii*). The scientific literature documents the extreme case in which this fungus species positions itself in order to exert "behavioral control" over ants, transforming them into "zombie ants," to provide its spores with maximal opportunity to infect foraging insects. "Inside the host, fungal cells damage the ant's muscles and central nervous system, causing a drunkard's walk, vegetation climbing, clamping to the underside of a leaf or twig, and finally death. The fungus then produces spores from a fruiting body on the back of the victim's head, discharged spores landing on ants on the ground below. . . . The zombie ant bites were synchronized near noon and the dead ants faced south."[8]

A voiceover emerges from the visual frenzy: "Secret deliriums/set your skull on fire/in the dead calm of intense heat./A formless, tangle knot unfolds/In the blazing lull."[9] The artists' laser projection and sound design activate an appearing-and-disappearing act with a surrealist penchant for uniting dissimilar objects, a system of analogies that connects to the mood of acedia; the apex of the sun as an emblem of that which the human eye cannot tolerate (Georges Bataille);[10] and the derangement of the senses that was a central concern of surrealist perspective, articulated by André Breton in "The Automatic Message" as a question: "How can one tolerate the distressing passage from the auditory to the visual?"[11] The idiosyncrasies of natural selection and the host-parasite relation of "zombie ant" to parasitic fungus, also timed with the particularity of noon, suggested the coupling of the literary and scientific imagination. Parasitology also engages a vocabulary around the question of the host that, as philosopher Michel Serres reminds us, does not distinguish between hospitality and hostility.[12] "You do not yet see what offerings I bring:/A useful dislocation of the mind . . . //I am the despot of the world because I have no shadow or remainder./I am the Meridian demon . . . /I drown you with sensation . . ."[13]

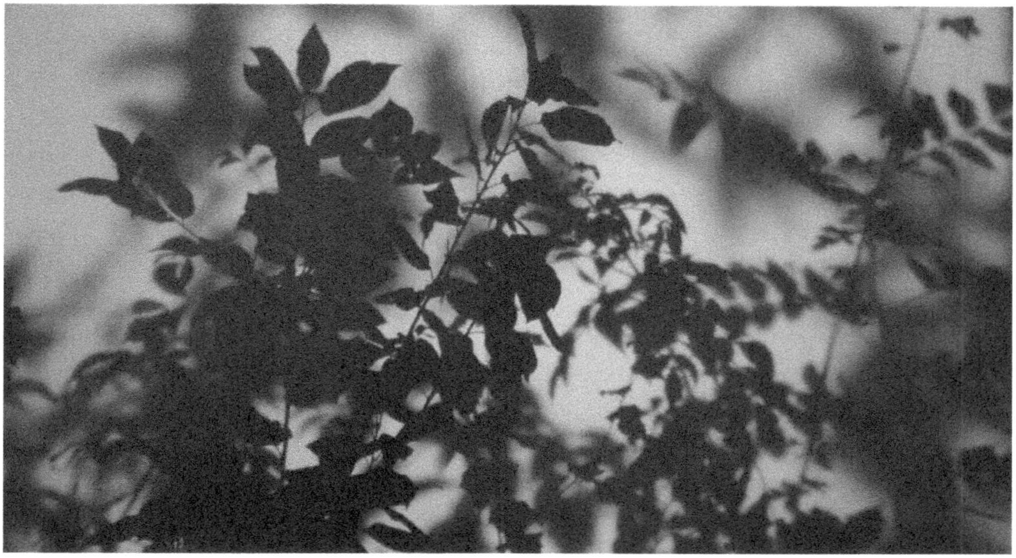

FIGURE 48. Allora & Calzadilla, *Penumbra (Shadow Study)*, 2019 (installation view), digital projection with sound, dimensions variable. Courtesy of Galerie Chantal Crousel, Paris, and Lisson Gallery, New York and London, photo by Paul Hester. © Allora & Calzadilla.

In a related work, *Penumbra* (2019/2020), a tone poem of projected forms with an acoustic counterpart, Allora & Calzadilla cast an animated sequence of shadow vignettes fading in and out over the blank walls of the gallery space, by turns assertive and ephemeral, in a visual sequence that captures the transience of shadow apparitions as if from a scattering of light and dark under a forest canopy as foliage intermittently trembles and obscures the sun's rays (fig. 48). A transatlantic narrative unites these two audiovisual works and others to the colonial history of France, the anticolonial resistance movements of Martinique, the cultural commitments in Paris around *Minotaure*, and the artistic formations in Fort-de-France around the journal *Tropiques*. A historic cargo-ship voyage of 1941 informs Allora & Calzadilla's work and serves as a structuring device for them to stage a scene, in their role as dramatists of history and visual metaphors; that is, in Nietzsche's view of history, "to think one thing with another, and weave the elements into a single whole, with the presumption that the unity of plan must be put into the objects if it is not already there."[14] This complex of references, encounters, correspondences, and alliances brings 1940s surrealism into relation with the anticolonial project and a Caribbean poetics that, through a nexus of material allusions, comment on the present. In *Tristes tropiques*, anthropologist Claude Lévi-Strauss had referred to the "end of one civilization, the beginning of another, and the sudden discovery of our present-day world that it is perhaps beginning to grow too small for the people inhabiting it."[15]

Lévi-Strauss recalls as well his efforts to embark, in 1941, on a transatlantic crossing during the German occupation of France in order to dodge the hazards of the Vichy government. In Marseille he learned that a boat managed by the Société Générale des Transport Maritimes "was about to leave for Martinique," the *Capitaine Paul-Lemerle*, which, overloaded with 350 people "crammed" together in what amounted to a small steamer, resembled a ship rather meant for the "deportation of convicts." Writing a decade after the fact, Lévi-Strauss recalls that, among the "'riff-raff,' as the gendarmes called them," was André Breton, with whom he was to develop "a lasting friendship."[16] After a month at sea and docking at Fort-de-France, the passengers were "interned in a camp called Le Lazaret," as though the Vichy authorities, in allowing them to leave France for Martinique, "had sent them a cargo of scapegoats" now put in the vindictive hands of the noncommissioned officers stationed there, whose one assignment "was to guard the gold of the Bank of France."[17]

Breton's account tells also of the *Capitaine Paul-Lemerle* voyage and Lazaret camp, but as events leading to a fortuitous circumstance: Having stopped "to buy a ribbon for [his] daughter" at a Fort-de-France fabric shop, but drawn to a publication on display with an unassuming cover, Breton eyed the first issue of *Tropiques*, the literary journal founded that year by Suzanne and Aimé Césaire and René Ménil under Vichy rule of the island colony Breton described as "coming apart, seemingly deprived of its essential organs." At first with no small amount of metropolitan aloofness and with a general skepticism of wartime's "intellectual degradation," Breton's attitude gave way to amazement at the radiance of what he found in *Tropiques*. In stark contrast to the pages of masochistic and servile writing "published in France during the preceding months" is the unprecedented voice of Aimé Césaire, whose impact on Breton is categorical: "All those mocking shadows were torn aside and dispersed; all the lies and derision fell in tatters. It was proof that, far from being broken or stifled, here the human voice rose up like the very shaft of light. . . . 'We are the kind,' Césaire announced, 'who refuse the shadow.'"[18]

A thickening of light and a refusal of shadows: the dynamic of radiance as an oppositional life force. In her essay "1943: Le Surréalisme et nous" Suzanne Césaire set into motion a defense of surrealism as a "total activity." She underscored the revolutionary and anticolonial vigor of its commitments, capable of freeing the mind "from the shackles of absurd logic and of so-called reason" while remaining "in the service of the largest and most thoroughgoing human emancipation [that could] be summed up completely in one single, magic word: freedom."[19] Surrealism was hence for her "as intransigent, as uncompromising as freedom itself."[20] Its mode of expression, its abundance of vivacity and courage, was the condition of "fruitfulness," a wager on an "immense" and "boundless" decolonized future inclined to transcend the "sordid antinomies of the present: whites/Blacks, Europeans/Africans, civilized/savages."[21]

Allora & Calzadilla's *Penumbra* materializes over wall space as tenuously and opaquely as the work alludes to the foregoing cultural archive. The durational apparition of shadow-foliage animates, dissembles, integrates, and dissolves. The projection overlaps the antimonies between France and Fort-de-France; that is, between the flora and landscape of Martinique and the urban confinement of Paris—its interior spaces, its apartment lifestyle.

The back pages of that 1936 issue of *Minotaure* with "The Noon Complex" by Caillois featured an unsigned article. Titled "La lumière et les plantes," its tonal register oscillates between the dry copy of an industry trade journal and that of a mock user's manual illustrating the optimal application of electrical indoor lighting for the maintenance of "plant organisms" in need of "ultraviolet rays that facilitate the absorption of chlorophyll—the crux of their subsistence."[22] Illustrating the text are photographs by André Kertesz: otherworldly compositions that frame urban domestic spaces with shadows cast by indoor plants through the auspices of "integrated" electric lighting, further estranging the instructional captions. One such caption encourages readers: "To grow plants with indoor lighting requires no extensive landscaping. With a little ingenuity, this floor lamp has been adapted to feature decorative planters."[23] The bitter irony of the article was to submit that, thanks to electricity, home plants and flowers now allowed metropolitans to "forget a little the deprivation of space and fresh air, greenery and country perfumes—namely nature"—bourgeois distractions, a form of camouflage, from France's involvement in the colonial enterprise.[24]

Breton met the Césaires the day after his encounter with *Tropiques*. About Aimé he remarked: "I can recall my quite basic initial reaction at finding him such a pure black in color, masked all the more at first sight by his smile." About Suzanne's essay in the first issue of *Tropiques*, "Léo Frobenius et le problème des civilisations," Breton had nothing to say, even as he glowed about her beauty, comparing it to "the flame on a bowl of punch."[25] He mentions, at any rate, an "excursion right into the interior of the island," a trek into its tropical rainforest. From one of its mountainous perspectives, he describes the "very materialization of the crucible in which poetic images powerful enough to move worlds are formed, with no other landmark in the tide of frantic vegetation than the great enigmatic canna flower, a triple heart quivering on the end of a spear." This was the vegetation that inspired the canonic painting *The Jungle* by Cuban artist Wifredo Lam, also among the company on the rainforest excursion. After his return to Havana from Europe via Martinique, Lam also illustrated Lydia Cabrera's 1942 Spanish translation of Césaire's *Cahier d'un retour au pays natal*. For her part, Suzanne Césaire animated, in the riveting prose of her essay "The Great Camouflage," the mythic status of the "heliconia shrubs and flowers of Absalon Forest." In her poetics of place, "life lights up in a vegetal fire. . . . Here the tropical vines rocking vertiginously, take on ethereal poses to charm the precipices, with their trembling fingertips they latch onto the ungraspable cosmic flurry rising all throughout the drum-filled nights. . . . [If] the flowers have known how to find just the right colors to leave one dumbstruck, if the tree-like ferns have secreted golden saps for their white crooks, rolled-up like a sex organ, if my Antilles are so beautiful, it is because the great game of hide-and-seek has succeeded."[26]

The hide-and-seek of the shadow play in *Penumbra* joins with the score created for the animation by composer David Lang, collaborator on this and other works by Allora & Calzadilla.[27] With its extended duration (forty-five minutes) and its reference to birdsong in call and response, sustained notes from two violins glide and abrade in tones that emerge and recede into the encompassing continuous timbre, a duration in contrast to the tenuous nature of projected foliage, as though one pitch were tentatively subordinate to the other, in what Justin Rito in another context has called David Lang's "rhythmic transformational system."[28] Following the flight that an audiovisual sensorium makes possible is crafted a narrative about fellowship in art and chance association (Caillois, Lévi-Strauss,

Breton, the Césaires, and Lam) traveling through time and projecting scenes of the past by way of shadow flowers and plant life in the present, enough for us to suspend the distinction between flora, environs, and our estimates of the human-made. What is longing but that light should give way to social interaction?

In his philosophical experiment of curatorial conception *Les immatériaux*, Jean-François Lyotard thought about that particular type of matter organized into digital information; about communication in the age of electronic techno-sciences; about the relationship between human beings and platform interface; and about the cognitive connection and dissonance with the substance of the habitable world. He wrote that "technology is not the cause of the decline of the modern figure; rather, it is one of its signs. Our grief is another of its symptoms. At the end of the eighteenth century, Europe and [US] America, in the name of the free and virtuous enlightened mind, claimed to spread light, law, and wealth over the human world. After two centuries of massacres and civil, international, world wars, we are now beginning to go into mourning for this arrogance" in the late style of "wise melancholy."[29]

Cultural histories subsist in the work of Allora & Calzadilla, a nexus of historical and material associations that prompt related meanings for their practice in the present. These narratives relate the attitudes voiced in the print platforms of *Minotaure* and *Tropiques*, and the partnership of Suzanne and Aimé Césaire, to multimedia works meant to transfigure particular moods of the European avant-garde into the critical confrontations between surrealism and anticolonial forms of meaning in the Caribbean context. For instance, after World War II and in the years after the journal *Tropiques* ceased publication, Aimé Césaire, in his *Discourse on Colonialism* (1955), plied the writings of Caillois as symptomatic of Western values and petty bourgeois malaise, incapable of a "humanism made to the measure of the world."[30] Césaire viewed the humanism of Caillois, its defense of Western integrity, as being so comprehensive as to be complicit in the colonial project that "works to *decivilize* the colonizer, to *brutalize* him in the true sense of the word, to degrade him, to awaken him to buried instincts, to covetousness, violence, race hatred, and moral relativism."[31]

Likewise, Suzanne Césaire's intensity of feeling for locale in language commensurate to the landscape and an "ungraspable cosmic flurry" belied the wartime affliction for which Caillois's acedia served as a stand-in—the colonial cover story serving to camouflage histories of violence "in the name of the free and virtuous enlightened mind [that] claimed to spread light, law, and wealth over the human world." The "mourning for this arrogance" that Lyotard remarks upon is a latter-day noon complex that remains in effect, still blurring lines between sorrow and stupefaction, pain and amazement, weariness and distress.[32]

Suzanne Césaire provides here a passage "to think about the other Caribbean islands." In "The Great Camouflage" she evoked a moment when "off the coast of Puerto Rico a huge cyclone begins to spin its way between the seas of clouds, with its beautiful tail sweeping rhythmically the semicircle of the Antilles."[33] The "unbearably beautiful" landscape and climes of the Caribbean that would keep concealed "the pattern of unfulfilled desires [that] has trapped the Antilles . . . from the time of the arrival of the conquistadors" to the "Black slave trade's infamy," with African-descendant peoples suffering most "from the degradations, the injustices, and the pettiness of colonial society." Even as natural forces or human volition may threaten those imagined futures, they were for Césaire as well the conditions that give way to "total insight."

Based in San Juan, Puerto Rico, since the mid-1990s, Allora & Calzadilla link sensory experience to the metaphoric value of materials; they embed substance with narratives that relate those amplitudes of cultural transmission over time while interrogating also the imagined futures that metaphor can make possible.

They compress sweeping histories of the colonial enterprise into material analogies, assemblages, and counterparts. Those point back to the irreversible episodes of conquest, beginning in 1511, on the island that is now Puerto Rico and the ongoing attributes of colonization owing to a European-imposed extraction economy that forced Taíno native peoples to plant crops and mine gold, catastrophically diminishing the Indigenous population—at the time of contact estimated at 30,000–60,000—through disease and brutal labor: the first 1530 census recorded 1,543 *indios*.[34] Tzvetan Todorov relates that Indian resistance led Spanish conquistador Oviedo y Valdés to view *caribes*—Indians, especially those who rebelled—not only as less-than-human, but as tantamount to "construction materials, wood, stone, or metal, in any case [to] inanimate objects."[35] Sylvia Wynter reminds us that it was "this initial, large-scale, one-sided accumulation of lands, wealth, power, and unpaid labor by the West that was to provide the basis" for the exponential disparities thereafter throughout the hemisphere, even centuries later, in the wake of Latin American independence from Spain and Portugal.[36] Photographs by Alexander Gardner, from his 1865 album *Rays of Sunlight from South America*, depict, from a considerable distance, groups of indentured Chinese miners standing at a precipice, overwhelmed by the surrounding enormity of the "Great Heap," the cliffs and crags cut into the side of one of the mountainous Chincha Islands off the southern coast of Peru, its surface composed of solidified guano, sometimes 200 feet deep, that had accumulated over time from the droppings left by the Guanay cormorant for which the islands served as home. Guano had become a highly valued commodity in a growing world market owing to its properties as a fertilizer; it was prized as well as a homoeopathic medicine that allegedly relieved the "itching of nostrils, back, thighs, genitals" or symptoms related to hay-fever.[37] The United States Guano Island Acts of 1855 had given US citizens the legal foundation and commercial incentive for the "peaceable possession" of land and resources beyond the political boundaries of the nation. In this capacity, any such unclaimed "island, rock, or key may, at the discretion of the President, be considered as appertaining to the United States."[38] Financial speculation led to conflicts between nations. Chile and Peru disputed possession of the Pacific Guano Islands; Venezuela and the Netherlands clashed over the Las Aves Archipelago; and Spain began to extract the guano found on the Mona and Monito Islands of Puerto Rico, including deposits of bat guano found in the islands' caves. The "exploitation and commercialization of guano" generated myths that lingered in the "collective imagination as a utopia" of unfulfilled promise for economic development in Puerto Rico.[39]

In *Manifest* (2020) Allora & Calzadilla produced two massive wall reliefs that use for a cast an actual ship engine once owned and operated by the Crowley Maritime cargo corporation (plate 31). Crowley's history can be traced to the guano extraction enterprise of the late nineteenth century, and the company's promotional materials describe certain innovations attributed to founder Tom Crowley, who, upon visiting South America in the 1890s, recommended more efficient cargo vessels. There he had observed "the methods used to lighter nitrate and guano from the numerous island and shoreside sites in Chile and Peru to ships anchored offshore."[40] For *Manifest* the artists created two molds shaped from the bisected engine, each mold cast in bat guano and solidifying agents. Protruding from opposite walls in relation to each other and to contrasting works in the gallery spaces of Allora & Calzadilla's 2020–21 exhibition *Specters of Noon* at the Menil Collection,[41] the resulting reliefs are each a tumult in suspended state, burnt umber in color, caked in surface values, and redolent of odors associated with fertilizer (nitrogen, potash, phosphoric acid).[42] The severed shapes of the engine bedplate, girders, frame, and connecting pipes coalesce into prodigious totems that suggest a devotional mood even as they expose materials once entangled in the dirty web of economic life. Georges Bataille had similarly sought to disrupt and make manifest the habits of thought in relation to materiality and meaning to "bring things down in the world."[43] *Manifest* serves as surrealist analogy that perversely unifies art and shit in order to ironize commodity forms as objects or functions, while never ceasing to be reservoirs of value, insofar as they provide, in Sarah Kofman's concise account, an "illusion of being autonomous once cut off from the processes of their own genesis."[44]

Manifest performs a worlding of the alleged autonomy of the artwork, even as its particular materiality disavows that independence. Similarly, regarding the guano industry associated with US expansionism, the work exposes the authority of individualism and entrepreneurship as a myth inseparable from the global relations on which it depends. Interdisciplinary scholar Lisa Lowe has examined how "free trade" as a liberal universal category concealed the interdependencies and historical complicities with "settler colonialism in North America and the West Indies and the African slave trade," as well as with the "importing of Chinese and South Asian indentured labor"—the global network Lowe portrays as the "intimacies of four continents."[45] Conditions that collapsed commerce and occupation led to the Spanish-American War, the occupation of Puerto Rico (fig. 49), and the final evacuation of Spanish troops from the island on October 18, 1898, when the American flag was hoisted by the US Army over the public buildings and forts of San Juan. Within a year, popular publications like *Harper's Pictorial History of the War with Spain* gave license to liberal narratives, citing pronouncements like those of the Commanding General of the United States Army: "The chief object of the American military forces [is not] to make war upon the people of a country that for centuries has been oppressed, but, on the contrary, to bring protection, not only to yourselves but to your property, to promote your prosperity, and bestow upon you the immunities and blessings of the liberal institutions of our government."[46] By mid-1900, Congress approved the Foraker Act, which

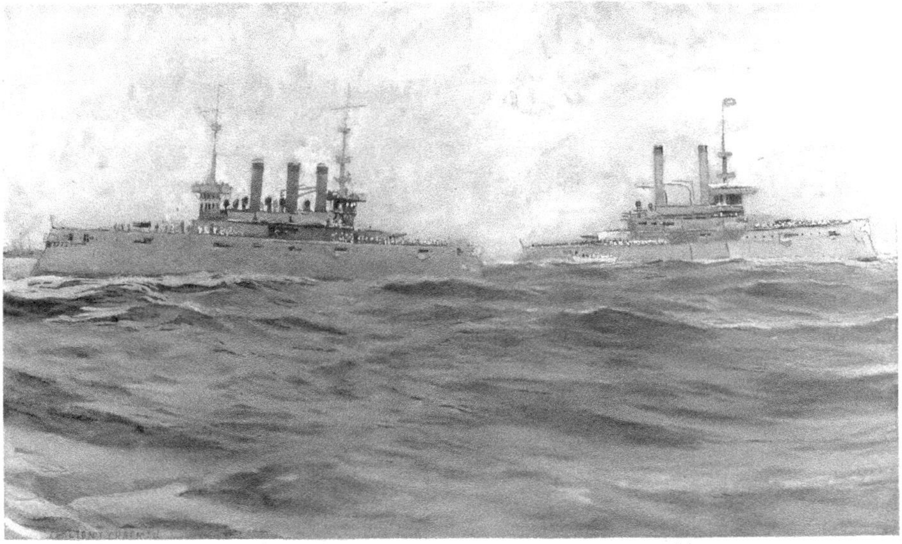

BEFORE THE BOMBARDMENT OF SAN JUAN—ADMIRAL SAMPSON TRANSFERS HIS FLAG TO THE *IOWA*, MAY 11, 5.10 P.M., SAN JUAN BEARING S.S.E. ABOUT SEVENTY MILES
DRAWN BY CARLTON T. CHAPMAN

FIGURE 49. "Before the Bombardment of San Juan," *Harper's Pictorial History of the War with Spain* (New York: Harper's and Brothers, 1899), 396.

> organized a civilian government for Puerto Rico, thus replacing the military government that had ruled the island from 1898 to 1900 [while imposing] a temporary tariff on goods moving between Puerto Rico and the United States amounting to 15 percent of the duties applicable to foreign goods entering the latter. . . . The significance of the temporary tariff included in the Foraker Act thus becomes evident: through the Foraker Act, Congress was organizing U.S. rule over Puerto Rico, but by imposing a tariff on goods coming from the island, it was treating it as *not* part of the United States. Through the Foraker Act, Congress both affirmed U.S. rule over Puerto Rico and defined the island as foreign territory.[47]

The subsequent 1917 Jones Act granted US citizenship to Puerto Ricans, but the law was met with opposition as it did not include future statehood. Therefore, if "Puerto Rico was not to be a state, US citizenship could be interpreted only as an attempt to block independence and perpetuate Puerto Rico in its colonial status." Historians César J. Ayala and Rafael Bernabe recount that the "extension of US citizenship did not constitute a promise of statehood but rather an attempt to exclude any consideration of independence. As Governor Arthur D. Yager put it, it meant "'that we have determined . . . that the American flag will never be lowered in Puerto Rico.'"[48] This, according to Pedro A. Malavet, was the groundwork for a "colonialism that establishes the condition of Puerto Ricans' strong cultural nationhood [in contrast to] their lack of legal sovereignty. Puerto Rico legally belongs to the United States, but has not been fully incorporated into it."[49]

In the ensuing century, that status has produced conditions of "extreme dependence on foreign investment" and has increasingly aggravated the island's status as a relatively impoverished region under US rule, despite cycles of economic insertion into the international free market through "unrestricted trade and unimpeded capital and labor mobility between Puerto Rico and the United States."[50] Patterns of underinvestment and debt-engineering continue, further compromising an already vulnerable infrastructure on the island. In the months prior to the 2017 devastation of Hurricane Maria, news stories reported that the economically unstable Puerto Rico Electric Power Authority (or PREPA) had "defaulted on a deal to restructure roughly $9 billion in bond debt" for antiquated generating plants. Moreover, as if any additional evidence were needed to call into question the perverse global logic of free trade, those plants had "burned *imported oil* to produce electricity."[51]

On the morning of September 20, 2017, Hurricane Maria made landfall on Puerto Rico, unleashing massive ruin that led to a desperate humanitarian crisis for the island's 3.4 million residents; it destroyed PREPA's distribution network, which resulted in a blackout in all parts of the island. In uncanny coincidence, on September 22, Allora & Calzadilla's exhibition *Foreign in a Domestic Sense* opened at their gallery in London. The artists relate the oxymoron "foreign in a domestic sense" to its first use when United States Supreme Court Justice Edward E. White so ruled as to provide legal sanction (*Downes v. Bidwell*, 1901) to "the US colonization of foreign territories through the ambiguous formulation of territorial non-incorporation."[52] The exhibition featured the first iteration of *Blackout*—a work that referred to previous power failures; a sculpture activated and completed by a performance scored for human voices. In the center of the gallery space a melted power transformer displayed "ceramic and copper insulators and rusty coils, exposed like splayed organs."[53] Suggesting as well a distorted snarl of potential destruction, the industrial ruin emitted a continuous low frequency known as mains hum, a "buzzing from old or improperly grounded electrical transformers."[54] In the 2020 iteration of *Blackout*, the power transformer no longer suggests the metallic equivalent of carnage; it overshadows human scale with imposing magnitude, a monolith—eleven feet high, nine feet wide, and seven feet deep—solidly in command of the surrounding space. This otherworldly ruin of an ossified technological imagination "half-encased in copper" suggests also the "apotheosis of electricity" that Wolfgang Schivelbusch described in his history of industrial lighting as a public utility that transformed street life and domestic space, since "social connections" thereafter ceased "to exist in the dark."[55] In counterpoint to such monumentality, collaborator David Lang activated the colossal object and its environment with a musical composition scored for "many voices." An unspecified number of vocalists inhabited the gallery space and tuned their voices to the humming electrical structure, each singer improvising pitch and duration to hover between the notes of A and B-flat. Structured loosely in "perpetual" or "infinite canon" form, Lang's score encourages "electrical" vocal sounds—"glitch, vocal fry, overtone, inhale"—in an arc beginning "not too loud" that crescendos to "very loud" and then concludes in whispers of diminishment, "sharp and percussive, with rests between." Chance and endurance determine how long the performance will last: It is "up to the singer if he or she will take 10 minutes to sing it or

10 hours."[56] The overlapping waves of fricatives and gutturals mimicking electricity are meant as metaphoric survivals, a utopian proxy for other voices lost to the "fiction of discourse" uttered by so many media analysts and lawmakers in times of humanitarian emergency.[57] The choral interplay between *Blackout* and *mains hum*—existing as they do in a provisional uncertainty of overlapping principal and secondary notes—is intended to rehearse and enliven what can or cannot be captured in the aftermath of catastrophe. In a book-length work written in the immediacy of Hurricane Maria's devastation, *While They Sleep (Under the Bed Is Another Country)*, poet Roque Raquel Salas Rivera voiced the unspeakable ruptures that natural disaster made visible: "one week after the hurricane we/'have different views on colonialism' . . . a fissure opens in the jones act/just long enough/to add sealant."[58] *Blackout* and *mains hum* similarly expose the unbearable contradictions between experience and outcome, between contemplation and action; that is, by extension, between faith in technological certainty, and the negligence that results in systemic collapse. Small wonder the artists and composer drew inspiration from the words of Benjamin Franklin: "In going on with these Experiments, how many pretty systems do we build, which we soon find ourselves oblig'd to destroy! If there is no other Use discover'd of Electricity, this, however, is something considerable, that it may help to make a vain Man humble."[59]

In the magnetic fields of power and failure, "electrified amazement" can describe a mood consistent with surrealist epistemologies. Georges Bataille applied those words to the incongruous shock of sight involved in contemplating the Upper Paleolithic depictions of human and animal forms discovered "by four Montignac boys" on September 12, 1940, in the Cave of Lascaux.[60] Allora & Calzadilla's most prodigious work in terms of scale, *Entelechy* (2020) comprises an uncanny coal-cast replica of a tree that, uprooted by rain and windstorm, exposed an entrance that led to that first encounter with the Lascaux cave paintings (plate 32). *Entelechy*'s collapsed roots and branches are configured in the combustible substance at the center of political debates today about industrial economies, labor, sustainable energy, and the precarious environment. The enormous tree shape haunts the gallery space with its sheer materiality—its physical proximity inescapable, although oriented to a more ominous impermanence. Art historian Petra Lange-Berndt reminds us that "the term material describes not prime matter but substances that are always subject to change, be it through handling, interaction with their surroundings, or the dynamic life of their chemical reactions."[61] *Entelechy*'s material presence serves as something akin to theater in the spectacular sense that Nietzsche was to think historically of "all things in relation to all others."[62]

The artists suggest that, on one important level, technological media, platforms, and projections (*Specters of Noon*, *Penumbra*) are elements no different from the materiality of coal, guano, iron filings, linen, silk, cotton, or copper. In this respect Allora & Calzadilla are inclined to recall former artistic interaction—the surrealist nexus of *Minotaure* and Martinique—in the desire to prompt the kind of public that comes into being in relation to metaphors, historical narratives, and "new arrangements with a nonhuman world" that today define the condition of human-machine interface.[63] To this end Lang's composition is energized with references to the birdsong of canaries—the species that traditionally signals immanent catastrophe—though "layered to achieve a saturated musical score: part machine, part animal, and part human."[64] Allora & Calzadilla take up the ecological crisis that confronts the human species today with relentless uncertainty. The future, heretofore imagined and practiced in the West as a vanishing point, invisible but infinite, now throws present historical understanding into confusion. In the sobering view of historian Dipesh Chakrabarty, climate crisis has destabilized the "age-old humanist distinction between natural history and human history . . . pointing to a figure of the universal that escapes our capacity to experience the world" as anything other than a "shared sense of catastrophe"—that is, as "negative universal history."[65]

If aesthetics has been at pains to destroy and preserve this distance between the material world and the imagination; if the surrealist order of the *unthought* was another name for knowledge aware of its relative status, then how are we to avoid the "momentary suspicion" Bataille described in view of Lascaux, that our drive to be of the world and apart from it is not "all a mirage, some deliberate trick?"[66] How to resist the inner commotion inclined to "paroxysm and resignation," to life "letting go into its opposite?"[67] How to account for all the little deprivations, and all the light and shade in the great camouflage that covers over the disparities of the universal human collectivity, the "ungraspable cosmic flurry" that is the unthought defined by present ecological crisis? In his writings about a "codified world," media philosopher Vilém Flusser once suggested that Lascaux serves as a cipher for what the "imagination" might mean: "the ability to reduce the world of situations to scenes. And vice versa: to decipher the scenes as substitutes for situations."[68] For Bataille, the dark caverns of prehistory provided a scene, a situation, or rather a fable that allowed him "to be wonderstruck" by the mark of human hands in search of fixity in substance. But the walls of Lascaux recede out of joint with the time now of *Entelechy*'s roots and branches; that is, with the speculative order of any "imperishable expression," or with evidence that would corroborate "enduring survival."[69] In this suite of multimedia works, some monumental, others discernable only "with light's star at its zenith," Allora & Calzadilla provide situations, scenes, and specters that lead to questions in the intolerable hour of noon—to discern whether symptoms are specific to a moment in time; whether complicity is possible between materials, techniques, and cultural archetypes; and whether the resulting forms, made to exist in fullness on the edge of decline, can serve to alter, wonderstruck, the course of understanding and action in the present.[70]

FIFTEEN

Luis Gispert: Radical Feedback

In a 2003 television commercial for a chief financial institution, an attractive young African American actress relaxes into the beige vinyl chair of a beauty salon or day spa as she fans her fingers to let the nail polish dry (fig. 50). Dressed in a pink pullover blouse and rolled-up blue jeans, she soaks her feet in the jet-bath prelude to a pedicure. As she directly addresses the camera, what follows produces a severe splinter between sight and sound. The lilted male inflection of an adolescent hacker confounds and displaces the expected cadence with the boast, "Firewall? Like that could stop me. Once I got hold of her account number, I couldn't spend it fast enough." The subsequent list of credit card expenditures is punctuated with intermittent snickers of nerdy laughter. The camera closes in on the visibly intonating Black woman ("Sandra T., Identity Theft Victim") while the irksome voice enumerates further counterfeit purchases, including the clincher: "twenty thousand dollars to complete my robot . . . my *girl* robot. [An inhaled high-pitched chortle.] This is going to be the best prom ever."

The television spot is compelling to the degree that, like the best commercials, it has visual appeal and provides narrative amusement. But in this particular ad there is so much more, especially the disconnect of social markers effected between a body and a vocal source foreign to the visible speaker, used for a service directed against credit card fraud. For a moment the commercial appeases anxieties about indeterminate identities within networks of high-speed communications by employing an audiovisual joke about the social coordinates of sex, ethnicity, class, and generation—no matter how collapsed or conflated these traditionally are by the promise of consumer subjectivity. The ad's astounding

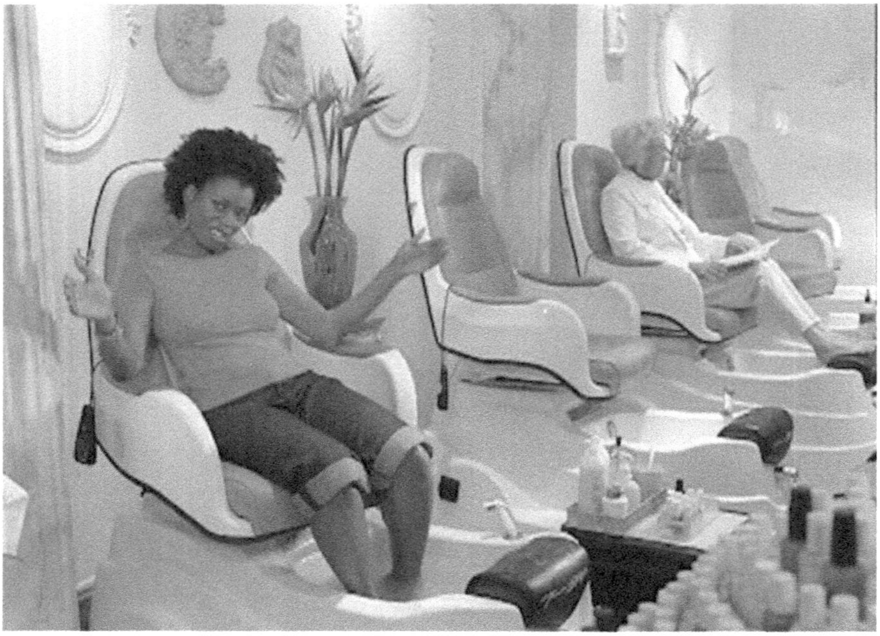

FIGURE 50. Citibank Identity Theft Commercial, Thomas Thomas Films, 2003.

feature is its self-awareness of the process whereby commodity culture and social identities are transposed, creating complex fields of reference.

Luis Gispert's work parallels this bit of popular culture—even as it draws from other aspects of advertising's sensual allure. His art understands the components that power the circuitry of image-making in a cultural economy whose values and denominations loop into each other, and whose aesthetic eclecticism is appropriate to social sampling. It reflects what Iain Chambers identifies as the relation between capitalism, mass culture, and the politics of consumerism when he claims that what is finally more significant "is less the *content* of advertising and its reference to the closed logic of commerce ('Buy Me!'), and more the evolving *possibility of its language* and the access it can provide to the wider dialogue of potential, of change, in which images can be chosen, adopted, adapted, inhabited and cast off like a set of clothes, like yesterday's fashion."[1]

From his large-scale photographs and personal spin on minimalism's "specific object" to his video installations and bold three-dimensional involvements with the logic of the museum space, Gispert's work interrogates social identities and their representation, as well as the language of subcultures when they become a visual commodity for art world consumption. Further claims engage the instability and unrest that exists between subject positions in a symbolic form of what might be seen as a kind of identity theft.

Gispert is an image-maker in the comprehensive sense of the word, shared as well by the film industry, public relations, and the mediated political sphere. The broad range of Gispert's methods—photographic, time-based, and sculptural—prompt a conversation between different formats in a structure of reference that is radically of the moment. In fact, it's hard to circumvent the initial impact of his startling iconography—images of cheerleaders and objects made of body-shop machinery or speaker-boxes. Because his practice poses important questions about US mainstream culture, about alternate representation, and about the art world in an age of multiculturalism, Luis Gispert has struck a sharp social, cultural, and art-historical chord.

Born in New Jersey and formerly based in South Florida, Gispert presently works out of Brooklyn, New York. A Cuban American, he belongs to a generation of artists whose development was in keeping with the accelerated changes in the Miami art world of the late 1990s. With access to substantial collections of contemporary art, both private and public, and to a thriving commercial gallery scene—sustained by the general material and cultural increase of Miami as a city linking North and South America—it was possible for emerging artists to view works by a roster of contemporary makers, with significant representation from Latin America and US Latinos.[2] These intensified formations provided Gispert with the enabling sources and techniques to conduct his own brand of archeology based on a literal and figurative trespass into the properties of two material cultures: those of the inner city and suburbia.

An early series of photographic diptychs, *Sneaking into Backyards* (1998–99) was produced in and around Miami-Dade County, and they are directly related to meanings suggested by the three-dimensional objects he produced during those same years. In the left panel of one pair, an image captures a young man—the artist himself—clad in a white T-shirt and navy-blue work khakis as he leaps over a chain-link fence into a residential backyard. Next to this, and in jarring contrast, is the picture of a garden sculpture: a kitschy pink hippopotamus, smiling at the viewer, a yellow sculpted bird perched upon its back. The documented "misdemeanor performance" questions social fears regarding crime in residential urban life as linked to systems of security and surveillance. But it layers this relationship to the practice of home adornment—a form of vernacular art that can betray the troublesome undertones of bourgeois social values surrounding real estate ownership. Gispert has stated that these images "were about the impossibility of making a genuinely subversive work of art," but in tandem with that series the artist constructed gray-felt speakers in the shape of objects that outwardly pertain to the domestic realm: a wood-and-felt audio speaker rises from the floor in the shape of an American dreamhouse.[3] With a distant family resemblance to the "specific object" of the minimalists, but for the unmistakable shape of the support and the sound technology it encloses, Gispert inverts a phrase that typifies Latino hospitality ("mi casa es tu casa") with the title *Your Home Is My Home* (1999), thus linking the threat of forced entry with the seepage of boombox culture into the home-sweet-homes of mainstream America and contemporary art.

This incorporation of stereo culture and hip-hop paraphernalia into the fantasies of sameness—with the not infrequent referencing of crime or criminalization—is the driving concern that gave way to an impressive series of large-format Fuji Flex prints produced while the artist pursued graduate studies at Yale. In his *Cheerleader Series* (2000–2002), Gispert employed models meant to unsettle viewer expectations and the standard masquerades of modern US American femininity. A symptom of Cold War compliance and voluntarism but also a "mutable pop icon,"[4] the figure of the cheerleader has been fetishized in all manner of media and print representations, from swimsuit calendars and sports-themed pornography, to television comedy and popular movies.[5] It is no coincidence that this authoritative "type" manages to signify so many registers of emotive possibility and the group dynamic contained in the term "pep squad." The success of Gispert's cheerleader cycle resides in the effect that it manages to strike—that of a tonal suspension between the allegedly jejune and the jubilantly affirming. Gispert's cheerleaders grant uplift in the literal and figurative sense—by way of suspension wires his cheerleader models levitate in recognizable or less overt art-historical references. The sequence sets out to defy any standard sense of physical prowess, to obscure the logic of photographic space, and to dispute interpretive habits—both formal and social—with a visual appeal that does not overburden the critical content.

In *Untitled (Car Girls)* (2000–2002), two cheerleaders avoiding each other's look and the lens of the camera are braced with seatbelts side by side in the claustrophobic back interior of a car, their hands meeting to touch. The two models are encapsulated in a moment of distress as though they were performers in a music video gone seriously awry. The cheerleaders are African American and Asian American—or are they both Latinas? "On what visual criteria do we make these assessments?" is the question these images ask. Bezzled out in thick rings, bracelets, and watches that harmonize with their snug identical outfits and long painted nails, the lavish gold strands around their necks are suspended in midair—at the end of one gold chain hovers a medal in the shape of an automatic pistol—as though the vehicle were spinning wildly out of control. The image is atypical of the series, but for the green backdrop that glows through the windows of the vehicle, as though the car were at the same time submerged underwater. The green backing—of the kind used in film to superimpose a screen projection—informs most of Gispert's camera-based images from this series, and the delight in such artifice is one that conflates undefined social space with the register of an advertising "product shot."

In the depth effect of that green environs, and with fingers interlocked in a twofold midair backflip, *Untitled (Fluid Exchange)* (2002) presents the poised bodies and dangling hair of two light-skinned cheerleaders who institute a symmetrical coupling. A floating visual torsion that pushes plausible dexterity to breaking point, the title suggests an oblique allusion to the delivery of force through a fluid medium, as from an engine to the wheels of an automobile, or in the transmission of a virus from one body to another. Even as they convey resilience to their contiguous condition, these female bodies hover at the brink of a public merger or disjointing. Inasmuch as his images revel in a patently cinematic and theatrical style, Gispert rehearses the politics of appearances that Guy Debord had in mind when, in *The Society of the Spectacle*, he wrote: "Like modern society itself, the spectacle is at once united and divided. In both, unity is grounded in a split."[6] Social and symbolic pressures of this kind are staged in high-pitched performances throughout the series.

The suspension wires serve a number of the cheerleader images to evoke all manner of baroque bodily gestures and composition (fig. 51), as in *Untitled (Tres)* (2001)—an arrangement that coalesces what appear to be an angelic apparition and the descent from the Cross. As the audacious red outfits of the three figures provide a retinal quiver fixed against the green surrounding, the viewer registers the ethnicity of these models as a legible

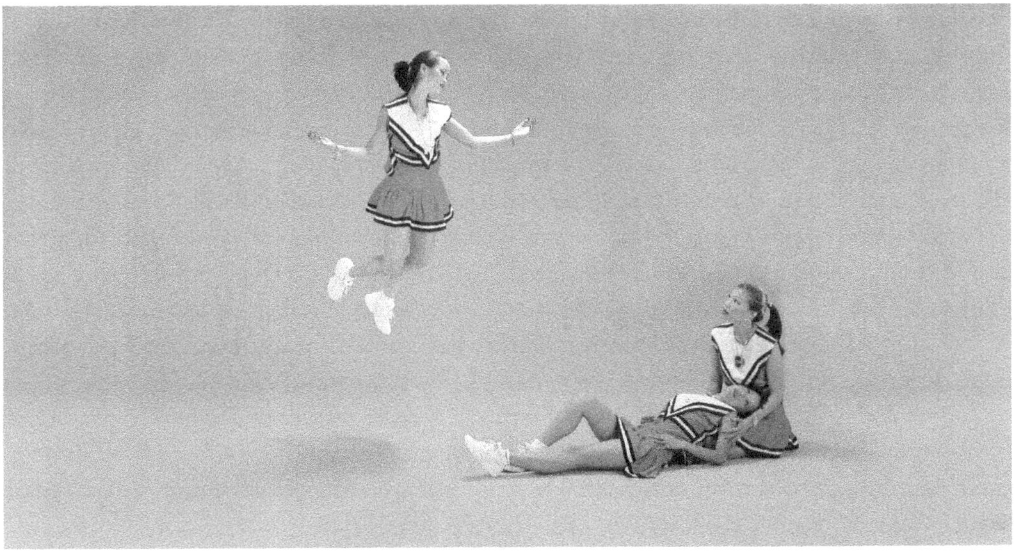

FIGURE 51. Luis Gispert, *Cheerleader Series, Untitled (Tres)*, 2001, color photograph. Courtesy of the artist.

text of variation in a tableau whose narrative is as preposterous as it is genuinely affecting. Like the deep meaning of hip-hop style that he insources, Gispert's baroque impulse functions not unlike colonial art of the Americas, both sacred and profane. In the words of Édouard Glissant, the elements of that art did not "occur as innovations in the representation of reality but as novel bits of information concerning a nature that was definitely 'new.'"[7] In contrast to the historic baroque of this hemisphere, which fused traits or cultural criteria made available by the various ethnic groups that came together in the new world, a contemporary baroque aesthetic, as compelled by an open-ended multicultural project, is underscored by Gispert with one of the most flagrant objects of social leveling: the uniform. Alert to the hazards inherent in any form of standardization, Gispert seeks a way in which photographic image-making has the unceasing power to frustrate conceptual assumptions about an obligatory relation between the picture's producer and the pictures produced. Gispert similarly claims today's representational system—one of postmodern sociocultural difference—to be in excess of those signs that by symbolic implication point to necessary subjects.

At this juncture it's worth recalling the identity-theft television commercial that was my starting point. In two color digital videos, *Block Watching* (2002) and *Can It Be That It Was All So Simple Then* (2002), Gispert upsets the continuity of voice and gaze to produce the kind of disagreement or ambivalence that informs the latter-day advertising image. In the first of these two time-based works, a cheerleader with long blond hair blowing back as in a fashion shoot—face directed at the camera—begins, after fussing with her fingernails, an amusingly bizarre vogue. In red-and- white cheerleader midriff top and miniskirt, covered in gold chains and medals around her wrists and neck rattling in unison with her hoop earrings, she gyrates with lips imperfectly synchronized to the distressing crank and loop of a car alarm's incessant siren—lips that alternately pout or smack in grimaces of sexual pleasure or annoyance. In this cleft performance, and its companion piece, Gispert tears apart what symbolically appears to belong to a predictable system of classification; he conflates severe urban negotiations with suburban ennui-naughtiness. The hazards of the street as a contained environment like the studio or gallery space belie the social markers of sight and sound as foreign to each other, and hence never inflexible as to what that can mutually mean. As to whose attempted theft could have triggered the alarm, it remains unclear: the cheerleader's colonization of a cultural environs to which she is alien, or the kind of body-snatching that transforms her into an image inscribed by so many contending community predicates.

In *Can It Be That It Was All So Simple Then*, a perverse script is enacted and lip-synched by a white, short-haired brunette in a cheerleader uniform, but devoid of any chunk accessories. A track by the Wu-Tang Clan begins with an onslaught of verbal male-to-male sexual violence, but as a self-aware, over-the-top send-up of a "torture, motherfucker" style that formerly had been unwitting of its suspect disposition.[8] Here, however, the posse banter is betrayed by incredulous laughter, as the brutal ante is progressively raised. The audio antagonism is representative of the bond between men that follows the logic of incarceration, where homosexual acts occur often "through rape or psychological coercion" and are hence not viewed "as acts of sexual orientation but as manifestations of control and domination, both reflections consistent with a 'gangsta mental' or gangster mentality."[9] The effect of such rivalry is one of arrest and fascination as we watch the animated cheerleader perform this shocking ventriloquism. Gispert goes to the hard core of social fears and fantasies activated between sexual subjects across the color line, even as he deflects and defuses the ideological powers that drive the allegedly incommensurate cultural economies here passing for each other (male-female; black-white; homosexual-heterosexual) in an unspeakable sadism neutralized by the cheerleader's final wink of an eye—yet another tribute to the language of advertising.

The stupefying coalitions between a visibly encoded body and the socially unconnected voice by which that surface is enabled to speak "off the subject"—as between a body politic and the officious power of its articulation—compels the psychic and political dimensions of Gispert's time-based works. Such trans-embodied voices produce a feeling of the uncanny Joan Copjec has described as an anxiety that "befalls us whenever we approach the *extimate* object in ourselves"—extimate in the sense of "they are in us that which is not us."[10] For psychoanalysis, objects like the gaze and voice are not identical to a subject but are the untenable possessions that feedback from what I see and hear into the function of looking and listening, at such a remove that deprives me of my selfsameness.

Insofar as the time-based works bear a resemblance to advertising images or video clips that beckon viewers to project themselves into a domain of meaning that cannot be completed, never mind how much we are made complicit, such viewer dispossession points again to Gispert's affinity for baroque practice. These strategies include the restless quality reflected at the level of the artist's faculties in various media formats, the concern for style as a productive structure, the interplay of violence and sensuality, and an impious but joyful confidence in the social field viewed not as a system of fixed meanings, but rather as an evolving visual and discursive regime whose uncertain interpretive warehouse reverberates into its own sound system of representation.

Gispert's image-making is committed to the cultural operations and meanings of style, but in a form of expression that is intentionally out of sync with its subject matter. If, as Ernst Gombrich once outlined for art history, the two main forces of style that make for change are "technological improvements" and "social rivalry," then hip-hop culture—with its origins in the science of sound manipulation and MC competitiveness—is the double writing with which Gispert participates in the production of meanings that he simultaneously reverses or transmogrifies into other markers in the US visual sphere.[11] In this respect his images are consistent with the overarching rap aesthetic that Tricia Rose describes as "a style nobody can deal with—a style that cannot be easily understood or erased, a style that has reflexivity to create counter-dominant narratives, [as well as] to fortify communities of resistance and simultaneously reserve the right to communal pleasures."[12] To the degree that Gispert enlists the visual construction or presentation of women to estrange and reorganize the social meanings most patently associated with both a hegemonic US mythology and a still largely male-inflected hip-hop subculture, the cheerleader uniform likewise becomes an inverted surrogate of athletic wear that, according to Nelson George, as "old school symbols of self-identification . . . gave way to status gear."[13] This is the line of flight, for example, that moves from the sundry articles sporting NFL and NBA logos to those of Tommy Hilfiger, FUBU, and Phat Farm. It is also the calculus whereby street style, the mediated sphere of music television, and the fashion industry have become increasingly more porous. To quote Iain Chambers again, and to account for the multiplicity of social markers employed by Gispert, this is the site out of which "subcultures once offered a 'strong' sense of stylistic opposition to the status quo [but have since] been extended and then gradually reworked into a wider sense of detailed differences; the 'Other' becomes more simply, but no less significantly, 'the others.'"[14] The multicultural, postmodern project has also its uncanny other in the capitalist production of desire and knowledge such that the style industries and the art world remain grounded in a split system whereby each force rapidly adjusts to the other's critique. Firewall? Like that could stop them.

Gispert has stated: "The part of pop culture that most appeals to me is the part that suggests that change is absolutely essential."[15] His work argues that popular culture and social politics are of a stylistic piece, such that any visible identity can only be a partial view. If style is the output and radical feedback that allows representation to authorize and undermine, his images compel viewers to rewrite narratives about the typologies in visual culture that both perpetuate and make ambivalent the certainties that inform our various social practices.

SIXTEEN

Geographies of Language and Light: Laura Aguilar, Raquel Gutiérrez

I've looked to Mexico City of the 1990s and to debates around the status of criticism, the role of the writer, and the changing art world late in the last millennium.

Discussed in public forums and in the written record were subjects of emergent impact: the complicity and antagonisms between artistic group formations, generational attitudes, global market forces and domestic commercial galleries, state and private museum cultures, regional and international systems of value, and initiatives and pedagogies that linked Mexico to art schools and cultural institutions in the United States, Europe, and beyond. These locations inform my own understanding of the role of art writing in terms of poetics and the historical imagination; they inform my own practice and life commitments along the borderlands of poetry, criticality, and art stories as they might be expressed in autobiography by art-historical means or memoir. What the late Franco-Mexican art historian Olivier Debroise had in mind when specifying the difference between a fanciful form of impressionistic writing and that of a literary or critical kind was a method, frame of reference, and genealogy of literary art writing associated with avant-garde language practices, consistent with the parallel life he led as an accomplished novelist and filmmaker.[1]

The domain of memoir leads me elsewhere today and by association to another scene of writing. Similarly, it enlivens homologies that blur the differences between literary, critical, and art-historical discourse but as reflected along the geopolitical borderlands of the US-Mexico divide. I turn to the particular effects derived from a style of writing inclined to map the relational and affective terrain of Chicanx/Latinx art through the lens of land use and commemoration in the US Southwest. In prose that demonstrates "how history continues to reveal itself in the contemporary art practices and national policies that animate the relational structures of the borderlands," poet, performer, and essayist Raquel Gutiérrez engages a "brown ontology" given to "art, music, space and institutionality" in a 2021 work of creative nonfiction entitled *Brown Neon*. In this cycle of interrelated first-person narratives, Gutiérrez speaks the personal loss and geopolitical "wounding" of history that prompts a kinship between artists and activists "through a labyrinth of damage towards one another . . . searching around in the dark for one another."[2]

As a participant witness, Gutiérrez animates a contemporary ethnography of the desert as a site for art practices, past and present, reflections on making through the lens of precarity and the process of grieving. Their essays relate an account of the present-day border crisis in interludes that time-stamp the Southwest desert landscape and its built environment, comprised as much by late modernist earthworks as by detention facilities serving as monuments to the surveillance state—but as a location as well for defiance though communities enlivened by the kinship of queer Brown cultural actors and social activists. In a discursive register that oscillates between the narrative and theoretical, and in a tone able to pivot from hard-boiled to self-effacing, Gutiérrez mobilizes a "protagonized self" in *Brown Neon*—all the while code-switching between roles as cultural critic and participant witness, and between sites of Brown ambivalence, pleasure, desire, and labor, with the particulars of "how we inhabit contested publics—whether it's receiving a subpar primary and secondary education, a predatory loan, or speaking in Spanish at the chain restaurant in a better-resourced adjacent neighborhood."[3] In the system of analogies that opens up between the illuminations afforded by neon—the festivity of night in the enclosures of bars as social space for queer and Brown desire, visual production, joy, and possibility—connected also to the materiality and relations of life in the key of Brown, Gutiérrez enlivens Chicanx/Latinx art practices, but in a form of argument that employs the metabolism of speech in scene structures that unite cultural worlds and their historical strata in Tucson, West Texas, New Mexico, and Southern California. By demystifying art objects as chiefly the aftereffects of contingent processes within Brown sites of inquiry, queer family, and the precarity of the present, Gutiérrez contributes to the art-historical account by means of a genre they denominate "ekphrastic memoir."[4]

An initial essay suite in *Brown Neon* assembles around the metaphor of desert grief. In passages that are a tribute to and lament for the passing of mentor figure Jeanne Córdova (publisher of the journal *Lesbian Tide* and butch feminist role model), Gutiérrez links the possibility of an intergenerational queer family narrative, one that explores the status of son as father to the man in the continuum of butch lesbian and trans-masculine expression, a rehearsal parallel to prospects for the intentional communities that make one's adulthood legible or illegible in years posterior to mentorship and the pedagogies of desire. Gutiérrez writes: "Our butchness was so ingrained in our queer bodies that we read as ladies only to a world that didn't really matter to us, that couldn't read the magic in the code we spoke with flesh and blood."[5] In the uncertain chronologies of grief, a romantic separation leads Gutiérrez in their memoir persona to connect heartbreak with the political emotions that coalesce along particular forms of alienation—"being cannibalized by multiple institutions wanting to extract the brown intelligence that 'earned' us a place in their ranks"—that is, the societal limits placed on cultural aspiration for Brown artists who, despite seeking economic stability, have been circumscribed by the conditions available to the creative precariat. This matter of feeling "stuck" is thematized and likened to an embodied process, thanks to insights attained through the physical prowess and material specificity of making adobe with a friend and fellow maker.[6]

In 2017 the author visits the Los Angeles–based multidisciplinary artist Rafa Esparza, then on a "summer residency" in West Texas fulfilling a "prestigious commission from Ballroom Marfa."[7] In their writing, Gutiérrez makes visible Esparza's method that calls on "ancestral knowledge as a way to bring brown, immigrant labor practices in the U.S. into the sightline of those [who] have been marginalized by the avant-garde and the art market."[8] Through a collage narrative of heartbreak and art-making, Gutiérrez expands the personal and political meanings of Esparza's practice to include real estate speculation and the art world's futures market. In describing the physical duress of adobe brickmaking, the writer discerns the degree to which a "semiotics of self-discovery and reinvention" and the supply chain of contemporary art are both contingent on land expropriation. Settlers colonized "territory inhabited by Shoshone, Washoe, and Ute Indians before and after the Treaty of Guadalupe Hidalgo," extractions that connect to US ascendency in the Cold War era, to Michael Heizer's *Double Negative* (1969) and Robert Smithson's *Spiral Jetty* (1970), both earthworks "seizing on the concept that there is nothing in that part of the Nevada desert except for an invitation to tear into the earth," such that the "architects of Land Art have reproduced a version of Manifest Destiny—one that stretches from the corners of Lower Manhattan to the desert of the Southwest." Additional lines in the desert sands connect the colonizing enterprise, political and economic asylum-seeking, and anti-immigration to the border-wall prototypes made by Swiss artist Christoph Büchel, and to the policies of gentrification and artwashing in Boyle Heights, Los Angeles. The centuries of forgetting "the way history is forced off the land" can obtain in the smallest of architectural details.[9]

For example, with Esparza's adobe works in view, Gutiérrez activates a series of associations referring to a home, one time the residence they and their partner shared, and to the so-called truth wall:

> [that] part of the room that exposes how the house is built. You see the unique materials that went into the skeleton—or how we know if the house has good bones. The truth wall reveals what we are surrounded by, showing its history in the sedimentary layers of adobe, bricks that live in the triangular crevice, deep in recess, high up where the wall touches the ceiling. An opening in a wall surface, the organic components within a wall, a century and its violences trapped behind spackle and stucco. A truth wall might help increase the property's value. In the era where our desires for sustainable, climate-conscious living come inside a gold-level package of mercenary marriages—we marry up even when we want to slum—a truth wall or truth window often serves as a decor option demonstrative of our own interiors.
>
> The truth wall silently nodded to the breakup that put it on the market.[10]

In the "115-degree summertime" of Southern Arizona, the locus of *Brown Neon*'s writing present, metaphors and flashpoints connect the anxiety and desires linked to living the precarious life of a Brown artist-activist in the No More Deaths movement. "The body here serves also," Gutiérrez writes, "as an ever-shifting part of the mutual aid machine that powers through one of the most harrowing physical landscapes in the world." Described are the looming ambivalence about capitalizing on migrant death for art making, gains and losses in the tense conversation between Mexican American and Indigenous communities, reflections in the ongoing ethics of whether and how migrant plight can or cannot be pictured. Insofar as "people come north because the alternative is death," works like Karlito Miller Espinosa's installation *Untitled (Corridor)* (2018) unsettle Gutiérrez in that they are a "reminder of the debt I owe the migrant, the uncomfortable intimacies that contour the histories between us, the circumstances that reinforce the tensions." Or, for example, in a narrative telling of the horizontal conflicts between progressives who have rallied around the phenomenon of "arts organizations that help scrub the stink of gentrification from developers seizing upon real estate opportunities," they wonder: "Do I sell out so you don't have to?" These and other sentences punctuate what is often repressed or unattainable in the authoritative mood of a typical art-historical account.[11]

The embedded meanings assemble in the final rehearsals of works by artists Shizu Saldamando, Sebastian Hernández, and—my focus here—the "photographer and chronicler of brown life," Laura Aguilar. The artist's death in 2019 from complications from diabetes ought to remind us, Gutiérrez relates, "of a U.S. healthcare system that brings into relief the depths of precarity [that] Chicana artists, intellectuals and cultural producers endure and succumb to"—Gloria Anzaldúa among them. In an essay entitled "Vessel Among Vessels: Laura Aguilar's Body in Landscape" and beginning with what they call the "conceptual ouroboros" of *Nature Self-Portrait #14* (1996), Gutiérrez draws a through line in Aguilar's work, a speculative art history that attaches desire and fantasy to criticality.

They argue that Aguilar's photographic self-portraits are "a quiet insurrection against policing engines that power the landscape, along with histories of violence against the Indigenous and Mexican people and otherwise marginalized bodies."[12] This vivid art-historical claim further reverberates through the situated subjectivity and embodied perspective on the space of composition that "ekphrastic memoir" inaugurates. It can be read in tandem with the interpretive framework and scholarship in the exhibition catalog *Laura Aguilar: Show and Tell*, the first comprehensive retrospective of Aguilar's opus, a "collection of her work spanning three decades. In photographs that are frequently political as well as personal," the curatorial statement encapsulates, "Aguilar offers candid portrayals of herself, her friends and family, and her Chicana/Latina and LGBT communities . . . using her nude body as an overt and courageous rebellion against the colonization of Chicana identities: racial, gendered, cultural, and sexual."[13]

Gutiérrez supplements these critical accounts with interiority and narrative, scale-shifting techniques and a syntax of feeling. They lend vocal amplitude to what Amelia Jones defines as the "structure of relationality" in Aguilar's "radical vulnerability" and attendant "psychic strategies of expulsion, projections and containment," or what Macarena

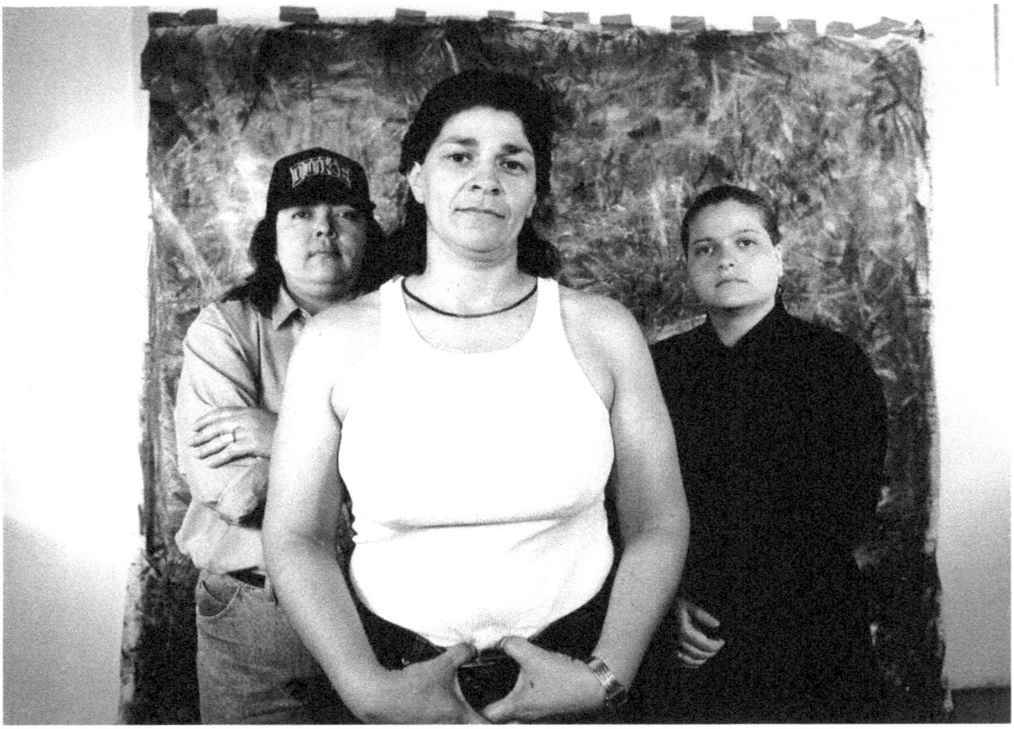

FIGURE 52. Laura Aguilar, *Plush Pony #2*, 1992. Courtesy of the artist and the UCLA Chicano Studies Research Center.

Gómez-Barris assigns as the "submerged perspective" and the "self-ecology" by which Aguilar "queers the mestizo body as discrete," so erasing "the boundaries between land, lived experience, and the social and ecological texture of the physical human self."[14] Gutiérrez orchestrates the interplay between their own experience as a Brown butch lesbian and the intergenerational memory atlas for which Aguilar's galleries of portraits and self-portraits serve. Gutiérrez's writing aligns with the process that gave way to Aguilar's photographic groups the *Latina Lesbian* series (1986–90) and the *Plush Pony* series (1992), that is, in "conversation between narrator and subject" that collapses a decade that separates Aguilar's photographs from lived experience Gutiérrez relates about their own kinships by choice (fig. 52). Her elective affinities comprise a narrative about queer desire and the pedagogies of self that materialize when, in 2001, Gutiérrez, a budding writer and performer, participates in a lesbian bar–sponsored softball team named Las Traviesas (The Rascals):

> When I came to the Plush Pony, the bar signaled what it meant to be a brown, gender nonconforming queer from East Los Angeles—it was a time and space when one could traffic in the promiscuity between the aspirational lesbian and the rough queer. My queer adolescence took place at the convergence between the higher educational options that gave the subjects in Latina Lesbians language and empowerment, and the roughness of barrio nightlife captured in the deep creases of the subjects' faces in the Plush Pony series.[15]

Gutiérrez provides testimony, embodiment of the anxieties and desire that mark the difference between what she validates as the "respectability close-up" of Aguilar's subjects in *Latina Lesbians* and the anonymity afforded the Plush Pony dykes, as a lesson in "how to inhabit our skins and to heed caution when skin became a liability." In the poetics of *Brown Neon*, the East Los Angeles lesbian bar softball league season "allowed for a nuanced inhabiting of an experience," writes Gutiérrez, that replicates "what Aguilar did representationally." These insights argue for a fictive developmental account that led Aguilar to produce the major works of the late 1990s and the 2000s and thereby "break open and into joy for her own brown abundance." As if by camera-generated double exposure, Gutiérrez transposes their own phantom anatomy and "wounding designation" onto Aguilar's "outlaw body," especially in relation to the *Grounded* series of color photographs (2006–7) "depicting Aguilar's body contracted and splayed in gestures that mirror the earthen spheroid formations in Joshua Tree National Park," what the author identifies as "respite and revolution in its wild hinterland of quiet intensity" (plate 33). In writing that similarly performs that "prison of wounding," the borders between subject and object blur, the lines between Gutiérrez and Aguilar overlap, as they walk together "unencumbered by the trapping of modernity through the shadows of Mojave yucca plants, ocotillos, and gravel trails—to piss in the wind and jerk off into the shadowy parts of the canyons—means that I could be as free as those who own the land on which I stand and make my own land art. . . . These are the ways I come to recalibrate how I see the vastness of my own body held in the center of the vastness of Joshua Tree."[16]

The memoir persona of *Brown Neon* gives verbal materiality—empathy, recognition, attachment—to the work of speculation in layered histories that include the mid-nineteenth-century Mormon pioneers who named the species of desert flora that early twentieth-century South Pasadena socialite Minerva Hamilton Hoyt used to christen the national park she worked for years to preserve.

Gutiérrez submits their "own affective assignations to the longing in the photographs of Aguilar in Joshua Tree, the ways the body sits, the subject's back to the camera as if in some heartbroken repose, the landscape embracing what's left of the body in wait and in the quietest of want." The prose here obliges an extended citation:

> I imagine that her coming to the desert meant making and taking an opportunity to be small. What might it mean to revel in the aura of smallness? To forget the bulldagger-in-a-china-shop policing of self for a moment and take in the safety offered in the eternity of sky above. In a city, in a dark, red-bulbed dancehall, a smoky bar in the bottoms of El Sereno, the large bodies of gender renegades are read as suspect in both appetite and desire. Good lays, bad citizens. Laura takes those suspicions and distills them in the photographs of her body, where she captures herself in the middle. She cropped many of the images to make her body appear as another presumed object taking its rightful place in the natural environment—another boulder, another mass of sediment containing the narrative of collision where two, three, or unknown numbers of cultures come to situate in the folds of her rippling belly or the stretch marks on her back. The largesse of that gesture seems only right to settle into a space like Joshua Tree, haven for the thing it's named after, and haven for embodied sites of excess. . . .

> What the body wants is the earthliest of desires and in Aguilar's bodily charge the desire is as immense as the rock formations it mirrors. In the interstitial space where my identity lives alongside my own desire to scrutinize, I wander on to Aguilar with eyes closed, her naked belly spilling over into the narcissistic mirrors on the surfaces of puddles that dot the New Mexican landscape in the *Nature Self-Portrait* series (1996) as if to plead to a lover or a swath of land, *Will you ever be mine?*[17]

Gutiérrez gives voice to Aguilar's body and its circumstance, between indwelling and social legibility, between borderland self-possession, sexed assertions, and enacted styles that can make the function of the image palpable by rehearsing nearness—phantasmatic and physical—in mediated or analog space. Emerging therein is a form of life in an empathic tense, a social engagement that, belated, will have occurred only by measure of a photograph's audible afterlife in ekphrastic memoir. The aggregate effects of alternating scenes and intonations reflect the uncertainty at stake when the first-person singular is discernable in the equivocations, misgivings, mood shifts, or fluctuations between the external and internal viewpoints; forces that confront in poetic form a once-imagined social unity—the humanity and duration, so to speak, that writing is able to contain. In the time span of its syllables, in the contact zone of its enactment, in the vocal enjoyment of pronouncing the written, the defense of one's inscape is the refusal to be judged, or for Gutiérrez, to be rendered out of the picture. Sounded embodiment is a material force—a holding place, a threshold—wherein is activated a series of arrivals and departures that lead from physical reality to sensory perception, and back. The method enlivens experience with situations and arguments that so unsettle the agreement of cause and effect as to approximate the life process—and by extension, the discontinuous flow of history—as movements that amend, delay, curve, and surprise.

Time will only allow me to rehearse in briefest detail the little marvel of illumination that is the final act of the essay—a phase shift by which Gutiérrez offers their dance partner, Laura Aguilar, to "another specter of working-class beauty and grace—the living ghost of Tejana pop queen Selena, a patron saint of joyful femme ebullience dancing in the foreground of another Joshua Tree" in the 1993 music video for the hit track "Amor Prohibido," directed by Cecilia Miniucchi, seven years prior to the *Grounded* series. In the briefest sketch, Gutiérrez reads Selena's "femme vulnerability" as being "situated in a classed conflict" reiterative of century-spanning colonial encounters, but together hand-to-hand now with Laura Aguilar in an uncanny desert choreography. (Freud on the uncanny: "So the dead *do* live on and appear on the scene of their former activities!"[18]):

> And thus, a dance emerges between star-crossed lovers of mixed economic backgrounds and blood—the butch lawyers and the femme sex workers of Aguilar's portraitures, the girl on the wrong side of the "Amor Prohibido" railroad tracks. This dance emerges and flirts with recognition and visibility, leaving the penumbra of anonymity in its wake. It gets choreographed between an austere landscape like Joshua Tree and its partner in brown excess; to see the movement of every wrinkle like it were desert mallow, every keloid like churro cholla, every bit of broken skin blooming in liberated relief. Laura Aguilar and Selena have both trafficked in those excessive intersections through a radical

> praxis of their brownness. This is a malleable brownness that sits and lays corpulently in the annals of art and popular culture, misperceived and misaligned as well as in the valleys of Joshua Tree, a mestizaje of suspicion where two bodies in a desert sing in similar and simultaneous registers of scarcity and plethora.[19]

In their ekphrastic memoir Gutiérrez performs interpretive potential of fantasy in the art-historical imagination, akin to the purpose of the anecdote, what Walter Benjamin described as a "street insurrection," which gives way in my view to self-discernment. This literary device is a critical invention insomuch as it resists the colonizing forces of social life conventionally rhymed in our productions of knowledge that "discipline the true life and confine it to barracks." *Brown Neon* finds a language of life in the historical imagination given to an "adequate and comprehensible . . . pathos of nearness" on a human scale.[20]

Michael Baxandall famously specified that any "language . . . is a conspiracy against experience in the sense of being a collective attempt to simplify and arrange experience into manageable parts."[21] The ekphrastic mood activates the interplay of subject and object; it makes palpable a selfhood—for a brief lapse in time—that can modify perception and reframe our view of art objects and the worlds of which they are evidence; fragments of history, as ordinary and extraordinary as the interaction with one's immediate circumstance. With tension and timing, the ekphrastic as memoir and mimicry seeks to re-enchant the communicability of experience in that contact zone with the past represented by processes imbued with the particularity of time and place—at once on the side of emergence in the world, and on the side of a spectral reception. *Brown Neon* reminds the historical account of the "interstitial space where my identity lives alongside my own desire to scrutinize" insomuch as I submit to wander now with Gutiérrez over "mirrors on the surfaces of puddles that dot the landscape as if to plead to a lover or a swath of land"—our common modernity a locus of moods in Brown and neon.[22] *Brown Neon* is the name assigned to objects and actions in the geographies of light and language, when we are able or inclined to give them the amplitude of relevance in our lives, as intimate as a lover or as contested as a swath of land. It is a category of things greater than the individual or object of inquiry, an ethics of what it means, in fact, to make of wonder and knowledge a choreography, a theater of memory, a valentine to all those former scenes that serve as placeholders for an attention to material, the experience of contingency, and the making of sharable selfhoods—"will you ever be mine?"

SEVENTEEN

Latinx Art in the Future Imperfect: *Axis Mundo*, Jennif(f)er Tamayo

You imagine the complex of time and place as ground given to invention, situations of exchange, things made with purpose or as improvised actions in arenas inclined to favor displays of furtive experience. You wonder what pressures conspire such that one form of life, and not another, so endures as to be acknowledged in hindsight. What objects and actors survive in memory over other eventualities indicative of an identical past? Whatever else compels the affirmation of history, a narrative drive seeks to arrange discontinuous events, actions, and artifacts into a plausible field of relation. Regarding his final book, *Before Pictures*, the late art historian and critic Douglas Crimp spoke candidly about the dilemmas of writing proper to objects, social exchanges, and historical description; about the question of tone or voice commensurate with argument and storytelling; about the perspective that wonders where exactly to begin any narrative and how to navigate the space between the idiosyncratic view and the common concern.[1] A distrust of the developmental account compels a form of curatorial practice toward accounts that work to reflect the incidental temporalities they describe; art histories that pursue alternate narrative or spatial techniques capable of connecting episodes around subjects and locations, in order to gain closer proximity, to inhabit the restless and unruly contemporary commitments to "the experimental exercise of freedom."[2]

These reflections came to mind around *Axis Mundo: Queer Networks in Chicano L.A.* and the exhibition's iteration in Houston at Lawndale Art Center (figs. 53–55).[3] Curators C. Ondine Chavoya and David Evans Frantz, in research that sought to offer the "first historical exhibition ever mounted on LGBTQ Chicana/o or Latina/o artists," found it imperative to deviate from the art-historical convention that lends focus to a circle of lesser-known artists in the orbit of an allegedly major figure.[4] And instead of organizing the exhibition "around an aesthetic or conceptual uniformity across multiple bodies of work by various artists," the curators assembled media as varied as Xeroxed flyers, music zines, mail-art postcards, fashion, videos, text-based art, photographs, and paintings.[5] The assembled works and ephemera, surreptitiously at times, pointed back to artist Edmundo "Mundo" Meza, whose brief life and work in East LA had until now remained largely invisible to the mainstream art world and to established Chicano/a formations of the 1970s and 1980s. These collaborations with Meza were "not always immediate or one-to-one, and thus some of the connections may appear unexpected or anomalous."[6] Nonetheless, Meza's attitudes, energies, and promise—cut short at the age of twenty-nine from complications due to AIDS—were central to connecting worlds of art and action in Los Angeles around the women's liberation movement, gay rights struggles, and El Movimiento, the social and aesthetic affirmation of identity for Mexican-descendant peoples in the United States. *Axis Mundo* proposed a narrative based not on categories, formations, and influence, but on encounters that led to chance associations and intentional kinships. The exhibition invited speculation about what a historical account can convey when the premise most resembles the ephemeral cohesions that drove alternate forms of society and belonging. It made visible a little-known archive of works and documents that tell the story of alliances, sites of experimentation, and incidents of conviviality. In Los Angeles, from the late 1960s to the early 1990s, these energies gave way to art making, nightlife, social-justice activism, punk music scenes, print publishing, and fashion innovations—all claims to a form of urban visibility—a right to the city—and to makeshift spaces that often parodied mainstream art and culture. Similarly, the curators designed gallery spaces to reflect the "queer synergies" and networks that led to a particular form of world making, at once "promiscuous and capacious."[7] In their curatorial essay, Chavoya and Frantz allude to "Julie Ault's fluid framework for what constitutes an artistic movement; 'shared concerns and overlapping agendas . . . social configurations as well as communication and degrees of collaboration between individuals—one thing leading to another, migration of ideas and models, generative social processes.'"[8] A sobering testament to the precarious fate of material culture and to the unpredictability of historical processes, *Axis Mundo* rehearsed the idea that "there are numerous reasons why artists are known or unknown," presenting the assembled work in such a way as to "de-center and destabilize canonical formations," prompting analogous occasions of display to spatialize and mirror the historical account.[9]

The result of multiyear research into institutional archives and personal collections that uncovered surprising finds and unexpected connections, *Axis Mundo* presented a memory-atlas of images and artifacts from an underground network that connected Mundo Meza to such figures of the Cold War–era Los Angeles avant-garde as Alice Bag, Vaginal Davis, Simon Doonan, Genesis Breyer P-Orridge, Ruby Ray, Zoe Leonard, Phranc, Pauline Oliveros, and Jack Vargas. The exhibition restaged the interweaving worlds of the Los Angeles DIY punk scene with Chicano conceptual art and vernacular traditions, including work that employed *rasquachismo*, an "aesthetic philosophy of the underdog," Chavoya explains,

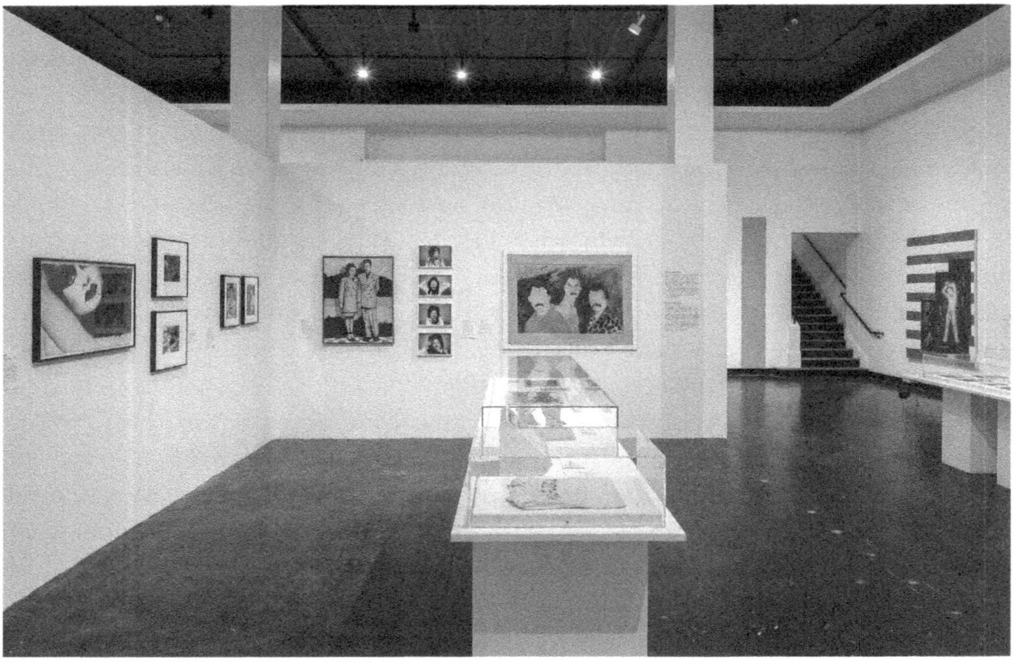

FIGURE 53. *Axis Mundo: Queer Networks in Chicano L.A.* (installation view), Lawndale Art Center, 2019. Photo by Nash Baker.

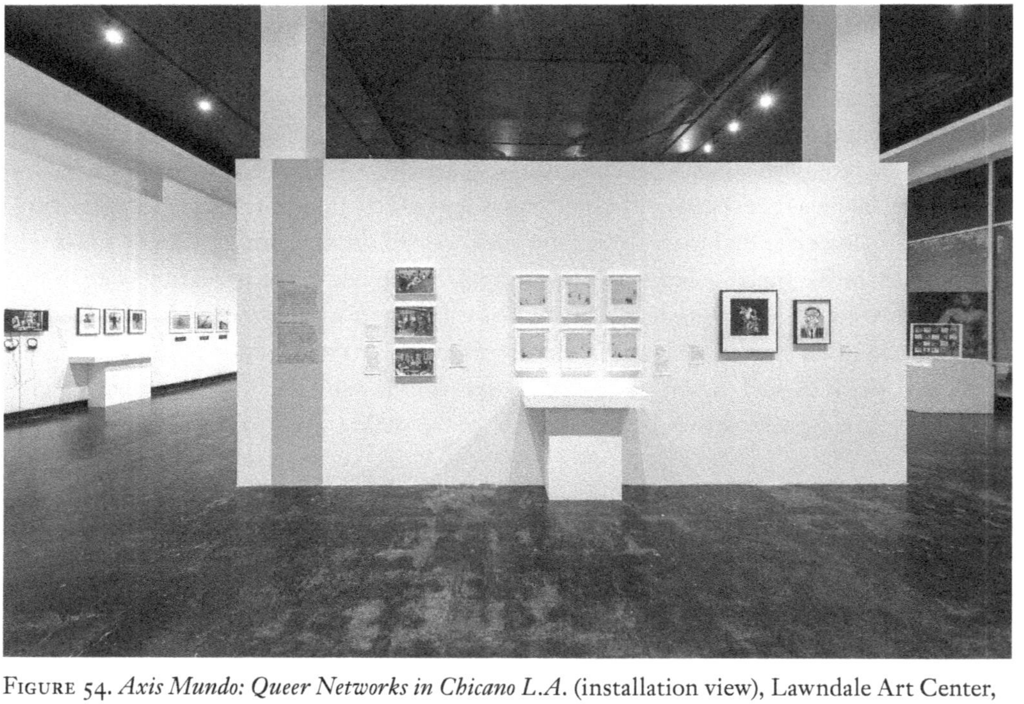

FIGURE 54. *Axis Mundo: Queer Networks in Chicano L.A.* (installation view), Lawndale Art Center, 2019. Photo by Nash Baker.

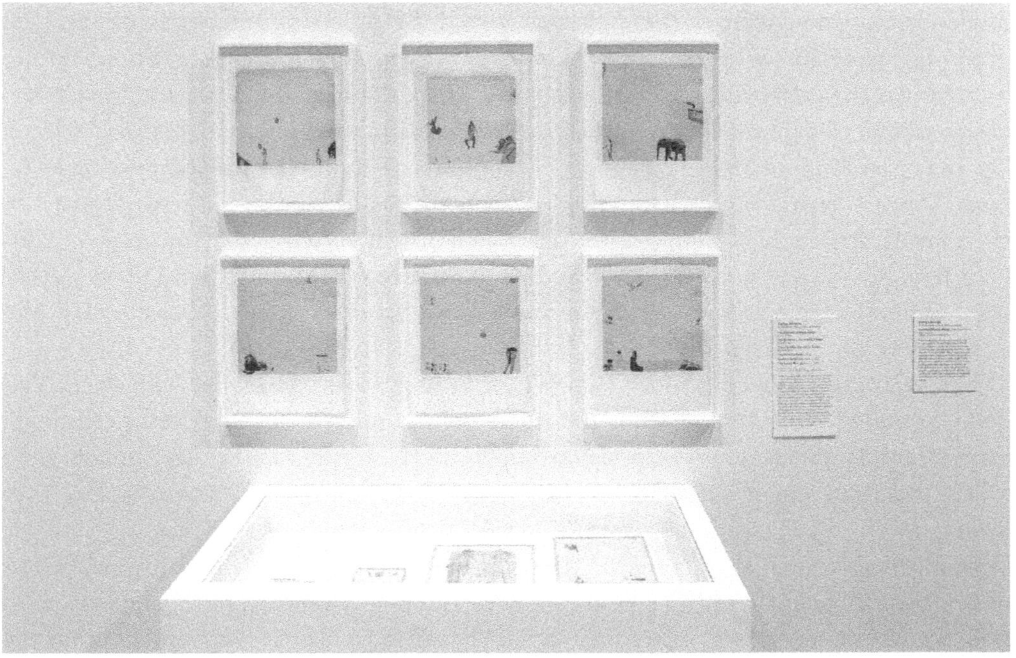

FIGURE 55. *Axis Mundo: Queer Networks in Chicano L.A.* (installation view: works on paper by Carlos Almaraz), Lawndale Art Center, 2019. Photo by Nash Baker.

"a making do that has to do with tactics and tenacity."[10] In constellations that connect histories of community organizing around questions of same-sex desire, modes of gender expression, and experimental art practices, *Axis Mundo* recovered queer Chicanx histories and artists' archives structured into thematic arrangements. The associations radiated outward from the self-fashioning proper to gay subcultures ("Chicano Chic"); to glam rock, punk music, and performance art scenes connecting the group Les Petites Bonbons, founded by Jerry Dreva and Robert Lambert, to the multimedia ethos around the band Nervous Gender, whose lead member, Gerardo Velázquez, produced paintings, graphic design, sound art, video, and poetry ("Art Meets Punk"). Similarly, such venues as Los Angeles Contemporary Exhibitions (LACE) were shown to have drawn connections between punk performances, arts advocacy, and AIDS activism.

Visual relationships in *Axis Mundo*'s curatorial design worked to reflect similar sorts of "queer synergy"—as, for instance, between the painting *Las Locas* (ca. 1980) by Teddy Sandoval and neighboring works on display. Sandoval's acrylic-and-mixed-media canvas depicts three anonymous men turned in half-body poses as though facing the lens during a camera shoot for an album cover. The scrawls and stray markings that speckle the background in pastel colors appear to resemble the effects, in color photography, of light in the interior of a discotheque captured by inadequate film speed. The shirtless, furry-chested middle figure wears green eyeshadow, his brows tweezed and arched in knowing assent. He looks on in decided contrast to the featureless faces of the stylishly attired companions to his left and right. All three sport prominent handlebar moustaches. Partially hidden in the anonymity of the nighttime crowd, Latino masculine attributes and the grooming associated with the "clone" aesthetic of 1970s and 1980s gay male subculture both affirm and contradict the flamboyance to which the title, *Las Locas*, alludes: a reference to screaming queens. Next to this work is photo documentation by Judith F. Baca of her 1975 performance *Vanity Table*, part of the Women's Building exhibition entitled *Chicanas, Venas de la Mujer.* Dressed to play the persona of La Pachuca, the artist gestures to the camera as though catching her reflection in a mirror, enacting a masquerade of Chicana ferocity—what Catherine S. Ramírez calls "aberrant femininity."[11] By turns she applies cosmetics, wields a switchblade, and adjusts her neckerchief, blouse collar, and upwardly voluminous hairdo.

Sandoval's *Las Locas* and Baca's *Vanity Table* prompt ideas continuous with Patssi Valdez's *Portrait of Sylvia Delgado* (early 1980s), the subject rendered in what Leticia Alvarado terms "high femme (aggressive) makeup," and with the "gender ambiguity" underscored by the male and female sitters in Jef Huereque's *My Parents in Their Matching Zoot Suits* (ca. 1973).[12]

Axis Mundo viewed the Southern California metropolis as home to simultaneous sites of heightened meaning within a larger national and global context. In this respect, a series of works on paper by Carlos Almaraz can be read as emblematic of the exhibition and its method. He produced, in 1970, a series of collages using tiny magazine cutouts sparsely distributed over a grid-paper surface, titling the small-format works with more than a hint of the grand theatrical gesture: *The Conscious Manipulator, The Children's Party with A Angel* [*sic*], *The Important But Clever Lover, The Queen's Own*, *Sweet Indulgence*, and *The Young Martyr.* Almaraz had moved from Los Angeles to New York City where, from 1965 to 1970, he rented a SoHo loft from Richard Serra and Nancy Graves, worked as an illustrator, gained exposure to the anti-art strains of Dada and Duchamp, the literary cubism of Apollinaire and Gertrude Stein, and an art world that saw pop art in critical decline but still robustly supported by a network of commercial galleries and collectors.

Struggles with depression led Almaraz back to Los Angeles where he reaffirmed a connection to his Mexican roots in the artistic energies of El Movimiento. In 1973 he worked with artist Judithe Hernández on a convention mural for Cesar Chavez and the United Farm Workers and became a founding member of the Chicano art collective Los Four (with Frank Romero, Gilbert Luján, and later, Beto de la Rocha).[13]

In the 1970 collage works, composed during the transitional period between New York and Los Angeles, Almaraz infused these diminutive works with homologies for same-sex desire and its consequences associated with danger, along with references to the animal kingdom and the divine, visually structured by foregrounding the margin or edge of the compositional field. In *The Conscious Manipulator* (plate 34), a male hand releases what appear to be large thimble-like forms into the air; simultaneously, a gray-scale magazine cutout of a 1960s beefcake, in full-frontal nudity, appears dwarfed in the lower right-hand corner by the encompassing surface grid and by a gargantuan cluster of table grapes nearby. In *The Children's Party with A Angel*, two depictions of lesbian sex—one in black and white, the other in color—feature couples whose bodies variously embrace and entangle, while an angel, as though lifted from a medieval book of hours, kneels in prayer with back turned to the scenes of seduction (fig. 56). In *The Young Martyr*, an art-deco locomotive charges headlong toward a courtly maiden—another art historical overlay—a truncated obelisk crowned with an obsidian sphere, and a photo cutout of a woman-identified model seated in partial undress, legs slightly parted. A pair of scissors floats above a 1950s pinup reclining face down in hose and garter belt, her body severed by the compositional grid of the collage. Other elements in the series include a fragment depicting a packet of Nestlé bittersweet chocolate; a flower-bearing child as though reproduced from a vintage Victorian greeting card; a handcrafted basket, a sign for Camel cigarettes, and a revolver; duplicate male nudes from 1950s bodybuilder magazines that doubled as gay erotica in the repressive climate of the Cold War; and disembodied female legs and other body parts transposed from mid-century soft-core print publications. In these collages, Almaraz arranged details derived from the mass media to serve as visual counterparts for the antagonisms that play out between fear and fantasy, between prohibitions and the "ground relative to one's desire."[14] These collages endure as emblems of the queer Mexican-descendant networks that prompted conversations in Los Angeles during the 1970s and 1980s about experience and experiment in art and creative action, driven by sexually nonconformist and ethno-racial demands for cultural equity, social inclusion, resource distribution, and forms of civic reciprocity. The collages argue for the social life of art on an axis that connects one's desire and locality to the larger world.

As with other artists in this exhibition, Almaraz died from AIDS-related complications.[15] In this respect *Axis Mundo* also served as a model for thinking about the intimacy of kinship and artistic practice linked to situations of catastrophe, trauma, and extreme transience. Art historian and theorist Robb Hernández has proposed that "AIDS's near obliteration of Chicanx avant-gardisms' queerer exponents yielded other modes of recordkeeping, custodial interventions, vernacular preservation, and storage technologies." In the "response to human loss" during the AIDS crisis, Hernández identifies an "archival body/archival space" that personifies "another state of *being, an approximation of human loss* in the articulation of accumulated records."[16] *Axis Mundo* made visible the radical contingency of persons and practices that comprise the meaningful narratives of a moment. The exhibition exposed the precarious nature of the historical account, accidental kinships or cultivated associations that will or will not have survived—the future imperfect—so as to document the incidents of sociability that eventuate in scenes of art and expressive culture.

Inasmuch as *Axis Mundo* looked at urban space as a model to think about histories of ethno-racial and sexual self-fashioning for Chicana/o/x identity, contemporary Latinx artists turn to the landscape of digital capitalism to give new meaning to queer Latinx personhood. Jennif(f)er Tamayo, a queer, formerly undocumented, Latinx writer and performer, has developed a multiplatform and multipart intervention, existing in iterations on the page and in the visuality of poetry-as-performance. The performer's transposed voice and body multiply as sites of corporal histories, media critique, identitarian loss of bearing, but also ancestral knowledge prone to ask questions about the violent legacies of slavery and settler colonialism that haunt the present and the specificity of

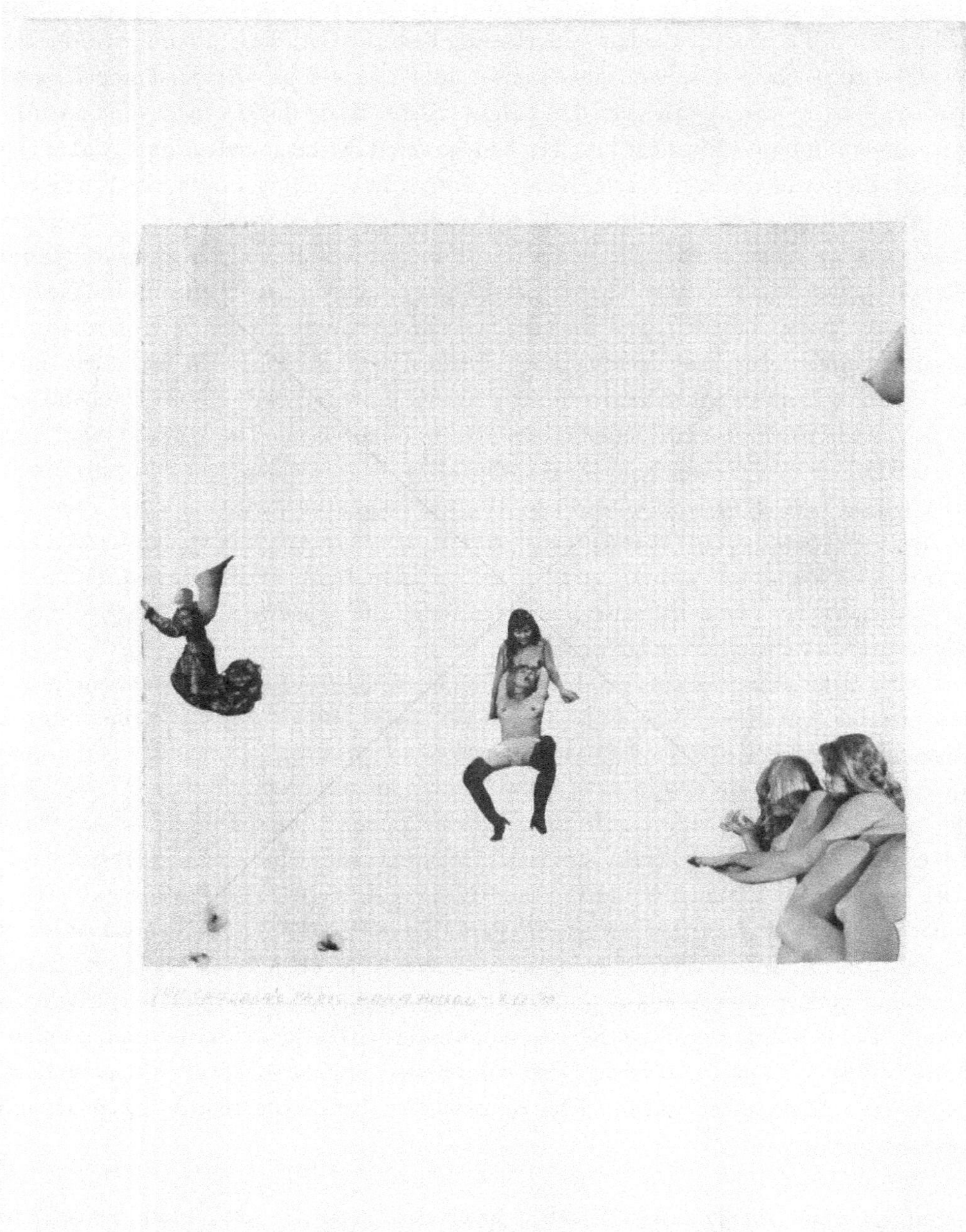

Figure 56. Carlos Almaraz, *The Children's Party with A Angel*, March 17, 1970, mixed-media collage on paper, 14 × 10 in. (35.6 × 26.7 cm). Collection of Elsa Flores and The Estate of Carlos Almaraz.

place. The body examined is also multipart: the artist's own, as figured in language, but also in relation to the Nickelodeon television animated character Dora the Explorer.

In an artist statement Tamayo writes that "If Nickelodeon's *Dora the Explorer* was, perhaps, a whitened fantasy of the late 1990s 'Latin-Explosion,' or an affective recuperation of Cuban migrant, Elián González, snatched back into the arms of U.S. empire, or a digital production of deracinated pan-Latinidad ready-made for mass consumption, then my various performance-poetry projects, loosely titled LA QUEERADORA, take on the digital properties of hyperlinks, glitching and meme-ing to develop a poetics of annotation that critiques *Dora the Explorer*'s enduring participation in the embodiment and deployment of global white supremacy as an infectious *virtual-corpo-reality*."[17]

In the poet's book-length work *YOU DA ONE* (2014/2017)—a print-based performance or theater of voices, what Della Pollock terms "performing writing"—Tamayo created an immersive textual space.[18] In typography that provides a harrowing, excessive, and deranging glimpse into the internet unconscious, celebrity delirium, rape culture, and the immigrant condition, the book is also an agonizing account of family trauma, a father-daughter interface or reckoning, immigrant narratives of return, in this case to Colombia, and textual orchestrations of melancholy, sarcasm, and fury. The book serves as a time-based and visual performance about the desire for access, world making, inaugural scenes, embodied actions, and about unacknowledged debts; chiefly the frame of performance that prompts affect-in-motion; with this in turn driving commitments between visual and vocal imaginations.

Similarly, in *LA QUEERADORA* (fig. 57), Tamayo examines the "racial project of U.S. Latinidad," as complicit with the nation-state's "capitalist and anti-Black enterprise," through the lens of the artist's own childhood and "the rise of mainstream internet culture." Tamayo has stated that insofar as the project of *latinidad* and internet culture "began to 'enter' households during the 80s and 90s," Dora the Explorer can serve "as a critical site of inquiry. A "'live-action' character [becomes] imbued with a digital materiality key to her production of Latinidad: fluid, placeless, and amorphous."[19]

In this alternate universe, a critical space of enactments, existing simultaneously on the printed page and in performance space, Dora's antithesis is the symbolic weapon of the law, the phallus of white supremacy. This "white cock" sets into motion a complex system of analogies that connects the surveillance state, the capitalist machine demanding fuel in the form of laboring immigrant bodies, to the Stephen Sondheim / Leonard Bernstein musical *West Side Story*. It transposes Freud's 1905 case study "Fragment of an Analysis of a Case of Hysteria" onto the Dream Act of 2011 (section C, paragraph 3), or vice versa, at any rate onto a queer or subordinate desiring subject lost in tyrannical nightmares of domination over a precarious or destitute life.

> I won't lie; like white cock, sometimes I want to crush hearts
> I want to stomp out all the love in all the hearts
> splatter crust broke hearts of my shiny baby sweetiemaks
> but the cost of permanent residency is good moral character
> in which good moral character is determined by a medical examination
> into the caliber of me 21st century pristine slut affect
> look at me: does it hang on me like drag, overcoatish

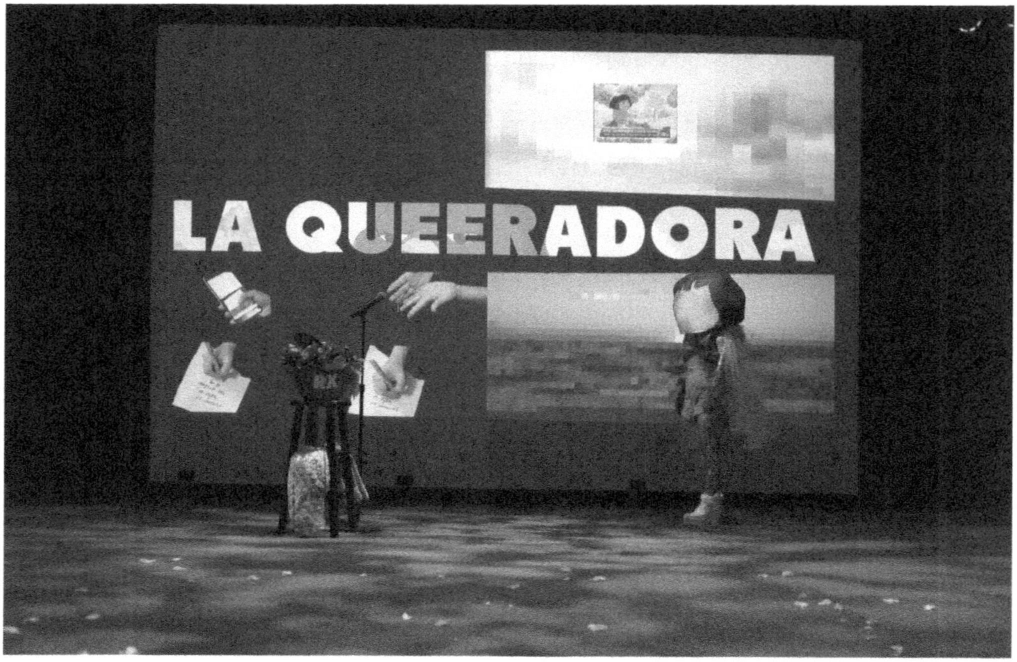

Figure 57. Jennif(f)er Tamayo, *LA QUEERADORA (Borderline)*, CounterCurrent 19, Houston, Texas, April 2019, performance. Courtesy of Cynthia Woods Mitchell Center for the Arts, Houston, Texas.

> like__________
> okay-perhaps I like white cock for its bald eagle qualities
> Its_______________
> the way in which white cock screams AMERIKA! AMERIKA!
> With its stick drizzle gold Drano paved streets
> I WANT TO LIVE IN AMERIKA
> EVERYTHING GREAT IN AMERIKA
> AI AI AI AI AI AI AI[20]

In the Houston CounterCurrent 2019 iteration of this work, and as a prelude to the performance proper of *LA QUEERADORA*, Tamayo participated in one of "Ten Tiny Dances" performed by various solo artists or duets at Houston's LGBTQ+ disco Rich's. This "night club" Dora swayed to disco, reggaetón, and cumbia as Tamayo wielded and finally destroyed a prop of the white phallus while taking swigs from a bottle of Colombian *aguardiente*. The printed page as well becomes a spectral site of reversals and substitutions, of writing un-writing itself, with Dora's selfhood "trapped in the ecosystem of my subjugation . . . an imagined body dematerialized." Dora ventriloquizes the obscene fantasy formations and the sinister thoughts of the US nation-state and its not so invisible corners of the cultural apparatus that would denigrate or fetishize: "(BROWN) BODIES ARE OVER (BLACK) BODIES ARE OVER (BROWN) BODIES ARE OVER GOD CAN ALL THE (BLACK & BROWN) BODIES BE THROWN OVER! because what better body than the body of the American Language what better body than the written word."[21]

In text-form the system of analogies unites Dora the Explorer to Ana Mendieta and to Ida Bauer (1882–1945), the Dora of Sigmund Freud's case study, and to the language of maternal indebtedness. In one section, Tamayo substitutes the name of Freud and other identifying terms with the characters Dora, Boots, Diego, and Swiper in an appropriation of "Dora: An Analysis of a Case Study of Hysteria" by Alex Gatlin. Past the halfway mark of Tamayo's forty-minute Houston performance (plate 35), the performer so disrobes from Dora's explorer drag into black lingerie as to conflate Madonna's 1984 iconic pop song "Borderline" with Gloria Anzaldúa's *La frontera.* This "borderland between/our subjectivities/a cave so grand it glitters/like a cut" cross-dresses into threshold space where "what one considers a border crisis a crisis of limits is really a crisis of the body and it, the body threatens limits and has its own limits brought into question."[22] The shifts in tone and mood are as abrupt as a newsfeed on social media, now intimate, now laughable, now sinister:

> Or, perhaps, consider my sister, DORA THE EXPLORER in Episode 18 Fairy Tale Land and The True Princesa in which Boots is drugged after he eats the fully grown abortada banana and turns into ZOMBIEBoots. And the gnomes ask do you know how to break the sleeping curse, DORA? You have to become a true princesa so you can save Boots, and then DORA says with a resting bitch face that says that's a lot of work, sure I'll save Boots, I'll become a true princess. Oh celestial DORA of our hearts Border Cross Dresser. DORA blank as white. DORA revised from heritage. I want to rip your sweet brown face off and stitch it on to the tiny sticky bodies at the borderlands and in a chorus so sick and dark it's like a mighty condor chanting HOLA YO SOY DORA! HOLA YO SOY DORA! HOLA YO SOY DORA! DORA DORA DORA THE EXPLORA. Imagine the chorus of the border crossers singing HOLA YO SOY DORA through their go-old lungs in some kind of communal misery that understands bodies are a way of reading. And this border crisis, this crisis of limits is the connection between: Hola yo soy DORA! and hola yo no puedo ser DORA yo no puedo ser DORA yo no puedo ser DORA!/tu/no/eres—[23]

The forty-minute version of Tamayo's *LA QUEERADORA* leads artist and audience to such syllables that would oblige a kind of physicality, a high metabolism, a gesture language in the locations of mass media derangement, or to the obscene underbelly of unwanted thoughts in a "future imperfect." By future imperfect I have in mind the view attributed to speculative writer and novelist William Gibson. "The future is already here," he claimed, "it's just not evenly distributed."

In practices like those of Tamayo and others, the materiality of the page and its concomitant voicing are critical border-spaces of poetry and art capable of energizing alternate geopolitical locations; borderland eventualities and hemispheric desires often staged across landscapes residual to the original brutality and theft of colonial settlement. A Latinx cultural poetics I have in mind appeals to a future imperfect rehearsed in imaginative failures to disavow the violent underside of the hemisphere's history. It obtains personas in the research imagination made possible by those artists for whom pattern language and speech so rekindle in the tangible present as to coalesce into that voice Michel de Certeau describes as moving "through an intermediary zone between body and language . . . strange interval, where the voice gives speech without 'truths,' and proximity a presence without possession."[24] This presence without possession is to ask what it means to engage an advanced poetic language of public imperative, and whether social engagement is necessarily manifest, specified, awaiting notice or, by contrast, created elsewhere in enacted speech, voiced by personas in time. This dual commitment between visual and vocal imaginations underlines complex patterns and experimental relationships animated in immediate or historic context between maker, institution, and audience: breaking the spell, so to speak, of human-made things and their means of circulation; it posits lyric drive as that unfamiliar vitality in which personhood can or cannot know itself as an axiomatic proposition of the historical uncanny. In opposition to forms of certainty over the "opaque landscape of anonymity," a Latinx poetics can bring together works that may suggest that in our embodied political identities the visual and the vocal are apt to coincide, but more likely to endure as mutually dissolving ostensible selfhoods. Here, *LA QUEERADORA* intones provisional parting words:

> these days i'm into negativity, like being less than, like being zero
> like the possibility of zero to be so lacking it burns holes on all it touches
> i imagine myself scorching
> zero, deflated,
> effervescent—a halo
> i believe in the power of nothing
> because first, fuck power
> and second, could i coronate myself with a glowing nothing
> i would do it forever, i am beautiful in the space of nothing in which I burn
> the cavity of me outlined in pink droopy leaflets, scorched
> from the inside out. don't touch me   i'm nothing.[25]

That *nothing* is neither a disintegration nor a vanishing. The *zero* circles back to enliven Latinx personhoods—a vocal, visual, and embodied *bricolage*—to empower the imagination, the underground place where, as Gloria Anzaldúa once insisted, the possibility of uniting all that is separate can happen and make happen.[26]

EIGHTEEN

Jesús Macarena-Ávila: The Essential Work

During his 2002 fellowship residency at the Ucross Foundation, and in advance of his Ucross Art Gallery exhibition, Jesús Macarena-Ávila prepared a pen-and-ink drawing to visualize the spatial design for his proposed installation (fig. 58). The sketch defined a maelstrom of amoebae shapes and other cell formations overwhelming a gallery wall, as though the accumulation had emerged from the floor below and so risen as to partially cover a grid of paintings, two rows, each comprising four square canvases. With arrows to indicate the placement of materials, bubble wrap applied with spray glue, Macarena-Ávila noted the analogies he intended by animating those spongy translucent forms cut from air-pocketed plastic sheets. He wrote: "Bubble-wrap represents 'flesh'/as a sacred skin—/the background is the landscape/colors hyperbolic substitutions/of clouds, land, prairie grass, sage, etc./my experience with the land, air, sky, and water at Ucross."[1] At once theorizing a corporeal, spatial, and environmental dynamic through the work's site specificity, "a working ranch at the confluence of three creeks" in Sheridan County, Wyoming, and on stolen land of the Lakota, Macarena-Ávila's preliminary sketch and installation decisively conveyed political stakes, effects that reverberate to this day while further connecting social realities of the past and present in a subsequent series of related works.[2]

Questions of skin and visibility inform his thought and practice, the figure-ground relationship through the long duration of racial and ecological violence in the colonial distributions that organize present-day geopolitics. In the years prior to his 2002 residency, following the September 11 attacks and the Bush administration's reality-manufacturing that led to the US Invasion of Iraq, Macarena-Ávila had delved into research on the

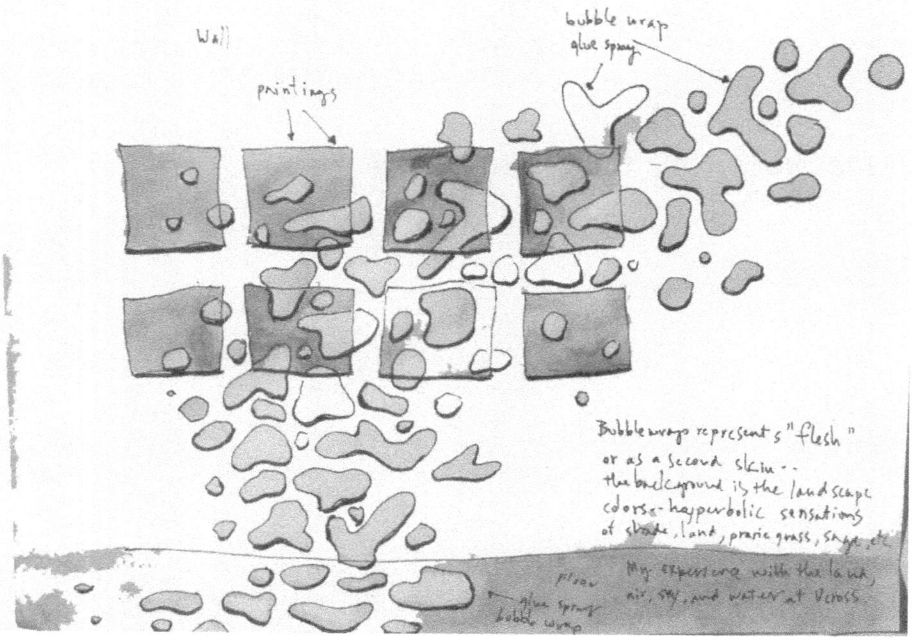

FIGURE 58. Jesús Macarena-Ávila, pen-and-ink drawing for proposed Ucross installation, 2002. Courtesy of the artist.

planetary effects of globalization and digital capitalism, including the impact of genetic engineering and biopiracy, as documented by agroecologist and anti-globalization advocate Vandana Shiva and by economic and social theorist Jeremy Rifkin, both of whom critiqued toxic agricultural practices increasingly employed for corporate profit.[3] Macarena-Ávila's application of bubble wrap in symbolic reference to a species of protective skin was grounded in the history of that material. Bubble wrap was patented in 1960 and made successful thanks to its use in freight packaging when first adopted by the IBM company, which had "recently introduced the 1401 unit—considered the Model T of the computer industry—and needed a way of protecting the delicate device during transit."[4]

Related as well is an incident that left indelible impressions. During his Ucross residency Macarena-Ávila was the target of racially motivated violence perpetrated by a pack of white youth who hurled rocks at the artist, possibly mistaking him for Muslim.[5] Even as he escaped the hate crime physically unharmed, the experience found inflection in two large-format mixed-media works produced at Ucross that feature overlays of bubble wrap covering the entire blood-red pictorial surface of *Surfer* (2002) or in biotic forms that double as psychic encroachments on a field of organic green (*Short Grass*, 2002). These collages communicated the hierarchies of power based on skin color and the visual ethics grounded in race and locality, ideologies connected to global markets and the distribution of bodies and commercial materials for which bubble wrap serves as proxy. In this, Macarena-Ávila's practice relates to the work of Sylvia Wynter, whose project has been to hold Western humanism accountable for the hierarchies that gave way to the present-day biocentric belief system of race, from the classificatory *casta* system, founded on colonization and subsequent racial mixing, or *mestizaje* in the Americas, to nineteenth-century biologized conceptions of the human, with the overrepresentation of "Man" by a white elite ethno-class beholden to the "local culture" of a Judeo-Christian West.[6] Like Wynter, Macarena-Ávila's practice derives a form of counter-modernism that views as imperative for the artist and intellectual to "disenchant" the dominant cultural model so as to re-enchant new worlds out of a current state of crisis.

He initiated the ongoing *Germscapes* series at a confluence of historical events during the first years of the new millennium, including the invasion and protracted wars in Iraq and Afghanistan, anthrax-related bioterrorism in the United States and the threat of biowarfare, as well as the 2003 outbreak of severe acute respiratory syndrome (SARS) that "shocked the world as it spread swiftly from continent to continent, resulting in [over] 8,000 infections, with approximately 10% mortality, and a devastating effect on local and regional economies."[7] With biting political humor, Macarena-Ávila deployed high-color contrast between the depiction of a central human figure or cultural object set against allover cell-patterned backgrounds that refer at once to warfare, camouflage, and the artist's earlier amoeba-shaped bubble-wrap surfaces. He gestured also to such art-historical antecedents as the 1970s borderlands Pop tableaux of Mel Casas in his numbered *Humanscape* paintings, as well as to mass media aesthetics and the direct appeal of Chicano poster art, in order to skewer the nation's chief executive in such oil-on-canvas works as *Germscapes: The Only Bush I Trust Is My Own* (2004).[8]

Another work, from 2006, *Germscapes: Big Bad Green (Vladimir Pasechnik)*—an ominous fatigues-colored protective gas mask over a field of bubble-forms ballooning pastel colors in rose, daffodil, and baby blue—referred to the Soviet defector who had alerted the West about Soviet commitments "to develop potential biological weapons that could spread diseases like anthrax, Ebola, Marburg virus, plague, Q fever and smallpox."[9] Similarly, *Germscapes: Knowledge (2281)* (2011) deploys a related color scheme and a central side-view image of a human brain so as to decry the assault on a culture's intellectual heritage. The State of Arizona's 2010 House Bill 2281 had targeted education in ethnic studies and Mexican American studies with preposterous claims that these disciplines promoted "the overthrow of the United States government" as well as "resentment toward a race or class of people."[10]

These earlier paintings connect to mixed-media works Macarena-Ávila produced in 2020, the year of the COVID-19 global pandemic, including *Germscapes: H.R. 6201 (Wenliang)*, a pencil-drawing tribute to Li Wenliang, the Chinese ophthalmologist who, as a public health vanguard, issued warnings about early SARS-CoV-2 infections in Wuhan. In *Germscapes: Essential Worker (Lorena Borjas, 1960–2020)* the artist renders a naturalistic portrait in pencil of Lorena Borjas—the transgender immigrant activist whose death was linked to the coronavirus (plate 36)—surrounded by an explosion of oblong magenta, flaxen, and navy-blue globules shaded with felt-tip markings. Macarena-Ávila thus combined tributes to the craft-activity aesthetic that provided an outlet in some households under lockdown and to the essential workers whose labor made such sheltering-in-place possible.[11]

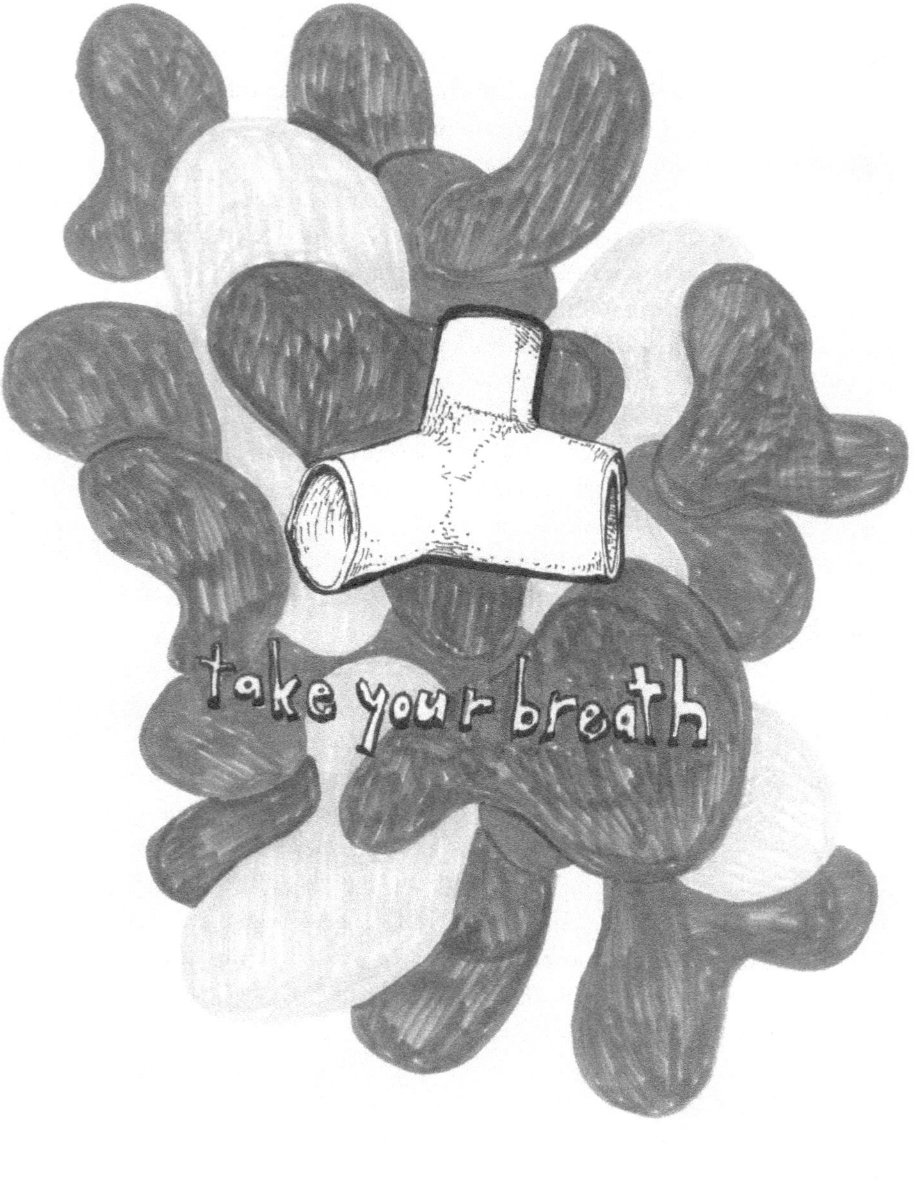

FIGURE 59. Jesús Macarena-Ávila, *Germscapes: Take Your Breath*, 2020, mixed media on paper, 8 × 11 in. Courtesy of the artist.

Through his ongoing research into activist history, the surveillance state, and health work—at times through the auspices of a semi-fictive global enterprise, the Instituto de Nuestra Cultura—Macarena-Ávila gives visual expression to those persistent residues of colonial violence, racial capitalism, and endlessly destabilizing warfare that together constitute the unremarked or camouflaged cellular horizon of the present system, its hierarchies of power and social rank also influencing and organizing the insulated bubble of the art world. Aligned with the writings of philosopher Peter Sloterdijk, who, in his opus *Spheres*, envisioned—even as the global COVID-19 pandemic was unimaginable at the time of writing—a "cellular world-bubble" comprising societies that resemble an "immune system of connected isolations" in a "telecommunicative integration of non-assembled people."[12] During the recent novel COVID-19 pandemic, at once an accelerated and deliriously slow-motion time span of uncertainty, loss, and foreboding, Macarena-Ávila returned to his *Germscapes* in a struggle to comprehend the exorbitant loss of life, as connected also to climate catastrophe, structural poverty, state criminality, and migration policies (fig. 59). He waged a searing critique of the Trump administration's incompetence and cruelty—the utter failure to meet its self-proclaimed "historic mobilization 'moving heaven and earth' to source and deliver vast amounts of medical supplies from overseas to pandemic hot spots in the United States."[13] He further pursued the *Germscapes* series in 2021 "as a response to idea of refuge," recreating "new digital compositions, collages of past *Germscapes* oil paintings (2003–2008)," compositions that were printed on canvas and later "installed at three specific Chicago neighborhoods and suburbs hosted by different community orgs: Little Village (Illinois Latino Voice), Edgewater (Haitian American Museum of Chicago), and Melrose park (Ecos Del Pacífico Afro Colombia)."[14] In this sense, Macarena-Ávila's various reiterations turned pictorial space into a location that rendered honorific tribute to those lost to the virus but remembered in vibrant striated auras that convey glimmers of cautious hope—that intangible practice of the possible.

NINETEEN

Christina Fernandez: Something Lost, Missing, or Unattainable

In a method that builds on prolonged, distinctly situated observations of urban space, uncovering secret histories from the visual record and public imagination, Christina Fernandez pursues her photographic practice with formal resolve and telling discernment. A pathway connecting her earliest work to the 2006–10 series produced in the East Los Angeles neighborhood of El Sereno and then to her more recent *American Trailer* (2021) sheds light on her intimate understanding of place, an orientation that forms a picture of Los Angeles from precise frames of encounter given to critical scenes of reflection. These works inform the present from the perspective of the foreclosure crisis and its deleterious effects on the Southern California landscape, for which a regional park imbued sight lines with the immiseration caused by the housing market collapse. Throughout, Fernandez has offered a series of visual definitions apt to account for public space in the landscapes of privacy and dispossession.

In 2007, as part of the public programming organized to accompany *Re-SITE-ing the West: Contemporary Photographs from the Permanent Collection* at the Los Angeles County Museum of Art, and as a prelude to the following year's exhibition *Phantom Sightings: Art After the Chicano Movement*, I had the opportunity to facilitate a LACMA conversation with Fernandez in a slideshow survey of her work. In preparation for the interview, and together with art historian Cristina Cuevas-Wolf, then LACMA's curator of education and public programs, we ambled through the Hammer Building galleries of *Re-SITE-ing the West* and considered works by John Pfahl, Lee Friedlander, Robert Adams, John Divola,

Anthony Hernandez, and an ample selection of Edward Ruscha's *Parking Lots* series.[1] We remarked on the paucity of women photographers and their work: Susan E. Evans (*Western Landscape*, 2004) and Cindy Bernard (*Topography: Dry Head Agate #9, Detail 1*, 1995). But the point was to pause, finally, in front of a grid comprising fifteen black-and-white images. The unity synthesized high-angle wide and eye-level medium perspectives ranging across the axes of near and far. Even an initial impression was enough to suggest a narrative, a system anyway, or what critic and curator Robert Sobieszek described once as "a strategy for picturing a landscape from multiple vantage points, indeterminable perspectives, and positions that are alternatively within and exterior to the principal subject."[2] Lewis Baltz's *Nevada* of 1977, unmistakable in its imposing scale, nearly seven feet high and five feet wide in its museum wall installation, unambiguous in its absence of human figures, seemed to confirm that "fundamental ambiguity in relation to the question of genre." Allen Sekula wondered with regard to Baltz and his work, "Is this a documentary photograph or an abstraction?"[3]

Sobieszek, the highly regarded photography historian and influential curator at LACMA for fifteen years, had passed in 2005. During his tenure at LACMA, beginning in 1990, he had significantly "increased the size of the museum's collection from 2,700 to more than 8,300 photographs through gifts and acquisitions that emphasized local and contemporary artists, including David Hockney and Cindy Sherman."[4] In his expansive writing on Baltz, framed by film references to John Ford's "desert epic *The Searchers* and Andrei Tarkovsky's postapocalyptic film *Stalker*," as well as to literary depictions of the landscape in T. S. Eliot, Samuel Beckett, Stephen King, William S. Boroughs, and Robert Smithson, he wrote that *Nevada* signaled a fundamental cultural change of perceptions regarding the land, environment, and history stripped of its halo, deprived of any future deliverance or redemption. Sobieszek argued that in the series, "synoptic and abbreviated in its scope," Baltz mobilized a "highly refined and clinical, if now seemingly unordered, vision" that allowed him to structure his subject: "a portion of bulldozed earth, various housing developments, a few newly completed houses, certain architectural details, and a roadside bar at night." In terms of broader art-historical inference, Sobieszek proposed that "the facades and front yards depicted in *Nevada* [had] something of the deadpan severity of a Donald Judd sculpture or the wry irony of an Edward Ruscha photograph of the 1960s."[5]

Standing in front of Baltz's *Nevada*—a storyboard monument to Cold War melancholy: optical and inner desolations prompted by industrialized expansion and an economy of overdevelopment, but also welcoming of visual contradiction and indeterminacy—Fernandez gained immediate presence of mind. She exhaled, referring to Baltz not so much in reverence as in matter of fact: "This is the master." Fernandez later explained that she had always thought of herself as a landscape photographer and that "Baltz's topographic work [had always been] a sort of reference point." Quizzically she added, "Strangely enough, I have only recently begun doing landscape work. But I have always been very heavily influenced by Baltz, and I do not know if it is the narrative or the grid that is often used in his work, or the sort of—these are very high-contrast prints. They are not credibly respectful of the zone system or anything like that, which I find very interesting in terms of landscape."[6]

Sobieszek had defined landscape photography, like that of Baltz and other photographers associated with the New Topographics, as having taken up matters of "measurement and calibration." In *Nevada*, a fluorescent light tube provides a scale of "measurable certainty in an otherwise incalculable vastness."[7] In this view, the focus was now "an entropic *terrain vague* where what is built is merged with what is unbuilt . . . where the positions of observer and inhabitant are confounded, and where past and present are intermingled."[8] For artists trained in the critical methods of the 1990s, the question of landscape served additionally to underscore questions of social hierarchy, cultural belonging, and the outsider-insider dynamic. In 1994 media theorist W. J. T. Mitchell refuted accepted ideas about landscape when understood solely as an object of contemplation. In the volume *Landscape and Power* Mitchell argued that to historicize and reimagine the question of landscape is to underscore its function as a verb, a picture-making "cultural practice and active process by which social and subjective identities are formed."[9] To the degree that a landscape "(whether urban or rural, artificial or natural) always greets us as space" or as an environment, it serves also as a spell, cast to conceal the experience of relation it produces with beholders. Persons "live and move" in the landscape and so gain a measure of being. However, as a vehicle for complex descriptions, the medium of landscape remains elusive in the "motion from one place or time to another." As a mechanism for asking what "we have done and are doing to our environment" and "what the environment in turn does to us," landscape serves as the site for examining "how we naturalize what we do to each other, and how these 'doings' are enacted in the media of representation."[10]

These are matters that have long compelled Fernandez, whose attitude aligns with a critical conception of landscape photography, even as a disavowal that allows her to engage the topographic by other means: "My attitude . . . has always been one of a landscape photographer, but yet most of my work has nothing to do with landscape."[11] Consider, for example, an early work (fig. 60): the multimedia site-specific *Arrivals and Departures* (1997), commissioned by inSITE97, the San Diego-Tijuana border initiative "committed to the production of artworks in the public sphere."[12] For *Arrivals and Departures*, conceived geographically in two parts—an installation in San Diego, an observation point in Tijuana—Fernandez installed a series of light boxes, videos, and other instructional media in the waiting area of the Greyhound Bus Terminal in San Ysidro, the San Diego district bordering Mexico. Archival photographs document two of the light boxes. One displays an image resembling a watercolor illustration of the kind found in mass-circulation magazines, or in an official government pamphlet. A paternalistic white judge, leaning over the court bench, issues his ruling to an anguished Brown youth pleading his case with arms outstretched. Another light box features a diagrammatic map of Mexico and the US Southwest with arrowed red lines specifying immigration routes linked to family surname narratives (A. Alvarez, Ma. Ramirez, J. P. Oñate, F. Ramos). A Sanyo television monitor displays a male figure in white shorts and striped T-shirt scaling the topmost ledge of the border wall extending into the Pacific Ocean made "of surplus helicopter landing pads, turned on their side and welded together."[13] In Mexico, Fernandez installed a telescope "in the style of a nineteenth-century nautical instrument," a lookout for surveilling the US side of the border. The "telescope was located in Colonia Libertad, which allowed immigrants who might

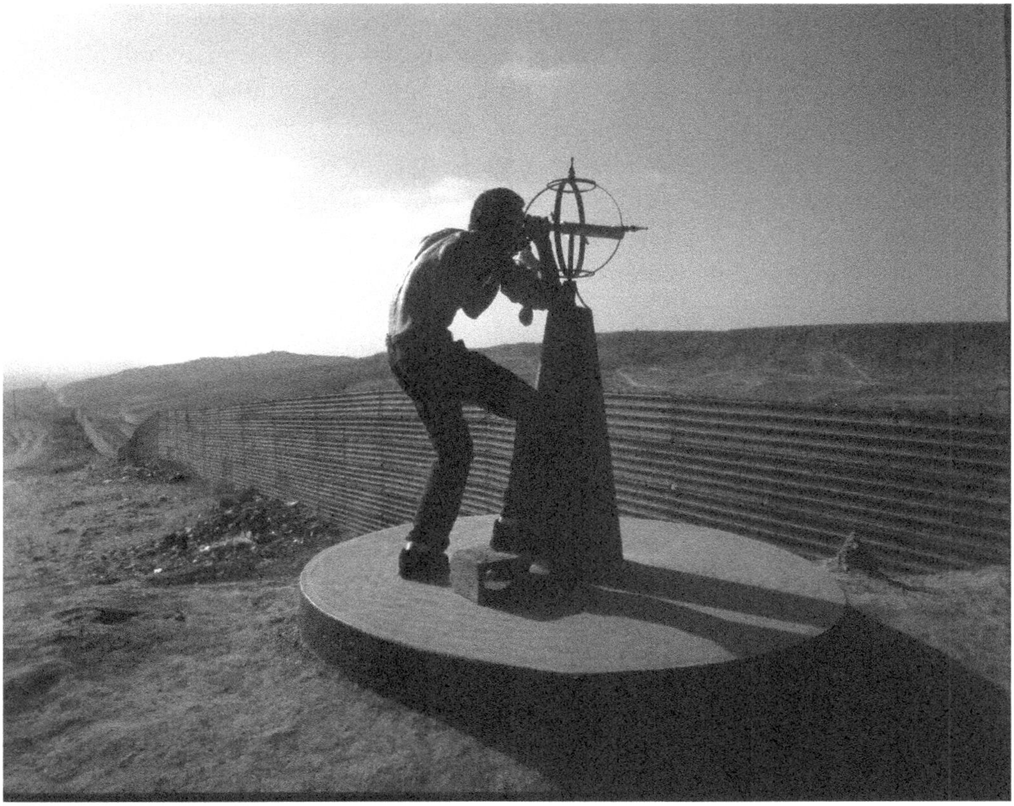

Figure 60. Christina Fernandez, *Arrivals and Departures*, 1997, site-specific installation. Courtesy of Christina Fernandez and Gallery Luisotti, color photograph by Philipp Scholz Ritterman, inSITE97.

be planning to cross the border to monitor the movements and location of US Border Patrol agents."[14] If, for W. J. T. Mitchell, a landscape representation can serve as "an instrument of cultural power," a way of seeing inseparable from the enforcements of a nation along geographic and political borders where the wishful thinking and clear-cut focus of citizenship blurs, Fernandez highlighted the uneven distributions defining the entitlement to "live and move" as experienced by some and not others in the liminal space between the United States and Mexico—in a reversal of customary insider-outsider distinctions.[15]

The staging of vision and the ethics of looking, as related to themes of disparity, estrangement, and exclusion, have been central to Fernandez in her work, most notably in the signature series of color prints she produced in 2002, *Lavandería 1–12* (plate 37). Her lens captured scenes of social abstraction; empty or near empty interior spaces so framed and partitioned as to turn semiprivate forms of labor and routine enacted in East Los Angeles laundromats, around the Boyle Heights, Montebello, and Pico Rivera neighborhoods, into public display observed from an exterior twilight perspective. Fernandez affirms that she was "interested in really basic things like repetition of form, the shine, the light, the fluorescent lighting, the shine of the stainless steel," that is, the particular "aesthetics of the laundromat."[16] The resulting photographs depicted brightly lit interiors in muted hues of off-white, yellow, gray-blue, and matte green; they captured ghostly figures in desolate common areas, with as many men as women doing laundry, upending expectations about culturally defined gender roles, machismo, and so-called women's work.

Using a conspicuous rule of thirds in strong vertical and horizontal lines, she framed the subjects behind the glass partition that featured foremost in the *Lavandería* photographs. The floor-to-ceiling storefront windowpanes bore the marks of graffiti made using chemical etching liquid, sold under brand names like Armour Etch or EtchAll, permanently inscribed into the glass, the letters obtaining a cloudy or "frosted" look, or oozing in heavy trickles, as though the surface writing were foreboding sweat or bloodshed. Some critics described the perspective, uniformly parallel to the picture plane, as though it meant to convey, even from the outside, a connection between photographer and subject.[17] The outside perspective further enhanced the illusion any fixed image is able to attain, abstracting prior scenes of inevitable exchange and negotiation the photographer conducted with laundromat management and customers, at least allowing her to properly position her 4 × 5 camera equipment as daylight receded. In her *Lavandería* images, Fernandez troubled the prospects as to what a still image can encapsulate about a particular site of human activity, and its relations of class, ethnicity, age, and gender in terms of the opacity that forms a bar separating the self from someone else, from a neighbor. She made visible the desire for transparency and interrelatedness, conveying the irreducible gap between insider and outsider, and as related to attendant calibrations of belonging in the built environments of Los Angeles. In *Lavandería*—with glass surfaces as the plane of focus, the workaday lifeways behind it blurring, even for photographed subjects who acknowledge the presence of the camera—there emerged a complex visual discourse about self-possession and dignity attained in daily acts. Also at play was the question of communicability in the ongoing terms that make a human being knowable or unknowable, especially in the immersive spaces to which persons are consigned when they are deprived of power.

We can read these images of life behind the partitions of graffitied glass in tandem with what Latinx philosopher María Lugones described as "complex communications" that thrive "on recognition of opacity and on reading opacity, not through assimilating the text of others to our own." Rather, with creative acts of mutuality, in "complex communication we create and cement relational identities, meanings that did not precede the encounter, ways of life that transcend nationalisms, root identities, and other simplifications of our imaginations."[18]

The question of embodied space for Fernandez—enclosures for living and working, or as a visual center point within a series of urban dispersions—led to a transitional inquiry and her 2004 series *Space Available*. In six black-and-white and four color photographs Fernandez documented the dismantled interiors and the progression of her move from one working space (Alhambra studio) to another (Spring Street studio): ladders, space heaters, rolls of paper towels, framed artworks wrapped in light-blue kraft paper, or glossy black garbage bags; flexible gooseneck lights, extension cords, and power strips; empty wooden frames and a cardboard flat file stacked in a corner against the wall; spools of pastel works on brown paper strewn on a hardwood floor. A bare, chalk-green wainscoting with its electrical outlet, flanked between two door frames, lent visual emphasis to a rectangle of debris on the floor below. There is, despite the flux and unsettled particularity of these images, the cruel irony that studio space here doubled into a narrative about processes hidden from view but transpiring all the same in the economic present of the transactional world—for which an interior can serve as secret sharer. Fernandez specified that the reduced color palette in the *Space Available* work was "not a jarring thing. I mean I am concerned about things like that in my work," she said, but made clear:

> In the print you would have to notice that there is this dark area around where something has been moved . . . and there are all kinds of stuff underneath your couch . . . or whatever was here and also where an artwork used to hang or is going to hang. . . . I wanted to say a little bit about living in LA as an artist and having to move into a studio and out of a studio and back into another space and the different types of spaces that you can use as an artist. And meanwhile, figuring out your studio space, changing from one studio to another, I felt like these images were full of potential. They are images of portent, like something is going to happen but it has not happened, or it never happened in terms of the artist studio. And that is pretty much what was happening with me as a photographer, so I wanted to document that in some way. I was still photographing.

The realm of the artist's studio was predictive of a social mood increasingly out of kilter, the consequence of "subprime" lending practices that had been fueling the housing market. Accounts in the *Los Angeles Times* reported on the worrisome increase in the number of Californians who, by October 2006, had fallen "sharply behind on their mortgages," more than doubling "in the third quarter" and "providing alarming evidence of weakness in the once-booming housing market."[19] The indelible images of what is referred to often as a "foreclosure epidemic" circulated in countless newspaper photographs and in television news footage: row after row of FOR SALE signs, then boarded-up windows, and finally dumpsters filled with furniture and abruptly discarded possessions lining the front of vacant homes so as to transform the topography of entire neighborhoods. By summer 2007, home foreclosures were soaring—17,408 assigned to the financial quarter ending in September—thus surpassing "a record set a decade earlier during a severe downturn." The following year, in March 2008, JPMorgan Chase agreed "to buy Bear Stearns Co. for a stunningly low $2 a share in a deal backed by emergency Federal Reserve funding to prevent the failure of the 85-year-old investment bank, which was dragged down by billions of dollars of mortgage-backed securities that went bad." Given the billions in worthless securities, by September 2008, the federal government took actions to bail out Fannie Mae and Freddie Mac, "government-chartered but privately owned firms that reported billions of dollars of losses on some $5 trillion worth of mortgage debt they own or guarantee." Thereafter, "Lehman Bros., an aggressive underwriter of mortgage-backed securities" had filed for bankruptcy protection, and Merrill Lynch agreed "to a $50-billion takeover by Bank of America—sending the Dow down 504 points the following Monday, the most since the September 2001 terrorist attacks."[20] US officials and the media spoke of the financial crisis, or Great Recession, which had stressed the financial system to catastrophic levels, with the euphemism of "downturn," as if so naming it, in tandem with the bailouts, could have prevented the "cascading home foreclosures, bank failures, massive layoffs, [and] diving stock prices," leading to economic meltdown.[21]

Lush undulating outlines divide the horizontals of the photograph into faraway and immediate planes of sun-drenched green, all of it culminating at a spot that overlooks the steep incline and dell below, a hill to the left in the distance (plate 38). A patch of homes with tiled roofs offers a visual puzzle of brown and brick-red, giving way to a clearing, an athletic field in the deep center of the scene, the composition in harmonic patterns of a daytime suburban idyll. From the field lights and intermittent juniper trees, a barely visible row of palms along the base of the hill leads the eye to a grassy incline counterposed by dry streaks along a slope at whose summit a few radio antennas pierce the cloud formations. Among the elements in the frame all coherence hinges on the tilted white stake in the foreground; a signpost filling the emphatic left third of the image. You discern the word *brokerage* under the half-hidden letters of the Coldwell Banker sign, a truncated phone number and URL further distressed by some graffiti scrawled in black permanent marker. The storybook idealism of the green urban-suburban enclave disintegrates from the viewpoint—all of it suggesting a kind of crucifixion on the mount. Daylight pools of illumination emanating from a source beyond the right of the frame direct the eye to the floral upholstery covering an abandoned sofa in the lower right. Its incongruous appearance in the scene imbues it with a will of its own, as though the object itself were detaining the downward momentum of the slope and the primary emphasis of your sight line.

Fernandez set her subsequent 2006 series in El Sereno, in northeast Los Angeles, a working-class Mexican and Mexican American neighborhood, "an enclave," in her description, "a beautiful little space with rolling hills, winding streets, and modest homes with front and backyards. . . . When I moved there in 2006, the gentrification process had not yet begun. It was simply a beautiful space that I could afford."[22] There, Fernandez began work on a series of photographs around the neighborhood, namely in Ernest E. Debs Regional Park in the Montecito Hills.

The particularity of place offered the photographer a series of contrasts to explore, not without ambivalence as to the compromised status of this park and its meanings, both past and present. The name *Sereno* itself suggested those contrasts, denoting serene in Spanish, but also a gang name (El Sereno Rifa). "You can go hiking and you forget you are in LA," she remarked, but then the minute you find yourself immersed in the experience, "you turn around and there is graffiti all over some eucalyptus tree, which is very odd too because eucalyptus trees shed," the bark so falling as to render the graffiti provisional. Hence, the graffiti artists committed over time—in a durational form of maintenance—to retagging the trees. "So, just talking about the peeling graffiti, the skin of the eucalyptus trees, I am really liking that right now. I am going to have to remember that."[23]

From the time of his arrival in 1937, German émigré Herman Schultheis—electrical engineer, Disney animator, and prolific cameraman—began photographing his newly adopted home, Los Angeles, documenting the city and its environs.[24] He left an invaluable archive of over six thousand prints that chronicle home life and leisure time with his wife Ethel in years prior to US involvement in World War II. However, the Schultheis archive is, overwhelmingly, a vast portrait of Los Angeles, depicting the city's idiosyncratic built environment, ethnic pluralism, consumer culture, and social relations; its leisure classes devoted to forms of popular entertainments or to the fantasy formations around the film industry; colonial pageantry, city street life, beach and freeway culture, as well as the industrial infrastructure of the urban landscape and the everyday labor of the dispossessed, including children. Among the profusion of pictures there is one—a view of Montecito Heights—that depicts trucks along the dry riverbed of the Arroyo Seco from Griffin and Montecito near the area later named Ernest E. Debs Regional Park (fig. 61). The Schultheis survey image predates the New Topographics by four decades, even as it betrays a visual grammar bearing a family resemblance to Lewis Baltz's 1977 *Element #11 (Lemmon Valley, Looking North)*. It makes visible the urban sprawl's in-between spaces by means of a perspective that necessarily collapses "art and geography through critical practices of mapping and photography."[25] Lewis Baltz had written of a "belief in the primacy of the photographic information" as manifest in a survey photograph like this one made by Schultheis of Arroyo Seco in Montecito Heights—the location of Fernandez's *Sereno* series in Ernest E. Debs Regional Park.

Together, images by Schultheis, Baltz, and Fernandez propose instead another temporality and counterforce to the narratives that photographic information alone cannot enable. Baltz wrote: "There is something paradoxical in the way that documentary photographs interact with our notions of reality. . . . Yet of course photographs, despite their verisimilitude, are abstractions; their information is selective and incomplete."[26] Los Angeles abstractions appear, therefore, in the form of flash tableaux related to land use, as placeholder surfaces for the long durations of history.

A eucalyptus tree, shedding bark, graffiti . . .

On Tongva land that was forcibly occupied by Spanish explorers in 1769, a river ran through the narrow arroyo, providing the precious resource of water to the village of Otsungna. There, Franciscan friars enslaved the Tongva to build the Mission San Gabriel Archangel, founded in 1771, and so imposed the mission's name on the Indigenous inhabitants, Gabrielinos, and called the arroyo El Rio Rosa de Castillo.

The enclave of present-day El Sereno is located on what served as the route from Mission San Gabriel Archangel to El Pueblo de Los Ángeles, founded by Spanish Governor Felipe de Neve, who had ordered the settlement of Los Angeles in 1781.

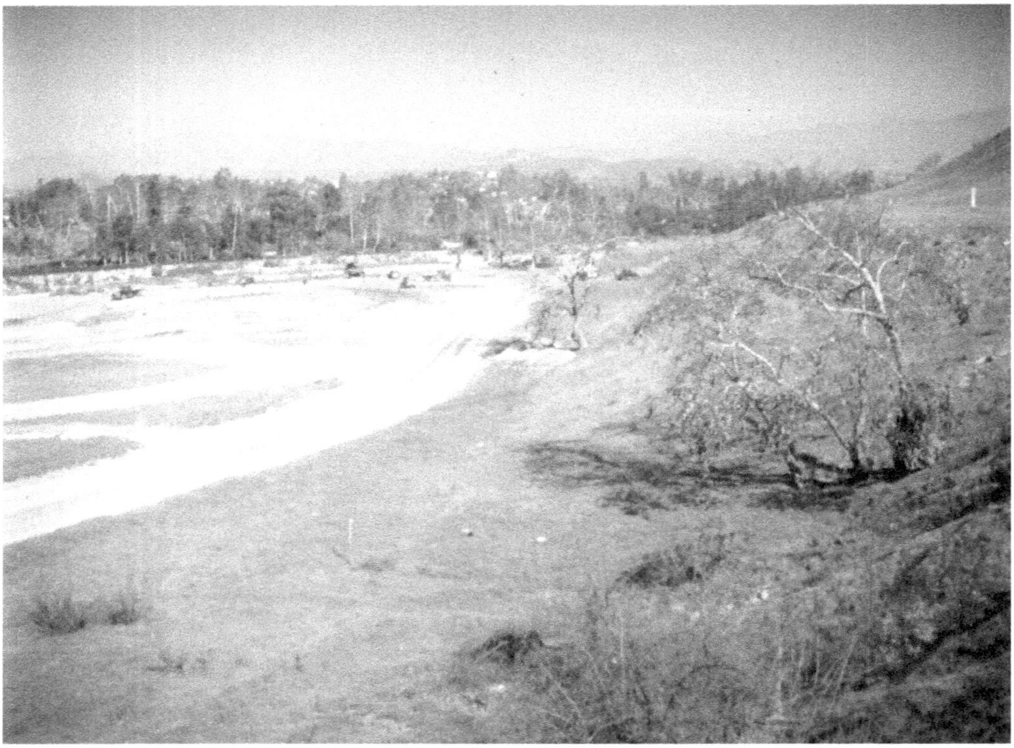

FIGURE 61. Herman Schultheis, *Arroyo Seco in Montecito Heights*, ca. 1938, silver gelatin print. Los Angeles Public Library Herman Schultheis Collection

In 1964, Mexican American journalist Rubén Salazar reported on Los Angeles Supervisor Ernest E. Debs, for whom the Montecito Hills Park was later renamed, and the delegation he led to Chihuahua, Mexico, celebrating with Chihuahua's Governor Práxedes Giner Durán and other Mexican officials the 182nd anniversary of the founding of Los Angeles. The Los Angeles delegation—"Walter Schaefer, representing Gov. Brown; Eddy S. Feldman, of the City Municipal Art Commission, representing Mayor Samuel W. Yorty, and Richard Rubio, East Los Angeles community leader"—joined the Mexican governor to participate "in the unveiling of a bronze plaque [to] mark the burial place of Gov. Felipe Neve." Salazar concluded with mention of a parallel celebration in Los Angeles scheduled to take place in the unspecified future but centered "in the Old Plaza, close to a statue of Gov. de Neve which was contributed to the city in 1931 by the California Parlor of the Native Daughters of the Golden West."[27]

A lifelong municipal politician in Cold War Southern California, Ernest E. Debs served on the Los Angeles County Board of Supervisors from 1958 to 1974. "I represent the richest of the rich, the poorest of the poor, and every nationality known to man in sizable numbers," he once claimed proudly.[28] Debs was known as much for his political prowess as for his personality variously described as colorful, tenacious, high-handed, or tempestuous, and for having spangled his conversation with a cascade of profanities. He began his career as a conservative Democrat, elected in 1942 to the state assembly representing Silver Lake. In that capacity he found himself having to disavow any relation to early twentieth-century labor leader and socialist Eugene V. Debs. He asserted: "We're not even remotely related. . . . Definitely, I'm against radicals and Communists. But at the same time I think the little fellow should get a fair hearing and a square deal—I'm for that, too."[29] Later, in 1947, "he was elected to the Los Angeles City Council from a largely Eastside district, serving for eleven years. A decade later, he ran for the Board of Supervisors, beating Edward R. Roybal, a seminal figure in Latino politics, after four recounts in a bitterly contested election." He consistently "won reelection to the board in the primaries of 1962, 1966 and 1970 by supporting cultural projects such as the Music Center, bilingual education, scholarships and improved parks," among them the self-named "282-acre Ernest E. Debs Regional Park in Montecito Heights."[30]

Reflecting on Roman Polanski and Robert Towne's 1973 neo-noir *Chinatown*, Thom Andersen, in *Los Angeles Plays Itself* (2003), wondered why "nostalgia has always been the dominant note in the city's image of itself. At any time in its history, Los Angeles was always a better place 'A long time ago' than in the present. What was new in the seventies was a nostalgia for what might have been, a sense that everything might have been different except for one defining event. We began to look for an originary sin. Robert Towne took an urban myth about the founding of Los Angeles on water stolen from the Owens River Valley and made it resonate."[31] In Robert Towne's filmscript to *Chinatown*, from an overpass named the Hollenbeck Bridge, private detective Jake Gittes "can see the muddy remains of a collapsed shack, its contents strewn" below in the Los Angeles River. "Downstream, there's the dresser, an oil drum, a Ford seat cushion, an Armour lard can, etc.—the trashy remains" of the homeless character, Shuhardt, one of the city's dispossessed, described as "a local drunk," and now missing or at least nowhere to be found. Jake Gittes, who has scrambled "down the embankment," now approaches a sheet of scrap metal "used as a roof of sorts." Lying "half over the storm drain and one wall" along "the bank of the river," the structure that once served as a shelter and makeshift home is actually "a sign that proclaims OWN YOUR OWN OFFICE IN THIS BUILDING $5000 to $6000."[32]

Around the half-hidden letters of a Coldwell Banker sign overlooking the seemingly peaceable suburban enclave, and in response to the subprime mortgage crisis that coincided with the six-year period she lived in El Sereno, Fernandez set herself to photograph "in-between spaces (of which there were many) where the refuse of outdated household items was dumped and people who could not afford even this modest community were forced to live outside. *Sereno* is absent of human figures and describes human presence through things left behind. By foregrounding the refuse against the backdrop of neighborhood homes, *Sereno* asks, 'Who is this place for? Who has access? Who does not?'"[33]

In *Sereno*, those questions obtain material support in a visual structure. An object, a deflated red Mylar balloon, for example, betrays the sparkle of its now-wrinkled shiny surface, by casting a lifeless state of suspense over waves of green grasses and straw-colored

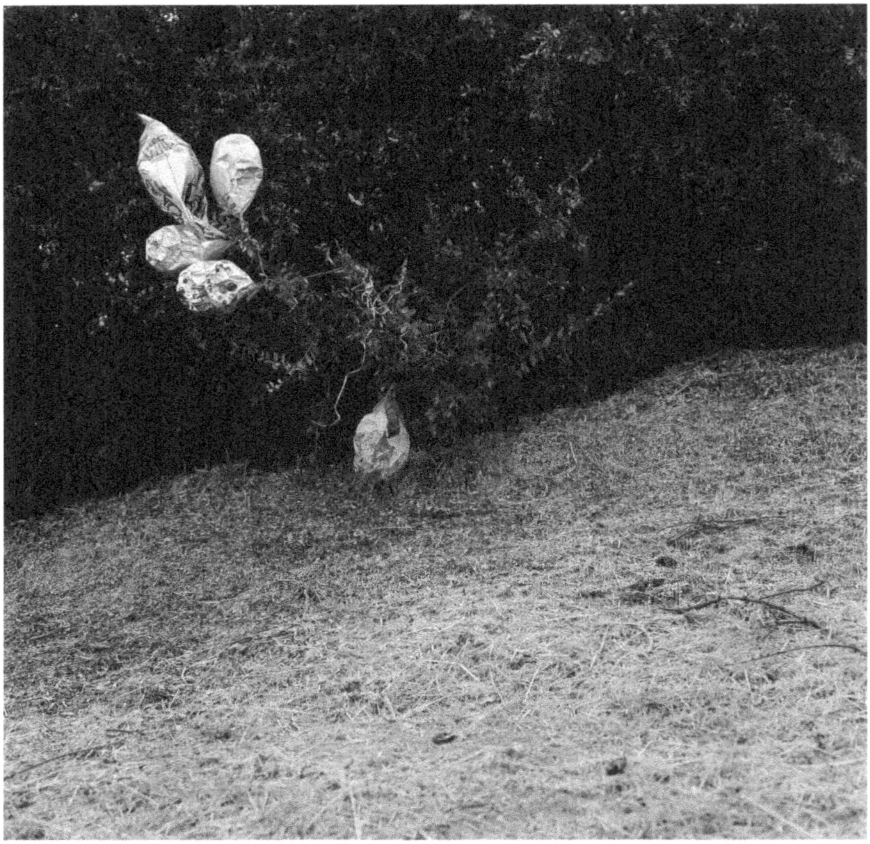

FIGURE 62. Christina Fernandez, *Sereno (Balloon II)*, 2009, black-and-white silver gelatin print. Courtesy of Christina Fernandez and Gallery Luisotti.

underbrush, the cloudless sky so occupying most of the upper frame as to distract from the vanishing point—two buildings from the Los Angeles skyline edging above the horizon line. Its companion piece in black and white (fig. 62) appears even more menacing, as though the five Mylar balloons, certainly the remainder of a long-forgotten celebration, were rather the forensic evidence of an unseen brutality. There are, in other images from the series, rhyming patterns of composition: a slope occupying two-thirds of the photographic field; the interplay between field of vision and field of action; accidental pools of light captured from a source that remains uncertain.

Whether a Styrofoam cup or abandoned television set, an object figures the middle distance and so establishes "an active, earthy, not-quite-human capaciousness" that philosopher Jane Bennett has ascribed to "vibrant matter," that "impersonal life that surrounds and infuses us," but also, the correlatives of that "painful, nagging feeling that something's being forgotten or left out."[34] In contrast to the "spectacular banality" often associated with a New Topographic view of suburbia, there is hardly a dispassionate note in these pictures.[35] Even a can of Painter's Touch spray paint—litter half buried under fallen foliage—appears in overhead close-up as something unbearably intimate but also in distressed tautological relation to the graffiti shed from the skin of eucalyptus trees. A consternation is evident in images of abandoned encampments, soggy mattresses, blankets, and bedsheets serving as shelter, strung to lower branches, remnants telling, in the alarming light of day, of lifeways observed by the unprotected and dispossessed. Like the connection doubling as disconnection in previous work by Fernandez—*Arrivals and Departures*; *Lavandería*—these images also point to the social relationship and to the "unbearable proximity" of a "community's fundamental particle, the neighbor."[36] Any trace of neighboring human existence attains—in the psychoanalytic view—the "proximity of the thing which, no matter how far away it is physically, is always by definition 'too close'" and thus apt to excite venal or violent inclinations.[37] In *Sereno*, Fernandez seeks to suspend these images between such abreactions and the "reciprocal habituation resulting from being neighbors, the processes of recognition—of identification—that are created thanks to proximity, to concrete coexistence in the same urban territory [and] to the great unknown that is everyday life."[38] At any rate the images recall the "horror and entrapment" artist Robert Smithson identified when camera and landscape join to release from an environs—"no matter how calm and lovely"—secret histories concealed as the "substrata of disaster."[39]

This dispersion in time, substrata of the photograph—as when an image eventuates in patterns of proximity or, so to speak, in a style of estrangement akin to a circle or a spiral. Is it an undersurface, an overlay?

Nearly a decade after the *Sereno* series, Fernandez circled back to the horizon line of precariousness and the logic of displacement, achieving formal correlation to the substrata of disasters that develop under the "systemic expulsions" resulting from the relentlessly advancing "mode of capitalist relations of production" over the uneven landscape of home ownership.[40] In 2017, the Pew Foundation had reported that of the 20 million Americans living in "manufactured homes . . . about two-fifths of those can be found in mobile home parks, mostly in suburbs and exurbs. But homeownership can be precarious for people who live in mobile home parks. Because they don't own the land beneath their houses or trailers, they have to move if the park closes down."[41] *American Trailer* of 2018 is the result of systematic photographic observations over an extended period—akin to the long durational form of graffiti artists retagging the trees of Ernest E. Debs Regional Park (plate 39). Collapsed into a single composite picture, head-on frontal views of a classic travel trailer contain a time lapse; from left to right, signs of former use and later abandonment reveal the trailer's white paint scorched around a missing window and tail end, damaged either by accidental fire or by arson. Seamlessly sutured by digital means, the large-format panoramic view appears—in the apt words of Robert Smithson—"confounded into a unitary chaos."[42] But Fernandez here seeks as well to underscore the perversity of aim that was specific to the New Topographic ideal. According to Lewis Baltz, "one of photography's most dramatic attributes [is] the power to isolate highly specific fragments from the flux of time, for the less theatrical but no less powerful attribute of scientific experiment."[43]

In her *Sereno* series and *American Trailer* Fernandez frames and mirrors embodied experience—her own and that of others—in the market-driven processes of abstraction, division, and alienation. Her photographs refute the commonsense claim that only human figuration can do justice to the body as an active agent in the ongoing happenings of history—photographically speaking, anyway, blurring the underlay and overlay, the question of figure and foreground. About her *Sereno* photographs Fernandez affirmed: "There is a homelessness about the images, the sense of something lost, missing, or unattainable."[44] With such narrative particularity she has organized a view that captures the competing processes of social production, land use, and everyday life under market forces, as well as the civic configurations and detachments that make up a habitus of human endeavor.

Her works have served also to make claims about the camera medium as a site for meanings that shape a cultural geography. With an ethical perspective prone to account at once for embodied urban fact, optical experience, and the contingencies of depiction, her images consistently extend the topographies of recognition: the visual and political differences between the overlooked and the under-photographed. In the ravaged landscape of advanced capital—in its "brutal divisions of the winners and losers"—New Topographic notions of "repeatability and verifiability" appear today as being mere fantasy formations liable at any moment to go up in smoke.[45]

ACKNOWLEDGMENTS

Most of the essays in this book enjoyed a previous life, either as catalog essays, as articles in journals, or as talks and lectures. My thanks to the following venues for supporting and hosting earlier versions of these essays:

1. *Diagonal and Self-Possessed: Group Portrait with Liminal Figures*

Presented at "Thinking Its Presence Conference" at the Poetry Center, University of Arizona, October 19, 2017.

Published on the Poetry Foundation website (June 18, 2018) in four parts: "Fighting for Fluency," "Societies of Alternate Belonging," "Diagonal & Self- Possessed," "Self-Portrait with Reflected Glimmer."

2. *"Everything I See Needs Rearranging": Los Angeles Snapshots*

Abridged version published as "Los Angeles Snapshots" in *Now Dig This! Art and Black Los Angeles 1960–1980*, ed. Kellie Jones (Los Angeles, New York: Hammer Museum, Prestel, 2011), 69–83.

3. *Mexico City: Art Stories with Roberto Bolaño*

Presented at "Roberto Bolaño and World Literature," a conference at the University of Warwick, UK, May 16–17, 2013.

Published as "Bolaño for Art Historians, 1990s Mexico City," in *Lana Turner: A Journal of Poetry & Opinion*, ed. Calvin Bedient and David Lau (Santa Monica, California) 10 (2019): 295–305.

4. *Family Resemblance in 1990s Mexico: Francis Alÿs,* The Fabiola Project

Unpublished; presented at the Menil Collection, Houston, Texas, December 16, 2016.

5. *Diaspora Assemblage: "Held Together by Stardust"*

Published in "A Questionnaire on Diaspora and the Modern," *October* (2023) (186): 106–12.

6. *Frameworks of Intelligibility: Latin American / Latinx Art*

Unpublished; presented at "Engaging Latinx Art: Methodological and Pedagogical Approaches," Museum of Fine Arts Houston–University of Houston NEH Summer Institute, June 6–18, 2022.

7. *The Latin American Photobook in Context*

Unpublished; presented at the Museum of Fine Arts Houston, Houston, Texas, April 1, 2017.

8. *Tropics of Broadband: Camera Culture and Experience in São Paulo*

Unpublished; presented at the Institute of Fine Arts, New York University, Latin American Forum, March 4, 2014.

9. *Printed Matters and Pop Art in América*

Published in *Pop América, 1965–1975*, ed. Esther Gabara (Durham, NC: Duke University Press, 2018), 124–37.

10. *Center of Gravity: José Clemente Orozco*

Published in *I Stand in My Place with My Own Day Here: Site-Specific Art at The New School*, ed. Frances Richard (Durham, NC: Duke University Press, 2019), 72–80.

11. *White Stone, Bramble, Gravity, Chance: Miguel Angel Ríos*

Published in *Gulf Coast: A Journal of Literature and Fine Art* 28, no. 2 (Summer/Fall 2016): 55–72.

12. *The Capture of Cuauhtémoc: David Alfaro Siqueiros, Leo Matiz, Javier de la Garza*

Published in *México una obra de arte* (Mexico City: Fundación BBVA, 2021).

13. Celia Álvarez Muñoz: "Ideas Are the Drivers"

Published in *Celia Álvarez Muñoz: Obras* (Houston: Art League Houston, 2020), 76–90.

14. Allora & Calzadilla: Wonderstruck on the Edge of Decline

Published as "Wonderstruck on the Edge of Decline: New Works by Allora & Calzadilla," in *Allora & Calzadilla: Specters of Noon*, ed. Michelle White (Houston and New Haven: The Menil Collection and Yale University Press), 66–79.

15. Luis Gispert: Radical Feedback

Published in Roberto J. Tejada, *Luis Gispert: Loud Image* (Hood Museum of Art, Dartmouth College; Hanover, NH: University Press of New England, 2004), 14–19.

16. Geographies of Language and Light: Laura Aguilar, Raquel Gutiérrez

Unpublished; abridged version presented at "Languages of Art History," International Committee Panel, Sonal Khullar (chair), College Art Association Conference, Chicago, February 15, 2020.

17. Latinx Art in the Future Imperfect: Axis Mundo, *Jennif(f)er Tamayo*

Published in *Gulf Coast: A Journal of Literature and Fine Art* 32, no. 1 (Winter/Spring 2020), 208–28.

18. Jesús Macarena-Ávila: The Essential Work

Published in *Jesús Macarena-Ávila: Germscapes: Covid-19 & Other Concerns* (Chicago: INC, 2021), n.p.

19. Christina Fernandez: Something Lost, Missing, or Unattainable

Published as "Something Lost, Missing, or Unattainable: In the Landscapes of Crisis with Christina Fernandez" in *Christina Fernandez: Multiple Exposures*, ed. Rebecca Epstein (Los Angeles, Seattle: UCLA Chicano Studies Research Center Press; University of Washington Press, 2022), 169–84.

An Andy Warhol Foundation Writers Grant, with its invaluable support and encouragement, made the conception and first framing of this book possible.

I extend the deepest gratitude to Richard Morrison and to the extraordinary team at Fordham University Press.

Special thanks to Eli Diner for his committed editorial excellence at various stages in the production of this book; and to Nancy Basmajian for her vigilant care and superlative clarity.

I've been the lucky beneficiary of conversations with Mary K. Coffey about art, art history, criticism, and theory for over two decades. Her foreword to this book is a dazzling gift.

I've been fortunate, as well, to participate, for over a decade, in an informal and evolving collective of researchers and writers on Latin American / Latinx art history and visual culture that has met intermittently at different locations to present current work in progress. My thanks to Claire F. Fox, Esther Gabara, Mary K. Coffey, Alejandra Uslenghi, Adele E. Nelson, Natalia Brizuela, Sergio Delgado Moya, Adriana Johnson, Natalia de la Rosa, George F. Flaherty, Camilo Trumper, Fernando Rosenberg, Laura G. Gutierrez, and China Medel.

Warmest thanks to a constellation of fellow writers—always generous with their time, supportive in their comments, and caring in their companionship: Alan Gilbert, Andrea Giunta, Chon Noriega, Dale Martin Smith, Esther Allen, J. Michael Martínez, Joel Bettridge, Joshua Escobar, Lalitha Gopalan, Margaret Randall, Matthew Stadler, Peter Ramos, Rachel Weiss, Ramón Gutiérrez, Raquel Gutiérrez, and Robb Hernández.

Sincerest acknowledgment for the inspiration, opportunity, and collaboration offered by so many others, among them Adrienne Perry, Carla Faesler, Carmen Giménez, Caroline Fowler, Cindy Peña, Darby English, David Breslin, David Dove, Derrick Cartwright, Dorothy Wang, Édouard Kopp, Edward Sullivan, Elisa Taber, Emily Butts, Frances Richards, Jennie Ash, Joanna Szupinska, Jon Evans, Justin Janice, Karen Farber, Katharine Barthelme, Kellie Jones, Laura Augusta, Lauren Greve, Leah Dickerman, Mari Carmen Ramírez, Michael Slosek, Michelle White, Molly Nesbit, Mónica Nepote, Naima J. Keith, Nicolas Lawrence, Ondine Chavoya, Paulina Rocha, Prageeta Sharma, Raphael Rubenstein, Rebecca Epstein, Rebecca Frazier, Rex Koontz, Sonal Khullar, Stephanie Mitchell, Surpik Angelini, and Toby Kamp.

For the horizon and promise of dwelling in relation, my love and gratitude to Michael Bryan.

NOTES

INTRODUCTION: DIAGONALLY SPEAKING

1. Photographs of photomechanical stencils provided by the artist. Correspondence with the author, June 18, 2020.

2. Álvarez Muñoz, correspondence with the author, June 18, 2020.

3. Alexander R. Galloway, "Along the Diagonal Line," post, July 22, 2022, http://cultureandcommunication.org/galloway/along-the-diagonal-line.

4. Jean d'Ormesson, "The Death of Roger Caillois," *Diogenes* 27, no. 105 (March 1979): 1–3. With the onset of World War II and at the invitation of Victoria Ocampo, Caillois lived as an exile in Buenos Aires (1939–46). His work had an impact not only in Argentina, "where he counted numerous friends whose works and thought he had made known in Europe," Jorge Luis Borges among them, but as well in Brazil, "whose Academy elected him to the seat previously occupied by André Malraux."

5. Roger Caillois, "Diagonal Sciences," in *The Mask of Medusa*, trans. George Ordish (Clarkson N. Potter, 1964), 9–15. Versions of "The Praying Mantis" and "The Three Functions of Mimicry" were first published in the surrealist journal *Minotaure*: see Roger Caillois, "La mante religieuse: De la biologie à la psychanalyse," *Minotaure* 5 (1934): 23–26; and Roger Caillois, "Mimétisme et psychasthénie légendaire," *Minotaure* 7 (1936): 510.

6. Claire F. Fox, "Commentary: The Transnational Turn and the Hemispheric Return," *American Literary History* 18, no. 3 (Fall 2006): 638–47.

7. Ramón A. Gutiérrez, "What's in a Name: The History and Politics of Hispanic and Latino Panethnicities," in *New Latino Studies Reader: A Twenty-First-Century Perspective*, ed. Ramón A. Gutiérrez and Tomás Almaguer (University of California Press, 2016), 20.

8. Olga Yatskevich, Russet Lederman, and Matthew Carson, eds., *CLAP!10 × 10 Contemporary Latin American Photobooks, 2000–2016* (10 × 10 Photobooks, Carnegie Museum of Art, Aperture Foundation, and Museum of Fine Arts, Houston, 2017).

9. Robert Duncan, "Often I Am Permitted to Return to a Meadow," in *The Opening of the Field* (New Directions, 1960), 7.

10. My involvement in both the attention practices and community building activated by Nameless Sound inform these pages (see https://www.namelesssound.org/).

11. Dale Martin Smith, *The Passenger* (Wave Books, 2026), 9, 32.

12. Friends of Attention's documents and public events can be accessed at https://www.friendsofattention.net/ and https://www.schoolofattention.org/about-1.

1. DIAGONAL AND SELF-POSSESSED: GROUP PORTRAIT WITH LIMINAL FIGURES

1. André Breton, *Mad Love* [1937], trans. Mary Ann Caws (University of Nebraska Press, 1987), 87.

2. Chris Marker, *Sans soleil/Sunless* [1983] (Argos Films, New Yorker Video, 1993).

3. Imamu Amiri Baraka, "Counterstatement to Whitney Ritz Bros," in *Black Art Notes*, ed. Tom Lloyd (n.p., 1971), 10–12.

4. Samira Kawash, *Dislocating the Color Line: Identity, Hybridity, and Singularity in African-American Narrative* (Stanford University Press, 1997), 130.

5. Rosa Alcalá, untitled statement, in *The Volta Book of Poets*, ed. Joshua Marie Wilkinson (Sidebrow Books, 2015), 1.

6. Philip Roth cited in Claudia Roth Pierpont, "The Book of Laughter," *New Yorker*, September 30, 2013.

7. Author's translation.

8. Dodie Bellamy, "My Mixed Marriage," *Village Voice*, June 27, 2000, 65.

9. Robert Duncan, "Often I Am Permitted to Return to a Meadow," in *The Opening of the Field* (New Directions, 1960), 7.

10. Walter Benjamin, *Escritos: La literatura infantil, los niños y los jóvenes* (Ediciones Nueva Visión, 1989), 98–99. Author's translation.

11. Sean Carrillo, "East to Eden," in *Forming: The Early Days of L.A. Punk*, by Claude Bessy et al. (Smart Art, 1999), 38.

12. Human Hands, *Trains vs. Planes* (Faulty Products, 1981), 7" 45 vinyl, n.p.

13. Human Hands, *Human Hands* (Independent Project Records, 1982), n.p.

14. Ira Robbins, "Human Hands" (review), Human Hands, *Hereafter* (Nate Starkman & Son, 1988), Trouser Press (online archive), https://trouserpress.com/reviews/human-hands/.

15. Human Hands, *Human Hands* (Independent Project Records, 1982), n.p.

16. Tomás Ybarra-Frausto, "Rasquachismo: A Chicano Sensibility," in *Chicano Art: Resistance and Affirmation, 1965–1985*, ed. Richard Griswold del Castillo, Teresa McKenna, and Yvonne Yarbro-Bejarano (Wight Art Gallery, University of California, 1991), 156–62.

17. Oscar Castillo, personal correspondence with author, June 2, 2010.

18. Victor Franco, oral history interview, July 1972, Smithsonian Archives of American Art, Washington, DC.

19. Rubén Salazar, "Black and Chicano Ties Worsen After Walkout at Santa Barbara," *Los Angeles Times*, September 15, 1969.

20. Ramón A. Gutiérrez, "Community, Patriarchy and Individualism: The Politics of Chicano History and the Dream of Equality," *American Quarterly* 45, no. 1 (March 1993): 46.

21. Karl Marx and Friedrich Engels, *The Communist Manifesto*, trans. Samuel Moore, introduction by Jodi Dean (Pluto Books, 2017), 54.

22. Sigmund Freud, *Three Contributions to the Theory of Sex*, trans. A. A. Brill (E. P. Dutton, 1962), 79.

23. Tzvetan Todorov, "No somos ni buenos ni malos, pero tiene sentido luchar: Entrevista con Todorov," *Letras Libres*, March 13, 2017, http://www.letraslibres.com/espana-mexico/revista/no- somos-ni-buenos-ni-malos-pero-tiene-sentido-luchar-entrevista-tzvetan-todorov. Author's translation.

24. Walter Benjamin, "Theses on the Philosophy of History" in *Illuminations*, trans. Harry Zohn (Schocken Books, 1969), 255.

25. Alex Nemerov, *Wartime Kiss: Visions of the Moment in the 1940s* (Princeton University Press, 2013), 2.

26. Ludwig Wittgenstein, "A Lecture on Ethics," *Philosophical Review* 74, no. 1 (1965): 12.

27. Judith Butler, *The Psychic Life of Power: Theories in Subjection* (Stanford University Press, 1997), 146.

2. "EVERYTHING I SEE NEEDS REARRANGING": LOS ANGELES SNAPSHOTS

1. Henry J. Seldis, "An Achievement 50 Years in the Making," *Los Angeles Times*, March 28, 1965.

2. Russell Lymes, "Los Angeles' Cultural Circus," *Harper's*, February 1964. Lymes, unconcerned with overstatement, adds: "'Why is the art gallery moving?' a local collector responded to a question from me. 'Obviously it is following the money.'"

3. "County Museum of Art to Be Opened March 31," *Los Angeles Times*, January 24, 1965; Seldis, "Achievement 50 Years in the Making," 4.

4. Mike Davis, *City of Quartz* (Vintage, 1992), 72.

5. Lymes, "Los Angeles' Cultural Circus."

6. Lymes, "Los Angeles' Cultural Circus."

7. The notion of an "idealist culture" is found in Siegfried Kracauer, "Cult of Distraction: On Berlin's Picture Palaces," trans. Thomas Y. Levin, *New German Critique* 40 (Winter 1987): 95.

8. Walter Benjamin, "Theory of Distraction," in *Selected Writings*, vol. 3, *1935–1938*, ed. Howard Eiland and Michael Jennings (Belknap, 2002), 141–42. The editors speculate as to the second term, when Benjamin writes, "Distraction and destruction [word conjectured] as the subjective and objective sides, respectively, of one and the same process/The relation of distraction to absorption must be examined." See also Kracauer, "Cult of Distraction," 95.

9. Art Berman, "Eight Men Slain, Guard Moves In," *Los Angeles Times*, August 14, 1965.

10. Rubén Salazar, "But He Recalls Race Problems," *Los Angeles Times*, August 23, 1965.

11. George Lipsitz, *Welcome to the Barrelhouse* (University of Minnesota Press, 2010), 86.

12. Johnny Otis, *Listen to the Lambs* (University of Minnesota Press, 2009), 62.

13. Otis, *Listen to the Lambs*, 77.

14. Otis, *Listen to the Lambs*, 186.

15. H. Edward Ransford, "Isolation, Powerlessness, and Violence: A Study of Attitudes and Participation in the Watts Riot," *American Journal of Sociology* 73, no. 5 (March 1968): 581–91.

16. Cornel West, "The Paradox of the Afro-American Rebellion," *Social Text* 9/10 (Spring–Summer 1984): 50.

17. Cortez adds: "The rebellions pointed out the need for social, economic, and political change. So it was time to recognize the need for change, a time to protest conditions, a time to reflect and cancel all conservative ideas, a time to drop the ball and chain, a time to go back to the root and use the Black freedom struggle as a foundation for art, a time to find another way of life. Many artists drew energy from the rebellion and produced works exploring the aftermath, the confrontations, the wounds, and the revolutionary ideas." Jayne Cortez, "In Her Own Words," in *Watts: Art and Social Change in Los Angeles, 1965–2002* (Haggerty Museum of Art, Marquette University, 2003), 33–34.

18. Lynn Spigel in "The Suburban Home Companion: Television and the Neighborhood Ideal in Postwar America" examines the changing notions of domestic and public space with the arrival of the television into a large number of US households after the Second World War, the subsequent reorganization of social space and the neighborhood in mass-produced suburbs like Levittown; so too TV's questionable democratic promise of a new, peaceably united community of viewers. This phenomenon coincides with notions about the larger virtual community constituted and united by US television. So, for example, many African American viewers in the segregated 1950s found television in the home a space in which they would not be discriminated against as they were in the outside world of racist America. Spigel also examines how the intrusion of the TV begins to determine male-female relationships in representations (advertisements, cartoons, and so forth) around the topic of television viewing. Lynn Spigel, *Welcome to the Dreamhouse: Popular Media and Postwar Suburbs* (Duke University Press, 2001), 31–59.

19. In *Listen to the Lambs*, Johnny Otis refers to Stanley "Saunders" even as the record shows he is referring to the author Stanley Sanders, who wrote "I'll Never Escape the Ghetto," *Ebony*, August 1967.

20. Otis, *Listen to the Lambs*, 56.

21. Otis, *Listen to the Lambs*, 56.
22. "Live and Let Live," track 8 on Love, *Forever Changes*, Elektra, 1967.
23. Andrew Hulktrans, *Forever Changes* (Continuum, 2003), 39.
24. Hulktrans, *Forever Changes*, 39.
25. Hulktrans, *Forever Changes*, 39.
26. A digital version of this image is archived as part of UCLA's *Changing Times: Los Angeles in Photographs, 1920–1990*, photo identification number: uclalat_1429_b572_232223. Even as it does not appear in any section of the *Los Angeles Times*, March 28, 1966, there is reason to suggest the image was made by *Times* staff photographer Joe Kennedy or Ben Olender. One of the works in the background setting appears to be by Betye Saar, from the period of her *View from the Sorcerer's Window* (1966).
27. Art Berman, "Junk from First Watts Riot Turned into Works of Art," *Los Angeles Times*, March 28, 1966, 3.
28. Art Berman, "Watts Easter Week Art Festival Puts Riot Debris to Cultural Uses," *Los Angeles Times*, April 8, 1966.
29. "'Watts Renaissance' Exhibit Opens Today," *Los Angeles Times*, April 3, 1966.
30. Berman, "Watts Easter Week Art Festival," 1.
31. Sigmund Freud, "The Uncanny," in *The Standard Edition of the Complete Psychological Works of Sigmund Freud*, vol. 17 (Hogarth Press and the Institute of Psychoanalysis, 1962), 220.
32. Freud, "The Uncanny," 220.
33. Stanley Sanders, "I'll Never Escape the Ghetto," *Ebony*, August 1967, 36.
34. Benjamin, "Theory of Distraction," 141.
35. Siegfried Kracauer, quoted in Walter Benjamin, "Review of Kracauer's *Die Angestellten*," in *Selected Writings*, vol. 2:1, ed. Marcus Bullock and Michael W. Jennings (Harvard University Press, 2004), 356.
36. "County Museum of Art to Be Opened March 31," *Los Angeles Times*, January 24, 1965, p. A.
37. Alexandra Schwartz, "'Second City': Ed Ruscha and the Reception of Los Angeles Pop," *October* 111 (Winter 2005): 35. "Ruscha has rejected such readings, insisting instead that he was primarily interested in capturing an image of paradoxical calm amid chaos. But Ruscha's choice of the celebrated new LACMA—and by association the local artistic community it symbolized—as the subject of this ambitious if ambiguous work indicates a certain willingness to serve as both a representative of and commentator on the city's burgeoning art scene."
38. Edward W. Soja, "The City and Spatial Justice," *Justice Spatiale / Spatial Justice*, no. 1 (September 2009).
39. "The Take-Over Generation," *Life*, September 14, 1962, 2.
40. "Take-Over Generation," 40.
41. *Visual Acoustics: The Modernism of Julius Shulman*, dir. Eric Bricker (New Video Group, 2010), 83 minutes.
42. "Four Outstanding Architect Houses," *Los Angeles Times*, Home Section, May 22, 1966.
43. According to Edwards, the owners of the house were Gerald and Arleen Rosen. Gerald Rosen was an attorney and his wife, Arleen, collected art; they later divorced and Gerald went east to New York, where he associated periodically with Edwards, and continued collecting his work. Mel met them about the time of LACMA's *5 Younger Artists* exhibition. Edwards relates that Arleen showed interest in the work, he later discovered, in part because she had grown up in Wyoming, where her father was a scrap metal dealer. Personal communication with the author, July 2, 2010.
44. Jack Jones, "Cultural Uprising Grows on Faith and Toil in Watts," *Los Angeles Times*, February 7, 1966.
45. D. H. Melhem and Jayne Cortez, "A MELUS Profile and Interview," *MELUS* 21, no. 1 (Spring 1996): 74.

46. Jayne Cortez, *Festivals and Funerals* (Phrase Text, 1971), n.p. The poems cited from this rare handmade artist-poet collaboration in the passages that follow are all unpaginated. For a survey of the poet's corpus, see Jayne Cortez, *Firespitter: The Collected Poems of Jayne Cortez* (Nightboat Books, 2024).

47. Georges Bataille, "The Solar Anus" and "Mouth" in *Visions of Excess: Selected Writings, 1927–1939* (University of Minnesota Press, 1985), 5–9, 59–60.

48. Cornel West, *Race Matters* (Beacon, 1993), 83.

49. Berman, "Watts Easter Week Art Festival." In the *Times* photographs, the facial expressions and body language of Mary Jane Jones and Nancy Godwin convey a guarded fascination whose framing in each case underscores the conditional unease of the figure-ground relation.

50. Henri Lefebvre, "The Right to the City," in *Writings on Cities*, trans. and ed. Eleonore Kofman and Elizabeth Lebas (Blackwell, 1996), 158; Soja, "City and Spatial Justice."

51. Rubén Salazar, "Latins' Image in Advertising Held 'Inferior,'" *Los Angeles Times*, October 20, 1969.

52. Rubén Salazar, "Anglo 'Integration' Rejected by Chicanos," *Los Angeles Times*, April 7, 1969.

53. Rubén Salazar, "Attack on Barrio, Ghetto Units Helps Explain Rising Alienation," *Los Angeles Times*, May 22, 1970.

54. Rubén Salazar, "Pachuco Folk Heroes—They Were First to Be Different," *Los Angeles Times*, July 17, 1970; Rubén Salazar, "Don't Make the 'Bato Loco' Go the Way of the Zoot Suiter," *Los Angeles Times*, June 19, 1970; Rubén Salazar, "Equal Chance to Education? Not Down in the Barrios," *Los Angeles Times*, June 12, 1970.

55. Rubén Salazar, "Chicano Must Be Nationalist to Last in U.S., Leader Says," *Los Angeles Times*, April 18, 1969; Rubén Salazar, "Thousands Cross Border," *Los Angeles Times*, August 31, 1969; Rubén Salazar, "Latin Group Presents 7 Demands to UCLA," *Los Angeles Times*, April 5, 1969.

56. Rubén Salazar, "Maligned Word: Mexican," *Los Angeles Times*, April 17, 1970; Rubén Salazar, "Who Is a Chicano? And What Is It the Chicanos Want?," *Los Angeles Times*, February 6, 1970.

57. Rubén Salazar, "No Middle Class Illusions," *Los Angeles Times*, February 3, 1969.

58. For a specific example, see Dale Rodgers Marshall, *The Politics of Participation in Poverty: A Case Study of the Board of the Economic and Youth Opportunities Agency of Greater Los Angeles* (University of California Press, 1971).

59. Rubén Salazar, "Chicanos Told to Fight Like Blacks for Respect," *Los Angeles Times*, April 9, 1969.

60. Ernesto Chávez, *"¡Mi Raza Primero!" (My People First!): Nationalism, Identity, and Insurgency in the Chicano Movement in Los Angeles, 1966–1978* (University of California Press, 2002), 66.

61. An inquest determined that Salazar's death was an "accident." Fellow writer and friend Hank López wrote:

> Initial reports indicated that a bullet that pierced his skull came from a crossfire between the police and some rioters who were holed-up in the restaurant-bar where his body was later found.
>
> But it later developed that he was shot through an open doorway by a high-velocity tear-gas missile that should never have been used by the police under such circumstances. In the words of the consultant for the Peace Officers Standards and Training Commission, such a weapon should never be used for crowd control, since it is designed for use against "barricaded animals"—hardly a term that could be used to describe a gentle human being like Ruben. (Enrique Hank López, "Ruben Salazar Death Silences a Leading Voice of Reason," *Los Angeles Times*, September 6, 1970.)

As recently as August 2010, *Los Angeles Times* reporter Robert J. López made efforts to view files relevant to Salazar's death; however, County Sheriff Lee Baca has refused to release eight boxes of records that could reveal how the *Times* columnist and KMEX-TV news director had long been under surveillance. Robert J. López, "Baca Refuses to Release Records Related to Times Journalist Ruben Salazar's Death," *Los Angeles Times*, August 9, 2010.

62. Tomás Ybarra-Frausto, "Rasquachismo: A Chicano Sensibility," in *Chicano Art: Resistance and Affirmation, 1965–1985*, ed. Richard Griswold del Castillo, Teresa McKenna, and Yvonne Yarbro-Bejarano (UCLA, Wight Art Gallery, 1991), 156.

63. *Los Four*, dir. James Tartan (1974), 16mm, 22:55, in *Los Four/Murals of Aztlán: The Street Painters of East Los Angeles* (Los Angeles UCLA Chicano Studies Research Center, Chicano Cinema and Media Series, vol. 1, 2004), DVD.

64. Dan Knapp, "KCET's Show for Chicano Viewers," *Los Angeles Times*, April 3, 1970.

65. Emory Holmes II, "A Pit Bull in the World of Fine Art; Cecil Fergerson Helped Rewrite the Definition of 'Artist' in Southern California as He Nurtured Up-and-Coming African American Talent. But Don't Think It's Been Easy," *Los Angeles Times Magazine*, February 14, 1999.

66. Holmes, "Pit Bull."

67. Josh Kun, "Vex Populi," *Los Angeles*, March 2003, 62–70.

68. Inasmuch as posters had established a communications network for the Chicano Arts Movement on the walls and windows of homes, offices, and storefronts—markers connecting private and public space, even as they promoted art exhibitions, concerts, theatrical productions, mass meetings, and rallies—poster artists expressed solidarity with oppressed peoples both at home and abroad, including those who opposed the war in Southeast Asia and supported liberation movements throughout Central America. Some examples include Rupert García's screen prints *Fuera de Indochina!* (Out of Indochina!) (1970), *Freedom for Political Prisoners (Angela Davis)* (1971), and *Allende, 1909–73* (1973); and Malaquías Montoya's *Viet Nam Aztlán Fuera* (1973) and *One Year of Military Dictatorship* (1977).

69. Jeff Spurrier, "Plugz: Back in Business," *Los Angeles Times*, January 10, 1982. In addition to Tito Larriva and Chalo Quintana of The Plugz, Alice Bag (Alice Armendariz) of The Bags, and San Diego band The Zeros, Latinos were an integral part of the LA punk scene from its beginnings. For a list of others, see Sean Carrillo, "East to Eden," in *Forming: The Early Days of L.A. Punk*, by Claude Bessy et al. (Smart Art, 1999), 38, quoted in further detail in chapter 1 of *Along the Diagonal*.

70. Richard Cromelin, Kristine McKenna, Don Snowden, and Robert Hilburn, "Rounding Up the L.A. Sound," *Los Angeles Times*, April 29, 1979; Kristine McKenna, "Plugz Keep on Plugging," *Los Angeles Times*, July 13, 1980.

71. "A Gain—A Loss," track 1 on The Plugz, *Electrify Me*, Plug Recordz, 1979.

72. George Lipsitz, "Not Just Another Social Movement: Poster Art and the Movimiento Chicano," in *American Studies in a Moment of Danger* (University of Minnesota Press, 2001), 171. Lipsitz writes that oppositional movements are successful insofar as they argue and encourage a contrary consciousness. They can account for shared experiences that make collective action imperative and make way for individuals who can find a place for themselves in the shared history of their social group, even as they prompt people "to take risks for systemic change." As well, they invert or satirize ideas and images that support the standard narrative.

73. Josh Frank, *In Heaven Everything Is Fine: The Unsolved Life of Peter Ivers and the Lost History of New Wave Theatre* (Soft Skull, 2009).

74. Kristine McKenna, "Remembrance of Things Fast," in *Forming: The Early Days of L.A. Punk*, by Claude Bessy et al. (Smart Art, 1999), 30.

75. *Punk Rock: How to Look Punk*, an undated fanzine of the time, submits: "That's why 'looking punk' is best achieved using ordinary things around the house. Search drawers, closets and attic, plus your friendly neighborhood thrift shops, for all varieties of PUNK JUNK to attach to your clothes (or mend holes and rips) . . . use safety pins (the symbol of punkdom), paper

clips and clothes pins . . . old badges, buttons, charms, soda can flip-flop tabs and war medals . . . bathtub plug chains, dog chains, hardware chains and locks . . . tumbler locks, bottle openers, rabbit's foot key chains and large antique hotel keys . . . bits of coiled rope, old neckties and broken shoestrings . . . studs, nuts 'n bolts, washers . . . toy daggers . . . all tied, pinned, clipped, taped or stapled to clothing, or worn as junk jewelry, in your own most individually creative fashion." Thanks to Rose Salseda-Gómez and Daniel Gómez for their joyous critical appreciation of this musical and artistic moment, and for providing access to this period gem.

76. Mark Spitz and Brendan Mullen, *We Got the Neutron Bomb: The Untold Story of L.A. Punk* (Three Rivers, 2001).

77. Quoted in Don Snowden, "Maverick Visions," *Los Angeles Times*, July 22, 1986.

78. Self-description by keyboardist John Dentino in "Fibonaccis Are Rota Rooters," *Los Angeles Times*, June 27, 1982.

79. Snowden, "Maverick Visions."

80. Snowden, "Maverick Visions." In writing about "the creative scene that is seldom seen or written about," Snowden adds: "Only a handful of local outlets, ranging from museums to underground rock clubs, exhibit fine-art videos and Jenkins' political thrust and Third World perspective often encountered stiff opposition there." Public access television on cable provided opportunities for artists like Jenkins to produce and air videos with content about the community. Jenkins considered his completed videos "rituals," and he christened his choppy style of editing (reminiscent of other cable-access productions like *New Wave Theater*) "doggereal."

81. West, *Race Matters*, 83.

82. Jenkins addressed this theme again in his 1979 MFA performance piece, *Just Another Rendering of the Same Old Problem.* See Paul Von Blum, "Ulysses Jenkins: A Griot for the Electronic Age," *Journal of Pan African Studies* 3, no. 2 (September 2009): 140–41.

83. Other members included saxophonist Harold (Stemsy) Hunter (original member of the rock group Electric Flag led by Buddy Miles) and David Strother on electric violin, Larry Tuttle on the Chapman Stick bass, and Jack Nathan on drums. Life in the Park with Debris was an early configuration of what later became Othervisions Art Band: a lineup comprising Michael Delgado on guitar and backup vocals, Oscar Del Pinal on bass, Brent Woten on drums, and Reyes Rodriguez (later founding director of Trópico de Nopal art gallery) on tracks and percussion; Ulysses Jenkins provided lead and backup vocals, as well as rhythm guitar. A track entitled "Sobriety" was co-penned with eventual front man of the Negro Problem, Mark Stewart, who with Heidi Rodewald produced several recordings as Stew, and wrote the 2009 Tony Award–winning musical *Passing Strange.* Prior to founding the Negro Problem, Stewart briefly played in a band with VinZula Kara called Primal Syntheses, and he had replaced Michael Delgado to collaborate with Jenkins on a CD entitled *Serendipity.* I am grateful to Ulysses Jenkins for providing this information.

84. Performing were Crono, Bob Dale, Todd Gray, Liz Rodriguez, Maren Hassinger, Ulysses Jenkins, Senga Nengundi, Frank Parker, and May Sun.

85. Ulysses Jenkins and Senga Nengudi Fittz, press release, "Chance Unfrozen," 1983. Manuscript provided by Ulysses Jenkins.

86. Artist's website: http://www.ulyssesjenkins.com/without.html (accessed September 5, 2010; site inactive on March 29, 2024).

87. Snowden, "Maverick Visions."

88. Snowden, "Maverick Visions."

89. Edward W. Soja, *Postmodern Geographies: The Reassertion of Space in Critical Social Theory* (Verso, 1989).

90. Pete Johnson, "Pop Records: Love's Third Album Out on Elektra," *Los Angeles Times*, February 25, 1968.

91. Rebecca Solnit, *Secret Exhibition: Six California Artists of the Cold War Era* (City Lights, 1991), ix, 85.

3. MEXICO CITY: ART STORIES WITH ROBERTO BOLAÑO

1. Born in Chile, Roberto Bolaño began his writing life in Mexico City, where he founded a short-lived poetry movement, *infrarrealismo*, remembered as often for its pranks as for its literary production, before moving to Spain, where he would eventually write the vast body of short fiction and novels for which he is remembered. Bolaño died at the age of fifty having produced an expansive list of work and was to become, posthumously, a publishing sensation in the English-speaking world and in Europe.

2. Roberto Bolaño, *The Savage Detectives*, translated from the Spanish with an introduction by Natasha Wimmer (Farrar, Strauss and Giroux, 2007), 168.

3. Bolaño, *Savage Detectives*, 139.

4. Ricardo Martínez, "Más allá de la última ventana: Los 'marcos' de *Los detectives salvajes* desde la poética cognitiva," in *Territorios en fuga: Estudios críticos sobre la obra de Roberto Bolaño*, ed. Patricia Espinosa H. (Frasis, 2003), 200. Author's translation.

5. Patricia Espinosa, "*Tres* de Roberto Bolaño: El crac de la posmodernidad," in *Territorios en fuga: Estudios críticos sobre la obra de Roberto Bolaño*, ed. Patricia Espinosa H. (Frasis, 2003), 170. Author's translation.

6. Bob Jessop, "Putting Neoliberalism in Its Time and Place," *Social Anthropology/Anthropologie Social* 21, no. 1 (2013): 68.

7. Klaus Biesenbach, "Mexico City: An Exhibition About the Exchange Rates of Bodies and Values," in *Mexico City: An Exhibition About the Exchange Rates of Bodies and Values* (P.S.1 Contemporary Art Center, 2003), 33.

8. Biesenbach, "Mexico City: An Exhibition," 36.

9. Carlos Monsiváis, *Mexican Postcards*, ed. and trans. John Kraniauskas (Verso, 1997), 138.

10. They included Joaquín Hernández Galicia, commonly known as "La Quina," and Eduardo Pesqueira Olea.

11. Anthony DePalma, "Despite Gains, Press Freedom in Mexico Is Still Limited," *New York Times*, November 20, 1994, sec. 1, p. 3.

12. DePalma, "Despite Gains," sec. 1, p. 3.

13. Anthony DePalma, "Disgraced Mexican Is Back, with Accusations of His Own," *New York Times*, October 8, 2000, sec. 1, p. 6.

14. DePalma, "Disgraced Mexican," sec. 1, p. 6.

15. Carlos Aguirre, *Images of Neoliberalism* (Galeria Nina Menocal, 1995).

16. Miguel Ventura, *Die Notizbücher der Mademoiselle Heidi Schreber* [The Notebooks of Mademoiselle Heidi Schreber] (New Interterritorial Language Committee, 1995).

17. Ventura, *Die Notizbücher.*

18. Miguel Ventura, Artist Statement, manuscript, 1994.

19. Sara Silver, "Mexican First Lady's Foundation Leaves Grey Areas," *Financial Times*, February 24, 2005, accessed online.

20. Sari Bermúdez, "Acknowledgment," in *Mexico City: An Exhibition About the Exchange Rates of Bodies and Values* (P.S. 1 Contemporary Art Center, 2003), 29.

21. Silver, "Mexican First Lady's Foundation."

22. Alphonso Lingis, *The Community of Those Who Have Nothing in Common* (Indiana University Press, 1994), 166–67.

23. Mario Vargas Llosa, "Why Does Latin America Fail?," *CATO Policy Report* 25, no. 1 (January/February 2003): 15.

24. Joan Copjec, *Read My Desire* (MIT Press, 1994), 200.

25. Cuauhtémoc Medina, "Mutual Abuse," in *Mexico City: An Exhibition About the Exchange Rates of Bodies and Values* (P.S. 1 Contemporary Art Center, 2003), 38–56.

26. Biesenbach, "Mexico City: An Exhibition," 36.

27. See Jo Tuckman, "Mexico's Drug Wars: Mystery Surrounds How Many Are Dying, and Who; Government Database Claims 35,000 Had Been Killed by December 2010, but Many Say Real Toll Could Be Much Higher," *The Guardian*, December 8, 2010, accessed online.

28. Bolaño, *Savage Detectives*, 162; 177; 233; 364; 474; 489; 557; 579.

29. Walter Benjamin, "Theses on the Philosophy of History," in *Illuminations*, trans. Harry Zohn; ed. and with an introduction by Hannah Arendt (Schocken Books, 1969), 255.

30. Benjamin, "Theses on the Philosophy of History," 255.

31. Stephen Greenblatt, "Towards a Poetics of Culture," in *The New Historicism*, ed. H. Aram Veeser (Routledge, 1989), 8.

32. Bolaño, *Savage Detectives*, 579.

4. FAMILY RESEMBLANCE IN 1990S MEXICO: FRANCIS ALŸS, *THE FABIOLA PROJECT*

1. In 1995 Alÿs also staged his performance "stroll" entitled *The Leak*, which "documents his walking through a working-class neighborhood in Sao Paulo carrying a punctured can of blue paint to leave a trail on the streets as a reminder of his transitory presence." H. Wendell Howard, "Saint Fabiola in Fiction, in History, in Portraiture," *Logos: A Journal of Catholic Thought and Culture* 14, no. 2 (Spring 2011), 82–95; 91.

2. James Brooke, "Arts Invade Rio for Earth Summit," *New York Times*, June 1, 1992: "'It's an excellent opportunity to get to know the range of contemporary Brazilian artists,' said Thomas M. Messer, director emeritus of the Solomon R. Guggenheim Museum, who came here to serve on the show's inter-American jury. On Tuesday, Mr. Bozano, president of Banco Bozano, Simonsen, is to distribute $600,000 in awards to the 12 prize winners, representing eight nations of the Americas."

3. Cuauhtémoc Medina and Roberto Tejada, "Lesa natura / Marred Nature," in *Lesa natura: Reflexiones sobre ecología* (Museo de Arte Moderno, 1993), 13.

4. Glassford had featured these works in the group exhibitions *Marcas* at the Galería de Arte Contemporáneo in 1991 and *Objeto/Sujeto* at Museo de Monterrey in 1993.

5. The founding members of Curare were Karen Cordero, Olivier Debroise, Rina Epelstein, James Oles, Ana Isabel Pérez Gavilán, Francisco Reyes Palma, and Armando Sáenz. Olivier Debroise and Cuauhtémoc Medina, eds., *La era de la discrepancia: Arte y cultura visual en México, 1968–1997* [The Age of Discrepancies: Art and Visual Culture in Mexico, 1968–1997] (Mexico City: Universidad Nacional Autónoma, 2006), 409.

6. Art critic Jean Fisher offers a similar suggestion: "Francis' use of the little narrative, the little fable, is incredibly important as a strategy showing us the importance of the detail of life; that life as it is lived with all the little incidents from which you may or may not take significance but are those things that build your sense of self within place. And what is so interesting to me and it does relate to the question of what is the poetics of Francis' work, is that he makes clear to us something about art-making as a process of thought. . . . Much of the work if not all of the work concerns boundaries, a certain kind of boundary violation if you like. . . . Walking is a material tangible way [to work with cities] of relating or inhabiting space even if temporarily; you know he never believes he belongs to a place." *Wide Details, on the Traces of Francis Alÿs*, directed by Julien Devaux (2006), 56 min.

7. In *The Practice of Everyday Life*, Michel de Certeau writes that "to practice space is to repeat the joyful silent experience of childhood; to overwrite the city with metaphor." Steven Rendall, trans. (University of California Press, 1988), 110.

8. Francis Alÿs, *Walking Distance from the Studio* (Antiguo Colegio de San Ildefonso, 2006), 18.

9. Debroise and Medina, *La era de la discrepancia*, 393.

10. Melanie Brkich, "One-on-One with Visiting Writer Susan Briante," *An Open Book: The Inprint Blog*, December 8, 2016, https://anopenbookblog.org/one-on-one-with-visiting-writer-susan-briante/.

11. Thomas Glassford, "Homeland Insecurity," *Mandorla: Nueva Escritura de las Américas/Mandorla: New Writing from the Americas* 8 (2005), 49–50.

12. *Francis Alÿs: The Fabiola Project*, May 21, 2016–October 28, 2018, The Menil Collection, Byzantine Fresco Chapel, Houston, Texas. The Byzantine Fresco Chapel housed frescoes dating from the thirteenth century, restored and installed in a building on The Menil Collection campus in February 1997, later removed and returned to Cyprus in March 2012. The Byzantine Fresco Chapel thereafter served as a contemplative space and site-specific venue. It has been off-view to the public since 2018.

13. Michel de Certeau, *The Writing of History*, trans. Tom Conley (Columbia University Press, 1988). "Such is the situation of the text. It does not escape the trial that it analyzes. It goes on with this trial and remains unable to find a sure, overlooking view protected from 'doubt.' It is not exempted from the struggle needed to 'take the place,' nor is it protected from the law that makes the eliminated element return" (328).

14. Michel de Certeau, *The Possession at Lodoun*, trans. Michael B. Smith (University of Chicago Press, 2000).

> How could history be sure? History books begin with a present. They are constructed on the basis of two series of data: on the one hand, the "ideas" we have about the past, ideas that are still conveyed by old material, but along pathways blazed by a new mentality; on the other hand, documents and "archives," remains saved by chance, frozen in collections that attach meanings to them that are also new. Between the two [emerges] the relation that makes history possible. [It] refers to a reality that once had a living unity, and no longer is, It is, in short, broken by an absence.
>
> Its form is in proportion to what it tells: a past. (7–8)

15. Francis Alÿs, curatorial statement for *Sleepers II* (2001), Art Gallery of New South Wales, Australia, https://www.artgallery.nsw.gov.au/collection/works/L2011.24/.

16. Elizabeth Grosz, "The Animal Sense of Family and Sexuality," paper presented at "What's Sex Got to Do with Family," CUNY Graduate Center, New York, October 5, 2009.

17. Allen Grossman, "The Death of the Beloved Companion: Brief Narrative on the Master Narrative of Poetic Knowledge," *Harvard Review* 2 (Fall 1992), 56.

18. Georges Didi-Humerman, cited in Michael Ann Holly, *The Melancholy Art* (Princeton University Press, 2013), 6.

5. DIASPORA ASSEMBLAGE: "HELD TOGETHER BY STARDUST"

1. Roberto Tejada, *Still Nowhere in an Empty Vastness: History + Metaphor* (Noemi, 2019).

2. Mari Carmen Ramírez, "Beyond 'The Fantastic': Framing Identity in U.S. Exhibitions of Latin American Art," in *Beyond the Fantastic: Contemporary Art Criticism from Latin America*, ed. Gerardo Mosquera (MIT Press, 1996), 230, 245n7.

3. Cecilia Vicuña, "The No," in *The Precarious: The Art and Poetry of Cecilia Vicuña*, ed. M. Catherine de Zegher, trans. Esther Allen (University Press of New England, 1997), 135.

4. Macarena Gómez-Barris, "Life Otherwise at the Sea's Edge," *Open Rivers: Rethinking Water, Place & Community* 13 (Spring 2019), https://libpubsdss.lib.umn.edu/openrivers/article/life-otherwise-at-the-seas-edge.

5. Claudia Sadowski-Smith and Claire F. Fox, "Theorizing the Hemisphere: Inter-Americas Work at the Intersection of American, Canadian, and Latin American Studies," *Comparative American Studies: An International Journal* 2, no. 1 (2004): 5–38.

6. Claire F. Fox, *Making Art Panamerican: Cultural Policy and the Cold War* (University of Minnesota Press, 2013), 35, 21.

7. Esther Gabara, *Errant Modernism: The Ethos of Photography in Mexico and Brazil* (Duke University Press, 2008).

8. Esther Gabara, *Non-Literary Fiction: Art of the Americas Under Neoliberalism* (University of Chicago Press, 2022), 42–43, 41.

9. Celia Álvarez Muñoz to Roberto Tejada, "What the Light Would Say: Conversation with Celia Álvarez Muñoz," in *Celia Álvarez Muñoz: Breaking the Binding* (Radius Books, 2023), 129.

10. Chon A. Noriega, "To Dwell on This Matrix of Places," in *Home—So Different, So Appealing*, ed. Chon A. Noriega, Mari Carmen Ramírez, and Pilar Tompkins Rivas (UCLA Chicano Studies Research Center Press, 2017), 24, 25, 26, 30, 58, 61.

11. Walter Benjamin, "The Storyteller," in *Illuminations*, trans. Harry Zohn (Schocken Books), 89.

12. Rachel Weiss, *Now What? Quandaries of Art and the Radical Past* (Fordham University Press, 2021), 49.

13. Gómez-Barris, "Life Otherwise at the Sea's Edge."

14. Weiss, *Now What?*, 172, 169–70.

6. FRAMEWORKS OF INTELLIGIBILITY: LATIN AMERICAN / LATINX ART

1. Derrick Cartwright, "Subwoofers, Subcultures, Subversions: A Conversation with Luis Gispert," in *Luis Gispert: Loud Image*, ed. Roberto Tejada (Hood Museum of Art), 23.

2. Chapter 8 offers a more extensive discussion of Luis Gipsert and his *Cheerleader* series.

3. Walter Mignolo, *The Idea of Latin America* (Blackwell, 2005).

4. Ramón A. Gutiérrez, "What's in a Name? The History and Politics of Hispanic and Latino Panethnicities," in *The New Latino Studies Reader: A Twenty-First-Century Perspective*, ed. Ramón A. Gutiérrez and Tomás Almaguer (University of California Press, 2016), 20.

5. Gutiérrez, "What's in a Name," 21.

6. Gutiérrez, "What's in a Name," 31.

7. Gutiérrez, "What's in a Name," 34.

8. Gutiérrez, "What's in a Name," 49.

9. Unattributed, "El Teatro Campesino en Berkeley," *El Malcriado: The Voice of the Farm Worker* (ed. Bill Esher and Daniel de los Reyes), no. 54 (January 1967): 16. Author's translation.

10. Tomás Ybarra-Frausto, "The Chicano Movement/The Movement of Chicano Art," in *Beyond the Fantastic: Contemporary Art Criticism from Latin America*, ed. Gerardo Mosquera (Institute of International Visual Arts, 1996), 173.

11. Rubén Salazar, "Who Is a Chicano? And What Is It the Chicanos Want?," *Los Angeles Times*, February 6, 1970.

12. Ybarra-Frausto, "Chicano Movement," 165.

13. Ybarra-Frausto, "Chicano Movement," 165.

14. Ybarra-Frausto, "Chicano Movement," 171.

15. Ybarra-Frausto, "Chicano Movement," 171.

16. Ybarra-Frausto, "Chicano Movement," 177.

17. Ybarra-Frausto, "Chicano Movement," 179.

18. Stuart Hall, "'In but Not of Europe': Europe and Its Myths," in *Selected Writings on Race and Difference*, ed. Paul Gilroy and Ruth Wilson Gilmore (Duke University Press, 2021), 377.

19. Ybarra-Frausto, "Chicano Movement," 181.

20. Rupert García, "Chicano Latino Wall Art: The Mural and the Poster," in *The Hispanic American Aesthetic: Origins, Manifestations, and Significance*, ed. Jacinto Quirarte (Research Center for the Arts and Humanities, University of Texas at San Antonio, 1983), 27.

21. Alicia Gaspar de Alba, *Chicano Art Inside/Outside the Master's House: Cultural Politics and the CARA Exhibition* (University of Texas Press, 1998), 25, 15.

22. Coco Fusco quoted in Gaspar de Alba, *Chicano Art Inside/Outside*, 23–24.

23. Gaspar de Alba, *Chicano Art Inside/Outside*, 26.

24. Gaspar de Alba, *Chicano Art Inside/Outside*, 41, 113.

25. Chapter 9 offers a brief description of this work and a comparative context for its reception.

26. Audre Lorde, "The Master's Tools Will Never Dismantle the Master's House," in *Sister Outsider: Essays and Speeches* (Crossing, 1984), 111.

27. Chon Noriega, "Barricades of Ideas: Latino Culture, Site-Specific Installation, and the U.S. Art Museum," in *Performing Hybridity*, ed. May Joseph and Jennifer Natalya Fink (University of Minnesota Press, 1999), 183.

28. Noriega, "Barricades of Ideas," 184, 186.

29. Noriega, "Barricades of Ideas," 186–87.

30. Noriega, "Barricades of Ideas," 191.

31. Noriega, "Barricades of Ideas," 192, 194.

32. Noriega, "Barricades of Ideas," 194. See also *Revelaciones/Revelations: Hispanic Art of Evanescence*, directed by Edin Velez, produced, written by Chon Noriega (Cinema Guild, 1995), DVD, 28 min. The film documents an exhibition held November 6–December 13, 1993, at the Herbert F. Johnson Museum of Art, Cornell University, Ithaca, New York. It features artists Maria Brito Avellana, Rimer Cardillo, Ronald González, Gronk, Daniel Joseph Martinez, Amalia Mesa-Bains, Raphael Montanez Ortiz, Pepón Osorio, Celia Alvarez Muñoz, and José Piedra.

33. E. Carmen Ramos, "Our America: The Latino Presence in American Art," Smithsonian Museum of American Art website, https://americanart.si.edu/exhibitions/our-america, accessed January 19, 2022.

34. E. Carmen Ramos, "The Latino Presence in American Art," *American Art* 26, no. 2 (Summer 2012): 12.

35. Alan Pelaez Lopez, "The X in Latinx Is a Wound, Not a Trend," *EFNIKS*, September 13, 2018, https://www.colorbloq.org/article/the-x-in-latinx-is-a-wound-not-a-trend.

36. Jennif(f)er Tamayo, *LA QUEERADORA* project proposal manuscript submitted to Cynthia Woods Mitchell Center for the Arts, Kathrine G. McGovern College of the Arts, University of Houston, phrase uncited on event page for "Countercurrent Festival," *Match*, posted February 20, 2019, https://matchouston.org/events/2019/la-queeradora.

7. THE LATIN AMERICAN PHOTOBOOK IN CONTEXT

1. Carol Armstrong, "*A Scene in a Library*: An Unsolved Mystery," *History of Photography* 26, no. 2 (Summer 2002): 98.

2. Carol Armstrong, *Scenes in a Library: Reading the Photograph in the Book, 1843–1875* (MIT Press, 1998), 1.

3. Armstrong, *Scenes in a Library*, 5.

4. William Henry Fox Talbot, *The Pencil of Nature* (Longman, Brown, Green and Longmans, 1844), 30. Digitized by Project Gutenberg, https://www.gutenberg.org/ebooks/33447.

5. Alejandro Castellano, "Statement," *Revelation, Uprising & Fiction: Hecho en Latinoamerica*, Zonezero website, accessed April 10, 2017, http://v1.zonezero.com/exposiciones/fotografos/revyficcion/acotacionen.html.

6. Cited in Castellano, "Statement."

7. Others included Jaime Ardila (Colombia), Mario García Joya and María Eugenia Haya (Cuba), Paolo Gasparini (Venezuela), and María Cristina Orive (Guatemala-Argentina).

8. Boris Kossoy interviewed by Paulo César Boni, *Discursos Fotográficos* 3, no. 3 (2007): 249–61. ("O colóquio se constituiu num marco importante para a fotografia da America Latina; um divisor de aguas entre o desconhecimento total que até então imperava acerca da produçao dos países vizinhos e, o principio de um relacionamento artístico, acadêmico e político, que a partir de então se iniciava.")

9. Darcy Ribeiro, "A América Latina existe?" *Ensaios insólitos* (L & PM, 1979), 217–25.

10. Pedro Meyer, "Palabras de presentación II Coloquio Latinoamericano de Fotografía," *Hecho en Latinoamérica: Segundo Coloquio Latinoamericano de Fotografía* (IINBA/SEP, 1982), 12. He writes: "No hay que olvidar que en contraste con Europa y Estados Unidos, América Latina por su misma pobreza y explotación se ha convertido en escenario de inmensas luchas sociales, revoluciones y represiones, por tanto contiene la gran semilla del futuro. La fotografía latinoamericana necesariamente se encuentra vinculada a estas realidades, ya sea directa o indirectamente, tendrá que rendir cuentas de sí misma y de su eventual aportación, como arte, como testimonio, como parte de la cultura de nuestra época." Author's translation.

11. Alan Riding, "Mexico's Middle Class Turns to Disco and Burgers," *New York Times*, January 13, 1982, sec. A, p. 2.

12. Raquel Tibol, "Homenaje a 'Río de Luz,'" *Proceso*, February 6, 1988. Author's translation. The original reads in full:

> Entre 1980 y 1981 el fotógrafo Pablo Ortiz Monasterio cuidó la publicación de algunos libros de fotografías coeditados por el Instituto Nacional Indigenista y el dispendioso Fondo Nacional para Actividades Sociales, como los de Mariana Yampolsky, Graciela Iturbide y el propio Ortiz Monasterio, con respectivos prólogos de Elena Poniatowska, Luis Barjau y José Manuel Pintado En agosto de 1984 el Fondo de Cultura Económica inició una colección dedicada a la fotografía: Río de Luz En tres años se publicaron quince libros, la mayoría dedicados a autores mexicanos, aunque figuran también algunos de otros países: *Yo, el ciudadano* de Nacho López, presentación de Fernando Benítez; *Los encuentros* de Víctor Flores Olea, presentación de Carlos Fuentes; *La raíz y el camino* de Mariana Yampolsky, presentación de Elena Poniatowska; *Sueños de papel* de Graciela Iturbide, presentación de Verónica Volkow; *Dulce sudor amargo* del brasileño Río Branco, con textos de Jean-Pierre Nouhaud en forma de carta al autor de las imágenes a color; *Escribir con luz* de Héctor García, presentación de Juan de la Cabada; en *Historia natural de las cosas* se reunieron fotografías de 50 autores y un breve texto de Alvaro Mutis; *Josep Renau fotomontador* presentado por Joan Fontcuberta, reunió parte de la serie Fatamorgana; del Archivo Casasola en la Fototeca del Instituto Nacional de Antropología e Historia salió la selección *Jefes, héroes y caudillos*, prologada por Flora Lara Klahr, donde la Revolución Mexicana queda documentada de manera soberbia, precisa y elocuente; *Espejo de espinas* de Pedro Meyer, presentación de Carlos Monsiváis; *Retornos a Oapan* del iraní Abbas, quien también escribió su bitácora mexicana entre diciembre de 1982 y agosto de 1985; *Casa santa* de Rafael Doniz, con un escrito notable de Antonio Alatorre; *Luces y tiempos* de Lázaro Blanco, presentación de Guillermo Samperio; *Cuba: dos épocas* de los cubanos Raúl Corrales y Constantino Arias, con dos sabios textos de María Eugenia Haya; el más reciente, terminado de imprimir el 15 de agosto de 1987, es *Al paso del tiempo* de José Luis Neyra, actual presidente del Consejo Mexicano de Fotografía, con texto introductorio de Jaime Moreno Villarreal.
>
> Los libros de Río de Luz, en un formato constante de 275 × 205 centímetros, han estado al cuidado de Pablo Ortiz Monasterio y fueron impresos con excepcional pulcritud en la Imprenta Madero.

13. Edward Ranney, "Recent Latin American Photography Books," *Latin American Research Review* 26, no. 3 (1991): 235.

14. Carlos Monsiváis, *The World of Agustín Víctor Casasola: Mexico, 1900–1938*, ed. Agustín Víctor Casasola (Fondo del Sol Visual Arts and Media Center, 1984), 38.

15. Michel de Certeau, *The Possession at Loudun*, trans. Michael B. Smith (University of Chicago Press, 2000), 9. To this effect, the French historian and philosopher wrote: "Thus a strangeness is deeply rooted in the substance of a society. . . . Perhaps it reveals an overall change that, once again, consists in exorcising or marginalizing the first symptoms of a crisis that progressively gives rise to a new order."

16. Julien Levy, *Memoir of an Art Gallery*, introduction by Ingrid Schaffner (MFA, 2003), 48.

17. Horacio Fernández, *The Latin American Photobook* (Aperture, 2011), 42.

18. Nacho López, "Yo, el ciudadano," in *Yo, el ciudadano* (Fondo de Cultura Económica, 1984), 13–16. Author's translation.

19. López, "Yo, el ciudadano," 13–16.

20. Fabienne Bradu and Graciela Iturbide, *Graciela Iturbide habla con Fabienne Bradu* (La Fábrica y Fundación Telefónica, 2003), 35.

21. Miguel Rio Branco, in conversation with Roberto Tejada, "Sweet Bitter Sweat: Miguel Rio Branco," *Aperture* 153 (Fall 1998): 74.

22. Branco, "Sweet Bitter Sweat," 74.

23. Raquel Tibol, "Cuatro libros de fotografías," *Proceso*, September 7, 1985, 54. Author's translation. The article was revised and included in Raquel Tibol, *Episodios fotográficos* (Libros de Proceso, 1989), 105–6.

24. Tibol, "Cuatro libros de fotografías," 54.

25. Iatã Cannabrava, 2º Fórum Latino-Americano de Fotografia de São Paulo (São Paulo, Itaú Cultural, press release, 2010), n.p. Also featured on the Fundação Catarinense de Cultura website: https://cultura.sc.gov.br/noticias/1417-noticias-mis/9940-9940-2-forum-latino-americano-de-fotografia-de-sao-paulo. Author's translation. The original reads:

> Após a realização pelo Itaú Cultural do 1º Fórum, em 2007, a fotografia brasileira intensificou sobremaneira sua rede de relações com os demais países da América Latina, gerando uma série de intercâmbios entre artistas, museus, curadores, galerias, festivais e encontros.
>
> A programação deste ano é, em boa parte, fruto dessas discussões e da própria história de nossa produção fotográfica.
>
> Com a expressão Fora de Casa, estamos falando de como, em pouco tempo, nossas origens se tornaram destinos [a diáspora europeia virou a diáspora latina]. Com Fora do Eixo mudamos o foco da discussão para o campo dos meios e suportes. As fronteiras antes bem delineadas entre a fotografia, o cinema e as artes plásticas se tornaram áreas comuns.
>
> Nesse vai e vem, estamos sempre tentando definir e redefinir uma fotografia latino-americana. Muitas vezes afirmamos até mesmo que ela não existe. No entanto, não conseguimos parar de falar e pensar nela! Será essa nomenclatura uma demarcação meramente geográfica ou um conceito, uma forma de representar o mundo moldada por questões intrínsecas à história (recente e conturbada) da região?
>
> Juntemos nessa discussão as novas plataformas de comunicação e produção que miscigenam ainda mais o caldeirão de nossa identidade imagética: as novas tecnologias, a internet e seus coadjuvantes (como as redes sociais), a tênue fronteira entre a imagem estática e a imagem em movimento. Tudo nos leva a cruzar as fronteiras o tempo todo, a experimentar mais livres que nunca.

26. Fernández, *Latin American Photobook*, 14.

27. Horacio Fernández, "Apresentaçao Fotolibro," 2º Fórum Latino-Americano de Fotografia de São Paulo/ 2nd Latin American Photography Forum of São Paulo, October 20–24, 2010.

28. The photobook bibliography includes Vince Aletti and David L. Strauss, *The Book of 101 Books: Seminal Photographic Books of the Twentieth Century* (PPP Editions in association with Ruth Horowitz, 2001); Martin Parr and Gerry Badger, *The Photobook: A History*, vols. 1–3 (Phaidon, 2004, 2006, 2014); and Manfred Heiting and Roland Jaeger, eds., *Autopsie: Deutschsprachige Fotobuecher 1918 bis 1945*, vol. 1 (Steidl Verlag, 2012). Another important antecedent was the exhibit organized by María Cristina Orive, *Libros fotográficos de autores latinoamericanos*, which formed part of the wider exhibition *Hecho en Latinoamérica*, Consejo Mexicano de Fotografía, Mexico City, Palacio de Bellas Artes, INBA, 1981.

29. Paolo Gasparini, quoted in Fernández, *Latin American Photobook*, 14.

30. Michel Butor, *Repertório*, trans. Leyla Perrone-Moises (Editora Perspectiva, 1974), 216. Author's translation.

31. Olga Yatskevich, Russet Lederman, and Matthew Cardon, eds., *CLAP! 10×10 Contemporary Latin American Photobooks 2000–2016* (10×10 Photobooks, 2016), 6.
32. Claudia Jaguaribe, *Aeroporto* (Codex, 2002), n.p. Author's translation.
33. João Castilho, *Hotel Tropical* (Artist's Edition, 2013), n.p. Author's translation.
34. Leo Marx, *The Machine in the Garden: Technology and the Pastoral Ideal in America* (Oxford University Press, 2000), 195. Marx coined the term "technological sublime" in the context of an increasingly mechanized landscape. He writes: "It is the new mechanized landscape itself which may be expected to induce this ideal state of mind . . . [a] progressive rhetoric, which also may be called the rhetoric of the technological sublime." Regarding the amount of data produced today, Google Gemini (AI) estimates that it ranges "from 2.31 to 328.77 million terabytes," a number that "translates to roughly 0.33 to 1.05 zettabytes per day" with "1 zettabyte [being] equal to 1 trillion terabytes. These figures include various data sources, including internet traffic, social media activity, sensor data, and video content. . . . Projections suggest the world generated around 120 zettabytes of data in 2023, with forecasts reaching 147 zettabytes in 2024 and 181 zettabytes in 2025." Google Gemini, accessed February 22, 2024.

8. TROPICS OF BROADBAND: CAMERA CULTURE AND EXPERIENCE IN SÃO PAULO

1. As discussed in previous pages, the monographs include those by Miguel Rio Branco, Bob Wolfenson, Marcelo Krasilcic, Caio Reisewitz, Alair Gomes, Claudia Andujar, Chris Bierrenbach, Rosângela Rennó, Luiz Braga, Arthur Omar, and Marcia Xavier, among others.
2. Other collectives include: Garapa (Leo Caobelli, Paulo Fehlauer, and Rodrigo Marcondes).
3. Boris Kossoy, "Hercules Florence, Pioneer of Photography in Brazil," *Image: Journal of Photography and Motion Pictures of the International Museum of Photography at George Eastman House* 20, no. 1 (March 1977): 16.
4. Kossoy, "Hercules Florence," 16.
5. Kossoy, "Hercules Florence," 13.
6. Douglas Crimp, "The Museum's Old/The Library's New Subject," in *The Contest of Meaning: Critical Histories of Photography*, ed. Richard Bolton (MIT Press, 1989), 3–14.
7. Alejandro Castellano, "Statement," *Revelación, revuelta, y ficción: Hecho en Latinoamérica*, Zonezero website, accessed April 10, 2017, http://v1.zonezero.com/exposiciones/fotografos/revyficcion/acotacionen.html. The first two Coloquios were held in Mexico City, in 1978 and then again in 1981, with later editions including the 1984 Coloquio in Havana, Cuba. See chap. 5, note 5.
8. Natalia Brizuela, *Fotografia e império* (Companhia das Letras, 2012), 18–20. Author's translation.
9. Roger Caillois, *Man, Play and Games*, trans. Meyer Barash (Free Press of Glencoe, 1961), 19.
10. Darcy Ribeiro, "A América Latina existe?" in *Ensaios insólitos* (L & PM Editores, 1979), 217–25.
11. Pio Figueiroa, *Olhar Indiscreto, Cia de Foto/Pio* (Belo Horizonte, Minas Gerais, Brazil: Pontifícia Universidade Católica, Jornalismo PUC TV, 2011), 12′25″. "Não há anulação do individuo no sistema de coletivo, pelo contrario há uma potencialização [potenciação, *sic*], já que esse estado é negociado tempo todo, assim o tempo todo, e não há como eu me anular no processo de coletivo porque ninguém vai dar conta de fazer o que faço" [0′01″–0′07″].
12. Armando Ismael Silva, *The Family Photo Album: The Image of Ourselves* (University of California, Irvine, 1996), 7–8.
13. Vilém Flusser, "The City as Wave-Trough in the Image-Flood," trans. Phil Gochenour, *Critical Inquiry* 31 (Winter 2005): 323–24.
14. Flusser, "City as Wave-Trough," 323–24.

9. PRINTED MATTERS AND POP ART IN AMÉRICA

1. Even as Randall and Mondragón often found they had to endure the "jealous and petty local literary scene" in Mexico that often overlooked their ambitious hemispheric efforts, they nonetheless knew the magazine was "very much a part of the world literary scene." "Editor's Note," *El corno emplumado* 21 (January 1967): 6. Literary historian Harris Feinsod writes that "just four years later, after Ernesto Cardenal declared the young countercultural poets Randall and Mondragón to represent 'la verdadera Unión Panamericana' (the true Pan-American Union) in the pages of their little magazine *El corno emplumado*, dozens of young poets flocking to Mexico City also thought they were assembling the 'First Gathering of American Poets' as an alternative to the Alliance for Progress." Harris Feinsod, *The Poetry of the Americas: From Good Neighbors to Countercultures* (Oxford University Press, 2017), 5. The roster of writers and artists featured in *El corno emplumado* is vast. It includes Ernesto Mejía Sánchez, Rochelle Owens, Homero Aridjis, Rachel Jodorowsky, Robert Kelley, Diane Wakoski, Anselm Hollo, Ernesto Cardenal, Kathleen Fraser, Paul Blackburn, Michael McClure, Thelma Nava, Ulises Carrión, Frank Lima, Lorenzo Thomas, and Jerome Rothenberg; as well as Elaine de Kooning, Leonora Carrington, Juan Soriano, Marisol, Franz Kline, and José Luis Cuevas, among others. For a brief discussion of Kurt Stavenhagen, a friend and neighbor of Diego Rivera, see Byron W. Knoblock, "Important Private Collection of Pre-Columbian Art in Mexico," *Central States Archaeological Journal* 3, no. 4 (April 1957): 143–46.

2. Feinsod, *Poetry of the Americas*, 2.

3. Dore Ashton et al., "A Symposium on Pop Art," *Arts Magazine*, April 1963, 37.

4. Ashton et al., "Symposium on Pop Art," 40. In advance of the 1962 MoMA Pop symposium, Peter Selz had announced in the press release that the discussion "dealing primarily with American artists" would address and "analyze the esthetics of the movement and its value as a meaningful comment on contemporary life as well as the problematic relationship of art to mass culture." Quoted in Museum of Modern Art, press release no. 138, December 3, 1962, MoMA Press Release Archives, https://www.moma.org/momaorg/shared/pdfs/docs/press_archives/3084/releases/MOMA_1962_0143_138.pdf.

5. *El corno emplumado: Una historia de los sesenta*, dir. Nicolenka Beltran and Anne Mette W. Nielsen (Mexico-Denmark: Ángulos Producciones, 2005).

6. Back matter, *El corno emplumado* 5 (January 1963): 160: "• codornices/• alimentos/• coches/• tortugas/• tortillas/• libros/• tintorería/• llaves al minuto/*en una palabra*, TODO."

7. Back matter, *El corno emplumado* 3 (July 1962): 143: "MATHIAS GOERITZ/está HARTO pero/TOMA/*Coca-Cola*."

8. The roster of artists included Consuelo Abascal de Lemionet, Benigno Alvarado, Octavio Asta, Francisco Ávalos, José Luis Cuevas, Pedro Friedeberg, Mathias Goeritz, Kati Horna, Inocencia (the hen), Agripina Maqueda, Jesús Reyes Ferreira, and Benito Rodríguez. The manifesto read as follows:

> The fed-ups reject any association with any artistic group, including, of course, the neo-dadaists who ignore that DADA is eternal. The fed-ups are also fed up with DADA. Its realism is of a MORAL nature.
>
> The fact that the fed-ups are exhibiting their work at the Antonio Souza Gallery does not imply identification on any of the parts. It's purely coincidental.
>
> If by any reason this exhibition would offend the sensibility of the people related to the arts, the fed-ups would like to categorically declare that their intention has never been that of hurting anybody. Their intentions are good. They're just fed up.
>
> We are fed up with the pretentious imposition of logic and of reason, of functionalism, of decorative calculus, and of the chaotic pornography of individualism, of the glory of the day, of the fashion of the moment, of vanity and of ambition, of bluff and of the artistic joke, of conscious and subconscious egocentrism, of fatuous concepts, of the exceedingly

> tedious propaganda of the isms and the ists, figurative or abstract. Fed up also with the preciosity of an inverted aesthetic; fed up with the copy or stylization of a heroically vulgar reality. Fed up, above all, with the artificial and hysterical atmosphere of the so-called art world, with its adulterated pleasures, its gaudy salons and its terrifying vacuum.
>
> We recognize the necessity of abandoning the illusory dreams of the glorification of the ego and of deflating art. We recognize that human work, at the present time, is most vigorous where the so-called artist less intervenes. We recognize, more and more, the importance of the service, or of any abnegated act based on a natural ethic, all logic aside—the cultivation of an orchard, the fulfilling of a professional duty, or the education of a child.
>
> We try to begin anew from below in a spiritual-sociological sense. All established values will have to be rectified: Believe without asking in what! Make, or at least try to make man's work become a PRAYER.

Mauricio Marcín, ed., *Estamos hartos (otra vez)* (Museo Experimental el Eco, 2014), 3.

9. See, for example, the exhibition organized by Soledad García and Daniela Berger, *La emergencia del pop: Irreverencia y calle en Chile*, Museo de la Solidaridad Salvador Allende, July–September 2016. Another advertisement in issue 20 was signed "el corno emplumado" and composed a protest list: "We Protest/ • the brutal police treatment, prison, illegal trial and pending death sentence against the peruvian guerilla leader HUGO BLANCO./ • the total ideological persecution which includes current closing of the national universities and university publishing houses in argentina./ • the wave of repression, blackmail and fear unleashed throughout the entire american continent by the state department of the united states of America." *El corno emplumado* 20 (October 1966): 134.

10. Jennifer Higgie, review of *Beau Geste Press*, CAPC, Bordeaux, France, *Frieze*, February 16, 2017, https://www.frieze.com/article/beau-geste-press. See also Donna Conwell, "Beau Geste Press," *Getty Research Journal* 2 (2010): 183–92.

11. *El corno emplumado* 19 (July 1966): 6. The original text in Spanish: "me reservo el derecho de retener todo premio o mención que reciba mi persona así como el dinero que se perciba de la venta de la misma." Author's translation.

12. *El corno emplumado* 22 (April 1967). The original text in Spanish: "Transformada el/alba cerré los/ojos y vi la/luna." Author's translation.

13. Ashton et al., "Symposium on Pop Art," 39.

14. The cover art of *El corno emplumado* 26 (April 1968) "reproduced the famous Cuban Protest Song poster by Alfredo Rostgaard of the rose with a drop of blood falling from a single thorn, already an icon of the times." Margaret Randall, finding aid note for volume 26, *El corno emplumado*, Open Door Archive, http://opendoor.northwestern.edu/archive/items/show/61.

15. Pilar García, collections curator at Museo Universitario Arte Contemporáneo, Mexico City, relates this fascinating detail in correspondence to Esther Gabara, curator of *Pop América: Contesting Freedom, 1965–1975*, dated December 18, 2017.

16. Antônio Henrique Amaral, *O meu e o seu: Impressões de nosso tempo: 7 gravuras originais* (Edição Mirante das Artes, 1967), n.p. The edition, which featured an essay by Ferreira Gullar, comprised three hundred copies with an additional twenty noncommercial copies lettered from A to L; and with the design of the metal encasing suggested by Ruben de Freitas Martins. Colophon reads: "Éste álbum, criado e produzido pelo artista, terminou de ser impresso aos cinco dias de Julho de mil novecentos e sessenta e sete nas oficinas de Gráfica Paulicéa, rua Casimiro de Abreu 575 em São Paulo, com a colaboração dedicada de todos os seus funcionários. A capa metálica nasceu de uma sugestão feita por Ruben Martins. O papel utilizado foi Super White 250 gramas de fabricação da indústria de Papel Leon Feffer S. A. O artista expressa admiração e reconhecimento a Adriano Van Moorsel e Durval F. Andrade pelo carinho e entusiasmo que demostraram pelo álbum, possibilitando sua execução./São Paulo, Julho de 1967."

17. The all-lowercase font style was pervasive in Latin America in the 1960s, as echoed in the typographic design of *El corno emplumado.*

18. Federico Morais, "A gravura brasileira: Os anos 60/70," in *Mostra da gravura brasileira* (Fundação Bienal de São Paulo, 1974), 44. Digitized in Documents of 20th-century Latin American and Latino Art, International Center for the Arts of the Americas at the Museum of Fine Arts, Houston, ICAA Record ID: 1110706.

19. Mário Pedrosa, "Gewgaws and Pop Art," in *Mário Pedrosa: Primary Documents*, ed. Glória Ferreira and Paulo Herkenhoff, trans. Stephen Berg (Museum of Modern Art, 2015), 201. Originally published as Mário Pedrosa, "Quinquilharia e Pop Art," *Correio da Manhã* (Rio de Janeiro), August 14, 1967.

20. Jayne Cortez, "In Her Own Words," in Jerome Fortier, *Watts: Art and Social Change in Los Angeles, 1965–2002* (Haggerty Museum of Art, Marquette University, 2003), 33–34.

21. Transcript of an oral history interview with Rupert García by Paul Karlstrom, 1995, Archives of American Art, Smithsonian Institution, https://www.aaa.si.edu/collections/interviews/oral-history- interview-rupert-garcia-13572.

22. Rubén Salazar, "Chicanos Would Find Identity Before Coalition with Blacks," *Los Angeles Times*, February 20, 1970.

23. Rubén Salazar, "Black-Brown Friction Growing," *Los Angeles Times*, October 26, 1969. See also Rubén Salazar, "Chicanos Told to Fight Like Blacks for Respect," *Los Angeles Times*, April 9, 1969:

> "Chicanos can learn from our black brothers, we can and must learn how to fight effectively for what we want. We have to get ourselves together in high school UMAS and in the community to become strong enough in our unity that 'the Man' will see and be afraid."
>
> This was the advice given Mexican-American youths by the underground newspaper *Chicano Student Movement* in its February issue. Since then UMAS (United Mexican-American Students) has been suspended from Roosevelt High School, following a peaceful sit-in which UMAS claims it did not lead.

24. Amiri Baraka, "Emory Douglas: A 'Good Brother,' a 'Bad' Artist," in *Black Panther: The Revolutionary Art of Emory Douglas*, ed. Sam Durant (Rizzoli, 2007), 169. The poster art of Emory Douglas shares both formal and social affinities with the art of Rupert García.

25. Smithsonian Archives of American Art, oral history interview with Rupert García (Oakland, CA, September/November 1995; June 1996; Paul J. Karlstrom, interviewer).

26. Sergio Mondragón and Margaret Randall, "Editor's Note," *El corno emplumado* 19 (July 1966): 5.

27. Pedrosa, "Gewgaws and Pop Art," 201.

10. CENTER OF GRAVITY: JOSÉ CLEMENTE OROZCO

1. José Clemente Orozco, *Cuadernos*, ed. Raquel Tibol (Secretaría de Educación Pública, 1983), 147. Author's translation.

2. Edward Alden Jewell, "The Frescoes by Orozco," *New York Times*, January 25, 1931.

3. José Clemente Orozco, *The Artist in New York: Letters to Jean Charlot and Unpublished Writings, 1925–1929*, trans. Ruth L. C. Simms (University of Texas Press, 1974), 13.

4. Alejandro Anreus, *Orozco in Gringoland: The Years in New York* (University of New Mexico Press, 2001), 106.

5. José Clemente Orozco, *An Autobiography* (University of Texas Press, 1962), 129.

6. Orozco, *Artist in New York*, 22.

7. Lois Wilcox, cited in Edward Alden Jewell, "About Orozco's New Frescos," *New York Times*, February 1, 1931.

8. The remark is a paraphrase from Tzvetan Todorov in "No somos ni buenos ni malos, pero tiene sentido luchar: entrevista con Tzvetan Todorov," trans. Aloma Rodríguez, *Letras Libres*, March 13, 2017, https://letraslibres.com/revista/no-somos-ni-buenos-ni-malos-pero-tiene-sentido-luchar-entrevista-con-tzvetan-todorov/. In his various writings, Todorov (1939–2017), like Orozco, was concerned with the role of artists and intellectuals in civic life and with cultural encounter and conflict.

11. WHITE STONE, BRAMBLE, GRAVITY, CHANCE: MIGUEL ANGEL RÍOS

1. Curatorial statement for "*A Morir ('til Death)* by Miguel Angel Ríos in collaboration with Rafael Ortega," Los Angeles Contemporary Exhibitions, October 15–December 10, 2004, LACE archive, https://welcometolace.org/lace/a-morir-til-death/. See also exhibition pamphlet, *Concentrations 49: Miguel Angel Rios*, Dallas Museum of Art, January 29–May 14, 2006, Portal to Texas History, University of North Texas Libraries, https://texashistory.unt.edu/ark:/67531/metapth307658/, accessed January 28, 2024; and Anne Martens, exhibition review, "Miguel Angel Ríos at Los Angeles Contemporary Exhibitions," *Flash Art*, January–February 2005, 116.

2. Victoria Verlichak, exhibition review, "Miguel Angel Ríos at Latin American Art Museum of Buenos Aires (MALBA)—Costantini Foundation," *Art Nexus* 8, no. 75 (December 2009–February 2010): 108–9.

3. In a related line of inquiry, art historian Claire Bishop critiques what she views as "one of the most persistent themes in contemporary art since the early 1990s . . . the proliferation of work that addresses 'ruined modernity' and 'failed utopias': in other words, a type of art that reformats iconic examples of twentieth-century architecture and design into painting, sculpture, photography, video, slide shows, archival installations." Claire Bishop, "Déjà Vu: Contemporary Art and the Ghosts of Modernism" (lecture, University of Houston, School of Art, the Contemporary Project series, September 17, 2015).

4. Joaquín Torres-García, "El nuevo arte de América," *Apex* 1 (July 1942): 11–16, reprinted in *The School of the South: The Torres-García Workshop and Its Legacy/La escuela del sur: El Taller Torres-García y su legado*, ed. Mari Carmen Ramírez (University of Texas and Museo Nacional Centro de Arte Reina Sofia, 1991), 57–62.

5. *Miguel Angel Ríos*: *Endless*, Sicardi Gallery, Houston, Texas, September 15–November 21, 2015. Another video work by Ríos, *Mecha* (2010), was concurrently on display at the Museum of Fine Arts, Houston, as part of the exhibition *Contingent Beauty: Contemporary Art from Latin America* (November 22, 2015–February 28, 2016). For commentary on this work, see Christopher Stackhouse, exhibition review, "Miguel Angel Ríos at Des Moines Art Center," *Art in America* (June–July 2012): 173:

> All of Ríos's videos resolutely blend gorgeous imagery with poetic treatments of human peril. *Mecha*, a ten-minute, two-channel projection, analogizes a diversional game called *tejo* to armed conflict. (In *tejo*, players toss weighted metal disks at targets stuffed with gunpowder, which explode when hit.) The opening frames of the video show men's arms throwing the disks. An ominous industrial cable spool rolls through a maze of wire fences in staged scenes of empty war-torn buildings and courtyards. The spool becomes an absurdly anthropomorphized villain as it moves either behind or in front of the men, who run haphazardly through obstacles amid sparks, fire and squads of warfare. Eventually, a video camera falls from the sky onto a Jasper Johns-like target painted on the spool, now stationary and on its side. Camera effects turn the surfaces of objects to a muddy yellow, which has the result of muting the violence. In this strange, beautiful, rhythmic alchemy of anxiety and pointless haste, Ríos presents disarming commentary on the futility of war.

6. The crew consisted of Lorenzo Rivera Flores, Adrián Rivera Flores, Ignacio Rivera Flores, Enrique Rivera Flores, Marco Rivera Flores, and Ramiro Rivera Flores.

7. The original handwritten script of the drawing in Spanish reads: "Toma # 6: Ataque frontal: Desde una montaña que se ve al fondo, miles de piedras vienen bajando directo hacia la cá-/mara y chocan con ella. Se levanta el polvo y la imagen se vuelve borrosa. Para esta toma es necesario/cernir polvo al paso de las piedras y es muy importante que no esté nublado para realizar la toma." Another, describing the stampede's terminus, reads: "Toma #12: Pensé en una toma en donde todas las piedras llegaran a un punto común, formando una montaña. Para esta toma emplearemos 4 cámaras. La de la izquierda para ver de frente como caen las piedras/la del centro, cámara GOPRO para ver las piedras más grandes. La de la derecha para ver el recorrido/de la piedras hacia abajo y la cámara C100 montada en grúa para hacer paneo de toda la acción."

8. "Los surcos de la tierra se parecen a las venas por donde fluye la sustancia tóxica."

9. E. M. Gómez Maillefert, "Folk-Lore de Oaxaca," *Journal of American Folklore* 36, no. 140 (April–June 1923): 199. "Para evitar que a las criaturas les causen mal de ojo, se les prende en la ropa, espinas de huizache (*Pithecolobium albicans* Benth)."

10. Total time of production for *Endless* was five and a half months: four to construct the massive bramble walls, and another month and a half of film production and editing.

11. Ruben Andersson, "Time and the Migrant Other: European Border Controls and the Temporal Economics of Illegality," *American Anthropologist* 116, no. 4 (December 2014): 795–809. See also Ruben Andersson, *Illegality, Inc.: Clandestine Migration and the Business of Bordering Europe* (University of California Press, 2014).

12. Yvonne Spielmann, "Video: From Technology to Medium," *Art Journal* 65, no. 3 (2006): 54–69.

13. Spielmann, "Video: From Technology to Medium," 58.

12. THE CAPTURE OF CUAUHTÉMOC: DAVID ALFARO SIQUEIROS, LEO MATIZ, AND JAVIER DE LA GARZA

1. Ramón López Velarde, "La suave patria," *El Maestro: Revista de cultura nacional*, México, no. 3 (June 1, 1921): 311–14. ". . . único héroe a la altura del arte.//Anacrónicamente, absurdamente" (author's translation); Carlos Pellicer, *Piedra de sacrificios: Poema iberoamericano* (1924) in *Obras: Poesía* (Fondo de Cultura Económica, 1981), 100; Carlos Pellicer, "Ode to Cuauhtémoc," transl. Tim Henderson, in *The Mexico Reader: History, Culture, Politics*, ed. Gilbert M. Joseph and Timothy J. Henderson (Duke University Press, 2002), 410.

2. David Alfaro Siqueiros, "Propósitos esenciales del Centro de Arte Realista Moderno," in *No hay más ruta que la nuestra: Importancia nacional e internacional de la pintura mexicana moderna*, 2nd ed. (Talleres Gráficos de la Secretaría de Educación Pública, 1978), 75.

3. Carlos Monsiváis, "El mundo soslayado (Donde se mezclan la confesión y la proclama)," introduction to Salvador Novo, *La estatua de sal* (Fondo de Cultura Económica, 2008), 29–30.

4. Federico Navarrete Linares, "Mestizo/Mestizaje" in *Teoría del color/Color Theory*, comp. Helena Chávez Mac Gregor, ed. Ekaterina Álvarez Romero, trans. Christopher Michael Fraga (Museo Universitario de Arte Contemporáneo, UNAM, 2015), 74–75.

5. Javier de la Garza, artist statement, *ZoneZero*, January 1995, http://v1.zonezero.com/magazine/essays/distant/ygarza2.html.

13. CELIA ÁLVAREZ MUÑOZ: "IDEAS ARE THE DRIVERS"

1. Quoted in Robert Craig Bunch, *The Art of Found Objects: Interviews with Texas Artists* (Texas A&M University Press, 2016), 14.

2. Álvarez Muñoz identified as early influences: "The text-based works of Jenny Holzer and Barbara Kruger I noticed. As well as the cruel photography of Diane Arbus, the narratives of

Duane Michals and early viewing of Gordon Parks in the *Life* magazines of the late fifties/ sixties." Bunch, *Art of Found Objects*, 14.

3. Christopher Bollen with Barbara Kruger, *Interview*, February 13, 2013, https://www.interviewmagazine.com/art/barbara-kruger.

4. Erving Goffman, *Gender Advertisements* (Harper & Row, 1979), 84, 50. See also Erving Goffman, "Gender Advertisements," in *Studies in the Anthropology of Visual Communication* 3, no. 2 (1976): 65–68.

5. Horace Mansion, *Old English Nursery Songs* (Brentano's, 1921).

6. Anita Brenner, *Idols Behind Altars: Modern Mexico and Its Cultural Roots* (Dover, 2002), 171.

7. The artist recalls as follows: "Only the headline is mine. We had a really great copywriter. Sat right next to her. Cannot recall her name. . . . Another quote from her to her teenage son, 'Some people have less sense, than money.'" Correspondence with the author, July 4, 2020.

8. Goffman, *Gender Advertisements*, 84.

9. Kobena Mercer, introduction to *Pop Art and Vernacular Cultures*, ed. Kobena Mercer (MIT Press and Iniva, Institute of International Visual Arts, 2007), 10.

10. Sol LeWitt, "Paragraphs on Conceptual Art," in *Sol LeWitt*, ed. Alicia Legg (Museum of Modern Art, 1978), 166.

11. Sol LeWitt, "Sentences on Conceptual Art," *0 to 9*, January 1969, 3–5. Digitized by Independent Voices, JSTOR, https://jstor.org/stable/community.28031925.

12. LeWitt, "Paragraphs on Conceptual Art," 166.

13. Sol LeWitt, *Autobiography* (Multiples and Lois and Michael K. Torf, 1980).

14. Nietzsche believed conceptual systems were inseparable from autobiography, that a hypothesis, while appearing neutral or absolute, is really just the "personal confession of its author and a kind of involuntary and unnoticed *mémoires*." *Beyond Good and Evil/On the Genealogy of Morality*, trans. Adrian Del Caro (Stanford University Press, 2014), 9.

15. Shifra M. Goldman and Luis Camnitzer, "The Columbus Quincentenary and Latin American Art: A Critical Evaluation," *Art Journal* 51, no. 4 (Winter 1992): 16–20. "A Continental Conference was organized by the Indigenous Alliance of the Americas on 500 Years of Resistance. A pan-Indian gathering, it was composed of representatives from 120 American Indian nations, as well as international and fraternal organizations, and it declared that 'the Indians of America have never abandoned our constant struggle against the conditions of oppression, discrimination and exploitation which were imposed upon us as a result of the European invasion of our ancestral territories.' It further stated that 'neither the invasion nor the regime has come to an end. Both continue to affect not only the Indigenous peoples but all the societies within the nations.'"

16. Marcos Sánchez-Tranquilino, foreword to *The Chicano Codices: Encountering Art of the Americas*, ed. Patricia Draher (Mexican Museum, 1992). The catalog included additional essays by Marcos Sánchez-Tranquilino ("The Chicano Codices: Feathered Reflections on an Aztlantic Archeology") as well as by poet and playwright Cherríe Moraga ("Codex Xeri: El momento histórico"). About the original installation at the Mexican Museum, Álvarez Muñoz related the following: "The piece suffered because I wasn't present to install. // The wall painting was very stiff & layout off. Even reproduction in book & documentation were off." Correspondence with the author, June 18, 2020.

17. Augusto F. Molina Montes, "The Building of Tenochtitlan," *National Geographic*, December 6, 1980, 762–63.

18. Eduardo Matos Moctezuma, "New Finds in the Great Temple," *National Geographic*, December 6, 1980, 770. Photographs by David Hiser.

19. "Rethinking the Apocalypse: An Indigenous Anti-Futurist Manifesto," Indigenous Action, March 19, 2020, https://www.indigenousaction.org/rethinking-the-apocalypse-an-indigenous-anti-futurist-manifesto. "We are the dreamers dreamt by our ancestors. We have

traversed all time between the breaths of our dreams. We exist at once with our ancestors and unbirthed generations. Our future is held in our hands. It is our mutuality and interdependence. It is our relative. It is in the creases of our memories, folded gently by our ancestors. It is our collective Dreamtime, and it is Now. Then. Tomorrow. Yesterday."

20. Jesús Macarena-Ávila, "'Postales' from the Edge: My Engagement with Celia Álvarez Muñoz," unpublished manuscript, July 2020.

21. Roberto Tejada, *Celia Alvarez Muñoz* (UCLA Chicano Studies Research Center and University of Minnesota Press, 2009), 63–67.

22. Correspondence with the author, June 18, 2020.

23. "On Empathic Pedagogies," in "Re–Directing: East X Empathic Pedagogies," e-flux Announcements, December 6, 2019, https://www.e-flux.com/announcements/296639/re-directing-east-x-empathic-pedagogies. See also La Red de Pedagogías Empáticas website, https://redpedagogiasempaticas.org.

24. David G. Savage, "Landmark Win for LGBTQ Workers' Rights," *Los Angeles Times*, June 16, 2020.

25. Walter Benjamin, *The Arcades Project*, ed. Rolf Tiedemann, trans. Howard Eiland and Kevin McLaughlin (Harvard University Press, 1999), 545.

26. Quoted in Bunch, *Art of Found Objects*, 15.

14. ALLORA & CALZADILLA: WONDERSTRUCK ON THE EDGE OF DECLINE

1. Roger Caillois, "The Noon Complex," in *The Edge of Surrealism: A Roger Caillois Reader*, ed. Claudine Frank (Duke University Press, 2003), 128.

2. Claudine Frank, introduction to *The Edge of Surrealism*, 5.

3. Caillois, "Noon Complex," 127. Caillois wrote:

> At noon, it would seem that life takes a pause, organic matter returns to an inorganic state, and everything blazes pointlessly and without ardor in a futile desire for luxury and display. Activity of any kind seems to involve unpleasant and risible agitation. All heartbeats have come to a halt. The supreme triumph of the positive forces dissolves into renunciation, their surging forth into slumber and their plenitude into resignation. The will to live withdraws somewhere unknown, as if absorbed by thirsty sands.
>
> This silent exaltation of every abdication, like a flood invincibly overwhelming all morality, swiftly drowns any uncertain inclination or remorse it might find. It is easy to perceive the seduction of such a scene for the asthenic personality—always prone to ask *What's the use?*

4. Caillois, "Noon Complex," 125–29.

5. Andrew Crislip, "The Sin of Sloth or the Illness of the Demons? The Demon of Acedia in Early Christian Monasticism," *Harvard Theological Review* 98, no. 2 (April 2005): 152.

6. Crislip, "Sin of Sloth," 147.

7. *Webster's Third New International Dictionary* (1976), s.v. "laser."

8. Tan-Ya Chung et al., "Zombie Ant Heads Are Oriented Relative to Solar Cues," *Fungal Ecology* 25 (February 2017): 22–28. For a discussion of the parasite-host interaction, see Sandra B. Andersen et al., "The Life of a Dead Ant: The Expression of an Adaptive Extended Phenotype," *American Naturalist* 174, no. 3 (2009): 424–33.

9. Sara Nadal-Melsió, "The Meridian Demon" (unpublished manuscript, 2019). The poem was composed for this video projection and assembled from fragments of works by authors Walter Benjamin, Roger Callois, Aimé Césaire, E. M. Cioran, and Gabriele D'Annunzio.

10. Georges Bataille, "The Solar Anus" (1931), in *Visions of Excess: Selected Writings, 1927–1939*, ed. Allan Stoekl, trans. Allan Stoekl with Carl R. Lovitt and Donald M. Leslie Jr. (University of Minnesota Press, 1985), 8.

11. André Breton, "The Automatic Message," in *Break of Day*, trans. Mark Polizzotti and Mary Ann Caws (University of Nebraska Press), 131.

12. Michel Serres, *The Parasite*, trans. Lawrence R. Schehr (Minneapolis: University of Minnesota Press, 2007), 193.

13. Nadal-Melsió, "Meridian Demon."

14. Friedrich Wilhelm Nietzsche, *The Use and Abuse of History*, trans. Adrian Collins, with an introduction by Julius Kraft (Bobbs-Merrill, 1957), 57, cited in Hayden White, "Interpretation in History," *New Literary History* 4, no. 2 (Winter 1973): 284.

15. Claude Lévi-Strauss, *Tristes tropiques*, trans. John and Doreen Weightman (Penguin Books, 1973), 22.

16. Lévi-Strauss, *Tristes tropiques*, 25.

17. Lévi-Strauss, *Tristes tropiques*, 27–28.

18. André Breton, "A Great Black Poet: Aimé Césaire," in *Refusal of the Shadow: Surrealism and the Caribbean*, ed. Michael Richardson and Krzysztof Fijalkowski (Verso, 1996), 192. Originally published as "Martinique charmeuse de serpents: Un grand poète noir," *Tropiques* 11 (May 1944): 119–26. The "Sommaire" to the first issue of *Tropiques* lists the following contributions: Aimé Césaire's "Présentation" and "Fragments d'un poème"; poetry by Charles Péguy; an essay by Georgette Anderson, "Mallarmé et Debussy: *L'après-midi d'un Faune* de Mallarmé et le prélude de Debussy"; "Naissance de notre art" by René Ménil; and Suzanne Césaire's "Léo Frobenius et le problème des civilisations." Brown University, Liberation Journal Index. Eleven issues of *Tropiques* were published from 1941 to 1945.

19. Suzanne Césaire, "1943: Surrealism and Us," in *Surrealist Women: An International Anthology*, ed. Penelope Rosemont, trans. Erin Gibson (University of Texas Press, 1998), 134.

20. Césaire, "1943: Surrealism and Us," 135.

21. Césaire, "1943: Surrealism and Us," 136.

22. "La lumière et les plantes," *Minotaure* 9 (October 1936): 66. Author's translation.

23. "La lumière et les plantes," 67. "Il n'est pas besoin de gros aménagement pour cultiver les plantes à la lumière intégrale. Avec un peu d'ingéniosité, ce lampadaire a été adapté à la decoration florale."

24. "La lumière et les plantes," 66.

25. Breton, "Great Black Poet," 192, 193.

26. Suzanne Césaire, "The Great Camouflage," in *The Great Camouflage: Writings of Dissent, 1941–1945*, ed. Daniel Maximin, trans. Keith L. Walker (Wesleyan University Press, 2012), 45. Originally published as "Le grand camouflage" in *Tropiques* 13–14 (1945): 267–73. The prose merits an extended citation:

> The heliconia shrubs and flowers of Absalon Forest bleed over the chasms, and the beauty of the tropical landscape goes to the heads of the poets passing by. Across the swaying latticed networks of the palms they can see the Antillean conflagration rolling across the Caribbean that is a tranquil sea of lavas. Here life lights up in a vegetal fire. Here on these hot lands that keep alive geological species, the fixed plant, passion and blood, in its primitive architecture, the disquieting ringing suddenly issue from the chaotic backs of the dancers. Here the tropical vines rocking vertiginously, take on ethereal poses to charm the precipices, with their trembling fingertips they latch onto the ungraspable cosmic flurry rising all throughout the drum-filled nights. Here the poets feel their heads capsize, and inhaling the fresh smells of the ravines, they take possession of the wreath of the islands, they listen to the sound of the water surrounding the islands, and they see tropical flames kindled no longer in the heliconia, in the gerberas, in the hibiscus, in the bougainvilleas, in the flame trees, but instead in the hungers, and in the fears, in the hatreds, in the ferocity, that burn in the hollows of the mountains.
>
> It is thus that the Caribbean conflagration blows its silent fumes, blinding for the only eyes that know how to see, and suddenly the blues of the Haitian mountains, of the

Martinican bays, turn dull, suddenly the most blazing reds go pale, and the sun is no longer a crystal play of light, and if the public squares have chosen the laceworks of Jerusalem thorn as luxury fans against the fieriness of the sky, if the flowers have known how to find just the right colors to leave one dumbstruck, if the tree-like ferns have secreted golden saps for their white crooks, rolled-up like a sex organ, if my Antilles are so beautiful, it is because the great game of hide-and-seek has succeeded, it is then because, on that day, the weather is most certainly too blindingly bright and beautiful to see clearly therein.

27. David Lang has worked with a variety of collaborators, including projects with rock musician Bryce Dessner (The National), Kronos Quartet, multi-instrumentalist Owen Pallett, Italian artist Ettore Spalletti, and British sound artist Scanner (Robin Rimbaud). See Robert L. Hubley, "David Lang and *the so-called laws of nature*" (PhD diss., University of Houston, 2015), 14–15.

28. Justin Rito, "Toward a Rhythmic Transformational System: David Lang's *cheating, lying, stealing*" (paper delivered at "Minimalism Unbounded!" the Fifth International Conference on Minimalist Music, University of Helsinki, September 23–27, 2015).

29. Jean-François Lyotard, "Les Immatériaux," *Art & Text* 17 (1985): 51.

30. Roger Caillois, "Illusions à rebours," *Nouvelle revue française*, December/January 1955. This article also led to a very public debate between Caillois, who implicitly posited the superiority of the West, and Lévi-Strauss, who aimed to defend an approach to civilization clear of all ethnocentrism. For a discussion of the debate, see Thierry Wendling, "Une joute intellectuelle au détriment du jeu? Claude Lévi-Strauss vs Roger Caillois (1954–1974)," *Ethnologies* 32, no. 1 (2010): 29–49.

Aimé Césaire, *Discourse on Colonialism*, trans. Joan Pinkham (Monthly Review Press, 2000), 73.

31. Césaire, *Discourse on Colonialism*, 35.

32. Lyotard, "Les Immatériaux," 51.

33. Césaire, "Great Camouflage," 39.

34. Karen F. Anderson-Córdova, "Aftermath of Conquest? The Indians of Puerto Rico During the Early Sixteenth Century," in *Ancient Borinquen: Archaeology and Ethnohistory of Ancient Puerto Rico*, ed. Peter E. Siegel (University of Alabama Press, 2005), 347.

35. Tzvetan Todorov, *The Conquest of America: The Question of the Other*, trans. Richard Howard (Harper & Row, 1984), 151.

36. Sylvia Wynter, "Unsettling the Coloniality of Being/Power/Truth/Freedom: Towards the Human, After Man, Its Overrepresentation—An Argument," *CR: The New Centennial Review* 3, no. 3 (2003): 291. Wynter refers to the present-day "20/80 wealth and power ratio between the world's peoples," saying, "this primary accumulation had been effected on the basis of a truth-for, or system of ethno-knowledge, that was no less non-veridical outside the viewpoint of its subjects than the premise the Portuguese and Columbus's voyages had only recently disproved—i.e., the premise that the Earth was nonhomogeneously divided into habitable within God's Grace and uninhabitable outside it."

37. National Museum of American History, "The Norie Atlas and the Guano Trade," https://americanhistory.si.edu/norie-atlas/guano-trade-objects. Archived link: https://wayback.archive-it.org/3340/20160510135323/http:/americanhistory.si.edu/norie- atlas/guano-trade-objects.

38. "Whenever any citizen of the United States discovers a deposit of guano on any island, rock, or key, not within the lawful jurisdiction of any other government, and not occupied by the citizens of any other government, and takes peaceable possession thereof, and occupies the same, such island, rock, or key may, at the discretion of the President, be considered as appertaining to the United States (R.S. § 5570.)." *United States Code: Guano Islands*, 48 U.S.C. §§1411–1419 (1988). Retrieved from the Library of Congress, www.loc.gov/item/uscode1988-019048008.

39. María Teresa Cortés Zavala and José Alfredo Uribe Salas, "Ciencia y economía del guano: La Isla Mona en Puerto Rico, siglo XIX," *Memorias* 22 (January 2014): 81–106.

40. Jean Gilbertson, *Two Men at the Helm: The First 100 Years of Crowley Maritime Corporation, 1892–1992* (Crowley Maritime Corporation, 1992), 25.

41. *Allora & Calzadilla: Specters of Noon*, Menil Collection, Houston, Texas, September 26, 2020–June 20, 2021.

42. C. F. Miller, "On the Composition and Value of Bat Guano," *Journal of Industrial & Engineering Chemistry* 6, no. 8 (1914): 664–65.

43. Georges Bataille, "Formless" (1929), in *Visions of Excess*, 31.

44. Sarah Kofman, *Camera Obscura: Of Ideology*, trans. Will Straw (Cornell University Press, 1999), 89.

45. Lisa Lowe, *The Intimacies of Four Continents* (Duke University Press, 2015), 5.

46. Nelson Miles, ed., *Harper's Pictorial History of the War with Spain*, vol. 2 (Harper's and Brothers, 1899), 396. Miles continues: "It is not our purpose to interfere with any existing laws and customs that are wholesome and beneficial to your people so long as they conform to the rules of military administration of order and justice. This is not a war of devastation, but one to give to all within the control of its military and naval forces the advantages and blessings of enlightened civilization."

47. César J. Ayala and Rafael Bernabe, *Puerto Rico in the American Century: A History Since 1898* (University of North Carolina Press, 2007), 26.

48. Ayala and Bernabe, *Puerto Rico in the American Century*, 57–58. The authors add: "The same point was made by William A. Jones (D-Va.), head of the House Committee on Insular Affairs; General Frank Mclntyre, head of the War Department's Bureau of Insular Affairs; and former governor Beekman Winthrop, among other participants in the congressional hearings. The House Committee report on the proposed legislation affirmed that 'Porto Rico [*sic*] has become permanent territory of the United States.' What Puerto Ricans desired was 'to legislate for themselves in respect to all purely local affairs.'"

49. Pedro A. Malavet, "Puerto Rico: Cultural Nation, American Colony," *Michigan Journal of Race and Law* 6, no. 1 (2000): 3.

50. Ayala and Bernabe, *Puerto Rico in the American Century*, 336.

51. Mary Williams Walsh, "Puerto Rico's Power Agency Defaults over Debt," *New York Times*, July 3, 2017. Emphasis added.

52. Press release, "Allora & Calzadilla 'Foreign in a Domestic Sense,'" Lisson Gallery London, September 22–November 11, 2017. The gallery copy further elaborates: "In a decision involving the foreign taxes oranges from Puerto Rico entering the port of New York should be subjected to, Supreme Court Justice White reasoned that 'while in an international sense Porto Rico was not a foreign country, since it was subject to the sovereignty of and was owned by the United States, it was foreign to the United States in a domestic sense, because the island has not been incorporated into the United States, but was merely appurtenant thereto as a possession.' For more than a century, this equivocation has been the basis for Puerto Rico's uneven access to constitutional rights and sovereignty." See: https://www.lissongallery.com/exhibitions/allora-calzadilla-foreign-in-a-domestic-sense.

53. Allora & Calzadilla, artists' description of work for *Allora & Calzadilla: Specters of Noon*, Menil Collection, Houston, Texas, September 26, 2020–June 20, 2021.

54. David Lang, *mains hum: for many voices* (Red Poppy, 2017).

55. Wolfgang Schivelbusch, *Disenchanted Night: The Industrialization of Light in the Nineteenth Century*, trans. Angela Davies (University of California Press, 1995), 221. He adds: "Darkness heightens individual perceptions, magnifying them many times."

56. Lang, *mains hum*.

57. Michel de Certeau, "Vocal Utopias: Glossolalias," trans. Daniel Rosenberg, *Representations* 56 (Autumn 1996): 29.

58. Roque Raquel Salas Rivera, *While They Sleep (Under the Bed Is Another Country)* (Birds, 2019), unpaginated.

59. Benjamin Franklin to Peter Collinson, May 9, 1753, New York Public Library, https://founders.archives.gov/documents/Franklin/01-04-02-0173.

60. "Marcel Ravidat, then eighteen years old, Jacques Marsal, and Simon Coencas, both fifteen, and Georges Agnel." Georges Bataille, *Lascaux; Or, The Birth of Art: Prehistoric Painting*, trans. Austryn Wainhouse (Skira, 1955), 137.

61. Petra Lange-Berndt, "How to Be Complicit with Materials," in *Materiality*, ed. Petra Lange-Berndt (Whitechapel Gallery; MIT Press, 2015), 12.

62. Friedrich Nietzsche, *Untimely Meditations*, trans. R. J. Hollingdale (Cambridge University Press, 1983), 91.

63. Allora & Calzadilla, artist statement, 2019, Menil Museum, Houston.

64. Allora & Calzadilla, artist statement, 2019, Menil Museum, Houston.

65. Dipesh Chakrabarty, "The Climate of History: Four Theses," *Critical Inquiry* 35 (Winter 2009): 222.

66. Bataille, *Lascaux*, 137.

67. Caillois, "Noon Complex," 128.

68. Vilém Flusser, "The Codified World," in *Writings*, ed. Andreas Ströhl, trans. Erik Eisel (University of Minnesota Press, 2002), 37.

69. Bataille, *Lascaux*, 12.

70. Caillois, "Noon Complex," 128.

15. LUIS GISPERT: RADICAL FEEDBACK

1. Iain Chambers, *Border Dialogues: Journeys in Postmodernity* (Routledge, 1990), 73. Emphasis added.

2. These include, among others, the work of figures such as José Bedia, Ana Mendieta, Felix Gonzalez-Torres, Doris Salcedo, Alfredo Jaar, Liliana Porter, and Eugenio Dittborn, all of whom have had significant representation in Miami collections. For a discussion of several of Miami's private holdings, see Phoebe Hoban, "Open Houses, Miami Style: 7BRs, Ocn Vu, WrldClass Art [*sic*]," *New York Times*, March 14, 2004; and Roni Feinstein, "Report from Miami," *Art in America*, December 2003. Of related importance is the Miami Art Museum's New Work series, documented in *Converge* (Miami Art Museum, 2000).

3. Luis Gispert with Derrick Cartwright, "Subwoofers, Subcultures, and Subversions: A Conversation with Luis Gispert," 24.

4. Gispert with Cartwright, "Subwoofers, Subcultures, and Subversions," 23.

5. Two films are relevant here in that they frustrate the semantic and social idealism of this icon: *But I'm a Cheerleader* (dir. Jamie Babbit, 1999), in which a "naive teenager is sent to rehab camp when her straitlaced parents and friends suspect her of being a lesbian," and *Bring It On* (dir. Peyton Reed, 2000), in which a "champion high school cheerleading squad discovers its previous captain stole all their best routines from an inner-city school and must scramble to compete at this year's championship." Plot descriptions are from Internet Movie Database, http://www.imdb.com.

6. Guy Debord, *The Society of the Spectacle*, trans. Donald Nicholson-Smith (Zone Books, 1995), 36.

7. Édouard Glissant, *Poetics of Relation* (University of Michigan Press, 2000), 78.

8. Wu-Tang Clan, "Method Man," track 9 on *Enter the Wu-Tang (36 Chambers)*, BMG/RCA, 1993.

9. Nelson George, *Hip Hop America* (Penguin Books, 1998), 44.

10. Joan Copjec, *Read My Desire: Lacan Against the Historicists* (MIT Press, 1994), 129.

11. Ernst Gombrich, "Style," in *The Art of Art History: A Critical Anthology*, ed. Donald Preziosi (Oxford University Press, 1998), 153.

12. Tricia Rose, "A Style Nobody Can Deal With: Politics, Style and the Postindustrial City in Hip Hop," in *Microphone Fiends: Youth Music and Youth Culture*, ed. Andrew Ross and Tricia Rose (Routledge, 1994), 85.

13. George, *Hip Hop America*, 160.

14. Chambers, *Border Dialogues*, 70.

15. Gispert with Cartwright, "Subwoofers, Subcultures, and Subversions," 23.

16. GEOGRAPHIES OF LANGUAGE AND LIGHT: LAURA AGUILAR, RAQUEL GUTIÉRREZ

1. Adela Salinas Salinas, "La crítica de arte en México" (roundtable debate with Raquel Tibol, Teresa del Conde, Olivier Debroise, Jorge Alberto Manrique, and Juan Acha), *Revista de la Universidad de México*, December 1991, 50–53.

2. Raquel Gutiérrez, *Brown Neon* (Coffee House, 2021), 42. Gutiérrez writes that this was "our way of dealing with all the shit we lost in the treaty," that is, the 1848 Treaty of Guadalupe Hidalgo. "The shit we took from other more vulnerable sectors of the archive."

3. Gutiérrez, *Brown Neon*, 133.

4. Raquel Gutiérrez, "On the Ekphrastic Memoir: Rendering an Insurgent Commons," public talk, Iowa City Public Library, April 7, 2023.

5. Gutiérrez, *Brown Neon*, 31.

6. Gutiérrez, *Brown Neon*, 42–43.

7. Rafa Esparza with Carmen Argote, Nao Bustamante, Beatriz Cortez, Timo Fahler, Eamon Ore Giron, and Star Montana: *Tierra. Sangre. Oro*, Ballroom Marfa, Texas, August 25, 2017–March 18, 2018.

8. Rafa Esparza's method is described as though an inheritance from an

> ancient how-to manual by the early Sonoran Desert dwellers, the Hohokam, who the Tohono O'odham and Pima tribes descend from, and early constructors of adobe shelters might instruct you to dig a shallow trench in the ground using a well-pointed digging stick and to pile all excavated material inside of the trench.
>
> Then fill that trench with a three-to-one mix of mud and broken stone, or river pebbles, tamping thoroughly to fill all of the nooks and crannies. Dampen the mix only as necessary, using only enough water to soften the mud to a stiff moldable consistency. A penalty is incurred for anyone using more than the minimum amount of water required. (Raquel Gutiérrez, *Brown Neon*, 54)

9. Gutiérrez, *Brown Neon*, 111.

10. Gutiérrez, *Brown Neon*, 53–54.

11. Gutiérrez, *Brown Neon*, 133.

12. Gutiérrez, *Brown Neon*, 138.

13. Press release for *Laura Aguilar: Show and Tell*, Vincent Price Art Museum, Los Angeles, September 16, 2017–February 8, 2018.

14. Amelia Jones, "Clothed/Unclothed: Laura Aguilar's Radical Vulnerability," in *Laura Aguilar: Show and Tell*, ed. Rebecca Epstein, cur. Sybil Venegas (UCLA Chicano Studies Research Center and Getty Foundation, 2017), 49–50; Macarena Gómez-Barris, "Mestiza Cultural Memory: The Self-Ecologies of Laura Aguilar," in *Laura Aguilar: Show and Tell*, 83.

15. Gutiérrez, *Brown Neon*, 140.

16. Gutiérrez, *Brown Neon*, 144.

17. Gutiérrez, *Brown Neon*, 145–46.

18. Sigmund Freud, "The Uncanny," in *The Standard Edition of the Complete Psychological Works of Sigmund Freud*, vol. 17 (Hogarth and the Institute of Psychoanalysis, 1962), 247.

19. Gutiérrez, *Brown Neon*, 148.

20. Walter Benjamin, *The Arcades Project*, trans. Howard Eiland and Kevin McLaughlin (Belknap, 1999), 545.

21. Michael Baxandall, *Giotto and the Orators: Humanist Observers of Painting in Italy and the Discovery of Pictorial Composition* (Oxford University Press, 1971), 44. A lineage links Raquel Gutiérrez's *Brown Neon* to the "travel essays in art" by Eileen Myles in *The Importance of Being Iceland* (Semiotext(e), 2009); the interpretive poetics illuminating "Black presences in European literature, visual art, and film" by Tisa Bryant in *Unexplained Presence* (Leon Works, 2007); the travelogue across several African cities that reconfigures the relationship of the photographic to time and place and between subject and object in *A Stranger's Pose* by Emmanuel Iduma (Cassava Republic, 2018); and the meditation on "loss, violence and rejuvenation, gender and sexuality" around the work of Felix Gonzalez-Torres's *"Untitled" (Orpheus Twice)* (1991), among others, in T. Fleischmann's memoir *Time Is the Thing a Body Moves Through* (Coffee House, 2019).

22. Gutiérrez, *Brown Neon*, 146.

17. LATINX ART IN THE FUTURE IMPERFECT: AXIS MUNDO, JENNIF(F)ER TAMAYO

1. Douglas Crimp, in public conversation with Dean Daderko, Contemporary Arts Museum Houston, November 12, 2016. Douglas Crimp, *Before Pictures* (Dancing Foxes and University of Chicago Press, 2016).

2. Mário Pedrosa, the late Brazilian art critic and theorist, referred to the practice of art and politics as the "experimental exercise of freedom." "O 'bicho-da-sêda' na produção em massa," *Correio da Manhã* (Rio de Janeiro), August 14, 1966: "Já faz bastante tempo que, tentando analisar o fenômeno, defini a arte de nossos dias como e exercício experimental da liberdade." ["Some time ago, in an attempt to analyze the phenomenon, I defined the art of our days as an experimental exercise of freedom." Author's translation.]

3. *Axis Mundo: Queer Networks in Chicano L.A.*, curated by C. Ondine Chavoya and David Evans Frantz, originated as part of Pacific Standard Time: LA/LA, an initiative of the Getty Foundation. The exhibition was organized by ONE National Gay & Lesbian Archives at the USC Libraries in collaboration with the Museum of Contemporary Art, Los Angeles, and organized as a traveling exhibition by Independent Curators International. The exhibition itinerary spanned the following dates and venues: MOCA Pacific Design Center and ONE National Gay & Lesbian Archives Gallery, West Hollywood, CA (September 9–December 31, 2017); Hunter College Art Galleries, New York (June 22–August 19, 2018); Vicki Myhren Gallery, University of Denver (September 13–December 2, 2018); Marjorie Barrick Museum of Art, University of Nevada, Las Vegas (January 11–March 16, 2019); Lawndale Art Center, Houston (April 6–June 2, 2019; Williams College Museum of Art, Williamstown, MA (September 6–December 9, 2019). *Axis Mundo: Queer Networks in Chicano L.A.* and the University of Houston CounterCurrent performance by Jennif(f)er Tamayo, discussed in this essay, formed part of Latino Art Now! 2019, a conference (University of Houston, April 4–6, 2019) and citywide series of art events cosponsored by the Inter-University Program for Latino Research and the University of Houston.

4. C. Ondine Chavoya and David Evans Frantz, "Axis Mundo: Constellations and Connections," in *Axis Mundo: Queer Networks in Chicano L.A.*, ed. C. Ondine Chavoya, David Evans Frantz, and Macarena Gómez-Barris (DelMonico Books-Prestel, 2017), 25.

5. Chavoya and Frantz, "Axis Mundo," 25.

6. Chavoya and Frantz, "Axis Mundo," 25.

7. Chavoya and Frantz, "Axis Mundo," 28.

8. Chavoya and Frantz, "Axis Mundo," 25.

9. Chavoya and Frantz, "Axis Mundo," 25.

10. Cited by Miss Rosen, "True Radicals: An Inside Look at LA's Queer Chicano Networks," *Huck*, June 19, 2018, https://www.huckmag.com/article/fascinating-look-inside-las-queer-chicano-networks.

11. Catherine S. Ramírez, *The Woman in the Zoot Suit* (Duke University Press, 2009), 56; cited in Leticia Alvarado, "Malflora Aberrant Femininities," in *Axis Mundo*, 101.

12. Alvarado, "Malflora Aberrant Femininities," 95.

13. Oral history interviews with Carlos Almaraz, February 6, 1986–January 29, 1987, Archives of American Art, Smithsonian Institution, Washington, DC.

14. Jacques Lacan, *The Ethics of Psychoanalysis, 1959–1960: The Seminars of Jacques Lacan, Book* 7, ed. Jacques-Alain Miller, trans. Dennis Porter (Norton, 1992), 319. "The only thing of which one can be guilty is having given ground relative to one's desire."

15. Chavoya and Frantz write: "Artists who passed during the heights of the epidemic include Carlos Almaraz (1941–1989), Steven Arnold (1943–1994), Tosh Carrillo (1941–1983), Mundo Meza (1955–1985), Ray Navarro (1964–1990), Richard Nieblas (1950–1994), Teddy Sandoval (1949–1995), Jack Smith (1932–1989), Jack Vargas (1952–1995), and Gerardo Velazquez (1958–1992). Additionally, artists Jerry Dreva (1945–1997), Tomata du Plenty (1948–2000), and Ricardo Valverde (1946–1998) died before their work could receive the robust attention and scholarship it warrants." "Axis Mundo," 35.

16. Robb Hernández, *Archiving an Epidemic: Art, AIDS, and the Queer Chicanx Avant-Garde* (New York University Press, 2019), 6, 22.

17. Jennif(f)er Tamayo, artist statement for *LA QUEERADORA Project* (unpublished, 2019). See also "CounterCurrent19: Jennif(f)er Tamayo: LA QUEERADORA," *The Buzz Magazines*, Houston, April 10, 2019, https://thebuzzmagazines.com/calendar-events/countercurrent19-jenniffer-tamayo-la-queeradora.

18. Jennif(f)er Tamayo, *YOU DA ONE*, 2nd ed., Akrilica series (Noemi, 2017).

19. Jennif(f)er Tamayo, artist statement for *LA QUEERADORA Project* (unpublished, 2019). See also "CounterCurrent19: Jennif(f)er Tamayo: LA QUEERADORA."

20. Rachel Eliza Griffiths, Jennif(f)er Tamayo, Cathy Linh Che, and Carolina Ebeid, *Ruth Stone House Reader I* (Monk Books, 2016), 55.

21. Griffiths et al., *Ruth Stone House Reader I*, 60.

22. Griffiths et al., *Ruth Stone House Reader I*, 63.

23. Griffiths et al., *Ruth Stone House Reader I*, 63.

24. Michel de Certeau, *The Writing of History*, trans. Tom Conley (Columbia University Press, 1988), 230, 241.

25. Griffiths et al., *Ruth Stone House Reader I*, 82.

26. Gloria Anzaldúa, *Borderlands: The New Mestiza* (Spinsters/Aunt Lute, 1987), 79.

18. JESÚS MACARENA-ÁVILA: THE ESSENTIAL WORK

1. Jesús Macarena-Ávila, "Ucross Installation Drawing," 2002, artist file provided to author in 2020. Macarena-Ávila relates that while at the Ucross residency he installed the sketch within his assigned studio and "invited all resident artists and UCross staff (cowboys/ranch hands) for an informal reception." Jesús Macarena-Ávila, correspondence with author, January 4, 2021. The Ucross Art Gallery, in a converted barn known as Big Red, had also mounted an exhibition, *Balancing Accounts: Crow and Gros Ventre Indian Ledger Art*, comprising thirty-five drawings from the Charles H. Barstow Collection from Montana State University–Billings. "Ucross Show Features Ledger Art of Native American Life," *Billings Gazette*, October 10, 2002.

2. “Ucross 40th Anniversary Campaign,” Ucross brochure, 2022, unpaginated on foundation website, https://www.ucrossfoundation.org/uploads/1/1/8/7/118757657/ucross_%7C_40th_anniversary_campaign.pdf.

3. Macarena-Ávila cites, among others, the following works: Vandana Shiva, *Biopiracy: The Plunder of Nature and Knowledge* (South End, 1997); and Jeremy Rifkin, *The Biotech Century: Harnessing the Gene and Remaking the World* (Jeremy P. Tarcher/Putnam, 1998).

4. David Kindy, “The Accidental Invention of Bubble Wrap,” *Smithsonian Magazine*, January 23, 2019, https://www.smithsonianmag.com/innovation/accidental-invention-bubble-wrap-180971325/.

5. Jesús Macarena-Ávila, correspondence with author, December 2, 2020.

6. Sylvia Wynter, “Unsettling the Coloniality of Being/Power/Truth/Freedom: Towards the Human, After Man, Its Overrepresentation—An Argument,” *CR: The New Centennial Review* 3, no. 3 (Fall 2003): 260. Wynter writes that “the struggle of our new millennium will be one between the ongoing imperative of securing the well-being of our present ethnoclass (i.e., Western bourgeois) conception of the human, Man, which overrepresents itself as if it were the human itself, and that of securing the well-being, and therefore the full cognitive and behavioral autonomy of the human species itself/ourselves.”

7. James W. LeDuc and M. Anita Barry, “SARS, the First Pandemic of the 21st Century,” *Emerging Infectious Diseases* 10, no. 11 (November 2004).

8. Other works include references to such historical and cultural figures as the women soldiers of the Mexican Revolution in *Germscapes: Adelita (Study)* (2008) and *Germscapes: Adelita* (2011); media capitalists in *Germscapes: Rupert Murdoch* (2011); firearms and gun violence in *Germscapes: SB1070 (Beretta)* (2011); labor organizers and radical socialists in *Germscapes: Lucia Gonzalez Parsons (HR 4437)* (2011–12); and to the influenza A virus subtype H1N1 in *Germscapes: H1N1* (2009).

9. Pearce Wright, obituary for Vladimir Pasechnik, *Guardian*, November 28, 2001.

10. House Bill 2281 (H.B. 2281), State of Arizona House of Representatives Forty-Ninth Legislature Second Regular Session, 2010, https://www.azleg.gov/legtext/49leg/2r/bills/hb2281s.pdf.

11. Other works on paper in the 2020 series include *Germscapes: take your breath*(2020); *Germscapes: Essential?* (2020); and *Germscapes: . . . move heaven and Earth . . .* (2020).

12. Peter Sloterdijk, “Cell Block, Egospheres, Self-Container,” trans. Daniela Fabricius, *Log*, no. 10 (Summer/Fall 2007): 90, 92, 89.

13. Amy Brittain, Isaac Stanley-Becker, and Nick Miroff, “White House’s Pandemic Relief Effort Project Airbridge Is Swathed in Secrecy and Exaggerations,” *Washington Post*, May 8, 2020.

14. Jesús Macarena-Ávila, correspondence with author, February 26, 2024. See the artist’s Instituto de Nuestra Cultura (INC.) Tumblr account: https://www.tumblr.com/institutodenuestracultura.

19. CHRISTINA FERNANDEZ: SOMETHING LOST, MISSING, OR UNATTAINABLE

1. The exhibition checklist comprised sixty works by other artists, including Emmet Gowin, James Turrell, Hank Wessel, David Berg, Thomas Barrow, Robert Glenn Ketchum, Miles Coolidge, Richard Misrach, Michael Light, David Maisel, and Mark Ruwedel. The LACMA website describes the exhibition as one that advanced “the dialogue about—and affirms the enduring mystique of—the place we call the West. By the 1970s, when most of the photographs on view were made, America’s postwar optimism had faded. Anxiety about potential nuclear annihilation grew as the cold war raged. With its weapons laboratories and test sites, the West was implicated in this new chapter of human history. Ravenous consumption sparked by American affluence further transformed the mythical guise of the Western landscape. Artists soon began to investigate our contradictory appetites for creation and destruction. Reflecting on the

realities of rapid development and exploring the terrain as object, the artists in this exhibition celebrate the West as a site in and of itself, with imposed illusions, allusions, and romantic pretensions laid to rest. This installation accompanies *The Modern West: American Landscapes, 1890–1950*." "Re-SITE-ing the West: Contemporary Photographs from the Permanent Collection," Los Angeles County Museum of Art, accessed June 7, 2021, https://www.lacma.org/art/exhibition/re-site-ing-west-contemporary-photographs-permanent-collection.

2. Robert A. Sobieszek, "Terminal Documents: The Early Desert of Lewis Baltz," in *Perpetual Mirage: Photographic Narratives of the Desert West* (Whitney Museum of American Art, 1996), 182.

3. Allan Sekula, "School Is a Factory," in *Photography Against the Grain: Essays and Photo Works, 1973–1983* (Press of the Nova Scotia College of Art and Design, 1984), 233.

4. Elaine Woo, "Robert Sobieszek, 62; Curator of Photography at LACMA," *Los Angeles Times*, July 16, 2005.

5. Sobieszek, "Terminal Documents," 181–82.

6. Christina Fernandez in conversation with Roberto Tejada, Los Angeles County Museum of Art, April 22, 2007. Fernandez added: "Lewis Baltz takes this idea of landscaping completely—I mean he holds true to some of it, like the long depth of field, horizon line placement, even using the rule of thirds in some of these photographs, but then he goes from very specific things like a cigarette butt and a window and a house to very wide angles, this almost panoramic shot at the very top and then back down into a smaller scale. I find it fascinating, and I love this piece for that, and I love Baltz's work for that." A slightly edited version of the conversation was published in *Christina Fernandez: Multiple Exposures*, cur. Joanna Szupinska; ed. Rebecca Epstein (UCR Arts; UCLA Chicano Studies Research Center, 2022), 201.

7. Sobieszek, "Terminal Documents," 182–83.

8. Sobieszek, "Terminal Documents," 182–83.

9. W. J. T. Mitchell, *Landscape and Power* (University of Chicago Press, 1994), 1.

10. Mitchell, *Landscape and Power*, 2.

11. Fernandez in conversation with Tejada.

12. inSITE97 was the third iteration of a borderlands site-specific public arts initiative. It comprised "forty-two commissioned projects and seventeen works, mostly developed by area artists," and all works "were open to the public from September 26 through November 30, 1997." inSITE97 enlisted four curators (Jessica Bradley, Olivier Debroise, Ivo Mesquita, and Sally Yard) "to conceptualize the framework" by selecting artists and coordinating "collaborations among twenty-seven institutions in San Diego and Tijuana." "inSITE97," INSITE, https://insiteart.org/insite97.

13. Peter Rowe, "Focus: Border Wall," *San Diego Union-Tribune*, January 27, 2017.

14. Christina Fernandez artist page, inSITE97, https://insiteart.org/people/christina-fernandez.

15. Mitchell, *Landscape and Power*, 2.

16. Fernandez in conversation with Tejada.

17. Jay Belloli, *Urban California* (Hanna S. Barsam Photography Invitational, Fresno Art Museum, 2015), 16.

18. María Lugones, "On Complex Communication," *Hypatia* 21, no. 3 (Summer 2006): 84.

19. "To the Brink and Back: A Financial Crisis Timeline," *Los Angeles Times*, September 9, 2018.

20. "To the Brink and Back."

21. Peter G. Gosselin, "Why This Downturn May Be No Run-of-the-Mill Recession," *Los Angeles Times*, January 13, 2008; Tom Petruno, "5 Years After Financial Crash, Many Losers—and Some Big Winners," *Los Angeles Times*, September 14, 2013. For a testimonial account from those most impacted, see Arthur Delaney, *A People's History of the Great Recession* (Huffington Post Media Group, 2011).

22. Jeanne Dreskin, "Christina Fernandez's Lines of Sight," *Aperture*, October 4, 2017, https://aperture.org/blog/christina-fernandez-interview/.

23. Fernandez in conversation with Tejada.

24. The Los Angeles Public Library is the repository of the Herman J. Schultheis collections. Its cataloger supplies the briefest summary of a life whose final episode was in keeping with the narrative logic of the cinema: "Herman J. Schultheis was born in Aachen, Germany in 1900, and immigrated to the United States in the mid-1920s after obtaining a Ph.D. in Mechanical and Electrical Engineering. He married Ethel Wisloh in 1936, and the pair moved to Los Angeles the following year. He worked in the film industry from the late 1930s to the mid-1940s, most notably on the animated features *Fantasia* and *Pinocchio*. His detailed notebook, documenting the special effects for *Fantasia*, is the subject of a 14-minute short-subject included on the film's DVD. In 1949, he started employment with Librascope as a patent engineer. Schultheis was an avid amateur photographer who traveled the world with his cameras. It was on one of these photographic [expeditions] in 1955 that he disappeared in the jungles of Guatemala. His remains were discovered 18 months later." Finding aid for the Herman J. Schultheis collection of international photographs, 1927–1950, Online Archive of California, https://oac.cdlib.org/findaid/ark:/13030/c8vt1xrz/.

25. Wendy Cheng, "'New Topographics': Locating Epistemological Concerns in the American Landscape," *American Quarterly* 63, no. 1 (March 2011): 151, 153.

26. Lewis Baltz, review of *The New West*, by Robert Adams, *Art in America*, March–April 1975, 41–42.

27. Rubén Salazar, "Debs Leads L.A. Group to De Neve Ceremony," *Los Angeles Times*, September 4, 1963.

28. Kenneth Reich, "Ernest E. Debs, 98; County Supervisor for 16 Years," *Los Angeles Times*, March 19, 2002.

29. "Ernest E. Debs No Relation to Eugene V. Debs," *Los Angeles Times*, March 27, 1947.

30. Reich, "Ernest E. Debs."

31. Thom Andersen, *Los Angeles Plays Itself*, film, 2003.

32. Robert Towne, *Chinatown and the Last Detail: Two Screenplays* (Grove, 1997), 48.

33. Dreskin, "Christina Fernandez's Lines of Sight."

34. Jane Bennett, *Vibrant Matter: A Political Ecology of Things* (Duke University Press, 2010), 3–4, 14.

35. Mary Warner Marien, *Photography: A Cultural History* (Harry N. Abrams, 2002), 355.

36. Kenneth Reinhard, "Toward a Political Theology of the Neighbor," in *The Neighbor: Three Inquiries in Political Theology* (University of Chicago Press, 2013), 38.

37. Slovoj Žižek, *Violence: Six Sideways Reflections* (Picador, 2008), 45.

38. Pierre Mayol, "The Neighborhood," in *The Practice of Everyday Life*, vol. 2, *Living and Cooking*, trans. Timothy J. Tomasik (University of Minnesota Press, 1998), 9.

39. Robert Smithson, "Art Through the Camera's Eye," in *Robert Smithson: The Collected Writings*, ed. Jack Flam (University of California Press, 1996), 371. He adds, citing the French poet Jean Cayrol, who wrote the narration to Alain Resnais's 1955 documentary film, *Night and Fog*, that the substrata petrifies a narrative that discloses "no story, no buoyancy, no plot."

40. Saskia Sassen, "Expanding the Terrain for Global Capital: When Local Housing Becomes an Electronic Instrument," in *Subprime Cities: The Political Economy of Mortgage Markets*, ed. Manuel B. Aalbers (Wiley-Blackwell, 2012), 73.

41. Sophie Quinton, "Why Some Cities Are Buying Trailer Parks," *Stateline*, Pew Charitable Trusts, 2017, https://www.pewtrusts.org/en/research-and-analysis/blogs/stateline/2017/10/24/why-some-cities-are-buying-trailer-parks. The author adds: "Even if a home can be safely moved, its owner may not be able to find an open lot nearby or be able to afford relocation costs,

which can run from $5,000 to $10,000, according to Prosperity Now, a Washington, D.C., nonprofit that studies and advocates for policies that help low-income people become more financially secure."

42. Robert Smithson, "A Tour of the Monuments of Passaic, New Jersey," in *Robert Smithson: The Collected Writings*, ed. Jack Flam (University of California Press, 1996), 71.

43. Baltz, review of *The New West*, 43.

44. Dreskin, "Christina Fernandez's Lines of Sight."

45. Sassen, "Expanding the Terrain for Global Capital," 76; Baltz, review of *The New West*, 43.

INDEX

Roberto Tejada is the author of poetry collections *Carbonate of Copper* (Fordham University Press, 2025), *Why the Assembly Disbanded* (Fordham University Press, 2022), *Todo en el ahora* (2015), *Full Foreground* (2012), *Exposition Park* (2010), and *Mirrors for Gold* (2006); as well as art and media histories that include *Still Nowhere in an Empty Vastness* (2019), *National Camera: Photography and Mexico's Image Environment* (2009), and *Celia Alvarez Muñoz* (2009). The recipient of a John Simon Guggenheim Memorial Foundation Fellowship (2021), he is the Hugh Roy and Lillie Cranz Cullen Distinguished Professor in Creative Writing and Art History at the University of Houston.